classic CHINESE AND ORIENTAL *cooking*

classic CHINESE AND ORIENTAL *cooking*

EDITED BY JEFF GROWMAN

NEW BURLINGTON BOOKS

A QUINTET BOOK

Published by New Burlington Books
6 Blundell Street
London N7 9BH

Exclusive to Coles in Canada

ISBN 1-85348-130-0

This book was designed and produced by
Quintet Publishing Limited
6 Blundell Street
London N7 9BH

Design: Richard Kelly
Editors: Jeff Growman, Belinda Giles
Editorial Assistant: Phillippa Growman

Typeset in Great Britain by
Central Southern Typesetters, Eastbourne
Manufactured in Hong Kong by Regent Publishing
Services Limited
Printed in Hong Kong by Leefung-Asco Printers
Limited.

This book contains material used in previous
publications.

CONTENTS

INTRODUCTION

Classic Chinese and Oriental Cooking is a practical introduction to the rich variety of Far Eastern dishes and cooking styles – written and presented specifically for the home cook who has no previous knowledge of Eastern cooking techniques or special ingredients. All cooking utensils and ingredients described are freely available in the West.

This book covers the distinctive cuisines of China, India, Japan, Malaysia, Singapore, Indonesia, the Philippines, Thailand, Korea, Burma, Kampuchea, Vietnam and Laos, with photographs that show finished dishes – many of which were shot on location in the countries of their origin.

Classic Chinese and Oriental Cooking is divided into four main chapters – China, India, Japan and Oriental Tour – and within each section, basic kitchen equipment, special ingredients, preparation and cooking techniques are described in detail. The recipes which follow have been carefully selected to offer variety and contrast, as well as presenting a delicious cross-section of dishes unique to each country or area.

The recipes – including dozens of vegetarian dishes – cover mouthwatering soups; a huge variety of rice and noodle dishes; vegetable, bean curd and egg specialities; fish and crustaceans; a great number of traditional poultry and game dishes; meat dishes both well-known and rare; and breads, snacks and desserts from the four corners of the Orient.

The magic aura of the East and its cuisine come alive in the pages of *Classic Chinese and Oriental Cooking* and will provide a constant source of appetizing dishes and inspiration for all creative home cooks.

CHINA

There *is* an abiding love of food among all Chinese: it verges on worship. The ways that ingredients are chosen, prepared, cooked and balanced are a constant way of 'saying grace', of offering thanks to the gods. And the speed with which this form of 'worship' – the taste for Chinese food – has spread throughout the Western world over the last 30 years is remarkable. Yet despite the popularity of Chinese food, Chinese cooking is still regarded by most Westerners as being difficult and requiring special talents – mainly because the techniques used are so different from those of Western cuisines. But this does not mean that they are more complex.

In Western-style cooking, individual foodstuffs are conditioned by heat until they are ready to eat: meat is roasted or grilled; vegetables are boiled or fried. Chinese cooking, on the other hand, is dominated by compound dishes. Ingredients are mixed and cooked in different ways. It is the method – rather than the ingredients themselves – that determines the nature of the final dish. Thus there is much more flavour- and texture-blending involved in Chinese cooking.

Most of the techniques used in Chinese cooking are the same as those used in the West, and those that are different form a few set patterns of using heat and marrying ingredients. The only completely different skill that needs to be mastered is stir-frying. Other techniques employed are quick, open steaming, steaming in a closed container and slow simmering. Red-cooking is simply slow-stewing in soy sauce. Each of these techniques is familiar to Western cooks.

The ingredients required will present no problem either. Most Chinese dishes can be prepared with no more than a handful of specifically Chinese ingredients, which are easily obtained from foodstores everywhere.

Many people may try to delude themselves that they 'eat to live', but the Chinese are honest enough to admit that they 'live to eat', and that a good appetite is a blessing.

A monument to the Chinese people: the Great Wall of China.

Left: *magnificent limestone mountains tower above the Li River in southern China.*
Above: *a busy corner of Peking market.*
Above right: *bamboo groves surround this house in Chengdu, western China.*
Right: *this is the famous Bund, or commercial centre which surrounds Shanghai harbour.*

◆ REGIONAL COOKERY ◆

Looking at a map of China, it is not difficult to understand why there should be such a large variety of different cooking styles throughout the country. The Chinese attach great importance to the use of fresh meat and tender young vegetables, so, because it was difficult to transport food and keep it fresh, each region was forced to make the best use of its own products. Every district has its own speciality, yet all these different forms and styles of cooking can be grouped under four main schools: Peking, Shanghai, Sichuan (Szechuan) and Guangzhou (Canton).

Peking (Northern School): *Besides the local cooking of Hebei (in which province Peking is situated), Peking cuisine embraces the cooking styles of Shandong (Shantung), Henan (Honan) and Shanxi, as well as the Chinese Moslem cooking of Inner Mongolia and Xinjiang (Sinkiang). Also, being the capital of China for many centuries, it became the culinary centre, drawing inspiration from all the different regional styles.*

Shanghai (Eastern School): *Also known as the Huaiyang School of the Yangtse River delta, with Shanghai as its culinary centre. This region covers the fertile lands of Anhui (Anhwei), Jiangsu (Kiangsu) and Fujian (Fukien). Fujian forms a school of its own, but sometimes is linked with the Southern School.*

The two provinces of Hubei (Hupeh)

Rinsed lamb fire pot

Three-layer shreds

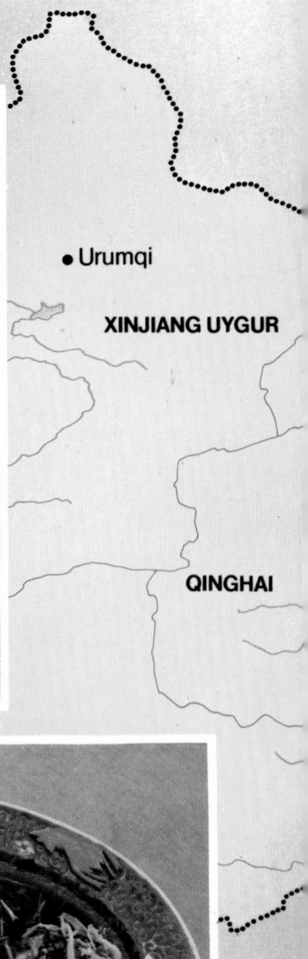

Liver paté soup

Steamed bass

◆ REGIONAL COOKERY ◆

and Jiangxi (Kiangsi) are sometimes grouped under this School because they both belong to China's 'Lands of Fish and Rice'.

Sichuan (Western School): *The Red Basin of Sichuan is one of the richest lands of China. Owing to its geographical position, it was practically inaccessible from the rest of China until recently, therefore it developed a very distinct style of cooking. Its richly flavoured and piquant food has influenced its neighbouring provinces of Hunan and Guizhou although the last two have a style of their own.*

Sichuan food has only recently been introduced to the outside world and has a strong following in both Japan and the United States.

Canton (Southern School): *The Pearl River delta, with Canton as the capital of Guangdong, is undoubtedly the home of the most famous of all Chinese cooking styles. Unfortunately its reputation has been damaged by a great number of so-called 'chop-suey' houses outside China. Authentic Cantonese food has no rival and has a greater variety of dishes than any other School. Because Canton was the first Chinese port opened for trade, foreign influences are particularly strong in its cooking.*

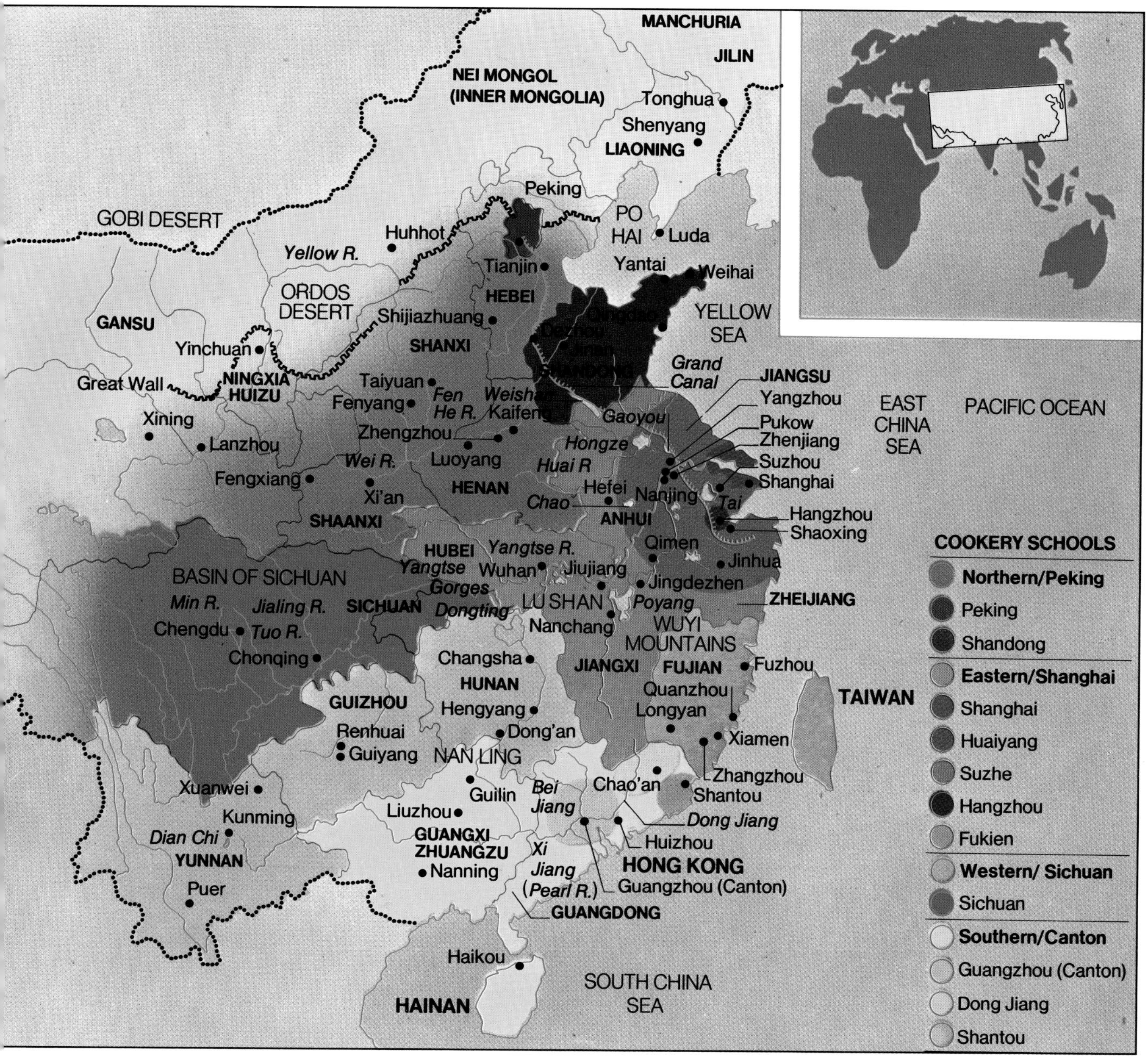

◆ KITCHEN EQUIPMENT ◆

The Wok

The best woks are traditional ones made of iron or carbon steel, with one long or two wooden side handles. The first is excellent for stir-frying since the cook can hold the wok yet is far away from the very hot oil, using a long-handled spoon, chopsticks or wok scoop to toss the ingredients. The two-handled wok is better for deep-frying or for steaming food because it is steadier to move when full of liquid. When buying a wok it is important that it should have deep sides, is fairly large, about 14 inches (35cm) in diameter, and that the metal is not too thin or stir-fried food will burn easily. Make sure your wok has a good fitting domed lid to use when steaming.

It is very important to season a wok before first cooking in it. Scrub it well to remove any protective coating, rinse, then dry it well. Place the wok over low heat, wipe it lightly with vegetable oil and let it heat for about 10 minutes. When cool, wipe the wok with absorbent kitchen paper to remove the dark film. Repeat the process until the paper wipes clean. Clean a seasoned wok in plain water without soap; never scrub it. Let the wok dry thoroughly over low heat before storing it. If the metal ever rusts, clean it with a scouring cream or fine sandpaper, rinse, dry and season it again. A wok brush is a stiff bundle of thin bamboo splints that is good for cleaning a wok.

Wok Stand

A wok stand is necessary for wok cooking when deep-frying and steaming, as it provides a steady base for the pan. The stand is also used with a two-handled wok for stir-frying. If cooking over gas, be sure to use a solid wok stand that has ventilation holes. It gives the wok stability and prevents the flame from going out.

***Far left:** double wooden-handled wok with wok brush; **left:** single-handled wok on wok stand with long-handled metal sieve and smaller perforated ladle; **below:** long wooden chopsticks for cooking on; chopstick stand and soft brush for cleaning woks.*

◆ KITCHEN EQUIPMENT ◆

Bamboo steamer

Bamboo steamers are placed on a metal or bamboo trivet over water. When the food is in place, the wok can be covered with its lid or with the steamer's own tight-fitting bamboo lid, which is necessary when more than one type of food, each in its own steamer, is stacked on top of the other. When new, wash then put the empty steamer over water and let it steam for five minutes.

Metal steamer

Metal steamers can be placed directly on the heat, fit snugly and have a tight-fitting lid. To prevent food sticking, place it on cheesecloth or in a heatproof dish.

Cooking pots

Chinese earthenware cooking pots, also known as sand pots, come in a variety of shapes and sizes, all with unglazed exteriors and lids. They can be used over low heat, as in making soup, but not in the oven. They will crack if hot, if put on a cold surface or if an empty pot is heated. Any heavy casserole makes a satisfactory substitute.

Mongolian hot pot

Mongolian hot pots, or fire-pots, heat stock or soup at the table from glowing charcoal under and in the middle of the pot. Small long-handled wire baskets or bamboo sieves or chopsticks are used to add and remove ingredients from liquid.

Above: *a vast selection of sandpots, in a Chinese kitchenware shop.*
Above right: *base and lid of a metal steamer;* ***right:*** *Chinese bamboo steamer with lid and ornate wooden cooking chopsticks.*

◆ KITCHEN EQUIPMENT ◆

Far left: *Chinese earthenware cooking pot with basket ladle;* **left:** *Mongolian hot pot with long-handled wire baskets for cooking.*

Resting on a chopping board, **below:** *small chopper (cleaver);* **below left:** *heavier, large chopper.*

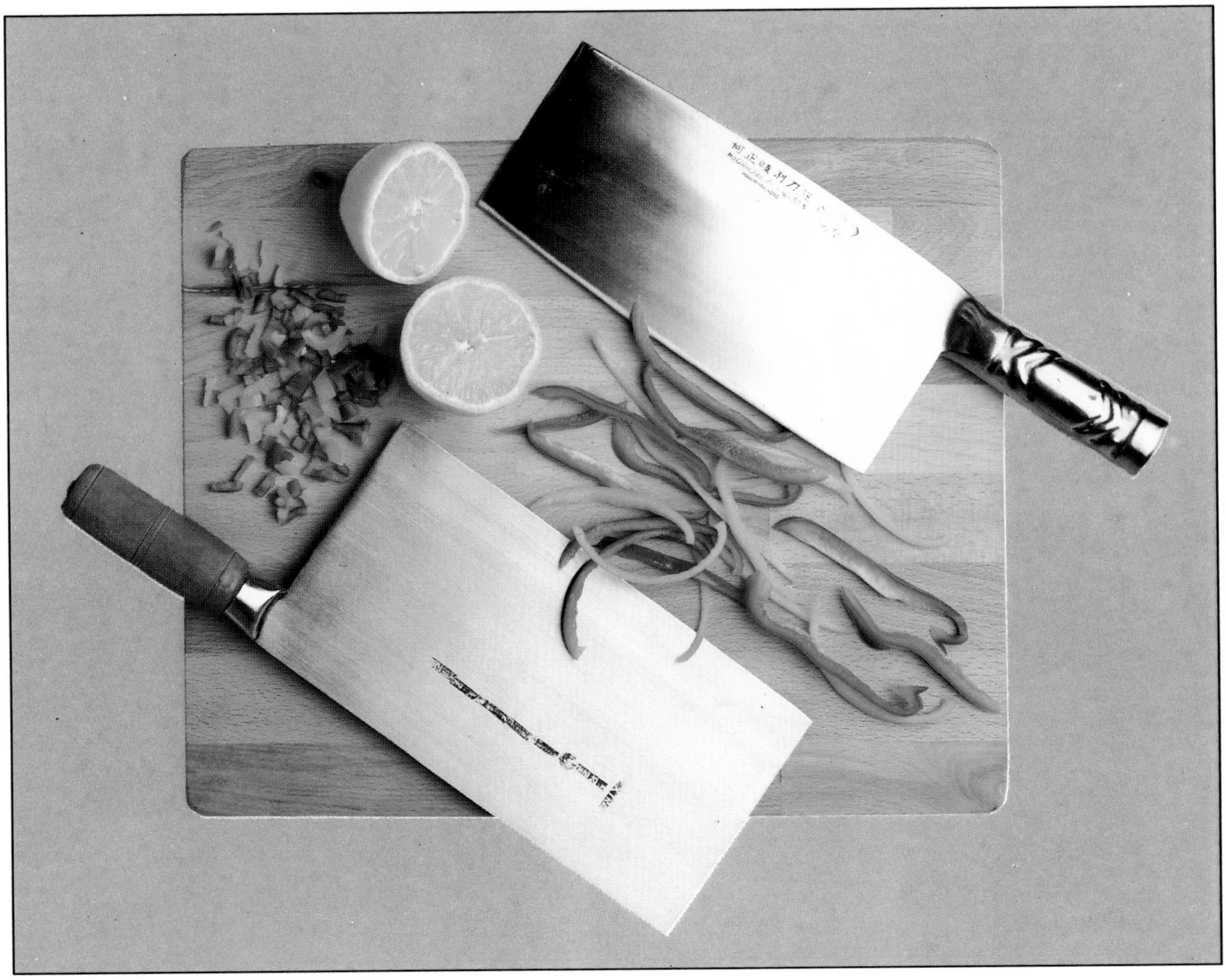

◆ KITCHEN EQUIPMENT ◆

Right: *metal ladle;* ***across from left to right:*** *bamboo sieve, basket ladle; wok scoop; glazing brush; larger wok scoop; whisk.*

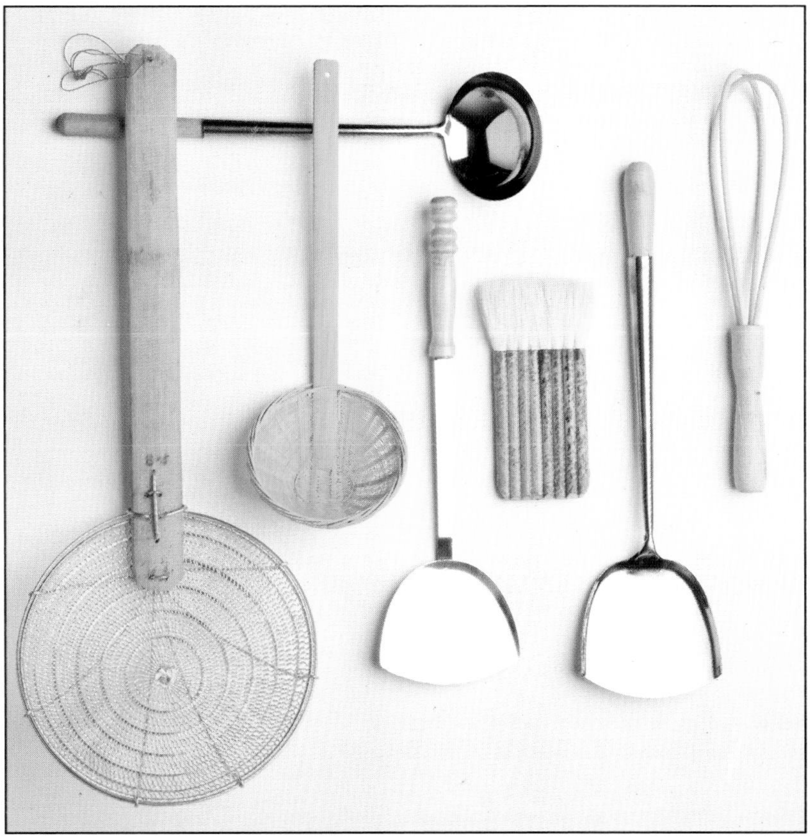

Sieves and ladles

Long-handled sieves and perforated ladles are useful for lifting food from hot oil, when steaming or straining noodles. A wok scoop is a long-handled metal disk perfect for stirring and serving up stir-fried food. A long-handled wooden spoon or metal spatula can also be used.

Choppers

Chinese choppers, or cleavers, come in two sizes: heavy ones for chopping through bones and tough ingredients and smaller, thinner and lighter ones for cutting vegetables and slicing meat. Chopping boards should be fairly thick and made of either hard wood or white acrylic. A wooden board needs regular oiling. An acrylic board is easier to clean.

Chopsticks

Chopsticks for cooking are wooden and long so that they don't conduct heat and distance the cook from hot fat and steam. For eating, chopsticks can be wooden, plastic or for special occasions, ivory. Chopstick stands are useful for resting chopsticks on and make a decorative addition to a Chinese meal.

◆ KITCHEN EQUIPMENT ◆

EATING CHINESE STYLE

A simple Chinese table setting including a soup bowl and spoon, a small shallow bowl for dip sauces, chopsticks and a small, deeper bowl for holding rice and other foods added from the several communal main dishes.

Below left: *to eat with chopsticks, hold the bowl close to the mouth to facilitate and grace the movements.*
Below right: *to use chopsticks, hold one chopstick towards its base between your thumb and index finger and against the middle of the fourth finger at its tip. This chopstick remains stationary. Hold the second chopstick similarly against your index finger, supporting it with your thumb like a pencil. The two thinner tips should be kept level, with the first or lower chopstick kept steady while you manipulate the second or upper chopstick to pick up the food.*

◆ SPECIAL INGREDIENTS ◆

Bamboo shoots: There are several kinds of bamboo shoots available in the West – all in cans only, which is a pity since they lose much of their crispy texture and flavour. Try to obtain Winter bamboo shoots; they are dug up from the cracked earth before the shoots grow to any great length or size, therefore they are extra tender and tasty. Spring bamboo shoots are much larger; they sometimes may reach several feet in length and 3–4 inches(7.5–10 cm) in diameter. Once the can is opened, the shoots may be kept in a covered jar of water in the refrigerator for several days. Braised bamboo shoots in cans should be eaten cold without any further cooking.

Bean-curd: Made from soaked yellow soy beans ground with water. A coagulant is added after some of the water is strained through muslin cloth, causing the ground beans to curdle and become firm bean curd. Usually sold in squares about 2½ × 2½ inches (6 × 6 cm), ¾ inch (2 cm) thick. Will keep a few days if submerged in water in a container and placed in the coldest part of the refrigerator. Dried bean curd skin is usually sold either in thick sticks or thin sheets. It should be soaked in cold water overnight or in warm water for at least an hour before use.

Bean sauce: Sometimes called 'Crushed bean sauce', this thick sauce is made from black or yellow beans, flour and salt. It is sold in tins and, once opened, must be transferred into a screw-top jar and then it will keep in a refrigerator for months. (N.B. Black bean sauce is very salty, while yellow bean sauce is sweeter with sugar added.)

Bean sprouts: Two kinds are available: yellow soy bean sprouts, only to be found in Chinese provision stores, and green mung bean sprouts, which can be bought from almost every large city supermarket. (Never use canned bean sprouts, they do not have the crunchy texture which is the main characteristic of bean sprouts.) They can be kept in the refrigerator for two or three days if bought fresh.

Cellophane or transparent noodles: Made from mung beans. They are sold in dried form, tied into bundles weighing from 2 oz (50g) to 1 lb (0.5 kg). Soak in warm water for five minutes before use.

Chilli paste: Also called 'Chilli purée'. Is made of chilli, soy bean, salt, sugar and flour. Sold in jars and will keep almost indefinitely.

Chilli sauce: Hot, red sauce made from chillis, vinegar, plums, salt and sesame.

Chinese cabbage: There are innumerable varieties of cabbage grown in China, of which only two or three types are available in the West. The one most commonly seen is known as celery cabbage or Chinese leaves, it has a pale green colour and tightly wrapped elongated head, two thirds of the vegetable is stem which has a crunchy texture; another variety has a shorter and fatter head with curlier, pale yellow leaves. Then there is the dark green-leaved variety, also with white stems, and the bright green-leaved variety with pale green stems, sometimes with a sprig of yellow flower in the centre which is very much prized by the Chinese. These last two varieties are sold only in Chinese stores.

◆ SPECIAL INGREDIENTS ◆

Chinese dried mushrooms: There are two main types of Chinese mushrooms: those that grow on trees, known as Fragrant or Winter Mushrooms; and those cultivated on a bed of straw, known as Straw Mushrooms. Fragrant or Winter Mushrooms are sold dried; they are used in many dishes as a complementary vegetable for their flavour and aroma. Soak in warm water for 20–30 minutes, squeeze dry and discard the hard stalks before use. Straw Mushrooms are available in cans, but are completely different in texture and flavour. The Western varieties of common or field mushrooms can be used as substitutes.

Dried shrimp: These are small to very small, and are sold cleaned, shelled and whole. They add a salty, savoury seasoning to dishes.

Five-spice powder: A mixture of anise seed, fennel, cloves, cinnamon and pepper. It is very strongly piquant, so use a very small amount each time. It will keep for years if stored in a tightly covered container.

Fresh coriander: Sometimes known as Chinese parsley, this plant is available in oriental stores, or in Italian grocers where it is called *cilantro*.

Ginger root: Sold by weight. Should be peeled and sliced or finely chopped before use. Will keep for weeks in a dry, cool place. Dried and powdered ginger is not a satisfactory substitute for fresh ginger.

Gluten: A high-gluten flour and water dough is soaked and kneaded in water to wash out the starch; the remaining gluten is porous like a sponge. It is cut into pieces to be used like dumplings to carry flavour and provide bulk in sauces.

Green hot chilli: Will keep fresh for a week or two in the vegetable compartment of the refrigerator in a plastic bag.

Green seaweed: This mosslike seaweed is dark green in colour. It is sold dried, in wads or in matted chips. When deep-fried in oil, it is crisp and has a toasted fragrance. Dried green cabbage leaves can be used as a substitute.

Hoisin sauce: Also known as barbecue sauce. Made from soy beans, sugar, flour, vinegar, salt, garlic, chilli and sesame.

Kao Liang liqueur: A spirit made from sorghum and millet. Brandy or vodka can be substituted.

Monosodium glutamate (MSG sometimes): This chemical compound, known as 'taste essence' is often used to heighten the flavour of food. It is rather frowned upon by true gourmets as it can wipe out the subtle distinction of a dish when used to excess.

Oyster sauce: A thick sauce made from oysters and soy sauce. Sold in bottles, will keep in the refrigerator indefinitely.

Red bean curd sauce: A thick sauce made from fermented bean curd and salt. Sold in cans or jars, will keep indefinitely.

Rice wine: Also known as Shaoxing wine, made from glutinous rice. Saké or pale (medium or dry) sherry can be substituted.

Salted black beans: Whole bean sauce, very salty.

Chinese dried mushrooms

Dried shrimp

Five-spice powder

◆ SPECIAL INGREDIENTS ◆

Ground and whole Sichuan peppercorns

Green seaweed

Wood ears

Sesame seed oil: Sold in bottles. Widely used in China as a garnish rather than for cooking. The refined yellow sesame oil sold in Middle Eastern stores has less flavour and therefore is not a very satisfactory substitute.

The most commonly used oils in China are vegetable oils such as soy bean, peanut or rape seed oils. The Chinese never use butter or meat dripping, although lard and chicken fat are used in some regional cooking, notably in the Eastern School.

Sichuan preserved vegetable: This is a speciality of Sichuan province. It is the root of a special variety of the mustard green pickled in salt and hot chilli. Sold in cans. Once opened it can be stored in a tightly sealed jar in the refrigerator for months.

Sichuan peppercorns: Reddish-brown peppercorns, much stronger than either black or white peppercorns of the West. Usually sold in plastic bags. Will keep indefinitely in a tightly sealed container.

Soy sauce: Sold in bottles or cans, this liquid ranges from light to dark brown in colour. The darker coloured sauces are strongest, and more often used in cooking, whereas the lighter is used at the table.

Golden needles (dried Tiger Lily buds): The buds of a special type of lily. Sold in dried form, should be soaked in warm water for 10–20 minutes and the hard stems removed. They are often used in combination with *Wood Ears.*

Tomato sauce: Quite different from Western tomato ketchup. Italian tomato paste (purée) may be substituted when fresh tomatoes are not available.

Water chestnuts: Strictly speaking, water chestnuts do not belong to the chestnut family, they are the roots of a vegetable. Also known as *horse's hooves* in China on account of their appearance before the skin is peeled off. They are available fresh or in cans. Canned water chestnuts retain only part of the texture, and flavour of fresh ones. Will keep for about a month in a refrigerator in a covered jar.

Water chestnut powder: A flour made from water chestnuts. Cornflour is a good substitute.

Wood Ears: Also known as *Cloud Ears* they are dried tree fungus. Sold in dried form, should be soaked in warm water for 20 minutes; discard any hard stems and rinse in fresh water before use. They have a crunchy texture and a mild but subtle flavour. According to the Chinese, Wood Ears contain protein, calcium, Phosphorous, iron and carbohydrates.

◆ PREPARATION AND TECHNIQUES ◆

Temperatures

The temperature of the cooking oil will also have to be varied according to the ingredients used and the dishes to be produced.

Hot pan with cold oil: Heat the pan until very hot, then add the cold oil. Put in the ingredients before the oil gets really hot and remove the ingredients after deep frying for a short time. This method requires the temperature of the oil to be 175–210°F (80–100°C). When you add the ingredients, there should be no smoke from the oil and no hissing sound. This method is used to prepare good cuts of meat as it helps to retain their natural flavour and preserves the tenderness of the meat.

Hot pan with hot oil: Heat the pan until very hot, then add the oil and heat it to a temperature of 350–425°F (180–220°C). The oil should start to smoke, and it will hiss if you stir it. This method is used to prepare seafood and food that requires a crunchy covering (often battered foods).

Medium heat with hot oil: Heat the pan until very hot, then heat the oil until it reaches a temperature of 225–330°F (110–170°C). A small amount of smoke will begin to come off the surface of the oil. This method is used for frying large pieces of meat, whole fish, chicken or duck.

Stir-frying

The ability to stir-fry is an important part of any Cantonese chef's skill. It is essential to heat the pan over maximum gas or electricity until it is extremely hot. Then add the necessary quantity of oil. When that is hot, add minced or chopped garlic, ginger and spring onion. As the mixture begins to cook, add the other ingredients, stir-fry and turn them to cook everything quickly and evenly. Sprinkle wine and sesame seed oil at the end to produce a fragrant smell.

Shallow frying

For shallow frying, heat the pan until it is extremely hot and then add oil. Lower the ingedient into the pan and, when it is slightly brown, reduce the heat to a minimum. Use this method to fry fish. It will stop the skin sticking to the pan and ensure an attractive appearance when it is served.

Deep frying

This is a popular technique in Chinese cooking. Strictly speaking, blanching the ingredients in oil can be regarded as deep frying. To deep fry you need, in most cases, adequate heat and hot oil to make the ingredients crunchy and tender. Be careful, however, with ingredients that are coated in batter: keep the temperature somewhat lower, otherwise you will overcook the outside of the food while the inside is still raw. In these cases, it might be better to use the 'soak-frying' method. Heat the oil, add the ingredients and turn off the heat. Let them soak for a while in the hot oil and then take them out. Reheat the oil until it reaches a temperature of 350–425°F (180–220°C) and then deep fry the ingredients for a second time, until done. This method is also known as double deep frying.

Steaming

There are two kinds of steaming. Short steaming, requiring high heat, and long steaming, requiring low heat. Some other Chinese cook

Above: *a Chinese housewife prepares a meal.*

◆ PREPARATION AND TECHNIQUES ◆

books may call long steaming 'double boiling' because the foods are contained in a closed receptacle. In some recipes, those calling for the steaming of a duck, chicken or a large piece of meat for example, you should use the low, medium heat until the ingredients are tender.

Boiling

This is a very simple method of cooking. Simply add water to cook the ingredients, exactly as you would cook soup, rice or porridge. If you want to make a bowl of clear meat soup, you must blanch the meat with boiling water first, then rinse it under cold water. Heat a bowlful of water in a pan and, when the water is boiling, put the ingredients into it. You should use the maximum heat at the start, reducing to medium heat and finally ending with low heat. This kind of soup is delicious once you have mastered the timing and the amount of water to add.

Braising

Cook ingredients over moderate heat with sufficient liquid to cover them. Reduce the liquid to 15 per cent of the original and add seasonings to make a sauce.

Stewing

Add more water or stock and use low heat to cook the ingredients until they are soft and tender. Once the liquid has nearly all evaporated – or reduced to 10–20 per cent – add seasonings, ingredients and flavouring to make the sauce.

Knife and cleaver

The ingredients in Chinese cooking are frequently prepared by using a knife or sharp cleaver. Many recipes are prepared by the 'cut-and-cook' method, which requires that equal attention is paid to both the cutting and the cooking. Whether you are preparing ingredients by cutting them into chunky pieces, or by slicing, thick shredding, fine shredding, dicing into cubes or mincing, you must always ensure that everything is of equal size. If you do not, then the quality of the cooking will be affected because of the uneven heating that will result.

You need a good sharp cleaver and a heavy chopping-board. Any good quality Chinese chopper will be more than adequate, and a traditional chopping board made of solid wood 5–6in (12–15cm) thick, is much better than the skimpy modern ones. Many Westerners are afraid of using a razor-sharp Chinese kitchen chopper. The secret for beginners is to avoid cutting horizontally. Instead, use your whole hand on the top of the blade, rather than chopping from the handle, and slice carefully into the ingredients at an angle. This is risk-free and easy, thanks to the sharpness of the blade.

Marinating

After cutting, the next stage in the preparation of food before actual cooking is marinating, sometimes called 'coating' or 'blending' in Chinese. The basic method is to marinate meat, fish or chicken in salt, egg-white and starch – usually water-chestnut flour, but cornflour is a good substitute. Sometimes sugar, soy sauce and wine are added. The purpose of this 'coating' is to preserve the vitamins and protein content in meat after it is finely cut up, while retaining its tenderness and delicacy.

◆ PREPARATION AND TECHNIQUES ◆

Seasonings

There are far too many seasonings to list here, but the most basic category of all are those made from soya beans. All kinds of soy sauce are made from beans, so are bean paste, preserved bean curd and preserved fermented black beans. You will begin to get the authentic Chinese flavour by combining any of the above with garlic, ginger and spring onion. Traditionally, Cantonese chefs enjoy using oyster sauce.

The following seasonings are sufficient: sweet soy sauce, soy sauce, oyster sauce, black bean paste, yellow bean paste, sesame seed oil, rice wine, pepper, sugar, rice vinegar and cornflour. Most ordinary Chinese dishes can be prepared using any of the above in combination with garlic, ginger and spring onions, and with dried orange peel.

Slicing: *this is probably the most common form of cutting in Chinese cooking. The ingredients are cut into very thin slices, not much bigger than an oblong stamp, and as thin as cardboard. When slicing meat, always cut across the grain – this makes it more tender when cooked.*

Slicing meat across the grain.

To preserve vitamins, always wash vegetables before cutting.

Shredding: *the ingredients are first cut into thin slices, then shredded into thin strips as small as matches but twice as long.*

Meat is shredded into thin strips.

Shredding bamboo shoots.

◆ PREPARATION AND TECHNIQUES ◆

Chopping: *the normal method of cutting a fowl is as follows:*

1 *Remove the two wings.*

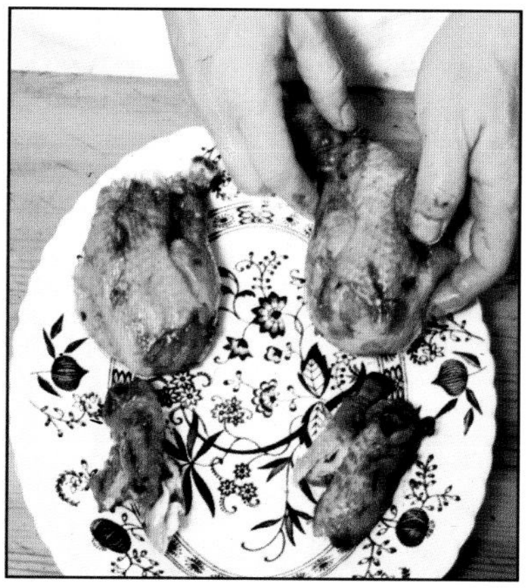

2 *Remove both the legs and thighs.*

3 *Separate the breast from the backbone.*

4 *Divide the breast into two sections.*

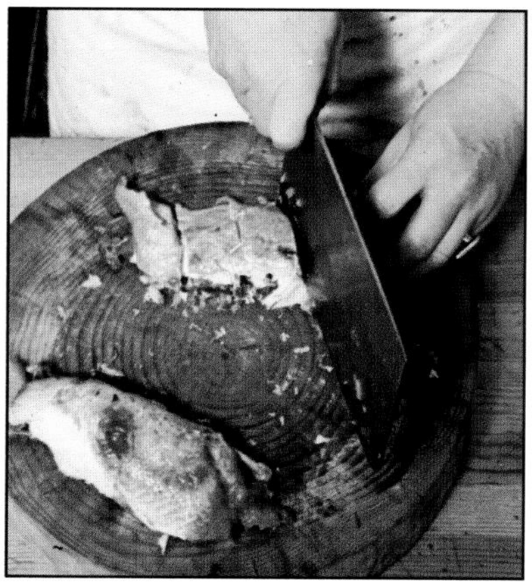

5 *Cut each breast into 3–4 pieces.*

6 *Cut each wing into 3 pieces and each leg into 5 pieces. Reassemble neatly.*

◆ PREPARATION AND TECHNIQUES ◆

Diagonal cutting: *carrots, celery, courgettes and asparagus are normally cut into diamond-shaped pieces.*

Carrots are cut diagonally.

Sweet peppers are cut into diamond-shaped pieces.

Dicing: *the ingredients are first cut into coarse strips about the size of French fries, then diced into small cubes.*

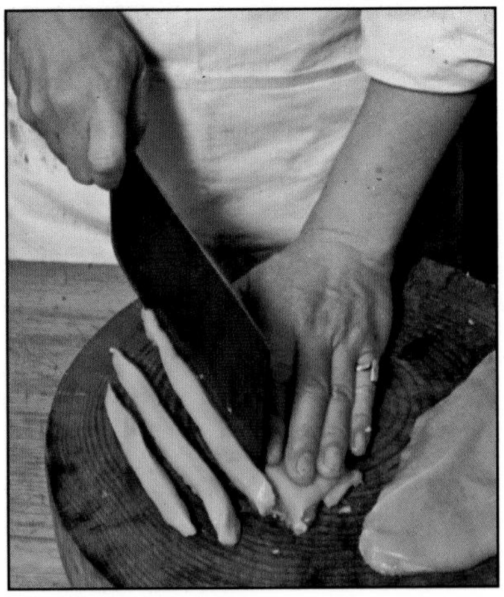

1 *Chicken breast is cut into strips.*

2 *Then cut crossways into small cubes.*

Mincing: *finely chop up the ingredients into small bits. Although it is much easier to use a mincer, the flavour is not quite the same.*

1 *Slices of pork are finely shredded and then coarsely chopped.*

2 *Mincing with a cleaver.*

◆ PREPARATION AND TECHNIQUES ◆

Steaming fish: *the Chinese steam almost all types of food including bread and dim sum, but they prize whole steamed fish above all. Served on its cooking dish, the fish juices blend with the seasonings and any marinade flavourings.*

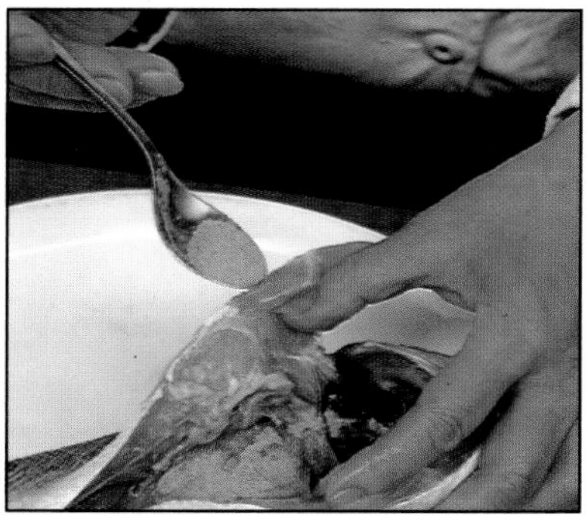

1 *Sprinkle the seasoning mixture inside the fish.*

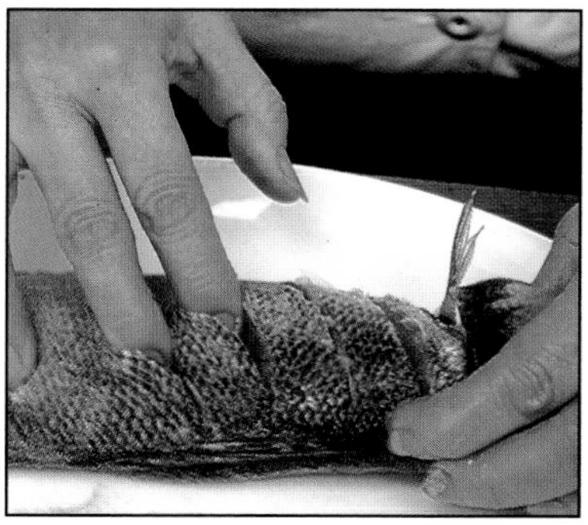

2 *Rub seasoning well inside the slits, and leave for the flavour to develop.*

3 *Season the outside of the fish.*

4 *Spread the spring onion and ginger garnish over the steamed fish.*

5 *Pour soy sauce over the fish. Repeat the process with dry wine or sherry. Finally, pour smoking hot oil over the fish to finish cooking.*

◆ PREPARATION AND TECHNIQUES ◆

Sweet and sour pork: *is an excellent example of wok cooking. The pork is first submerged in hot deep oil to fry it crisply. The pineapple and pepper pieces are stir-fried in a separate wok or skillet, then the sweet and sour sauce is stirred in. When the sauce thickens, the pork is added and tossed in the sauce.*

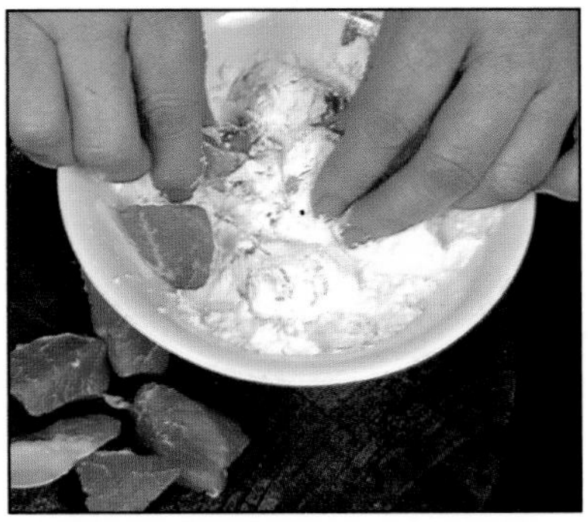

1 *Roll the pieces of pork in cornflour on all sides.*

2 *Coat the pieces well in a smooth egg and cornflour batter.*

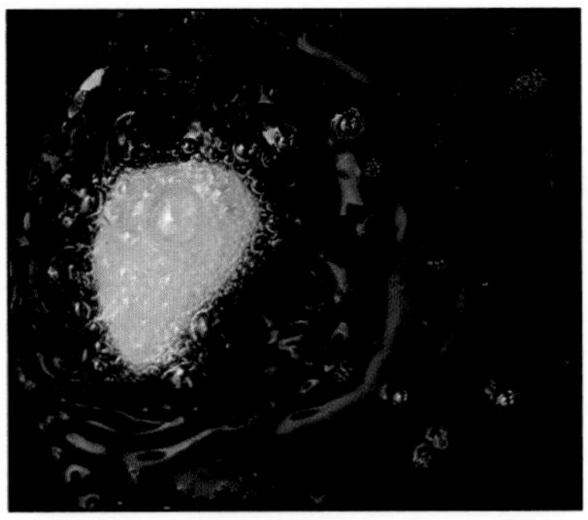

3 *To test if the oil is hot enough, drop in a slice of peeled ginger – Chinese style. It should bubble instantly.*

4 *Lower the battered pork into the oil with a slotted spoon and deep-fry. When cooked, remove, drain on absorbent kitchen paper and keep warm.*

5 *Stir-fry the vegetables quickly. Then stir in the sweet and sour sauce.*

6 *Add the fried pork to the sauce. Turn and stir for 1 minute.*

◆ PREPARATION AND TECHNIQUES ◆

Deep-frying: *properly carried out, seals the surface of the food and prevents the flavours of the food escaping into the oil; the cooked food itself will be crisp and non- greasy.*

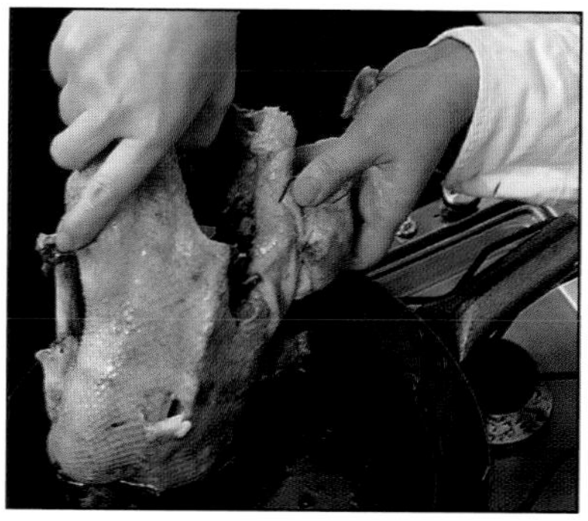

1 Aromatic and Crispy duck *Carefully lower the steamed duck into the hot oil.*

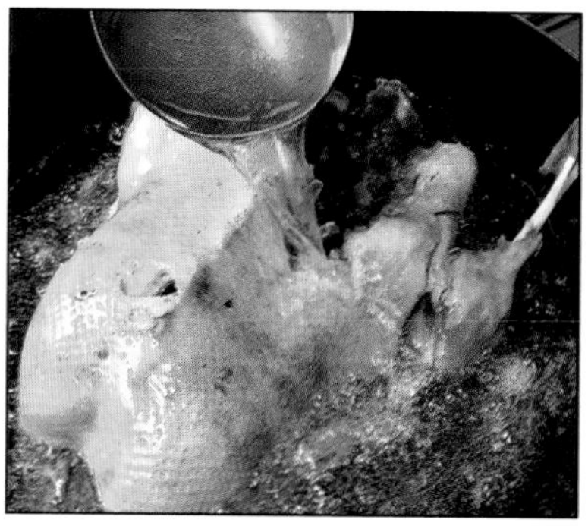

2 *Ladle hot oil repeatedly over the partly submerged duck to ensure even crisping.*

Stir-frying: *Practically all vegetables are cooked in this way.*

1 Blanched noodles stir-fried in seasoned oil *Add the cooked, drained noodles to the oil in the wok.*

2 *Turn the noodles frequently to ensure even cooking.*

Marinating: *this is sometimes called 'coating' or 'blending' in Chinese. The basic method is to marinate meat, fish or chicken in salt, egg white and cornflour. Sometimes sugar, soy sauce and wine are added. The purpose of marinating is to preserve the vitamins and protein content in meat after it is cut up, while retaining its tenderness and delicacy.*

Mixing the cornflour mixture with pork.

Soy sauce is added to the marinade.

◆ PREPARATION AND TECHNIQUES ◆

Rice: *is a staple food throughout China especially in the south and west. White, long grain rice is preferred to short or glutinous varieties for most meals as long, properly cooked fragrant grains are a perfect complement to other dishes served. To enjoy it at its best, be sure to use ordinary long grain rice that needs to be washed before cooking in preference to instant or pre-cooked varieties which lack flavour.*

1 **Egg-fried rice:** *fry in the beaten eggs until barely set.*

2 *Add plain boiled rice to the egg.*

3 *Add spring onions and other ingredients to the mixture.*

4 *Season with soy sauce.*

5 *Turn and mix over low heat.*

◆ PREPARATION AND TECHNIQUES ◆

Making spring rolls:
1 *Cut each spring roll skin in half diagonally.*
2 *Place about 2 tsp of the filling on the skin about a third of the way down, with the triangle pointing away from you.*

3 and 4 *Lift the lower flap over the filling and roll once.*

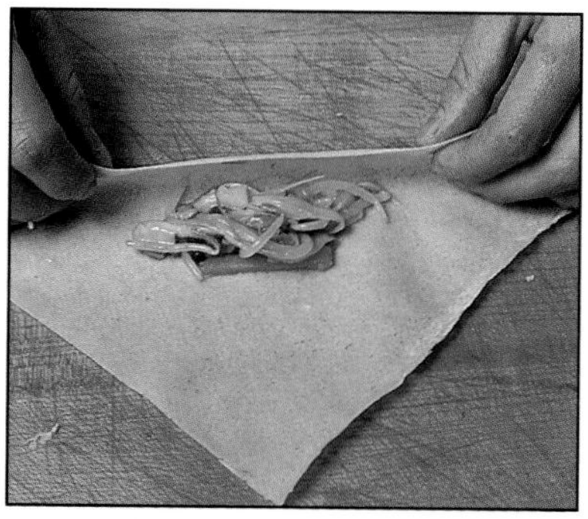

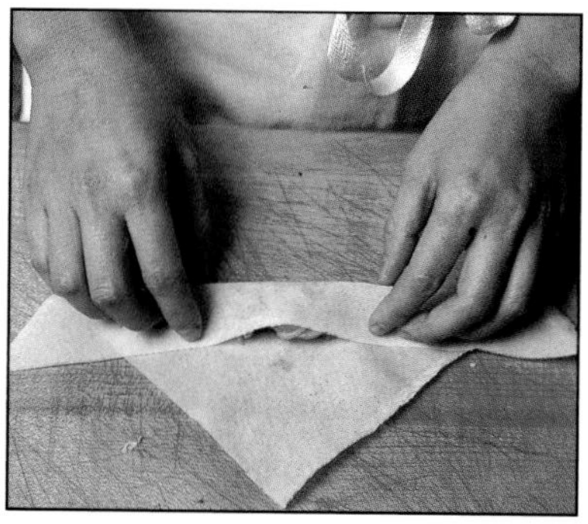

5 and 6 *Fold in both ends.*

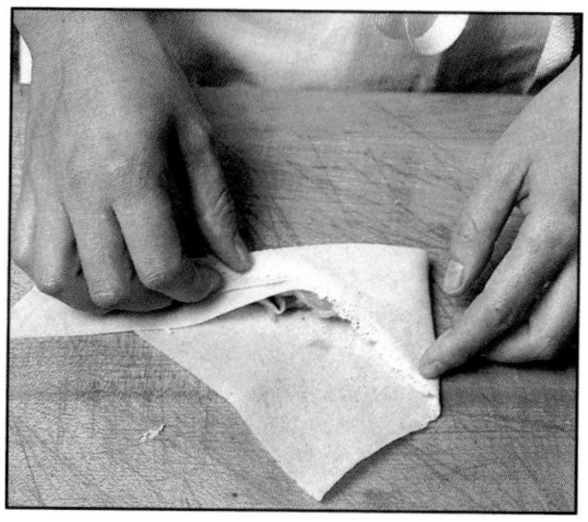

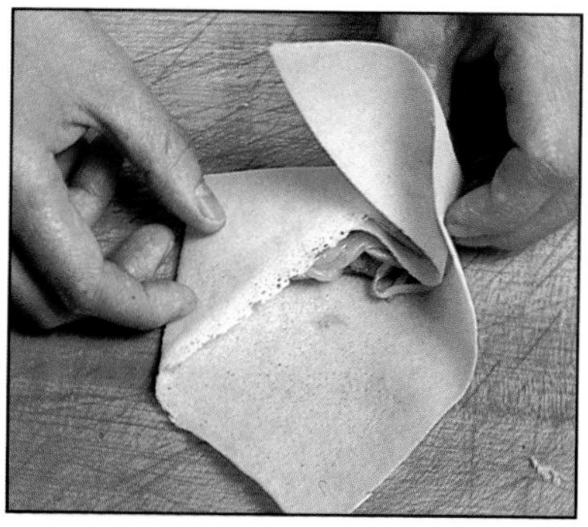

7 *Roll over once more. Brush the upper edge with a little flour and water paste.*
8 *Roll over into a neat package. Repeat until all the filling is used up. These can be kept in the refrigerator for a couple of days or frozen for up to 3 months.*

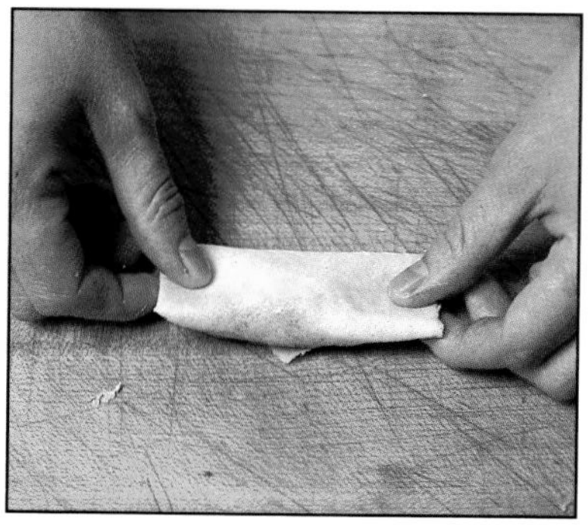

GOOD STOCK

SERVES 12

3–4lb (1.5–1.75kg) chicken (broiler if available) or duck carcass or spareribs
Scant 3¼pt (2lt) water
3–4 slices fresh root ginger

Remove the breast meat and the 2 legs from the chicken. Boil the remaining carcass of the chicken in 3 pt (1.75 lt) of the water for 20 minutes. Remove from the heat and add ¼ pt (150 ml) cold water. (The adding of the cold water causes the fat and impurities to cling together, making them easier to remove.) Skim the surface of all scum which rises to the top. Add the ginger and continue to simmer gently for about 1½ hours. After about an hour of simmering, remove the chicken carcass from the stock. Mince the leg meat and the breast meat separately. Add the leg meat to the stock at this stage. Simmer for 10 minutes, then add the breast meat and simmer for about 5 minutes. Strain the stock through a fine sieve or muslin.

DOUBLED-BOILED PIGEON, HAM AND BLACK MUSHROOM SOUP

DOUBLE–BOILED PIGEON, HAM AND BLACK MUSHROOM SOUP

SERVES 4–6

2 pigeons
8oz (225g) lean pork
6 medium black mushrooms
1½oz (40g) ham
3 slices fresh root ginger
1tbsp Chinese yellow wine
1pt (600ml) chicken stock
2–3tbsp oil

Clean the pigeons thoroughly. Cut out the breast meat and save it for a stir-fried supreme of pigeon. Blanch the lean pork and pigeons in boiling water for 2 minutes and rinse under the tap for 1 minute. Soak the black mushrooms in warm water for about 30 minutes until they have softened. Discard the stems and cut the caps into evenly sized pieces.

Put all ingredients in a heavy pot or casserole with a lid, add the stock and an equal amount of water, and cover and steam over medium heat for 3 hours. Double boiling is the favourite Cantonese way of preparing soup. The Cantonese believe that it not only makes the flavour richer but increases the nutritional value.

DRIED BEAN CURD SKIN AND VERMICELLI SOUP

SERVES 4–6

½oz (15g) dried bean curd skin
1oz (25g) golden needles (dried, tiger-lily buds)
¼oz (5g) black moss
2oz (50g) bean thread vermicelli
1½pt (900ml) water
1tsp salt
2tbsp light soy sauce

1tbsp rice wine or dry sherry
1tsp fresh root ginger, finely chopped
2 spring onions, finely chopped
2tsp sesame seed oil
fresh coriander to garnish

Soak the bean curd skin in hot water for 30–35 minutes and then cut it into small pieces. Soak the lily buds and black moss in water separately for about 20–25 minutes. Rinse the lily buds until clean. Loosen the black moss until it resembles human hair.

With a pair of scissors, cut the vermicelli into short lengths.

Bring the water to the boil in a wok or large pot, and add all the ingredients together with the seasonings. Stir until well blended. Cook the soup for 1–1½ minutes. Add the sesame seed oil and serve hot, garnished with coriander.

DRIED BEAN CURD SKIN AND VERMICELLI SOUP

DUCK AND CABBAGE SOUP

SERVES 4–6

1 duck carcass (plus giblets if available)
1lb (450g) Chinese cabbage
2 slices fresh root ginger
salt and Sichuan pepper

Break up the carcass, place it together with the giblets and any other bits and pieces in a large pot or pan; cover it with water, add the ginger root, bring it to the boil. Skim off the impurities floating on the surface and let it simmer gently with a lid on for at least 45 minutes.

About 20 minutes before serving, add the washed and sliced cabbage. Season, then serve.

BEEF BROTH TOMATO SOUP

SERVES 4–6

3oz (75g) lean beef
1½tsp salt
1½tbsp cornflour
½ egg white
4tbsp vegetable oil
6 firm medium tomatoes
2 spring onions
2pt (1.2lt) good stock (see recipe)
3–4 slices fresh root ginger
1 chicken stock cube
1½tbsp light soy sauce
pepper to taste
1 egg
1tsp sesame seed oil

Cut the beef into very thin slices. Rub with the salt and cornflour, then toss in the egg white. Heat the vegetable oil in a wok or frying pan. When moderately hot, gently fry the beef for 30 seconds, then drain. Cut each tomato into 6 pieces. Cut onions into ½ inch (1 cm) sections.

Bring the stock to the boil in a wok or saucepan. Add the ginger, crumbled stock cube, beef, soy sauce, pepper, spring onion and tomatoes. Simmer for 2 minutes and then pour the beaten egg into the soup in a thin stream. Finally, add the sesame seed oil. Stir and serve immediately.

◆ SOUPS ◆

YELLOW FISH SOUP (OR WHOLE FISH SOUP)

SERVES 4–6

1 trout (or sea bass, bream etc), about 1½lb (700g)
2tsp salt
1tsp ground ginger
1tsp pepper
5oz (150g) leeks
4 slices fresh root ginger
2oz (50g) canned bamboo shoots
vegetable oil for deep-frying
2pt (1.2lt) good stock (see recipe)
1tbsp drained, canned chopped snow pickles
2tbsp light soy sauce
3tbsp wine vinegar

Clean the fish thoroughly. Rub the inside and outside well with salt, ground ginger and pepper. Leave to season for 20 minutes. Clean the leeks and shred. Shred the ginger and bamboo shoots.

Heat the oil in a wok or deep-fryer. When hot, fry the fish for about 7–8 minutes until beginning to brown and become crispy. Remove and drain on absorbent kitchen paper. Heat the stock in an oval-shaped flameproof casserole, wok or similar pan. Lower the fish into the stock. Bring to the boil, add the leeks, ginger, bamboo shoots and pickles, and simmer for 5–6 minutes. Sprinkle on the soy sauce and vinegar, continue to simmer for a further 5–6 minutes.

Ladle the soup and vegetables from the casserole into individual rice bowls and eat with rice and fish.

HOT AND SOUR SOUP

SERVES 4–6

2–4oz (50–100g) lean pork
1–2oz (25–50g) canned bamboo shoots
4 medium dried Chinese mushrooms
1tbsp dried shrimps
1–2 cakes fresh bean curd
1 egg
2 spring onions
2pt (1.2lt) good stock (see recipe)
3tbsp fresh or frozen shrimps
1tsp salt
2 stock cubes
2tbsp peas
1tsp sesame seed oil

HOT AND SOUR SOUP

◆ SOUPS ◆

Hot and sour mixture
2tbsp soy sauce
3tbsp vinegar
2tbsp cornflour
4tbsp water
pepper to taste

Shred the pork and bamboo shoots into 1 inch (2.5 cm) strips. Soak the dried mushrooms and dried shrimps separately in hot water to cover for 25 minutes. Drain, reserving the soaking water. Discard the tough stalks from the mushrooms, then cut the caps into slices a similar size to the pork. Add the soaking water to the stock. Cut the bean curd into ½ inch (1 cm) cubes. Beat the egg lightly with a fork for 15 seconds. Roughly chop the spring onions. Mix the hot and sour mixture together in a bowl.

Bring the stock to the boil in a wok or saucepan. Add the pork, dried shrimps and mushrooms and simmer for 10 minutes. Add the fresh or frozen shrimps, bean curd, bamboo shoots, salt, crumbled stock cubes, peas and spring onions. Continue to cook for 3–4 minutes, then stir in the hot and sour mixture which will thicken the soup. Gently pour the beaten egg over the surface of the soup in a thin stream. Sprinkle the soup with sesame seed oil and serve immediately.

TRIPE, SQUID AND PEA SOUP

SERVES 4–6

8oz (225g) dried squid
3tsp salt
3 slices fresh root ginger
12oz–1lb (350–450g) tripe (pork or beef)
12oz (350g) peas
1½pt (900ml) good stock (see recipe)
1 chicken stock cube
1½tbsp cornflour blended with 4tbsp water
salt and pepper to taste
1tsp sesame seed oil

Soak the dried squid in warm water to cover for 3 hours. Place the salt and ginger in a saucepan with 2 pt (1.2 lt) water. Bring to the boil and add the tripe. Simmer for 1½ hours. Drain the tripe and squid, then cut into matchstick–sized shreds. Purée the peas in a liquidizer.

Place the squid in a saucepan with ½ pt (300 ml) boiling water. Simmer until the liquid in the pan has been reduced by half, about 15 minutes. Add the tripe and stock and simmer gently for 30 minutes. Add the pea purée and crumbled stock cube. Heat and stir gently for 10 minutes. Add the blended cornflour and salt and pepper to taste. Stir in the sesame seed oil. Continue to cook for 2 minutes, stirring.

CRAB MEAT SOUP

SERVES 5–6

6–7oz (175–200g) crab meat, fresh or frozen
2 slices fresh root ginger
2 spring onions
1 cake fresh bean curd
8oz (225g) young spinach
2tbsp vegetable oil
1½pt (900ml) good stock (see recipe)
1 chicken stock cube
1tsp salt
pepper to taste
2tbsp cornflour blended with 5tbsp water

Flake the crab meat, thawing first if necessary. Coarsely chop the ginger. Cut the spring onions into ½ inch (1 cm) shreds. Cut the bean curd into cubes. Wash the spinach, removing any tough stems and discoloured leaves.

Heat the oil in a wok or saucepan. When hot, stir-fry the ginger and spring onion for 30 seconds. Add the crab meat and stir-fry for 15 seconds. Pour in the stock. Add the crumbled stock cube and the salt and pepper. Bring to the boil, stirring. Add the spinach and bean curd. Bring contents to the boil again, stirring, then simmer gently for 2 minutes. Stir in the blended cornflour and cook until thickened.

CRAB MEAT SOUP

◆ SOUPS ◆

BEAN CURD, HAM, MUSHROOM AND SPINACH SOUP

SERVES 4–6

6oz (175g) carton frozen spinach
4 medium dried Chinese mushrooms
3–4oz (75–100g) ham
2–3oz (50–75g) button mushrooms
2tbsp cornflour
2 cakes fresh bean curd
1½pt (900ml) good stock (see recipe)
1½tsp salt
pepper to taste
1 chicken stock cube
1tbsp light soy sauce
1tsp sesame seed oil

Thaw the spinach and roughly chop. Soak the dried mushrooms in hot water to cover for 25 minutes. Drain, reserving the soaking liquid. Discard the tough stalks and cut the mushroom caps into shreds. Cut the ham and fresh mushrooms into similar shreds. Blend the cornflour with the mushroom soaking water. Cut the bean curd into 1½ inch (4 cm) cubes.

Bring the stock to the boil in a wok or saucepan. Add the fresh and dried mushrooms, bean curd, salt, pepper and crumbled stock cube. Bring back to the boil and add the spinach, ham, soy sauce and blended cornflour. Cook over gentle heat for 3–4 minutes. Sprinkle with sesame seed oil and serve.

EGG–FLOWER SOUP

SERVES 4–6

1 clove garlic
2 slices fresh root ginger
3 spring onions
1 egg

EGG-FLOWER SOUP

1tsp salt
pepper to taste
1¾pt (1lt) good stock (see recipe)
1 chicken stock cube
1tsp sesame seed oil

Finely chop the garlic, ginger and spring onions. Lightly beat the egg with a fork for 30 seconds, then sprinkle with a pinch of salt and pepper.

Heat the stock in a wok or saucepan. Add the garlic, ginger and crumbled stock cube. Bring to the boil and simmer for 3 minutes. Pour the beaten egg in a very thin stream, along the prongs of a fork, and trail it over the surface of the soup. When the egg has set, sprinkle the soup with spring onion, remaining salt and pepper and the sesame seed oil.

DEEP–FRIED BEAN CURD AND WOOD EAR SOUP

SERVES 4–6

2oz (50g) deep-fried bean curd, or 1 cake fresh bean curd
½oz (15g) wood ears (tree fungus)
1pt (600ml) water
1tsp salt
1tbsp light soy sauce
1 spring onion, finely chopped
1tsp sesame seed oil

Use either 2 packets of ready-made deep-fried bean curd (there are about 10 to each 1 oz [25 g] packet), or cut a cake of fresh bean curd into about 20 small cubes and deep-fry them in very hot vegetable oil until they are puffed up and golden. Cut them in half. Soak the wood ears in water until soft (this will take about 20–25 minutes) and rinse until clean.

Bring the water to the boil in a wok or large pot. Add the bean curd, wood ears and the salt. When the soup starts to boil again, add the soy sauce and cook for about 1 minute. Garnish with finely chopped spring onion and sesame seed oil. Serve hot.

CHINESE CABBAGE SOUP

SERVES 4–6

9oz (250g) Chinese cabbage
3–4 dried Chinese mushrooms, soaked in warm water for 30 minutes
2tbsp oil
2tsp salt
1tbsp rice wine or dry sherry
1½pt (900ml) water
1tsp sesame seed oil

Wash the cabbage and cut it into thin slices. Squeeze dry the soaked mushrooms. Discard the hard stalks and cut the mushrooms into small pieces. Reserve the water in which the mushrooms have been soaked for use later.

Heat a wok or large pot until hot, add oil and wait for it to smoke. Add the cabbage and mushrooms. Stir a few times and then add the salt, wine, water and the mushroom soaking water. Bring to the boil, add the sesame seed oil and serve.

CHICKEN AND PRAWN BALL SOUP

SERVES 4–6

½lb (225g) uncooked prawns
2oz (50g) pork fat
2oz (50g) chicken breast meat
2oz (50g) cooked ham
½ cucumber
2 egg whites
1½tbsp cornflour
1 slice fresh root ginger, peeled and finely shredded
2tbsp rice wine or dry sherry
2tsp salt
1½pt (900ml) stock

Shell the prawns and finely mince to a pulp. Mince the pork fat and chicken breast meat. Finely chop the ham. Slice the cucumber thinly.

Mix ½ tbsp cornflour with 4 tbsp water, add the minced chicken breast and 1 egg white, blend well. This is called chicken purée.

Mix together the prawns, pork fat, the remaining cornflour, egg white, finely chopped root ginger, 1tbsp rice wine or sherry and 1tsp salt; blend well.

Bring the stock to the boil, then reduce the heat and put in the prawn and pork fat mixture made into small balls about the size of walnuts. Increase the heat to bring it back to the boil. Now add the remaining salt and rice wine or sherry, then reduce heat again and simmer gently for about 10 minutes.

Stir the chicken purée and add it to the soup, stirring all the time so it does not form into lumps.

Add the ham and cucumber; turn up the heat to bring to a rapid boil; serve in a large bowl.

RIGHT: CHINESE CABBAGE SOUP

◆ SOUPS ◆

BEAN SPROUT SOUP

SERVES 4–6

8oz (225g) fresh bean sprouts
1 small red pepper, cored and seeded
2tbsp oil
2tsp salt
1pt (600ml) water
1 spring onion, finely chopped

Wash the bean sprouts in cold water, discarding the husks and other bits and pieces that float to the surface. It is not necessary to top and tail each sprout. Thinly shred the pepper.

Heat a wok or large pot, add the oil and wait for it to smoke. Add the bean sprouts and red pepper and stir a few times. Add the salt and water. When the soup starts to boil, garnish with finely chopped spring onion and serve hot.

PEKING SLICED FISH PEPPER POT SOUP

SERVES 4–6

8oz (225g) white fish fillets
1½tsp salt
1tbsp cornflour
1 egg white
2 slices fresh root ginger
1 clove garlic
2 spring onions
vegetable oil for deep-frying
1½pt (900ml) chicken stock
½tsp salt
¼tsp monosodium glutamate
3tbsp wine vinegar
½tsp pepper

Cut the fish into 1½×1 inch (4×2.5 cm) slices. Dust with the 1½ tsp salt and the cornflour, and wet with the egg white. Finely chop the ginger and garlic. Coarsely chop the spring onions.

Heat the oil in a wok or deep-fryer. When hot, lightly fry the coated fish for 1 minute. Remove and drain. Bring the stock to the boil in the wok or saucepan. Add the ginger, garlic, remaining salt and monosodium glutamate, if using, and bring back to the boil for 1 minute. Add the fish, vinegar and pepper and simmer for 3–4 minutes. Pour into a heated tureen, sprinkle with spring onions and serve.

SWEETCORN AND ASPARAGUS SOUP

SERVES 4–6

6oz (175g) white asparagus
1 egg white
1tbsp cornflour
2tbsp water
1pt (600ml) water
1tsp salt
4oz (100g) sweetcorn
1 spring onion, finely chopped, to garnish.

Cut the asparagus spears into small cubes. Beat the egg white lightly. Mix the cornflour with the water to make a smooth paste. Bring the water to a rolling boil. Add the salt, sweetcorn and asparagus. When the water starts to boil again, add the cornflour and water mixture, stirring constantly. Add the egg white very slowly and stir. Serve hot, garnished with finely chopped spring onions.

CUCUMBER SOUP

SERVES 4–6

½ cucumber
2oz (50g) black field mushrooms
1pt (600ml) water
1½tsp salt
1tsp sesame seed oil
1 spring onion, finely chopped

Split the cucumber in half lengthwise, and thinly slice but do not peel. Wash and slice the mushrooms, but do not peel. Bring the water to the boil in a wok or large pot. Add the cucumber and mushroom slices and salt. Boil for about 1 minute. Add the sesame seed oil and finely chopped spring onion, stir and serve hot.

LEFT: BEAN SPROUT SOUP
RIGHT: CUCUMBER SOUP

◆ SOUPS ◆

CHINESE MUSHROOM SOUP

SERVES 4–6

6 dried Chinese mushrooms
2tsp cornflour
1tbsp cold water
3 egg whites
2tsp salt
1pt (600ml) water
1 spring onion, finely chopped

Soak the dried mushrooms in warm water for 25–30 minutes. Squeeze them dry, discard the hard stalks and cut each mushroom into thin slices. Reserve the water in which the mushrooms were soaked for use later.

Mix the cornflour with the water to make a smooth paste. Comb the egg whites with your fingers to loosen them.

Mix the water and the mushroom soaking water in a pan and bring to the boil. Add the mushrooms and cook for about 1 minute. Now add the cornflour and water mixture, stir and add the salt. Pour the egg whites very slowly into the soup, stirring constantly. Garnish with the finely chopped spring onions and serve hot.

BACON AND BAMBOO SHOOT SOUP

SERVES 4–6

4oz (100g) unsmoked streaky bacon in one piece
6oz (175g) bamboo shoot tips
2oz (50g) seasonal greens
1tbsp rice wine or dry sherry
½tsp monosodium glutamate
1tsp salt
1tbsp lard
1pt (600ml) water

Dice the bacon into small cubes and the bamboo shoot tips into small triangles. Bring water to the boil; put in both the bacon and bamboo shoots at the same time; add wine or sherry, then reduce heat and simmer for 10 minutes. Add greens, monosodium glutamate and salt; increase heat to high again and when the soup starts to boil put in the lard and serve.

LIVER PÂTÉ SOUP

SERVES 4–6

½lb (225g) pig's liver
2 egg whites
1tbsp rice wine or dry sherry
1tsp salt
1¼pt (650ml) stock
salt and pepper to taste

Chop the liver into a pulp; squeeze it through a muslin cloth; mix it with 1 tbsp stock and the egg whites; add wine or sherry and salt. Place in a bowl and steam for 15 minutes; by then it will have become a solid liver pâté; let it cool.

Place the liver pâté on the bottom of a large soup bowl; cut it into small squares (but keep the whole pieces together). Bring the stock to the boil and gently pour it over the liver. Season with salt and pepper and serve.

THREE PEARLS SOUP

SERVES 4–6

4oz (100g) chicken breast meat
1 egg white
2tbsp milk
1½tbsp cornflour
2oz (50g) peas
2 red tomatoes
1pt (600ml) stock
1tbsp rice wine or dry sherry
1tsp salt
½tsp monosodium glutamate
1tsp chicken fat

Remove all white tendon and membrane from the chicken meat, finely mince it into a pulp, mix it with ½ tbsp cornflour and milk, add the egg white and blend it all together well.

Skin tomatoes by dipping in boiling water and cut into small cubes the same size as the peas.

Bring the stock to a rolling boil, add the peas and tomato, bring it back to the boil, then remove it from the flame. Now use a single chopstick to pick up a little bit of chicken mixture at a time and flip it into the stock until all the chicken is used up and you end up with lots of tiny chicken balls the size of peas. Then place the pan back on a high heat and bring the stock to a boil. Mix the rest of the cornflour in a little water and add to the soup together with salt, rice wine or sherry and monosodium glutamate. When it starts to boil again, all the 'three pearls' will float on top; add the chicken fat and serve.

Should you use ham instead of tomato, you will still have the three colours of white, green and pink.

PORK AND BAMBOO SHOOT SOUP

SERVES 4–6

½lb (225g) unsmoked bacon in one piece
1lb (450g) leg of pork in one piece
1lb (450g) bamboo shoots
3½pt (2lt) water

Place the two pieces of meat in a large pot; add the water, bring to a rolling boil, skim off the scum and reduce the heat to moderate. Replace the lid and simmer for about 2–3 hours, then add the bamboo shoots, cut into chunks, and continue cooking for 20–30 minutes.

When serving, you should be able to pull small pieces of the meat off with your chopsticks or with a serving spoon. The preserved pork or bacon should not taste too salty and the fresh pork should have acquired some of the flavour of the preserved pork. The bamboo shoots should taste fantastic, having absorbed the flavours of both.

OPPOSITE: LIVER PÂTÉ SOUP

WONTON SOUP

SERVES 6–8

40 wontons
1¼tbsp dried shrimps
1tbsp peanut oil
4 slices fresh root ginger
1½pt (900ml) chicken stock
2tsp sugar
2tsp sesame oil
4–6tsp light soy sauce
2tbsp spring onions, chopped

Soak the dried shrimps in ½ pt (225 ml) hot water for 30 minutes. Heat 1 tbsp oil in a pot or casserole and add the ginger and dried shrimps, stirring until the aroma rises. Add the chicken stock plus the water used to soak the shrimps. Bring the contents to the boil, reduce the heat and simmer for 30 minutes. Add the sugar and keep warm in the pot.

Use four or six soup bowls and put into each ¼ tsp sesame oil, 1 tsp light soy sauce and 1 tsp chopped spring onion. Set aside.

Bring 4 pt (2.5 lt) water to the boil. Add the wontons. Reduce the heat to medium and simmer for 5 minutes. Remove with a perforated spoon and divide them equally among the soup bowls. Add the soup and serve.

YIN AND YANG VEGETABLE SOUP

SERVES 4–6

1¼lb (550g) spinach leaves
1tsp bicarbonate of soda
9oz (250g) button mushrooms
4oz (100g) chicken breast meat
1 egg white
2tsp salt
4tbsp peanut oil
2tsp Chinese yellow wine
1½pt (900ml) chicken stock
6tbsp cornflour

Blanch the spinach for 2 minutes in 1 pt (600 ml) boiling water with 1 tsp bicarbonate of soda added. Remove and rinse under the tap for 1 minute. Drain the leaves before chopping them finely. Set aside. Chop the mushrooms finely. Set aside. Finely mince the chicken breast and mix with the egg white and 1 tsp salt. Set aside.

Heat 2 tbsp oil in a pan. Sauté the minced spinach for 3 minutes, add 1 tsp of Chinese yellow wine and 1 tsp of salt and stir together. Add 1 pt (600 ml) chicken stock to the pan, having first mixed 3 tbsp of the stock with 3 tbsp cornflour. Bring the stock to the boil and slowly stir in the cornflour.

Place an S-shaped piece of greased cardboard in the centre of a soup tureen to divide the bowl into two. Pour the spinach soup into one side of the bowl, holding the cardboard upright by placing a glass of water against it on the empty side.

Heat 2 tbsp oil. Add the mushrooms, sauté for 1 minute and add 1 tsp of Chinese yellow wine. Take 3 tbsp of the remaining stock and mix with 3 tbsp cornflour. Add the

YIN AND YANG VEGETABLE SOUP

rest of the chicken stock to the pan, bring to the boil and slowly stir in the blended cornflour. When it boils, stir in the minced chicken and mix well.

Pour the chicken soup into the other half of the soup tureen, first removing the glass of water. Take out the cardboard as gently as possible. The one bowl of soup is then presented and served in the two colours of Ying and Yang.

MINCED BEEF, CELERY, CHIVES AND NOODLES IN SOUP

SERVES 4–6

9oz (250g) Chinese celery
9oz (250g) Chinese white chives or the white part of leeks
1¼lb (550g) dried white wheat flour thick noodles
1pt (600ml) chicken stock, boiling
4tbsp peanut oil
1¼lb (550g) minced beef
2tsp spring onions, chopped
2tsp fresh root ginger, chopped
2tsp Sichuan pickle, chopped
1tbsp dark soy sauce
2tsp chilli oil
2tsp Sichuan peppercorn powder
4tbsp chicken stock

Chop the celery and white chives or leeks into shavings. Set aside.

Bring 4 pt (2.5 lt) water to the boil and add the noodles. Reduce the heat to medium and cook for 5–6 minutes. Transfer the noodles to a large pan of cold water, stirring to keep them separate. Drain the noodles and return them to a pan of boiling water and cook for a further 2 minutes. Test with your fingers to see if they are cooked: they should be firm but also soft and easy to break. When they are cooked remove and drain them and divide them among four or six bowls.

Add 1 pt (600 ml) of boiling chicken stock to the noodles in the bowls.

Heat the oil in a pan, add the minced beef and stir-fry quickly over high heat. Add the chopped celery and chives and, continuing to stir, cook for 30 seconds. Add the remaining ingredients, including an additional 4 tbsp chicken stock, stir and bring the contents to the boil. Ladle over each bowl of noodles and serve one bowl to each diner.

PICKLED CABBAGE AND CHICKEN CLEAR SOUP

SERVES 4–6

9oz (250g) pickled cabbage
9oz (250g) chicken breasts

Marinade
1 egg white
1tbsp light soy sauce
½tsp sesame seed oil
1tsp cornflour
1½pt (900ml) chicken stock
½pt (225ml) water
4 slices fresh root ginger

Soak the pickled cabbage in salted water for 2 hours. Rinse under the tap, squeezing several times. Cut into strips.

Cut the chicken breast meat into thin slices. Mix the marinade, add the chicken and set aside.

Put the chicken stock, water, ginger and cabbage in a pot and bring to the boil. Reduce the heat and simmer for 15 minutes.

Bring ¾ pt (450 ml) water to the boil. Add the chicken slices, stir to separate and remove immediately. Drain the chicken and transfer the pieces to the soup in the pot. Simmer for 3 minutes and serve.

OX TAIL SOUP

SERVES 4–6

1 ox tail
1 chicken (boiler)
½lb (225g) carrots
6pt (3lt) water
1oz (25g) fresh root ginger, crushed
1tbsp Sichuan peppercorns
4tbsp rice wine or dry sherry
salt to taste

Trim off the excess fat on the ox tail and cut into pieces. Cut the carrots into thick chunks.

Place the ox tail in a large pot with water, bring to the boil, skim off the scum; add root ginger, Sichuan peppercorns, wine or sherry and chicken. Reduce heat when it starts to boil; simmer for 4 hours or more, turning the chicken and ox tail over every hour or so. Add the carrots in the last 20 minutes of cooking time. Discard chicken before serving; add salt to taste.

RIGHT: MINCED BEEF, CELERY, CHIVES AND NOODLES IN SOUP

CHICKEN LIVER MOUSSE CLEAR SOUP

CHICKEN LIVER MOUSSE CLEAR SOUP

SERVES 4–6

8oz (225g) chicken livers
5 egg whites
1 egg yolk
1½pt (900ml) chicken stock
1tsp salt
2tsp Chinese yellow wine
¼tsp pepper
½tsp sesame seed oil

Finely mince the chicken livers and run them through a sieve. Add the 5 egg whites and the egg yolk to ¾ pt (450 ml) chicken stock. Stir to mix well together in a basin. Add the salt, yellow wine, pepper and sesame seed oil, stir and blend thoroughly.

Grease the bottom of a medium-sized soup tureen and transfer the mixture to it to steam over medium heat until set, which will take 7–8 minutes. Heat the remaining chicken stock and place it in a large soup tureen. Transfer the chicken liver mousse to the large tureen, taking care not to damage the mousse in the transfer. Serve for eating throughout the meal.

AROMATIC CHIU CHOW RICH FISH SOUP

SERVES 4–6

5oz (150g) fillet of pomfret (sea bream) or other white fish
4oz (100g) squid
1tsp sesame seed oil
1tsp salt
1 fillet dried sole
2–3tbsp peanut oil
2 medium black mushrooms
1 Chinese celery
1pt (600ml) chicken stock
8oz (225g) plain cooked rice

Cut the fillet of pomfret or whichever white fish you are using into thick slices and cut the squid into bite-sized pieces. Mix the fish and squid with 1 tsp of sesame seed oil and 1 tsp of salt.

Break or chop the fillet of dried sole into tiny pieces and deep-fry with 2–3 tbsp oil over low heat until crisp. Drain and set aside.

Soak the black mushrooms in hot water for 30 minutes. Remove and discard the stems and cut the caps into fine shreds. Chop the celery coarsely. Bring the chicken stock to the boil and add the celery, black mushrooms and rice. When the soup boils again, add the sliced fish and squid and when it boils again, sprinkle with chopped dried fish.

ROAST DUCK BONE, CABBAGE AND MUSHROOM SOUP

SERVES 4–6

1 roast duck carcass (from Peking Duck)
2lb (1kg) Chinese cabbage
4–6 medium black mushrooms
1tbsp peanut oil
1pt (600ml) chicken stock
1½pt (900ml) water
3–4 slices fresh root ginger
salt and pepper

Chop the duck bones into 3 inch (7 cm) pieces and cut the Chinese cabbage into 2×3 inch (5×7 cm) pieces.

Soak the black mushrooms in hot water for 30 minutes. Remove stems.

Blanch the duck pieces in boiling water for 3 minutes. Remove.

Heat the peanut oil in a pan and stir-fry the Chinese cabbage for 2 minutes. Remove and set aside.

Bring the chicken stock and water to the boil. Add all the ingredients and simmer for 1½ hours. Season with salt and pepper to taste. Serve in a large bowl for diners to help themselves.

◆ ◆ ◆

◆ RICE AND NOODLES ◆

FRIED RICE CHIU CHOW STYLE

SERVES 4–6

4oz (100g) Chinese kale, stem only
4tbsp peanut oil
2tbsp fresh-root ginger, shredded
4oz (100g) shrimps, shelled and deveined
2 eggs, lightly beaten
8oz (225g) cold plain cooked rice
2tbsp shrimp sauce
8 tbsp chicken stock

Dice the stems of the Chinese kale into small pieces. Heat the oil in a pan and add the shredded ginger, shrimps and Chinese kale, stir-frying them for 1 minute. Add the eggs (beaten for 10 seconds) and, when they are partly set, add the cold plain rice. Stir-fry over a very high heat. Scramble the eggs, breaking them into tiny pieces with your spoon or spatula.

Add the shrimp sauce and chicken stock and stir-fry over reduced heat for a further 3–5 minutes. Serve.

FRIED RICE CHIU CHOW STYLE

YIN AND YANG RICE

SERVES 4–6

Marinade
1 egg white
1tbsp cornflour
1tsp sesame seed oil
1tsp salt
8oz (225g) chicken breast
9oz (250g) shrimps, shelled and deveined
4tbsp peanut oil
1tbsp fresh root ginger, shredded
2 eggs, beaten
8oz (225g) cold plain cooked rice
2tbsp light soy sauce
½pt (300ml) chicken stock
½pt (300ml) peanut oil
2oz (50g) peas
1tsp salt
1tsp fresh root ginger, chopped
1tsp garlic, chopped

White sauce
8tbsp chicken stock
2tbsp milk
1tbsp cornflour
1tsp salt

Red sauce
1½tbsp tomato ketchup
8tbsp chicken stock
1tbsp cornflour
1tsp sugar
1tbsp light soy sauce

Mix together the marinade ingredients in a bowl. Shred the chicken breasts and add to half of the marinade. Set aside.

Clean the shrimps and pat them dry. Mix them with the other half of the marinade in a bowl and refrigerate for 30 minutes.

Heat 4 tbsp oil in a pan and add 1 tbsp shredded ginger. When hot, add the beaten eggs and, when the eggs are partly set, add the rice. Stir-fry for 2 minutes, breaking up the egg with a spatula. Add the soy sauce and chicken stock and keep on stir-frying for 3 minutes. Transfer to a large dish.

Heat ½ pt (300 ml) oil in a pan. Add the shrimps, stirring to separate. Remove and set aside. Add the chicken to the oil, again stirring to separate. Remove and set aside. Cook the peas in 8 tbsp water with 1 tsp salt for 5 minutes. Drain and set aside.

Heat 1 tbsp oil in the pan and add ½ tsp garlic. When the aroma rises, return the shrimps and peas to the pan. Add the white sauce ingredients and bring to the boil. Pour over one half of the dish of fried rice, using an S-shaped piece of foil to keep the sauce to one side of the dish.

Heat 1 tbsp oil in the pan and add ½ tsp ginger and ½ tsp garlic and when the aroma rises, return the chicken to the pan. Add the red sauce and bring to the boil. Pour over the fried rice on the other side of the foil. Remove the foil and serve.

◆ RICE AND NOODLES ◆

FUKIEN CRAB RICE

SERVES 6–8

1 bowl cooked glutinous rice
2 bowls cooked long grain rice
8–12oz (225–350g) young leeks
3 slices fresh root ginger
2 cloves garlic
2 medium crabs, about 3lb (1.5kg)
¼pt (150ml) vegetable oil
1oz (25g) lard
1tsp salt
⅓pt (200ml) good stock (see recipe)
1 chicken stock cube
2tbsp tomato purée
1tsp paprika
1tbsp light soy sauce
¼pt (150ml) dry sherry
1tbsp cornflour blended with 2tbsp water

Place the bowl of glutinous rice in a saucepan with 1½ bowls of water. Bring to the boil and simmer very gently for 15 minutes. Add this rice to the cooked long grain rice and mix together. Clean and cut the leeks slantwise into 2 inch (5 cm) sections. Shred the ginger. Coarsely chop the garlic. Chop each crab through the shell into 12 pieces, cracking the claws with the side of the chopper. Discard the dead men's fingers.

Heat the oil in a wok or large frying pan. When very hot, add the crab pieces and turn them around in the hot oil for 3 minutes. Drain. Pour away the oil to use for other purposes, leaving 2 tbsp. Add the lard and reheat the wok or pan. When hot, stir-fry the ginger and garlic over medium heat for 15 seconds. Add the leeks and salt and stir-fry for 1 minute. Pour in the stock and sprinkle in the crumbled stock cube, then add the tomato purée, paprika, soy sauce and sherry. Bring to the boil, stirring, and return the crab pieces to the pan. Cook over medium heat for 3 minutes. Add the blended cornflour, turn and stir a few times until thickened.

Place the mixed rice into a medium two-handled wok with a lid, or a large flameproof casserole. Pour the crab and leek mixture over the rice. Place the wok or casserole over a low heat, cover and cook gently for 5 minutes. Bring the container to the table for serving.

BASIC FRIED RICE

SERVES 4

2 medium onions
2–3 rashers of bacon
2 spring onions
3 eggs
5tbsp vegetable oil
3tbsp peas
2 bowls plain boiled rice
1tsp salt

Peel and thinly slice the onions. Cut the bacon across the lean and fat into matchstick-sized strips. Cut the spring onions into ¼ inch (0.5 cm) shreds. Lightly beat the eggs.

Heat 2½ tbsp of the oil in a wok or frying pan. When hot, stir-fry the onion and bacon over medium heat for 1 minute. Add the peas and continue to stir-fry for 45 seconds. Add the cooked rice and toss and turn for 45 seconds. Remove from the heat. Heat the remaining oil in a separate small wok or pan. When hot, add half the spring onions and stir over medium heat for 30 seconds. Pour in the beaten egg. Tilt the pan, so that the egg flows evenly over the bottom of the pan. After 1 minute, when the eggs have nearly set, sprinkle with the salt and the remainder of the spring onions. Stir and lightly scramble the eggs. When set, transfer the egg mixture to the rice. Stir and turn over medium heat for 1 minute.

YANCHOW FRIED RICE

YANCHOW FRIED RICE

SERVES 5–6

1 recipe Basic Fried Rice (see recipe)
1 medium red pepper
2–3oz (50–75g) bean sprouts
3oz (75g) fresh or frozen medium or large prawns
2–3oz (50–75g) canned straw mushrooms or 4oz (100g) fresh button mushrooms
1 medium courgette
2½tbsp vegetable oil
2tbsp sweetcorn
3oz (75g) fresh or frozen shrimps
¾oz (20g) lard or butter
1½tbsp light soy sauce

Repeat the Basic Fried Rice recipe. Cut the red pepper into ¼ inch (0.5 cm) pieces. Wash and dry the bean sprouts. Cut each shrimp into 2–3 pieces. If using button mushrooms, quarter them. Cut the courgette into 8 sections, then further divide in quarters.

Heat the oil in a wok or frying pan. When hot, stir-fry the pepper, mushrooms, bean sprouts, courgette, shrimp and prawns over high heat for 1½ minutes. Add the lard and light soy sauce and continue to stir-fry over medium heat for 1½ minutes. Turn the contents into the pan containing the fried rice. Reduce the heat to low, turn and stir together for 30 seconds.

SHANGHAI VEGETABLE RICE

SERVES 5–6

2 cups long grain rice
1lb (450g) green cabbage or spring greens
1½tbsp dried shrimps
about 8oz (225g) Chinese sausages
2tbsp vegetable oil
¾oz (20g) lard
1½tsp salt

Wash and measure the rice. Simmer in the same volume of water for 6 minutes. Remove from the heat and leave to stand, covered, for 7–8 minutes. Wash and dry the cabbage. Chop into 1½×3 inch (4×7.5 cm) pieces, removing the tougher stalks. Soak the dried shrimps in hot water to cover for 7–8 minutes, then drain. Cut the sausages slantwise into 1 inch (2.5 cm) sections.

Heat the oil and lard in a deep saucepan. When hot, stir-fry the shrimps for 30 seconds. Add the cabbage and toss and turn for 1½ minutes until well coated with oil. Sprinkle the cabbage with the salt. Pack in the rice. Push pieces of sausage into the rice. Add 4–5 tbsp water down the side of the pan. Cover and simmer very gently for about 15 minutes. Transfer to a heated serving dish.

◆ RICE AND NOODLES ◆

VEGETARIAN SPECIAL FRIED RICE

SERVES 4–6

4–6 dried Chinese mushrooms
1 green pepper, cored and seeded
1 red pepper, cored and seeded
4oz (100g) bamboo shoots
2 eggs
2 spring onions, finely chopped
2tsp salt
4–5tbsp oil
2lb (900g) cooked rice
1tbsp light soy sauce (optional)

Soak the dried mushrooms in warm water for 25–30 minutes, squeeze dry and discard the hard stalks. Cut the mushrooms into small cubes. Cut the green and red peppers and the bamboo shoots into small cubes. Lightly beat the eggs with about half of the spring onions and a pinch of the salt.

Heat about 2 tbsp of oil in a hot wok, add the beaten eggs and scramble until set. Remove. Heat the remaining oil. When hot, add the rest of the spring onions followed by all the vegetables and stir-fry until each piece is covered with oil. Add the cooked rice and salt and stir to separate each grain of rice. Finally add the soy sauce, blend everything together and serve.

SHANGHAI EMERALD FRIED RICE

SERVES 4–6

8oz (225g) spring greens or cabbage
2tsp salt
4½–5½tbsp vegetable oil
2 eggs
2 spring onions
1lb (450g) cooked rice (see recipe)
2tbsp chopped ham
¼tsp monosodium glutamate (optional)

Wash and finely shred the cabbage. Sprinkle with 1½ tsp of the salt. Toss and leave to season for 10 minutes. Squeeze dry. Heat 1½ tbsp of the oil in a wok or pan. When hot, stir-fry the cabbage for 30 seconds. Remove from the pan. Add 1 tbsp oil to the wok or pan. When hot, add the beaten eggs to form a thin pancake. As soon as the egg sets, remove from the pan and chop. Chop the spring onions.

Heat 2–3 tbsp oil in a wok or pan. When hot, stir-fry the spring onion for a few seconds. Add the rice and stir with the spring onion. Reduce the heat to low, stir and turn until the rice is heated through. Add the cabbage, egg and ham. Stir and mix them together well. Sprinkle with monosodium glutamate, if using, and remaining salt. Stir and turn once more, then sprinkle with remaining egg.

PLAIN COOKED RICE GRUEL OR CONGEE

SERVES 4–6

2 cups or bowls long grain white rice
10 cups or bowls water

Wash and rinse the rice, drain well. Place in a deep heavy pot or pan and add the water. Bring to the boil, reduce the heat and simmer very gently, uncovered, for 1½ hours, stirring occasionally. By this time, the rice will be fairly thick and porridgy; suitable for serving for breakfast or late supper. Serve accompanied by pickled or salted foods.

VEGETARIAN NOODLES IN SOUP

SERVES 4–6

8oz (225g) water chestnuts
4oz (100g) straw mushrooms
4oz (100g) white nuts
3tbsp oil
1tsp salt
1tsp sugar
1tbsp light soy sauce
1tsp sesame seed oil
8oz (225g) egg noodles or vermicelli

Drain the ingredients if they are canned and cut the water chestnuts into thin slices. The straw mushrooms and white nuts can be left whole.

Heat the oil in a hot wok or frying pan. When it starts to smoke, add the vegetables and stir-fry for a few seconds. Add the salt, sugar and soy sauce and continue stirring. When the gravy begins to boil, reduce the heat and let it simmer gently.

Cook the noodles in boiling water. Drain and place them in a large serving bowl. Pour a little of the water in which the noodles were cooked into the bowl – just enough to half-cover the noodles. Then quickly pour the entire contents of the wok or frying pan over the top. Garnish with the sesame seed oil and serve hot.

BEGGARS' NOODLES

SERVES 6

3 spring onions
3tbsp soy sauce
3tbsp wine vinegar
1lb (450g) wheat flour noodles, flat or Ho Fen noodles, or spaghetti

Sauce
3tbsp peanut butter
2tbsp sesame paste
3tbsp sesame seed oil

Coarsely chop or shred the onions. Mix the soy sauce and vinegar together. Mix the peanut butter, sesame paste and sesame seed oil together.

Place the noodles in a saucepan of boiling water and simmer for 10 minutes, or spaghetti for about 10–12 minutes. Drain.

Divide the hot noodles into 4–6 heated large rice bowls. Sprinkle evenly with the spring onion. Add a large spoonful of the peanut butter and sesame mixture to each bowl of noodles. Pour 1 tbsp of soy sauce and vinegar mixture over contents of each bowl.

OPPOSITE: BEGGARS' NOODLES

◆ RICE AND NOODLES ◆

TEN VARIETY FRIED RICE

SERVES 4–6

½lb (225g) rice
4oz (100g) shrimps
4oz (100g) cooked ham or pork
2 spring onions
3 eggs
salt
4oz (100g) peas
2tbsp soy sauce

Wash the rice in cold water just once, then cover it with more cold water so that there is about 1 inch (2.5 cm) of water above the surface of the rice in the saucepan. Bring it to the boil; stir to prevent it sticking to the bottom of the pan when cooked. Replace the lid tightly and reduce the heat so that it is as low as possible. Cook for about 15–20 minutes.

Peel the shrimps, dice the ham or pork into small cubes the size of the peas. Finely chop the onions. Beat up the eggs with a little salt; heat up about 1 tbsp oil and make an omelette; set aside to cool. Heat up the remaining oil, stir-fry the finely chopped onions, followed by the shrimps, ham or pork, and peas; stir, adding a little salt, then add the cooked rice and soy sauce. Add the omelette, breaking it into little bits. When everything is well blended it is ready to serve.

ABOVE LEFT: TEN VARIETY FRIED RICE
ABOVE RIGHT: FRIED RICE-NOODLES

BRAISED E-FU NOODLES WITH SHREDDED PORK AND MUSHROOMS

SERVES 4–6

2oz (50g) fillet of pork
1tsp cornflour
2 medium black mushrooms
4oz (100g) chives
1½pt (900ml) boiling water
12oz (350g) E-Fu noodles
3–4tbsp peanut oil
1tbsp fresh root ginger, shredded

Sauce
1tbsp oyster sauce
1tbsp light soy sauce
1tsp dark soy sauce
1tsp sesame seed oil
½tsp sugar

Mix the sauce ingredients together in a bowl. Cut the fillet of pork into matchstick-sized shreds and add 1 tbsp of the mixed sauce and 1 tsp of cornflour. Mix well and set aside.

Soak the black mushrooms in hot water for 30 minutes. Remove and discard the stems and cut the caps into shreds. Set aside. Cut the chives into 1½ inch (3 cm) pieces and set aside. Bring the water to the boil and add the E-Fu noodles. Parboil until soft. Remove, drain and dry the noodles with absorbent kitchen paper.

Heat 3–4 tbsp oil in pan. Add the shredded ginger and fillet of pork

◆ RICE AND NOODLES ◆

and stir-fry for 1 minute. Add the mushrooms, stir and continue to cook for a further minute. Return the E-Fu noodles to the pan and add the remainder of the sauce. Stir and mix the ingredients together, simmering over medium heat until all the water is absorbed by the noodles.

Sprinkle the chives over the noodles and cook for 30 seconds. Transfer to a plate and serve immediately.

PRAWNS AND NOODLE BALLS

MAKES 15

4oz (100g) Chinese rice vermicelli (beehoon)
8oz (225g) peeled prawns
½tsp sugar
2oz (50g) pork fat
few slices fresh root ginger
salt and pepper
very little, lightly beaten egg white
oil for deep frying

Crush the beehoon finely and leave in a dry place. Mince the prawns (use a food processor for this), sprinkle with sugar. Mince the pork fat with fresh ginger, add the prawns with seasoning and bind together. Use wetted hands to form into even, bite-sized balls. Chill well, and roll in crushed beehoon just before frying in hot oil. Cook for about 3–4 minutes until cooked through, or steam in a bamboo steamer over hot water for 30 minutes.

PEKING JA CHIANG MEIN NOODLES

SERVES 4–6

1 medium onion
2 slices fresh root ginger
2 cloves garlic
4 spring onions
6 inch (15cm) section cucumber
1lb (450g) wheat flour noodles (like spaghetti)
4tbsp vegetable oil
8oz (225g) minced pork
½tsp salt
1tbsp yellow bean paste
1tbsp soy sauce
4tbsp good stock (see recipe)
1tbsp cornflour blended with 3tbsp water

Coarsely chop the onion, ginger and garlic. Cut the spring onions into 2½ inch (6 cm) sections (dividing the larger stalks in half or a quarter). Cut the cucumber into matchstick-sized shreds. Place the noodles in a saucepan of boiling water and simmer for 8–10 minutes. Drain. Rinse the noodles under running cold water to keep separate.

Heat the oil in a wok or large frying pan. When hot, stir-fry the onion and ginger for 1 minute. Add the garlic and pork and stir-fry over medium heat for 3 minutes. Add the salt, yellow bean paste and soy sauce. Stir and cook for 3 minutes. Mix in the stock and continue to cook for a further 3 minutes. Pour in the blended cornflour, stirring until thickened.

Reheat the noodles by dipping them in boiling water for 15 seconds, then drain thoroughly. Arrange them on a large heated serving dish. Pour the sauce into the centre of the noodles. Arrange the shredded cucumber and spring onion sections on either side of the sauce.

FRIED RICE-NOODLES

SERVES 4–6

1lb (450g) rice-noodles
1oz (25g) dried shrimps
2oz (50g) pork
2oz (50g) bamboo shoots
3–4 small dried Chinese mushrooms
2oz (50g) celery
1oz (25g) leeks
1tsp salt
2tbsp soy sauce
4tbsp stock
4tbsp oil

Soak the rice-noodles in warm water until soft; soak the dried shrimps and mushrooms. Cut the pork, bamboo shoots and leeks into match-stick sized shreds.

Stir-fry the pork, bamboo shoots, shrimps, celery and leeks in a little hot oil; add salt and stock; cook for about 2 minutes, remove.

Heat up the remaining oil; stir-fry the rice-noodles for about 2–3 minutes; add the other cooked ingredients and soy sauce; stir for a further 2 minutes until there is no juice at all left; serve hot.

SHANGHAI COLD-TOSSED NOODLES

SERVES 3–4

2tbsp dried shrimps
3tbsp dry sherry
3tbsp light soy sauce
2tbsp wine vinegar
1½tsp red chilli oil
2 spring onions
1lb (450g) freshly made noodles or 12oz (350g) wheat flour noodles
2½tbsp Sichuan hot Ja Chai pickles, coarsely chopped
2tbsp snow pickles, coarsely chopped
1½tbsp winter pickles, coarsely chopped
1½tsp sesame seed oil

Soak the dried shrimps in hot water to cover for 5 minutes. Drain and coarsely chop. Add the shrimp to the sherry and leave to soak for 15 minutes. Mix the soy sauce, vinegar and red chilli oil together. Cut the spring onions into ½ inch (1 cm) shreds.

Place the freshly made noodles in a saucepan of boiling water and blanch for 3 minutes; if using wheat noodles, simmer for 5–6 minutes. Remove from heat and leave to soak in the hot water for a further 5–6 minutes. Drain and cool.

Spread the noodles on a large serving dish. Sprinkle them evenly with the chopped pickles, shrimps and sherry, then the soy sauce mixture. Finally, add the spring onion shreds and sesame seed oil.

To serve the Chinese way, the diners mix and toss the noodles they require and transfer it to their bowls, adjusting any additional seasonings of soy sauce, red chilli oil or vinegar.

◆ RICE AND NOODLES ◆

CHINESE CABBAGE, MUNG BEAN NOODLES, DRIED SHRIMPS AND SHREDDED PORK

SERVES 4–6

1¼lb (550g) Chinese cabbage
4oz (100g) mung bean noodles
2oz (50g) dried shrimps
2oz (50g) fillet of pork

Seasoning
1tsp salt
2tsp cornflour
½tsp sesame seed oil
½tsp sugar

3–4tbsp peanut oil
3–4 slices fresh root ginger
1½pt (900ml) chicken stock
1tsp salt
2tsp Chinese yellow wine

Cut the Chinese cabbage into ½×2 inch (1×5 cm) pieces. Soak the mung bean noodles and the dried shrimps in water for about 15 minutes until they are softened. Shred the fillet of pork and mix the meat with the seasoning ingredients. Heat 3–4 tbsp oil in a clay pot or a wok and add the

ginger slices and shredded fillet of pork, stirring to separate. Then add the dried shrimps.

Add the Chinese cabbage, stir and mix well. Pour in the chicken stock and bring the contents to the boil. Reduce the heat and simmer for 15 minutes. Add the mung bean noodles and simmer for a further 2–3 minutes. Finally add salt and Chinese yellow wine and serve.

BRAISED TRANSPARENT PEA-STARCHED NOODLES

SERVES 4–6

5 large dried Chinese mushrooms
4oz (100g) transparent pea-starched noodles
2tsp dried shrimps
3 slices fresh root ginger
3 spring onions
4oz (100g) lean pork
2tbsp vegetable oil
½pt (300ml) good stock (see recipe)
1 chicken stock cube
2tbsp light soy sauce
1½tbsp vinegar
½tsp salt
¼tsp pepper

Soak the dried mushrooms in hot water to cover for 25 minutes. Drain and discard the tough stalks. Cut the mushroom caps into shreds. Soak the noodles in hot water to cover for 3 minutes, then drain. Soak the dried shrimps in hot water to cover for 5 minutes. Cut the ginger and spring onions into similar sized shreds as the mushrooms. Dice the pork.

Heat the oil in a wok or frying pan. When hot, stir-fry the shrimps, ginger, pork and mushrooms over a medium heat for 1½ minutes. Add the spring onions, stock, crumbled stock cube and soy sauce. Bring to the boil and simmer gently for 4–5 minutes. Add the noodles, vinegar, salt and pepper. Stir and mix the contents evenly and continue to simmer for another 4–5 minutes.

SICHUAN NOODLES WITH PEANUT SAUCE AND VEGETABLES

SERVES 6

1lb (450g) fresh egg noodles or dried noodles, cooked according to packet instructions
4tbsp oil for frying

Sauce
2 large tbsp crunchy peanut butter
1tbsp hot oil and 1tsp sesame seed oil

Garnish
a handful of dry fried peanuts, lightly crushed
2 spring onions, shredded
4oz (100g) bean sprouts, blanched in boiling water for 1 minute, rinsed in cold water and drained
¼–½ cucumber, cut into small chunks
a few radishes

Plunge the noodles into boiling water for 1 minute. Rinse with cold water and leave on one side to dry. Meanwhile prepare the sauce by blending the peanut butter with hot oil and sesame seed oil to a smooth paste. Prepare the garnishes. Now fry the noodles in two or three lots in hot oil. Flatten out on one side and, when hot, turn over and fry on the other side. Keep warm while cooking the other noodles. Pile onto a large platter and pour over the sauce — mix lightly then scatter with peanuts and spring onions. Arrange the bean sprouts, cucumber and radishes either around the noodles or in separate bowls.

TEN TREASURE TAPESTRY NOODLES

SERVES 5–6

2 rashers of bacon
2–3oz (50–75g) pork
2oz (50g) beef or lamb
2oz (50g) chicken
1tsp salt
2tbsp cornflour
1 egg white
2oz (50g) canned bamboo shoots
2 sticks celery
2 spring onions
2–3oz (50–75g) French beans
4 dried Chinese mushrooms
5tbsp good stock (see recipe)
4tbsp soy sauce
8–12oz (225–350g) packet egg noodles or wheat flour noodles
4tbsp vegetable oil
1½oz (40g) lard
1tbsp rice wine or dry sherry
1tsp sesame seed oil

Shred the bacon. Cut the pork, beef and chicken into similar matchstick-sized shreds. Rub the meats with the salt. Dust with the cornflour. Coat with the egg white. Cut the bamboo shoots and celery into similar matchstick-sized shreds. Cut the spring onions into 1 inch (2.5 cm) sections, separating the white parts from the green. Top and tail the French beans and parboil in boiling water for 2 minutes. Drain. Soak the dried mushrooms in hot water to cover for 25 minutes. Drain and discard the tough stalks. Cut the mushroom caps into shreds. Blend the remainder of the cornflour with the stock and 1 tbsp soy sauce. Place the noodles in a saucepan of boiling water and simmer for 4 minutes. Drain.

Heat the oil in a wok or large frying pan. When hot, stir-fry the pork, chicken, beef, bacon and white parts of the spring onion over high heat for 2½ minutes. Remove two-thirds of the contents and put aside. Add all the vegetables and ½ oz (15 g) of the lard to the wok or pan and stir-fry for 2 minutes. Stir in 2 tbsp soy sauce and half the blended cornflour. Cook for 1 minute. Pour in the noodles, turn and mix for 1½ minutes until the noodles are heated through. Heat the remaining lard in a separate wok or pan. When hot, add the green parts of the spring onion and the reserved two-thirds meat mixture. Stir-fry over high heat for 1 minute. Pour in the remainder of the soy sauce and stir-fry for 30 seconds. Add the remainder of the blended cornflour, the sherry and sesame seed oil. Continue to stir and mix for 30 seconds.

Spread the noodle mixture on to a large heated serving dish. Pour over the meat mixture from the second pan.

BASIC CHOW MEIN

SERVES 4–6

12oz–1lb (350–450g) wheat flour or rice flour noodles
8oz (225g) lean pork
½tsp salt
4½tbsp vegetable oil
2oz (50g) drained, canned snow pickles
8oz (225g) bean sprouts
2 spring onions
¾oz (20g) lard
2tbsp soy sauce
1tbsp sesame seed oil

Parboil the noodles in a saucepan of boiling water for 5 minutes, or 3 minutes for rice flour noodles. Drain. Cut the pork into matchstick-sized shreds. Sprinkle with salt. Rub with 1 tsp of the oil. Coarsely chop the pickles. Wash and drain the bean sprouts. Cut the spring onions into 1 inch (2.5 cm) sections.

Heat the vegetable oil in a wok or large frying pan. When hot, stir-fry the pork and pickles for 2½ minutes. Remove half the contents and put aside. Pour all the noodles into the pan to turn and stir for 2½ minutes. Transfer to a heated serving dish. Add the lard to the wok and return the reserved pork and pickles. Add the spring onions and stir-fry for 30 seconds over high heat. Add the bean sprouts, soya sauce and sesame seed oil. Continue to stir-fry for 1½ minutes.

Spoon the stir-fried ingredients over the noodles. Toss before serving.

BEEF CHOW MEIN

SERVES 4–6

12oz (350g) packet wheat flour noodles or egg noodles
12oz (350g) steak, eg, fillet, rump or sirloin
2tbsp soy sauce
pepper to taste
3 slices fresh root ginger
2 spring onions
4tbsp vegetable oil
¾oz (20g) lard
1tbsp hoisin sauce
2tbsp good stock (see recipe)
1½tbsp rice wine or dry sherry
1tbsp cornflour blended with 2 tbsp water

Place the noodles in a saucepan of boiling water and simmer for 5 minutes. Drain. Cut the beef into 2×1 inch (5×2.5 cm) very thin slices. Rub with the soy sauce and pepper to taste. Shred the ginger. Cut the spring onions into 2 inch (5 cm) sections, separating the white from the green parts.

Heat 3 tbsp of the oil in a wok or frying pan. When hot, stir-fry the ginger and white parts of the spring onion for 30 seconds. Add the beef slices, spread them over the wok or pan, and stir-fry over high heat for 1½ minutes. Remove from the pan. Add the lard, hoisin sauce, remaining soy sauce and stock to the wok. Bring to the boil, stirring. Pour the noodles into the pan, toss and stir until heated through. Spread out on a heated serving dish. Add the remaining oil, green parts of the spring onions, sherry and beef to the wok or pan. When boiling, pour over the blended cornflour and turn the beef over a few times. Spoon the beef mixture evenly over the noodles.

MANCHURIAN BOILED AND BRAISED LAMB NOODLES

SERVES 6–8

1lb (450g) leg of lamb
2 slices fresh root ginger
1½tbsp cornflour
4tbsp vegetable oil
1½lb (675g) mutton
3 medium onions
3 cloves garlic
12oz (350g) young leeks
1 chicken stock cube
1tsp salt
12oz (350g) wheat flour noodles
½oz (15g) lard
2tbsp soy sauce
½tbsp yellow bean paste
1tbsp red chilli oil
1tbsp prepared English mustard

Cut the lamb into 1½×1 inch (4×2.5 cm) thin slices. Finely chop the ginger. Dust and rub the lamb with the ginger, cornflour and 1 tbsp of the vegetable oil. Cut the mutton into 1 inch (2.5 cm) cubes. Slice the onions. Coarsely chop the garlic. Clean and cut the leeks into 1 inch (2.5 cm) sections.

Parboil the mutton in a saucepan of boiling water for 5 minutes. Drain. Place the mutton in a flameproof casserole and add 1½ pt (900 ml) water, the crumbled stock cube, salt and onion. Bring to the boil and simmer gently for 1¼ hours or until the stock is reduced by a quarter. Place the noodles in a saucepan of boiling water and blanch for 3 minutes. Drain and add to the mutton. Cook for 10 minutes.

Meanwhile, heat the remaining oil in a wok or frying pan. When hot, stir-fry the leeks for 2 minutes, then push to the sides of the pan. Add the lard to the centre of the wok or pan. When hot, stir-fry the lamb and garlic over a high heat for 1 minute. Add the soy sauce and yellow bean paste and stir-fry with the lamb for 1 minute. Mix the leeks with the lamb and stir-fry for 1 minute.

Pour the noodles and mutton into a deep-sided heated serving dish. Pour the lamb and leeks over them. Trickle the red chilli oil and mustard in a criss-cross pattern over the dish.

◆ ◆ ◆

◆ VEGETABLES, BEAN CURD AND EGG ◆

PRECIOUS THINGS CASSEROLE

SERVES 4–6

4–6 medium black mushrooms
4tbsp peanut oil
3–4 slices fresh root ginger
2oz (50g) dried shrimps
9oz (250g) Chinese cabbage
1½pt (900ml) chicken stock
2oz (50g) bamboo shoots, sliced
2oz (50g) ham
2oz (50g) cooked chicken, sliced
2oz (50g) cooked prawns
2oz (50g) abalone, sliced
2tsp salt
1tsp sesame seed oil

Soak the mushrooms in hot water for 30 minutes. Remove and discard the stems and set the caps to one side.

Heat the oil in a clay pot. Add the ginger slices, dried shrimps and Chinese cabbage cut into strips ½×3 inch (1×7 cm) and cook for 2 minutes.

Add the chicken stock, bring to the boil and cook over a medium heat for 10 minutes. Add the sliced bamboo shoot, mushrooms and ham and continue to cook over a medium heat for 15 minutes. Add the cooked chicken, prawns, abalone, salt and sesame seed oil. Serve.

VEGETARIAN CASSEROLE

SERVES 4–6

9oz (250g) aubergine
4oz (100g) French beans
9oz (250g) Chinese cabbage
6 medium black mushrooms
2oz (50g) mung bean noodles
½pt (300ml) peanut oil
4 pieces sweet dried bean curd
4 slices fresh root ginger
1tsp garlic, chopped
2tbsp red fermented bean curd
¾pt (450ml) chicken stock or water
2 pieces fried bean curd
1tsp salt
1½tbsp cornflour blended with 1½tbsp water
1tsp Chinese yellow wine
1tsp sesame seed oil

Cut the aubergine into long, thick strips, the French beans in half and the cabbage lengthwise into quarters. Soak the black mushrooms in hot water for 30 minutes. Remove and discard the stems and cut the caps in half. Soak the mung bean noodles in hot water for 10 minutes.

Heat the oil in a pan and fry all the vegetables for 1 minute over a high heat. Remove, drain and set aside. Sauté the sweet dried bean curd over a low heat until slightly browned. Remove and set aside.

Heat 2 tbsp oil in a clay pot and add the ginger and garlic. Break the fermented red bean curd into pieces and add 2 tablespoons to the pot, stirring over a high heat to release the aroma.

Place all the vegetables in the clay pot and cook, stirring continuously, for 2 minutes. Add the chicken stock or water, place the fried bean curd and sweet dried bean curd sheets on top of the vegetables and bring to the boil. Cover the pot, lower the heat and simmer for 10 minutes.

Add the mung bean noodles and salt, recover the pot and cook for another 2 minutes over high heat. Stir in the softened cornflour, add the Chinese yellow wine and sesame seed oil and serve.

BELOW TOP: PRECIOUS THINGS CASSEROLE
BELOW BOTTOM: VEGETARIAN CASSEROLE

◆ VEGETABLES, BEAN CURD AND EGG ◆

STUFFED GREEN PEPPERS

SERVES 4–6

½lb (225g) pork
4oz (100g) fish fillet
1lb (450g) small round green peppers
1tsp salt
1tbsp rice wine or dry sherry
1tbsp soy sauce
1tbsp cornflour
2tsp sugar
1 clove garlic, crushed
½tbsp crushed black bean sauce
2tbsp oil

Finely chop the pork and fish; mix with a little salt and cornflour.

Wash the green peppers; cut them in half and remove the seeds and stalks. Stuff them with the meat and fish mixture; sprinkle with a little cornflour.

Heat up 1 tbsp oil in a flat frying pan; put in the stuffed peppers, meat side down; fry gently for 4 minutes, adding a little more oil from time to time. When the meat side turns golden, add the crushed garlic, bean sauce, rice wine or sherry, sugar and a little stock or water. Simmer for 2–3 minutes, then add soy sauce and a little cornflour mixed with cold water. Serve as soon as the gravy thickens.

STEAMED CAULIFLOWER

SERVES 4–6

1 medium-sized cauliflower
1tsp salt
1tbsp rice wine or dry sherry
1tbsp sesame seed oil
1 cube fermented red bean curd

When choosing cauliflower, make sure the leaves that curl round the flower are bright green and not withered. Bright leaves show that the cauliflower is fresh. Wash the cauliflower well under the cold water tap, trim off the hard root and discard the tough outer leaves. Keep a few of the tender leaves on as they add to the colour and flavour.

Place the cauliflower in a snugly fitting bowl. Mix salt, wine and sesame seed oil and pour them evenly over the cauliflower, covering its entire surface. Place the bowl in a steamer and cook over high heat for 10–15 minutes.

To serve, remove bowl from the steamer. Crush the fermented red bean curd with a little sauce and pour it over the cauliflower. You should be able to break the cauliflower into florets either with a spoon or a pair of chopsticks. Serve hot.

BUDDHA'S FRY

SERVES 6–8

½oz (15g) dried Chinese mushrooms
½oz (15g) golden needles (dried tiger lily buds)
½oz (15g) wood ears (tree fungus)
1oz (25g) dried bean curd skin
2oz (50g) fresh straw mushrooms
2oz (50g) bamboo shoots
2oz (50g) Chinese cabbage or celery
2oz (50g) mange-tout, or French beans
2oz (50g) broccoli or cauliflower
2oz (50g) carrots
4tbsp vegetable oil
2tbsp soy sauce
½tbsp sugar
1tsp monosodium glutamate
1tbsp cornflour
¼pt (150ml) mushroom stock

Soak all the dried ingredients in separate bowls; cut the larger dried mushrooms into 4 pieces, smaller ones can be left uncut. Cut the golden needles in half; tear the bean curd skin into pieces roughly the same size as the wood ears. Cut all the fresh vegetables into a roughly uniform size.

Heat up about 2 tbsp oil; stir-fry the dried mushrooms, golden needles, bamboo shoots, mange-tout and carrots for about 1 minute, add about half the soy sauce and sugar; stir a few times more, then add about half of the monosodium glutamate and stock. Cover and cook for about 1 minute; mix in ½ tbsp cornflour to thicken the gravy, then dish it out and keep warm.

Meanwhile heat up the remaining oil and stir-fry the other ingredients (ie, wood ears and bean curd skin, fresh mushrooms, Chinese cabbage and broccoli), add the remaining soy sauce, sugar, monosodium glutamate and stock. Cover and cook for about 1 minute, then add ½ tbsp of cornflour, blend well and put it on top of the first group of vegetables. Garnish with sesame seed oil and serve.

Ideally these two groups of vegetables should be cooked simultaneously, for there will be a loss of quality if the gap between the finishing time of each is too long.

BRAISED BAMBOO SHOOTS

SERVES 4–6

1½lb (700g) fresh bamboo shoots
1oz (25g) green seaweed, or 4oz (100g) green cabbage
1 slice fresh root ginger, peeled and finely chopped
1lb (450g) lard for deep-frying
2tbsp oyster sauce
1½tbsp sugar
1tsp monosodium glutamate
1tbsp rice wine or dry sherry
4tbsp chicken stock
1tbsp sesame seed oil

Peel off the skin of the bamboo shoots and discard the tough parts of the root. Cut them into small slices about ¼ inch (5 mm) thick, then into strips about 1½ inch (3.5 cm) long. Finely chop the seaweed or cabbage and ginger root.

Warm up the lard, deep-fry the bamboo shoots for 1–2 minutes, then reduce heat and continue cooking for 2–3 minutes. When their colour turns golden, scoop them out and drain.

Keep about 2 tbsp of lard in the wok or pan, increase the heat and put in the seaweed or cabbage and ginger root, followed by the bamboo shoots; add the oyster sauce, sugar, monosodium glutamate and rice wine or sherry, blend well. Add the chicken stock, bring it to the boil, then reduce heat and let it simmer until almost all the juice is evaporated. Now increase

◆ VEGETABLES, BEAN CURD AND EGG ◆

the heat again, add the sesame seed oil, stir a few times and serve.

THE TWO WINTERS

SERVES 4–6

1oz (25g) dried Chinese mushrooms
4oz (100g) winter bamboo shoots
2tbsp soy sauce
½tbsp sugar
1tsp monosodium glutamate
4tbsp mushroom stock
3tbsp vegetable oil
½tbsp cornflour
½tbsp sesame seed oil

Try to select mushrooms of a uniformly small size. Soak them in warm water; squeeze dry and keep the water as mushroom stock.

Cut the shoots into thin slices not much bigger than the mushrooms.

Heat up the oil until it smokes; stir-fry the mushrooms and bamboo shoots for about 1 minute; add soy sauce and sugar, stir, add mushroom stock. Bring it to the boil and cook for about 2 minutes; add monosodium glutamate and cornflour. Blend well, then add sesame seed oil and serve.

STRING BEANS IN GARLIC SAUCE

SERVES 4–6

14oz (400g) string beans
1 large or 2 small cloves garlic
3tbsp oil
1tsp salt
1tsp sugar
1tbsp light soy sauce

BRAISED BAMBOO SHOOTS

Trim the beans. Leave them whole if they are young and tender; otherwise, cut them in half. Crush and finely chop the garlic.

Blanch the beans in a pan of lightly salted boiling water, drain and plunge in cold water to stop the cooking and to preserve the beans' bright green colour.

Heat the oil in a wok or frying pan. When it starts to smoke, add the crushed garlic to flavour the oil. Before the colour of the garlic turns dark brown, add the beans and stir-fry for about 1 minute. Add the salt, sugar and soy sauce and continue stirring for another minute at most. Serve hot or cold.

◆ VEGETABLES, BEAN CURD AND EGG ◆

SHANGHAI SPRING ROLLS

SERVES 12

6 dried Chinese mushrooms, soaked in warm water for 30 minutes
2 cakes fresh bean curd
8oz (225g) finely minced pork
peanut or corn oil for frying
8oz (225g) cooked prawns, chopped coarsely
½tsp cornflour, mixed to a paste with 1tbsp light soy sauce
3oz (75g) each bamboo shoots and water chestnuts, sliced finely
3oz (75g) bean sprouts
6 spring onions, finely chopped
a little sesame seed oil
12 spring roll wrappers, thawed and separated, covered with damp cloth
deep fat for frying
hoisin sauce for dipping

Drain the mushrooms, remove stalks and cut into fine matchstick-like pieces; slice the bean curd similarly. Fry the minced pork in a little hot oil until it changes colour, stirring all the time. Cook for 2–3 minutes. Add the prawns, then the cornflour paste and keep breaking up the mixture with a slice. Now add the bamboo shoots, water chestnuts, bean sprouts and spring onions over a high heat, stirring all the time. Add the mushrooms and bean curd. Taste for seasoning and stir in the sesame seed oil away from the heat. Allow to cool before filling the spring roll wrappers. Deep-fry in the same way and drain them one by one on absorbent kitchen paper. Serve hot with hoisin sauce for dipping.

PICKLED VEGETABLES

Use four to six of the following vegetables, or more:

cucumber
carrot
radish or turnip
cauliflower
broccoli
green cabbage
white cabbage
celery
onion
fresh root ginger
leek
spring onion
red pepper
green pepper
string beans
garlic
8pt (4lt) boiled water, cooled
6oz (175g) salt
2oz (50g) chilli peppers
3tsp Sichuan peppercorns
2fl oz (50ml) Chinese distilled spirit (or white rum, gin or vodka)
4oz (100g) fresh root ginger
4oz (100g) brown sugar

Put the cold boiled water into a large, clean earthenware or glass jar. Add the salt, chillies, peppercorns, spirit, ginger and sugar.

Wash and trim the vegetables, peel if necessary and drain well. Put them into the jar and seal it, making sure it is airtight. Place the jar in a cool place and leave the vegetables to pickle for at least five days before serving.

Use a pair of clean chopsticks or tongs to pick the vegetables out of the jar. Do not allow any grease to enter the jar. You can replenish the vegetables, adding a little salt each time. If any white scum appears on the surface of the brine, add a little sugar and spirit. The longer the pickling lasts, the better.

VEGETARIAN 'LION'S HEAD' CASSEROLE

SERVES 4–6

4 cakes fresh bean curd
4oz (100g) fried gluten
2oz (50g) cooked carrots
4–5 dried Chinese mushrooms, soaked
2oz (50g) bamboo shoots
6 cabbage or lettuce hearts
5 large cabbage leaves
1tsp fresh root ginger, finely chopped
2tbsp rice wine or dry sherry
1tbsp salt
1tsp sugar
1tsp white pepper (ground)
2tsp sesame seed oil
1tbsp cornflour

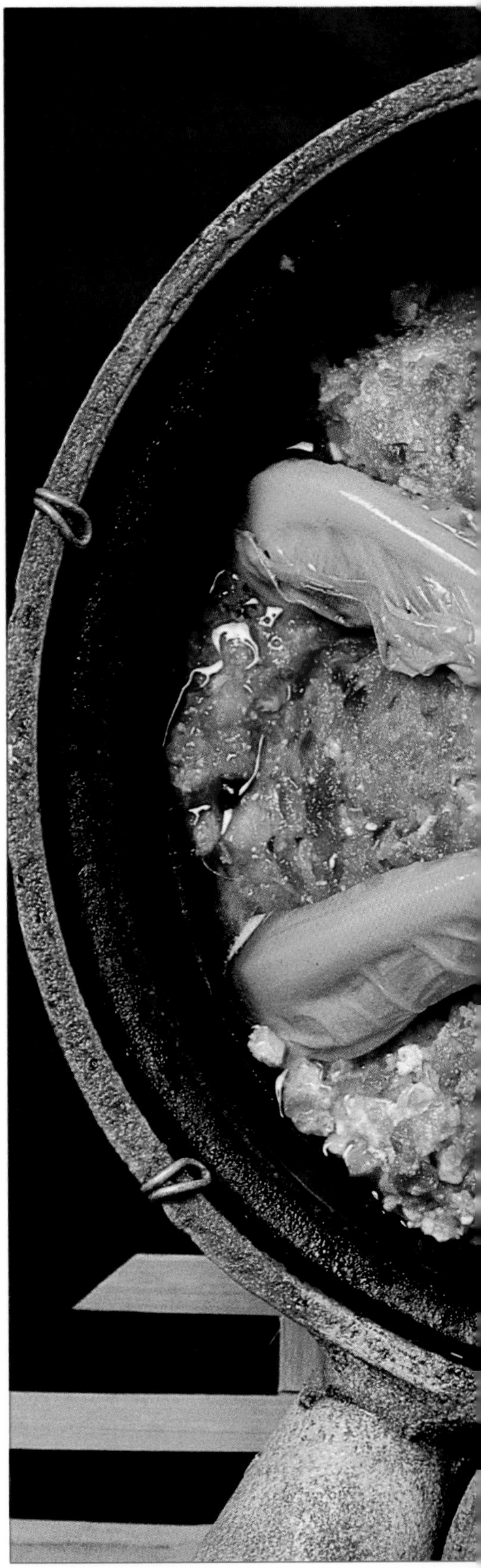

◆ VEGETABLES, BEAN CURD AND EGG ◆

1oz (25g) ground rice or breadcrumbs
oil for deep-frying
Plain flour for dusting

Squeeze as much liquid as possible from the bean curd using cheese cloth or muslin and then mash. Finely chop the gluten, carrots, mushrooms and bamboo shoots. Place them with the mashed bean curd in a large mixing bowl. Add 1 tsp salt, the finely chopped root ginger, ground rice, cornflour and sesame seed oil and blend everything together until smooth. Make 10 'meatballs' from this mixture and place them on a plate lightly dusted with flour. Trim off any hard or tough roots from the cabbage or lettuce hearts.

Heat the oil in a wok or deep-fryer. When hot, deep-fry the 'meatballs' for about 3 minutes, stirring very gently to make sure that they are not stuck together. Scoop out with a slotted spoon or strainer and drain.

Pour off the excess oil leaving about 2 tbsp in the wok. Stir-fry the cabbage hearts with a little salt and sugar. Add about 1 pt (600 ml) water and bring to the boil. Reduce the heat and let the mixture simmer.

Meanwhile, line the bottom of a casserole with the cabbage leaves and place the 'meatballs' on top. Pour the cabbage hearts with the soup into the casserole and add the remaining salt, ground pepper and wine or sherry. Cover, bring to the boil, reduce the heat and simmer for 10 minutes.

To serve, take off the lid and rearrange the cabbage hearts so that they appear between the 'meatballs' in a star-shaped pattern.

VEGETARIAN 'LION'S HEAD' CASSEROLE

◆ VEGETABLES, BEAN CURD AND EGG ◆

HOT AND SOUR CUCUMBER — SICHUAN STYLE

SERVES 4–6

1 cucumber
1tsp salt
2tbsp sugar
2 tbsp vinegar
1 tbsp chilli oil

Split the cucumber in two lengthwise and then cut each piece into strips rather like potato chips. Sprinkle with the salt and leave for about 10 minutes to extract the bitter juices.

Remove each cucumber strip. Place it on a firm surface and soften it by gently tapping it with the blade of a cleaver or knife.

Place the cucumber strips on a plate. Sprinkle the sugar evenly over them and then add the vinegar and chilli oil just before serving.

VEGETARIAN SPRING ROLLS

1 pack of 20 frozen spring roll skins
8oz (225g) fresh bean sprouts
8oz (225g) young tender leeks or spring onions
4oz (100g) carrots
4oz (100g) white mushrooms
oil for deep-frying
1½tsp salt
1tsp sugar
1tbsp light soy sauce

Take the spring roll skins out of the packet and leave them to defrost thoroughly under a damp cloth. Wash and rinse the bean sprouts in a bowl of cold water and discard the husks and other bits and pieces that float to the surface. Drain. Cut the leeks or spring onions, carrots and mushrooms into thin shreds.

To cook the filling, heat 3–4 tbsp of oil in a preheated wok or frying pan and stir-fry all the vegetables for a few seconds. Add the salt, sugar and soy sauce and continue stirring for about 1–1½ minutes. Remove and leave to cool a little.

To cook the spring rolls, heat about 2½ pt (1.5 lt) oil in a wok or deep-fryer until it smokes. Reduce the heat or even turn it off for a few minutes to cool the oil a little before adding the spring rolls. Deep-fry 6–8 at a time for 3–4 minutes or until golden and crispy. Increase the heat to high again before frying each batch. As each batch is cooked, remove and drain it on absorbent paper. Serve hot with a dip sauce such as soy sauce, vinegar, chilli sauce or mustard.

These spring rolls are ideal for a buffet-style meal or as cocktail snacks.

HOT AND SOUR CUCUMBER – SICHUAN STYLE

◆ VEGETABLES, BEAN CURD AND EGG ◆

SAN SHIAN — 'THE THREE DELICACIES'

SERVES 4–6

9oz (250g) winter bamboo shoots
4oz (100g) oyster or straw mushrooms
10oz (275g) fried gluten or deep-fried bean curd
4tbsp oil
1½tsp salt
1tsp sugar
1tbsp light soy sauce
1tsp sesame seed oil
fresh coriander leaves to garnish (optional)

Cut the bamboo shoots into thin slices. The oyster mushrooms can be left whole if small; otherwise halve or quarter them. Straw mushrooms can be left whole.

Heat the oil in a hot wok or frying pan, swirling it so that most of the surface is well greased. When the oil starts to smoke, add the bamboo shoots and mushrooms and stir-fry for about 1 minute. Add the gluten or bean curd together with salt, sugar and soy sauce. Continue stirring for 1–1½ minutes longer, adding a little water if necessary. Finally add the sesame seed oil, blend well and serve hot.

This dish can also be served cold. In that case, you might like to separate the three main ingredients, arrange them in three neat rows and garnish with fresh coriander.

QUICK-FRIED FRENCH BEANS WITH DRIED SHRIMPS AND PORK

SERVES 4–6

1½lb (675g) French beans
2tbsp dried shrimps
1tbsp chopped Sichuan Ja Chai hot pickle
vegetable oil for deep-frying
¾oz (20g) lard
3tsp garlic, chopped
3oz (75g) minced pork
3tbsp good stock (see recipe)
1tbsp soy sauce
½tbsp sugar
2tsp salt
3tbsp water
1tsp sesame seed oil
2tsp vinegar
2tbsp chopped spring onions (optional)

Trim the French beans. Soak the dried shrimp in hot water to cover for 20 minutes. Drain and chop. Finely chop the pickle.

Heat the oil in a wok or deep-fryer. When hot, fry the beans for 2 minutes. Remove and put aside. Pour away the oil to use for other purposes. Heat the lard in the wok or frying pan. When hot, add the garlic and stir a few times. Add the pork, shrimps, stock and pickle and stir-fry for 2 minutes. Stir in the soy sauce, sugar, salt and water. Add the French beans and turn and toss until the liquid in the pan has nearly all evaporated. Sprinkle with the sesame seed oil, vinegar and spring onions. Turn and stir once more, then serve.

VEGETARIAN SPRING ROLLS

◆ VEGETABLES, BEAN CURD AND EGG ◆

STIR-FRIED BEAN SPROUTS WITH GREEN PEPPERS

SERVES 4–6

1lb (450g) fresh bean sprouts
1 small green pepper, cored and seeded
1–2 spring onions
3tbsp oil
1tsp salt
1tsp sugar

Wash and rinse the bean sprouts in cold water, discarding the husks and other bits and pieces that float to the surface. Cut the green pepper into thin shreds. Cut the spring onions into short lengths.

Heat the oil in a hot wok until smoking. Add the spring onions and green pepper, stir a few times, and then add the bean sprouts. Continue stirring.

After about 30 seconds, add salt and sugar, and stir a few times more. Do not overcook because the sprouts will become soggy. This dish can be served either hot or cold.

ABOVE: CHINESE CABBAGE WITH CHILLIES
RIGHT: FU YUNG CAULIFLOWER

STIR-FRIED SPINACH AND BEAN CURD

SERVES 4–6

8oz (225g) spinach
2 cakes fresh bean curd
4tbsp oil
1tsp salt
1tsp sugar
1tbsp soy sauce
1tsp sesame seed oil

Wash the spinach well, shaking off the excess water. Cut up each cake of bean curd into about 8 pieces.

Heat the oil in a wok. Fry the bean curd pieces until they are golden, turning them over once or twice gently. Remove them with a slotted spoon and set aside.

Stir-fry the spinach in the remaining oil for about 30 seconds or until the leaves are limp. Add the bean curd pieces, salt, sugar and soy sauce, blend well and cook for another 1–1½ minutes. Add the sesame seed oil and serve hot.

AUBERGINE WITH SICHUAN 'FISH SAUCE'

SERVES 4–6

1lb (450g) aubergines
4–5 dried red chilli peppers
oil for deep-frying
3–4 spring onions, finely chopped
1 slice fresh root ginger, peeled and finely chopped
1 clove garlic, finely chopped
1tsp sugar
1tbsp soy sauce
1tbsp vinegar
1tbsp chilli bean paste
2tsp cornflour, mixed with 2tbsp water
1tsp sesame seed oil

Soak the dried red chillies for 5–10 minutes, cut them into small pieces and discard the stalks. Peel the aubergines, discard the stalks and cut them into diamond-shaped chunks.

Heat the oil in a wok and deep-fry the aubergines for 3½–4 minutes or until soft. Remove with a slotted spoon and drain.

Pour off the oil and return the aubergines to the wok with the red chillies, spring onions, root ginger and garlic. Stir a few times and add the sugar, soy sauce, vinegar and chilli bean paste. Stir for 1 minute. Add cornflour and water mixture, blend well and garnish with sesame seed oil. Serve hot or cold.

FU-YUNG CAULIFLOWER

SERVES 4–6

1 large cauliflower
2 egg whites
4oz (100g) minced breast of chicken
4tbsp good stock (see recipe)
1½tbsp cornflour blended with 4tbsp water
salt and pepper to taste
4tbsp milk

Remove the cauliflower stalk. Cut the cauliflower into florets. Beat the

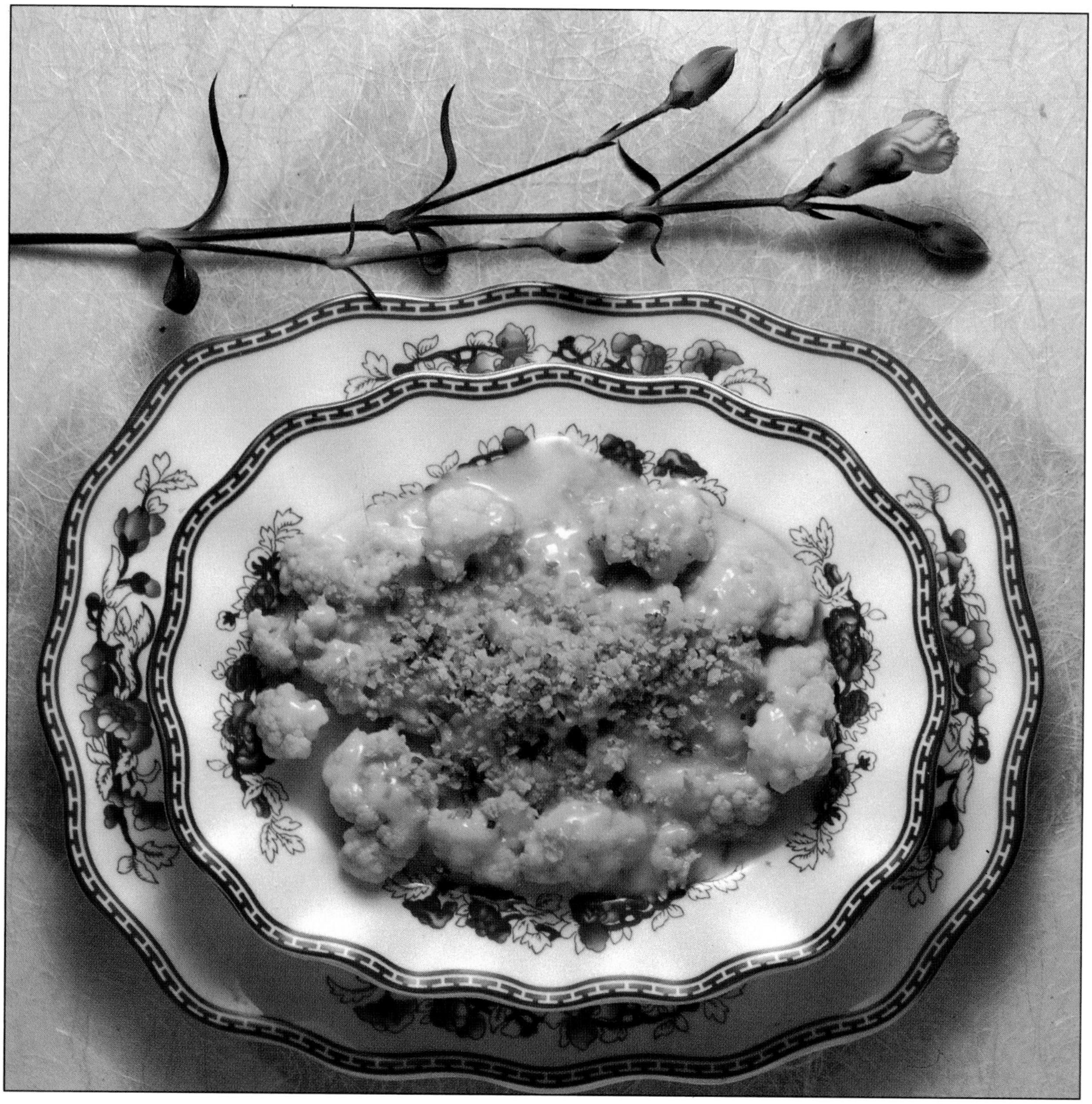

egg whites until nearly stiff. Mix in all the remaining ingredients thoroughly. Lightly beat together.

Place the cauliflower florets in a saucepan of boiling water and simmer for 7–8 minutes. Drain. Put the cauliflower in a wok or pan. Add the egg white and chicken mixture. Bring to the boil, reduce the heat and gently simmer for 3 minutes, stirring and turning gently.

Transfer the cauliflower to a heated dish and pour the sauce over. If liked, sprinkle with chopped spring onion and finely chopped ham or presoaked, chopped dried shrimps.

CHINESE WHITE CABBAGE WITH CHILLIES

SERVES 5–6

1 Chinese white cabbage, about 3½lb (1.5kg)
3 small fresh red chillies
2 dried red chillies
1½tsp Sichuan peppercorns
2tsp salt
½tsp sesame seed oil
1tbsp vegetable oil

Chop the cabbage coarsely, discarding the tougher parts. Coarsely chop the chillies, discarding the seeds. Pound the peppercorns lightly. Place the cabbage in a large bowl, sprinkle evenly with the salt, chillies and peppercorns. Toss to mix. Refrigerate for 2–3 days before serving. Sprinkle the cabbage with the oils; toss well and serve.

◆ VEGETABLES, BEAN CURD AND EGG ◆

ABOVE: BEAN CURD WITH MUSHROOMS

BRAISED AUBERGINES

SERVES 4–6

10oz (275g) aubergines
1pt (600ml) oil for deep-frying
2tbsp soy sauce
1tbsp sugar
2tbsp water
1tsp sesame seed oil

Choose the long, purple variety of aubergine, rather than the large round kind, if possible. Discard the stalks and cut the aubergines into diamond-shaped chunks.

Heat oil in a wok until hot. Deep-fry the aubergine chunks in batches until golden. Remove with a slotted spoon and drain.

Pour off excess oil leaving about 1 tbsp in the wok. Return the aubergines to the wok and add the soy sauce, sugar and water. Cook over a fairly high heat for about 2 minutes, adding more water if necessary. Stir occasionally. When the juice is reduced to almost nothing, add the sesame seed oil, blend well and serve.

STIR-FRIED COURGETTES

SERVES 4–6

1lb (450g) courgettes
3tbsp oil
2tsp salt
1tsp sugar
2tbsp water

Do not peel the courgettes; just trim off the ends. Split the courgettes in half lengthwise and cut each length diagonally into diamond-shaped chunks.

Heat the oil in a wok. When the oil starts to smoke, put the courgettes in and stir-fry for about 30 seconds. Add the salt and sugar and cook for a further 1–1½ minutes, adding a little water if necessary. Serve hot.

BEAN CURD WITH MUSHROOMS

SERVES 4–6

4 cakes fresh bean curd
3–4 medium dried Chinese mushrooms
1tbsp sherry
4tbsp oil
1tbsp soy sauce
1tsp cornflour
½tsp salt
½tsp sugar
1tsp sesame seed oil

Soak the dried mushrooms in warm water for about 30 minutes. Squeeze them dry and discard the stalks. Keep the water for use as stock. Slice each square of bean curd into ¼ inch (6 mm) slices and then cut each slice into 6 or 8 pieces.

Heat the oil in a wok and stir-fry the mushrooms for a short time. Add about ¼ pt (150 ml) of the water in which the mushrooms have been soaking. Bring to the boil and add the bean curd with the salt and sugar. Let it bubble for a while and then add the sherry and the sesame seed oil. Mix the cornflour with the soy sauce and a little water in a bowl and pour it over the bean curd in the wok so that it forms a clear, light glaze. Serve immediately.

BEAN CURD WITH CRAB MEAT AND PEAS

SERVES 4–6

2 cakes fresh bean curd
2 spring onions
5–6oz (150–175g) crab meat
2½tbsp vegetable oil
1tbsp fresh root ginger, finely chopped
1tbsp peas
salt and pepper to taste
2tsp light soy sauce
1tbsp rice wine or dry sherry
3tsp cornflour blended with 3tbsp good stock (see recipe)

Cut the bean curd into ¼ inch (0.5 cm) slices, then quarter each slice. Shred the spring onions. Flake the crab meat.

Heat the oil in a wok or frying pan. When hot, stir-fry the ginger for 10–15 seconds. Stir in the crab meat and peas and stir-fry for 45 seconds. Add the bean curd pieces, spring onions, salt and pepper to taste, soy sauce and sherry, and toss and turn for 1½ minutes. Sprinkle with the blended cornflour, and toss for a further 45 seconds.

BELOW: BEAN CURD WITH CRAB MEAT AND PEAS

◆ VEGETABLES, BEAN CURD AND EGG ◆

'POCK MARKED WOMAN' BEAN CURD

The 'pock-marked woman' was the wife of a well-known chef who worked in western China about a hundred years ago; it was she who created this dish.

SERVES 4–6

3 cakes fresh bean curd
¼lb (100g) minced beef (or pork)
¼tsp salt
1tsp salted black beans
1tbsp chilli paste
3tbsp stock
1 leek or 3 spring onions
½tbsp soy sauce
1tbsp cornflour
Sichuan pepper, freshly ground

Cut the bean curd into ½ inch (1 cm) square cubes; blanch for 2–3 minutes to get rid of its plaster odour; remove and drain. Cut the leek or onions into short lengths.

Heat up the oil until smoking; stir-fry the minced beef or pork until it turns dark in colour; add salt, stir a few times, then add salted black beans. Crush them with the cooking ladle to blend well with the meat, then add chilli paste; continue stirring. When you can smell the chilli, add stock followed by the bean curd and leek or onions. Reduce heat; cook gently for 3–4 minutes; add soy sauce and cornflour mixed in a little water; stir gently to blend well and serve with freshly ground Sichuan pepper as a garnish.

STEAMED STUFFED BEAN CURD

SERVES 6–8

3 cakes fresh bean curd
1tbsp dried shrimps
1 clove garlic
4oz (100g) minced pork
¼tsp salt
pepper to taste
½tbsp vegetable oil
1 egg white
12 medium fresh or frozen prawns or shrimps

Sauce
1½tbsp vegetable oil
1½tsp fresh root ginger, finely chopped
2tbsp spring onions, coarsely chopped
3tbsp good stock (see recipe)
1tbsp oyster sauce
½tbsp light soy sauce
1tsp sesame seed oil

Cut each cake of bean curd into 4 pieces. Scoop out a deep hollow in the centre of each piece, about halfway through. Soak the dried shrimps in hot water to cover for 5 minutes, then drain and finely chop. Crush the garlic. Mix the pork, garlic, shrimps, salt, pepper, half of the oil and the egg white together in a bowl. Spoon this mixture into the bean curd and place a whole prawn or shrimp firmly on top.

Arrange the 12 pieces of stuffed bean curd on a heatproof dish, place in a steamer and cook for 20 minutes. Meanwhile, heat the oil for the sauce in a small pan. When hot, add the ginger, spring onion, stock, oyster sauce and soy sauce. Bring to the boil and stir well. When the bean curd is ready, add the sesame seed oil to the sauce and pour it evenly over the bean curd.

BASIC PLAIN STIR-FRIED OMELETTE

SERVES 4–6

4–5 eggs
½tsp salt
pepper to taste
4–5tbsp vegetable oil
1½tbsp spring onion, finely chopped
1½tbsp good quality dark soy sauce

Break the eggs into a bowl with the salt and pepper and beat lightly with a fork. Heat the oil in a wok or frying pan. When hot, pour in the eggs. When the edges of the egg begin to set, continue to cook over medium heat for a further 15 seconds. Stir and turn the mixture over several times until it is almost set and then arrange on a heated dish. Sprinkle the omelette evenly with chopped spring onion and soy sauce.

STIR-FRIED CHINESE OMELETTE WITH TOMATOES

SERVES 4–6

4–5 eggs
½tsp salt
pepper to taste
1 medium onion
3 medium tomatoes
4–5tbsp vegetable oil
1tsp sesame seed oil
1½tbsp spring onion, finely chopped
1½tbsp good quality dark soy sauce

Break the eggs into a bowl with the salt and pepper and beat lightly with a fork. Peel and finely slice the onion. Cut each tomato into 8 segments.

Heat the vegetable oil in a wok or frying pan. When hot, gently stir-fry the onion for about 30 seconds, then add the tomatoes. Spread evenly over the bottom of the pan. Pour over the beaten egg and allow to flow over the base of the pan. When the edges of the egg have begun to set, gently turn and stir several times, allowing any uncooked liquid to come in contact with the surface of the pan. Sprinkle on the sesame seed oil and arrrange the omelette on a heated dish. Sprinkle over the chopped spring onion, with extra spring onion shreds if liked, and soy sauce and serve.

STIR-FRIED EGGS WITH OYSTERS

SERVES 4–6

5–6 eggs
½tsp salt
2tsp fresh root ginger, chopped
4–5oz (100–150g) fresh or canned oysters
2 spring onions
3tbsp vegetable oil
1oz (25g) lard
1tbsp rice wine or dry sherry

Break the eggs into a bowl with half the salt and beat lightly with a fork. Mix the ginger and remaining salt with the oysters and marinate for 15 minutes, then drain. Coarsely chop the spring onions.

Heat the oil and lard in a wok or frying pan. When hot, stir-fry the ginger, oysters and spring onions for 1 minute. Pour in the eggs and, when they are almost set, stir a few times and sprinkle on the wine or sherry. Cook for a further 30 seconds and serve.

STIR-FRIED CHINESE OMELETTE WITH ONION AND BACON

SERVES 4–6

4–5 eggs
½tsp salt
pepper to taste
1 medium onion
2 rashers of bacon
4–5tbsp vegetable oil
1½tbsp spring onion, finely chopped
1½tbsp dark soy sauce

Break the eggs into a bowl with the salt and pepper and beat lightly with a fork. Peel and finely slice the onion. Derind and finely slice the bacon.

Heat the oil in a wok or frying pan. When hot, stir-fry the onion and bacon for about 1½ minutes. Spread evenly over the bottom of the pan. Pour over the beaten egg and allow to flow over the base of the pan. When the edges of the egg have begun to set, gently turn and stir several times, allowing any uncooked liquid to come in contact with the surface of the pan. Arrange on a heated dish, sprinkle over the spring onion and soy sauce and serve.

STIR-FRIED PRAWN 'SOUFFLÉ'

SERVES 4–6

8oz (225g) king prawns, fresh or frozen, shelled
1tsp salt
pepper to taste
5tbsp vegetable oil
2tsp cornflour
2 cloves garlic
3 spring onions
4 eggs
1tbsp rice wine or dry sherry

Sprinkle the prawns with the salt, pepper, ½ tbsp of the oil and dust with the cornflour. Crush the garlic. Cut the spring onions into 1 inch (2.5 cm) sections. Beat the eggs in a bowl.

Heat the remaining oil in a wok or frying pan. When hot, stir-fry the garlic and prawns for 1½ minutes. Pour in the beaten egg and let the egg flow over the surface of the pan. Reduce the heat to low, sprinkle on the spring onions and cook for 1½ minutes. When the eggs are almost set, toss with a metal spoon. Sprinkle on the sherry and place on a heated serving plate.

PRESERVED EGGS AND GROUND PORK

Preserved eggs are sometimes called ancient or thousand-year-old eggs. In fact they are duck's eggs preserved in a mixture of alkali, lime ashes, mud and other materials. After a few months the chemicals penetrate the eggshell, turning both the white and yolk a dark brownish-green colour. Normally they are served uncooked. Children and Westerners do not always find them to their taste to start with.

SERVES 2–4

2 Chinese preserved eggs
½lb (250g) pork
1tbsp oil
1½tbsp soy sauce
1tsp sesame seed oil

Remove the mud covering the eggshells, then clean them in water thoroughly before cracking them. Coarsely chop the eggs and the pork, keeping the two ingredients separate.

Heat the oil and fry the pork. When its colour changes, put in the chopped eggs, add the soy sauce and mix well. Stir for 3–4 minutes; add sesame seed oil and serve.

STIR-FRIED CHINESE OMELETTE WITH TOMATOES

FRIED 'POCKETED' EGGS

SERVES 4–6

4 eggs
2–3tbsp oil
1tbsp light soy sauce
1 spring onion, finely chopped

Heat the oil in a hot wok or frying pan and fry the eggs on both sides. Add the soy sauce and a little water and braise for 1–2 minutes. Garnish with spring onion and serve hot.

Taking a bit of the egg and finding the yolk inside the white is rather like finding something in a pocket — hence the name of this dish.

BOATMEN'S EGG OMELETTE

SERVES 4–6

7 eggs
1tsp salt
pepper to taste
8tbsp vegetable oil
1tbsp onion, finely chopped
3tbsp cooked crab meat
3tbsp fresh, shelled shrimps
3tbsp peas
2tbsp spring onion, finely chopped
1½tbsp soy sauce

Break the eggs into a bowl with the salt and pepper and beat lightly with a fork. Heat 3 tbsp of the oil in a wok or frying pan. When hot, stir-fry the onion for a few seconds. Add the crab meat and spread evenly over the bottom of the pan. Pour in one third of the eggs and cook until almost set. With the aid of a fish slice, transfer to a heated dish. Reheat the wok or pan with about 2 tbsp of oil and, when hot, add the shrimps. Spread over the bottom of the pan and then pour on another third of the eggs. Cook until almost set, then stack on top of the first 'pancake'. Reheat the wok or pan with about 2 tbsp of oil and, when hot, add the peas and spring onions. Stir-fry for a few seconds, then spread evenly over the bottom of the pan. Pour in the remaining egg and cook until almost set, then stack on top of the other 2 pancakes.

Cut the 'triple pancake' into 8 segments. Sprinkle with soy sauce.

FRIED 'POCKETED' EGGS

◆ VEGETABLES, BEAN CURD AND EGG ◆

BRAISED TEA-EGGS

MAKES 12 EGGS

12 eggs
2tsp salt
5tbsp soy sauce
2–3 star anise
1½tbsp red tea leaves (the better the quality tea, the better the result)

Boil the eggs in warm water for 5–10 minutes. Remove and gently tap the shell of each egg with a spoon until it is cracked finely all over. Put the eggs back into the pot and cover with fresh water. Add salt, soy sauce, star anise and tea leaves. Bring to the boil and simmer for 30–45 minutes. Let the eggs cool for a while in the liquid.

When you peel the shells off, the eggs will have a beautiful marbled pattern.

BASIC STEAMED EGG AND FANCY STEAMED EGGS

SERVES 4–6

2 eggs
½pt (300ml) good stock (see recipe), or water
salt and pepper to taste
1tbsp soy sauce
1tbsp spring onion, finely chopped

Optional extras
2–3tbsp shredded crab meat or prawns
1–2tbsp chopped ham
1–2tbsp petits pois

The most basic Chinese steamed egg dish consists of no more than 2 eggs mixed with ½ pt (300 ml) stock or water in a dish with seasoning added and cooked in a steamer for about 15 minutes, or until the custard has set. It is then topped with a spoonful of soy sauce and a scattering of chopped spring onion.

A more elaborate version consists of using the best grade stock, perhaps with a little shredded crab meat or prawns added. After steaming, the top of the custard should be set and firm enough so that more prawns or crab meat can be arranged on top, together with some chopped ham and petits pois. The dish is then returned to the steamer for a further 3–4 minutes. After the second steaming, a large pinch of chopped spring onion is sprinkled over the top. When cooking this dish, never use too many eggs, as this will cause the custard to become too firm and hard after steaming.

PAN-FRIED EGG DUMPLING WITH MINCED PORK AND SHRIMPS

SERVES 4–6

6 eggs

Marinade
1tbsp egg white (from main recipe)
1tsp salt
1tsp cornflour
½tsp sesame seed oil
4oz (100g) fillet of pork, minced
8oz (225g) shrimps, shelled and deveined
1 medium onion
½pt (300ml) peanut oil
1tbsp chopped coriander

Break the eggs into a mixing bowl, reserving 1 tbsp egg white for the marinade. Beat the remainder lightly. Make the marinade in a separate bowl and mix the minced pork with half of the mixture.

Clean the shrimps. Pat them dry and mix with the other half of the marinade. Keep refrigerated for 30 minutes.

Chop the onion and set it aside.

Heat the oil in a pan. Add the shrimps, stirring to separate, and remove them when their colour has changed. Drain and set aside.

Sauté the minced pork for 2 minutes. Remove and set aside. Sauté the chopped onion for 1 minute. Remove and set aside.

Mix the pork, shrimps, onion and coriander with the beaten egg. Heat 1 tbsp of oil in the pan and put 2 tbsp of the egg mixture in the pan to form one dumpling. Fry it gently over a medium heat, turning it over gently until both sides are nicely golden-brown. Make 2 or 3 at a time and continue until all the ingredients are used. This simple but effective recipe will make 8 or 10 dumplings in all.

CHINESE CABBAGE SALAD

SERVES 4–6

1 small Chinese cabbage
2tbsp light soy sauce
1tsp salt
1tsp sugar
1tbsp sesame seed oil

Wash the cabbage thoroughly, cut into thick slices and place in a bowl. Add the soy sauce, salt, sugar and sesame seed oil to the cabbage. Toss well and serve.

COLD TOSSED CUCUMBER SALAD

SERVES 4-6

1 medium cucumber
2tsp salt
2tbsp sugar
3tbsp vinegar
1tbsp vegetable oil
2¾tbsp sesame seed oil

Cut the cucumber slantwise into ⅛ inch (3 mm) slices or cut into 2 inch (5 cm) shreds. Place in a large bowl and sprinkle evenly with salt. Leave to season for 30 minutes. Pour away any water from the cucumber. Sprinkle the cucumber with sugar and vinegar, and toss together. Just before serving, add the oils. Toss well and sprinkle with presoaked, chopped dried shrimps, if liked.

FANCY STEAMED EGGS WITH CRABMEAT AND PETIT POIS

◆ VEGETABLES, BEAN CURD AND EGG ◆

◆ VEGETABLES, BEAN CURD AND EGG ◆

STEWED GLUTEN IN SWEET BEAN SAUCE

SERVES 4–6

See the recipe for Fried Gluten

11oz (300g) gluten in small pieces
3tbsp oil
1tbsp dark soy sauce
1tbsp sugar
1tsp five-spice powder
2tbsp rice wine or dry sherry
1tbsp sweet bean paste
1 slice fresh root ginger, crushed
2tsp sesame seed oil

Boil the gluten pieces in a pan of water for about 4–5 minutes or until they float to the surface. Remove and drain off as much water as possible.

Heat the oil in a hot wok or pan. When hot, add the boiled gluten, stir for a few seconds and then add the soy sauce, sugar, five-spice powder, wine, sweet bean paste, crushed root ginger and about 4 floz (125 ml) water. Bring to the boil and cook over high heat for 20–25 minutes or until there is very little juice left, stirring now and again to make sure that each piece of gluten is well covered by the gravy.

Add the sesame seed oil, blend well and serve hot or cold.

FRIED GLUTEN

SERVES 4–6

2lb (1kg) flour
1tbsp salt
18–19fl oz (500–550ml) warm water
oil for deep-frying
1tsp salt
1tsp sugar
1tbsp light soy sauce
¼tsp monosodium glutamate (optional)

Sift the flour into a large mixing bowl. Add the salt and the water gradually to make a firm dough. Knead until smooth and then cover with a damp cloth and leave to stand for about 1 hour.

Place the dough in a large colander or sieve and run cold water over it while you press and squeeze the dough with your hands to wash out as much of the starch as you can. After 10–15 minutes of this hard work, you will end up with about 11 oz (300 g) gluten. Squeeze off as much water as you can and then cut the gluten into about 35–40 small pieces. These can be cooked either by deep-frying or boiling (or they can be steamed or baked).

Heat the oil in a wok or deep-fryer. When hot, deep-fry the gluten in batches — about 6 to 8 at a time — for about 3 minutes or until they turn golden. Remove and drain.

Pour off the excess oil, leaving about 1 tbsp in the wok. Return the partly cooked gluten to the wok, add salt, sugar and soy sauce (and the monosodium glutamate if used), stir, and add a little water if necessary. Braise for about 2 minutes. Serve hot or cold.

◆◆◆

◆ FISH AND CRUSTACEANS ◆

FRIED BASS IN SWEET AND SOUR SAUCE

SERVES 2–4

1 sea bass weighing about 1½–2lb (0.75–1kg)
1tsp salt
2tbsp flour
oil for deep-frying

Sauce
2tbsp sugar
2tbsp vinegar
1tbsp soy sauce
½tbsp cornflour
2tbsp stock or water

Garnish
2 spring onions
2 slices fresh root ginger, peeled
1 small red pepper
fresh coriander

Clean and scale the fish, slash both sides diagonally at intervals. Rub salt both inside and out, then coat with flour.

Thinly shred the onions, root ginger and red pepper.

Deep-fry the fish in hot oil until golden; place it on a long dish.

Pour off the excess oil from the wok, put in the sauce mixture and stir until smooth, then pour it over the fish. Garnish with shredded onions, root ginger, red pepper and coriander.

FISH-HEAD CASSEROLE

SERVES 4–6

1 fish-head weighing about 1lb (450g)
2oz (50g) lean pork
3–4 dried Chinese mushrooms, soaked
2 cakes fresh bean curd
2 slices fresh root ginger
2 spring onions
1tsp salt
2tbsp rice wine or dry sherry
1tbsp sugar
2tbsp soy sauce
2tbsp flour
½pt (300ml) stock
oil for deep-frying

Garnish
spring onions
red chilli
fresh coriander

Discard the gills from the fish-head; rub some salt both inside and out; coat the head with flour.

Cut the pork, mushrooms, bean curd and root ginger into small slices; cut the onions into short lengths.

Deep-fry the fish-head over a moderate heat for 10 minutes or until golden. Remove.

Heat a little oil in a sand-pot or casserole. Put in the root ginger and onions, followed by pork, mushrooms and bean curd; stir for a while, then add rice wine or sherry, sugar, soy sauce, stock and the fish-head; bring it to the boil; add a little salt; reduce heat; simmer for 7 minutes.

Garnish with onions, red chilli and fresh coriander. Serve in a sand-pot or casserole.

ABOVE RIGHT: FRIED BASS IN SWEET AND SOUR SAUCE
RIGHT: FISH-HEAD CASSEROLE

◆ FISH AND CRUSTACEANS ◆

SLICED ABALONE IN OYSTER SAUCE WITH LETTUCE

FRIED GROUPER WITH VEGETABLES

SERVES 4–6

¾lb (350g) grouper or other firm white fish steak
4oz (100g) seasonal greens
1 carrot
2–3 dried Chinese mushrooms, soaked
1 slice fresh root ginger, finely chopped
1 spring onion, cut into short lengths
1tsp salt
1 egg white
2tbsp soy sauce
2tbsp rice wine or dry sherry
1tbsp sugar
½tbsp cornflour
1tsp sesame seed oil
oil for deep-frying

Mix the fish steak with a little salt, the egg white and cornflour.

Wash and cut the greens, cut the carrot into thin slices and cut each mushroom into 2 or 3 pieces.

Deep-fry the fish pieces until lightly golden; scoop out and drain.

Pour off the excess oil leaving about 2 tbsp in the wok, stir-fry the root ginger, onion, greens, mushrooms and carrot; add salt; blend well. Now add the fish pieces with soy sauce, rice wine or sherry and sugar; stir gently for 3–4 minutes, then thicken the gravy with cornflour mixed with a little water. Finally add sesame seed oil and serve.

RED-COOKED SHAD

SERVES 3–4

1 shad (bass can be substituted) weighing about 1½lb (700g)
3tbsp lard for frying
3tbsp soy sauce
1tbsp sugar
2tbsp rice wine or dry sherry
2oz (50g) bamboo shoots, cut into small slices
2–3 dried Chinese mushrooms, soaked
1tsp salt
2 spring onions
2 slices fresh root ginger, peeled
1tbsp cornflour
½pt (300ml) water

Clean the shad or bass, wash and dry it thoroughly. Cut it into slices of uniform thickness.

Warm up the lard, coat the skin of fish with soy sauce and fry for 5 minutes. Turn it over, add the remaining soy sauce, sugar, rice wine or sherry, bamboo shoots, mushrooms, salt, onions, root ginger and water; bring it to the boil and bubble over a high heat for 5 minutes. Reduce heat and simmer for 15 minutes; by then the juice should be reduced somewhat. Remove the fish onto a plate, add the cornflour to thicken the gravy, then pour it over the fish and serve.

SLICED ABALONE IN OYSTER SAUCE WITH LETTUCE

SERVES 4–6

1¼lb (550g) canned abalone
5fl oz (140ml) peanut oil
1tbsp salt
1¼lb (550g) lettuce
2–3 slices fresh root ginger
1–2 cloves garlic
1tbsp Chinese yellow wine
2tbsp oyster sauce
1tsp dark soy sauce
1tsp sesame seed oil
1tsp sugar
4tbsp chicken stock
4tbsp abalone stock
1tsp Chinese yellow wine
1tbsp cornflour

Stand the unopened can of abalone in plenty of water and boil for 3 hours. Remove the abalone from the can, saving 4 tbsp of juice to make the sauce. Trim the abalone into thin slices and set aside.

Heat 4 tbsp of oil and the salt with 1½ pt (900 ml) water in a pan. Bring to the boil and blanch the lettuce leaves for 1 minute. Remove, drain thoroughly and place on a serving dish.

Heat 6 tbsp of oil in the pan and add the ginger and garlic. Remove and discard the garlic when it has turned brown. Add the abalone slices and 1 tbsp of Chinese yellow wine and sauté them lightly.

Add the remaining ingredients, stir and cook for 30 seconds over medium heat. Transfer to the serving dish with the lettuce.

◆ FISH AND CRUSTACEANS ◆

FISH IN WINE-LEE SAUCE

SERVES 4–6

1½lb (700g) fillet of white fish such as sea bass, cod, turbot or halibut
½ egg white
2tsp cornflour
3–4 wood ears (tree fungus)
6fl oz (175ml) peanut oil

Sauce
3tsp rice wine or 2tsp wine-lee paste if available
1tsp salt
1½tbsp sugar
8fl oz (300ml) stock
1tbsp cornflour dissolved in 2tbsp water

Cut the fish fillet into six pieces and mix it with egg white and 2 tsp of cornflour. Soak the mushrooms in water for 30 minutes and cut them into small pieces.

Heat a pan until it is very hot. Pour in the peanut oil to heat for 20 seconds and add the sliced fish to fry for 15 seconds. Remove and drain away the oil. Add 1 tbsp of peanut oil, the sauce, the fish and the mushrooms. Finally add the cornflour to the pan to thicken the sauce. Serve.

ABALONE STEAK IN OYSTER SAUCE

SERVES 4–6

2 cans abalone
3–4tbsp peanut oil
3–4 slices fresh root ginger
1–2 cloves garlic
1tbsp Chinese yellow wine
2tbsp oyster sauce
1tsp sugar
2tbsp cornflour

Boil the abalone in the tins for 5 hours over a low heat in 6–7 pts (3–4 lt) of water before opening the cans. Cut the abalone in slices ½ inch (1 cm) thick. Save 8 tbsp of liquid in the cans as a base for the sauce. Heat 3–4 tbsp of oil in a pan and add the ginger and garlic, frying them until browned. Remove and discard. Add the Chinese yellow wine and liquid from the abalone to the pan and stir in the oyster sauce, sugar and cornflour mixed with 2 tbsp of water. Finally, add the abalone slices, stir well to mix with the sauce and serve.

Abalone is always one of the star dishes on a banquet menu. Canned abalone is recommended for this recipe as some of the dried varieties are expensive and complicated to prepare. If you wish you make take the abalone from the can without first boiling it, but you will have to cut it into thinner slices, not exceeding ⅛ inch (3 mm), or the texture will be too tough and rubbery for you to enjoy.

ABALONE STEAK IN OYSTER SAUCE

STEAMED GROUPER WITH HAM AND MUSHROOMS

SERVES 4–6

1½–1¾lb (700–800g) grouper or sea bass
2tsp salt
¼tsp pepper
6tbsp peanut oil
12 medium dried Chinese mushrooms
5oz (150g) ham
4 slices fresh root ginger
4 spring onions
2tbsp light soy sauce
2tbsp rice wine or dry sherry

Clean the fish, remove the bones and cut the flesh into about 12 evenly sized pieces. Mix the salt and pepper with 2 tsp of oil and rub the mixture over the fish pieces.

Soak the dried mushrooms in hot water for 30 minutes. Remove and discard the stems and cut the caps slantwise into 3 thin slices. Cut the ham into thin slices of a similar size.

Shred the ginger and spring onion into matchstick-sized pieces and arrange half of the pieces as a bed on an oval, heatproof plate. Place the fish pieces, alternating with slices of ham and mushroom, over the ginger and spring onion and put the plate in a steamer. Steam vigorously for 10 minutes and pour away any excess liquid that has accumulated during the steaming.

Sprinkle the soy sauce and wine or sherry over the fish, ham and mushroom and lay the remaining spring onion shreds on top.

Heat 5 tbsp of oil in a small pan and add the remaining shredded ginger. Stir the ginger in the boiling oil for 30 seconds, remove and discard the ginger and pour the hot oil over the fish, ham and mushroom. Serve.

◆ FISH AND CRUSTACEANS ◆

FISH WITH SWEET AND SOUR SAUCE

SERVES 4–6

A whole fish such as bream or red snapper, weighing about 2lb 3oz (1kg), or fish steaks,
1oz (25g) seasoned flour
oil for shallow frying

Sauce
3tbsp tomato ketchup
1tbsp sugar
2tbsp rice wine or dry sherry
1tbsp soy sauce
2tbsp vinegar
2tsp cornflour
7fl oz (200ml) water
salt
2tbsp oil
1 clove garlic, crushed
1 small onion, peeled and siced
½in (1cm) piece fresh root ginger, scraped and cut into shreds
1–2 slices pineapple, cut into fine chunks
few water chestnuts or lychees, cut into wedges
¼ each red and green pepper, deseeded and cut into strips
1 red chilli, deseeded and cut into fine shreds
fresh coriander to garnish

If using steaks or fish make sure that they are of uniform thickness for even cooking. Ask the fishmonger to gut the fish, leaving the head and tail on, but trimming off the fins. Clean and dry, then dust the steaks or whole fish with seasoned flour and fry in hot oil for 5 minutes on each side or until cooked through. Set aside and keep warm while preparing the sauce.

Blend the tomato ketchup with sugar, rice wine and sherry, soy sauce and vinegar. Blend the cornflour with some of the water to a paste. Stir into the tomato mixture and add the remaining water. Add a pinch of salt. Heat the oil, fry the garlic and onion without browning for 1 minute. Fold in the cornflour sauce mixture and stir until the sauce is smooth and thickens. Reduce the heat, stir in the ginger pineapple, water chestnuts or lychees, red and green pepper and chilli. Pour over the fish, laid out on a serving platter, and garnish attractively with fresh coriander.

SMOKED WHITE FISH FRENCH STYLE

SERVES 4–6

1¼lb (550g) white fish, such as turbot

Seasonings
4tbsp western sauce (see recipe below)
¼tsp white pepper
1tsp onion powder
1tsp sugar
1tsp sherry
1tbsp butter

Garnish
½ lettuce
2 tomatoes
4 pieces ham (about 4oz [100g] each)
2–3tbsp mayonnaise

Cut the fish into 4 big pieces. Mix the seasonings together and marinate the fish in the mixture for 7–8 hours or overnight.

Drain the fish and bake it in a moderate oven (350°F/180°C/Gas Mark 4) for 15 minutes. Butter the fish on both sides for a further 10 minutes. Shred the lettuce and slice the tomatoes. Halve each piece of ham. Put the fish on a hot plate and garnish with lettuce, tomatoes, ham and mayonnaise.

To make western sauce, finely shred 4 oz (100 g) each of celery, carrot and onion and 2 bay leaves. Add the shredded vegetables to ½ pt (300 ml) chicken stock and cook over medium heat until the liquid has reduced by about 50 per cent. (This dish is shown opposite without garnish.)

BRAISED CARP

SERVES 2–3

1 carp weighing about 2lb 3oz (1kg) or bream, gutted and scaled, but head and tail left on
salt
fat for deep-frying
1in (2½cm) fresh root ginger, scraped, sliced and cut into slivers
2 cloves garlic, crushed
6 spring onions, roots removed, white part left whole and tops cut into strips
1tbsp light soy sauce
½pt (300ml) fish or chicken stock
1tbsp cornflour
rice wine or dry sherry to taste
seasoning to taste
1 red chilli, deseeded and cut into fine strips
fresh coriander to garnish

Slash the flesh of the fish at ½ inch (1 cm) intervals on each side, dry on absorbent kitchen paper and rub lightly with salt. Lower carefully into the hot fat and cook for 5 minutes, then lift out onto a platter lined with absorbent kitchen paper. Pour off all except 3 tbsp of the oil and fry the ginger, garlic and white parts of the spring onion. Stir in soy sauce and stock. Replace the fish in the pan and cook for a further 15–20 minutes or until tender. Lift the fish onto a serving platter. Blend the cornflour into a paste with water and stir into the pan to thicken the sauce. Add rice wine or sherry and seasoning to taste. Pour this sauce over the fish and garnish with the spring onion tops, chilli and coriander.

FISH ROLLS

SERVES 4–6

8oz (225g) filleted sole
4 medium dried black mushrooms
¼tsp salt
1tsp oil

Seasonings
½tsp salt
1½tsp cornflour
½ egg white

1oz (25g) ham
1½oz (40g) bamboo shoots
¾pt (450ml) peanut oil (to fry fish rolls)
½tsp garlic, chopped
½tsp fresh root ginger, chopped

Sauce
2tbsp stock

1tbsp oyster sauce
2tsp soy sauce
1tsp rice wine or dry sherry
1tsp cornflour

Cut the fish into pieces approximately 1¾ × 2½ inch (4 × 6 cm).

Soak the mushrooms in a small bowl of hot water for 30 minutes. Add ¼ tsp of salt and 1 tsp of oil to the mushrooms and steam them for 10 minutes. Shred the mushrooms, discarding the stems.

Mix the seasoning ingredients and coat the fish thoroughly with the mixture. Slice the ham and the bamboo shoots to matchstick-sized shreds about ¾ inch (2 cm) long.

Place a combination of the ham, bamboo shoots and mushrooms in the centre of each fish fillet. Roll the fish up around the mixture and dust with flour.

Heat the peanut oil until very hot and fry a few fish rolls for 10–20 seconds until they become golden. Remove and set aside. Repeat until all the fish rolls are fried.

Reheat the pan until it is very hot and pour in 1 tbsp of peanut oil. Add the garlic and ginger to sauté. Return the fish rolls to the pan. Mix the sauce ingredients and add to the pan, turning the fish rolls over in the boiling sauce over a high heat for 10 seconds. Serve as an accompaniment to soup.

YANGTZE FISH SALAD

SERVES 5–8

1lb (450g) fish fillets, eg, cod, haddock, sole, turbot
1½tsp salt
1 egg
2oz (50g) cornflour
3 slices fresh root ginger
3 stalks celery
3 spring onions
4oz (100g) bean sprouts
vegetable oil for deep-frying
2tbsp light soy sauce
1½tbsp wine vinegar

SMOKED WHITE FISH FRENCH STYLE

1tbsp chilli sauce
1tbsp sesame seed oil

Cut the fish into thin slices, then cut the slices into matchstick-sized strips. Rub in the salt, coat with the beaten egg and dust with the cornflour. Cut the ginger into thin shreds. Cut the celery into thick matchstick-sized strips. Blanch the celery in a pan of boiling water for 1½ minutes, then drain. Cut the spring onions into 2 inch (5 cm) sections. Wash the bean sprouts and drain thoroughly.

Heat the oil in a wok or deep-fryer. When hot, fry the fish in 2 batches for about 2 minutes. Drain.

Place the celery and bean sprouts in the base of a deep-sided dish. Arrange the strips of fish, like French fries, in one layer on top. Sprinkle with the ginger, spring onions, soy sauce, vinegar, chili sauce and sesame seed oil. Toss the salad before eating.

STEAMED WHOLE FISH WRAPPED IN LOTUS LEAVES

SERVES 4–6

1 whole fish, about 2lb (1kg)
1½tbsp dark soy sauce
2 lotus leaves
3tbsp vegetable oil

Garnish and sauce
3–4oz (75–100g) canned snow pickles
3 slices fresh root ginger
2 spring onions
2 fresh chillies
2tbsp light soy sauce
2tbsp rice wine or dry sherry
6tbsp good stock (see recipe)
2tsp sugar

Clean the fish and dry well. Rub inside and out with the soy sauce. Shred the pickles, ginger, spring onions and fresh chillies, discarding seeds. Soak the lotus leaves in warm water for 10 minutes to soften. Drain.

Heat the oil in a wok or frying pan. When hot, stir-fry pickles, spring onions, ginger and chillies over medium heat for 1 minute. Add the soy sauce, rice wine or sherry, stock and sugar, bring to the boil and stir for 30 seconds. Place the fish on the lotus leaves. Pour half the contents of the wok or pan over the length of the fish. Turn the fish over and pour over the remainder. Wrap the fish completely in the lotus leaves. Secure by tying with string. Place in a steamer and steam for 25 minutes.

SQUIRREL FISH

SERVES 4–6

1 whole fish, 1½–2lb (700–900g)
3 slices fresh root ginger
1½tsp salt
pepper to taste
3–4tbsp cornflour
vegetable oil for deep-frying

Sauce
2tbsp wood ears (tree fungus)
6 medium dried Chinese mushrooms

2 spring onions
1oz (25g) lard
1oz (25g) drained, canned bamboo shoots
3tbsp soy sauce
1tbsp sugar
4tbsp good stock (see recipe)
2tbsp wine vinegar
2tbsp rice wine or dry sherry

This dish derives its name from the fact that, when cooked and served, the fish's tail curves up like a squirrel's.

Clean the fish and slit open from head to tail on the underside so that it lays flat. Cut 7–8 deep slashes on one side of the fish and only 2 on the other side. Finely chop the ginger. Rub the fish inside and out with the salt, pepper and ginger, then coat in the cornflour. Soak the wood ears and mushrooms separately in hot water to cover for 25 minutes. Drain and discard the tough stalks. Cut the mushroom caps into shreds. Finely slice the wood ears. Cut the spring onions into 2 inch (5 cm) sections.

Heat the oil in a wok or deep-fryer. When hot, gently fry the fish over medium heat for 4 minutes, then reduce the heat to low. Meanwhile, melt the lard in a smaller wok or pan. When hot, stir-fry the wood ears, mushrooms, spring onions and bamboo shoots over medium heat for 1½ minutes. Add the soy sauce, sugar, stock, vinegar and wine or sherry. Stir the ingredients over low heat for about 2 minutes. Raise the heat under the wok containing the fish and fry for another 2 minutes. The tail should have curled by now due to the uneven amount of cuts on the fish. Lift out the fish, drain and place on a heated dish.

STEAMED WHOLE FISH WRAPPED IN LOTUS LEAVES

◆ FISH AND CRUSTACEANS ◆

STEAMED FISH WITH GARNISH

SERVES 4–5

1 whole fish, about 1½–2lb (700–900g)
2tsp salt
pepper to taste
1½tbsp fresh root ginger, finely chopped

Garnish and sauce
2–3 spring onions
3 slices fresh root ginger
3 large fresh or dried Chinese mushrooms (optional)
1tbsp rice wine or dry sherry
2½tbsp soy sauce
4tbsp vegetable oil

Clean the fish and dry well. Rub inside and out with the salt, pepper and finely chopped ginger. Leave to season for 30 minutes. Shred the spring onions and ginger. Slice the mushroom caps; if using dried, soak first in hot water for 25 minutes.

Place the fish on a heatproof dish and put into a steamer. Steam vigorously for 10 minutes. Remove the dish from the steamer and pour away any excess water which has collected. Pour the rice wine or sherry and soy sauce down the length of the fish and garnish the fish with the spring onions, mushrooms and ginger. Heat the oil in a small pan and, when smoking hot, pour it in a thin stream down the length of the fish over the spring onions, mushrooms and ginger. The fish is brought to the table on the dish in which it was cooked.

SAUTÉD FISH STEAKS WITH GARNISH

SERVES 4–6

1½–2lb (700–900g) fish, cut into 4–6 steaks
2tsp salt
pepper to taste
6tbsp vegetable oil
5 slices fresh root ginger

Garnish and sauce
4 medium dried Chinese mushrooms
2 spring onions
1¼oz (35g) lard
2tbsp onion, coarsely chopped
1½tbsp fresh root ginger, chopped
4oz (100g) minced pork
3tbsp soy sauce
4tbsp good stock (see recipe)
2tbsp rice wine or dry sherry

Clean and dry the fish steaks. Rub with the salt, pepper and 1 tbsp of the oil. Soak the dried mushrooms in hot water to cover for 25 minutes. Drain and discard the tough stalks. Cut the mushroom caps into matchstick-sized shreds. Cut the spring onions into 1 inch (2.5 cm) sections.

Heat the remaining oil in a wok or frying pan. When hot, add the ginger slices and spread out evenly to flavour the oil. Lay the fish steaks in the hot flavoured oil and shallow-fry or sauté for 2 minutes on each side. Pour away any excess oil and remove from the heat. Heat the lard in a separate pan. When hot, stir-fry the chopped onion, ginger and mushrooms for 1 minute. Add the minced pork and stir over high heat for 3 minutes. Mix in the soy sauce, stock, wine or sherry and spring onion. Bring to the boil and continue to stir-fry for 1 minute. Meanwhile, reheat the first pan and return the fish steaks to it. Heat through, then pour the sauce and garnish over the fish. Transfer contents to a heated serving plate.

BRAISED WHOLE FISH IN HOT VINEGAR SAUCE

SERVES 4–6

2 slices fresh root ginger
1 whole fish, 1½–2lb (700–900g)
1tsp salt
pepper to taste
4tbsp vegetable oil

Sauce
3 slices fresh root ginger
1½oz (40g) canned bamboo shoots, drained
½ red pepper
1 small carrot
1 green chilli
2 dried chillies
2 spring onions
1oz (25g) lard
2tbsp light soy sauce
3tbsp good stock (see recipe)
6tbsp vinegar
½tbsp cornflour blended with 2tbsp water

Finely chop the 2 slices of ginger. Clean the fish and dry well. Rub evenly inside and out with salt, pepper, chopped ginger and 1 tbsp of the oil. Leave to season for 30 minutes. Shred the 3 slices of ginger, bamboo shoots, red pepper, carrot, chillies, discarding seeds, and spring onions.

Heat the remaining oil in a wok or frying pan. When hot, fry the fish for 2½ minutes on each side. Remove and drain. Add the shredded ginger, bamboo shoots, red pepper, carrot, chillies and spring onions to the remaining oil and stir-fry over medium heat for 1 minute. Add the lard, soy sauce, stock and half the vinegar and cook for another minute. Lay the fish back in the wok or pan and cook gently for 2 minutes on both sides, basting. Transfer the fish to a serving dish. Stir the remaining vinegar into the wok, then add the blended cornflour, stirring over high heat until the sauce thickens.

Pour the sauce from the wok over the length of the fish and garnish with the shredded vegetables.

BEAN CURD FISH IN CHILLI SAUCE

SERVES 2–3

1lb (450g) mullet or mackerel
2 spring onions, white parts only
1 clove garlic
2 slices fresh root ginger
2 cakes fresh bean curd
1tsp salt
4tbsp oil
2tbsp chilli paste
1tbsp soy sauce
2tbsp rice wine or dry sherry
2tbsp cornflour
12fl oz (350ml) stock

Cut the heads off the fish and remove the backbone; crush the garlic, cut it and the root ginger into small pieces; cut the onion whites into short lengths.

Cut each bean curd into about 10 pieces. Blanch them in boiling water; remove and soak them in stock with salt.

Heat up the oil until hot; fry the fish until both sides are golden; put them to one side; tilt the wok, and put in the chilli paste. When it starts to bubble, return the wok to its original position, push the fish back, add soy sauce, wine or sherry, onion, root ginger, garlic and a little stock — about 4 fl oz (100 ml). At the same time add the bean curd taken from the stock and cook with the fish for about 10 minutes.

Now pick out the fish with chopsticks and place them on a serving dish, then quickly mix the cornflour with a little cold water. Add to the wok to make a smooth sauce with the bean curd; pour it all over the fish and serve.

CHRYSANTHEMUM FISH POT

SERVES 4–6

4oz (100g) fish maw
4oz (100g) chicken breast meat, boned and skinned
2 chicken gizzards
½lb (225g) pig's tripe
4oz (100g) Bêche-de-mer
4oz (100g) mange tout
½lb (225g) spinach leaves
2oz (50g) fresh coriander
2 slices fresh root ginger, peeled
2–3 spring onions
2tsp salt
1tsp Sichuan pepper, freshly ground
3½pts (2lt) stock (see recipe)

BRAISED WHOLE FISH IN HOT VINEGAR SAUCE

1 large dry chrysanthemum (white or yellow)

Cut the fish maw, chicken gizzards, Bêche-de-Mer and tripe into slices. Wash the cabbage, mange tout, spinach and coriander; cut them into small pieces.

Finely chop the ginger root and onions; place them with salt and pepper in a small bowl.

Bring the stock to a rolling boil in the fire-pot; arrange the meat and vegetables in the moat. They will only need to be cooked for about 5 minutes. Everybody just helps themselves from the pot with chopsticks, and dips their helping in the 'four seasonings' before eating it.

Use the chrysanthemum as a decoration.

◆ FISH AND CRUSTACEANS ◆

SWEET-SOUR CRISP FISH

SERVES 2–3

1 carp (or freshwater fish) weighing 1½lb (700g)
2tbsp rice wine or dry sherry
4tbsp soy sauce
2oz (50g) cornflour
1 clove garlic
2 spring onions
2 slices fresh root ginger
2 dried red chillies, soaked
1oz (25g) bamboo shoots
2–3 dried Chinese mushrooms, soaked
oil for deep-frying
1½tbsp sugar
1½tbsp vinegar
4fl oz (100ml) stock

Clean the fish; make 6 or 7 diagonal cuts as deep as the bone on each side of the fish. Marinate in rice wine or sherry and 2 tbsp of soy sauce for 5 minutes; remove and wipe dry. Make a paste with 1½ oz (40 g) cornflour and water and coat the entire fish evenly.

Finely chop the garlic, 1 onion and slice root ginger. Cut the other onion and root ginger into thin shreds. Cut the soaked red chillies (discarding the seeds), bamboo shoots and mushrooms all into thin shreds.

Heat up the oil to boiling point, pick up the fish by the tail, lower it head first into the oil, turn it around and deep-fry for about 7 minutes or until golden; remove and drain.

Pour off the excess oil leaving about 2 tbsp in the wok; add finely chopped onion, root ginger, garlic and red chilli, bamboo shoots and mushrooms followed by the remaining soy sauce, sugar, vinegar and stock. Stir a few times, then add the remaining cornflour mixed with a little water; blend well to make a slightly thick smooth sauce.

Place a cloth over the fish, press gently with your hand to soften the body, then put it on a serving dish and pour the sauce over it; garnish with onion and root ginger shreds.

STEAMED LOBSTER

SERVES 2–4

1 lobster weighing about 1½–2lb (700–900g)

Sauce
2 spring onions, finely chopped
2 slices fresh root ginger, finely chopped
1tsp salt
1tsp sugar
½tbsp cornflour
1tsp sesame seed oil
4tbsp stock
freshly ground Sichuan pepper
1tbsp oil

Steam the lobster for 20 minutes. Leave to cool, then split in two lengthwise, and cut each half into four pieces.

Crack the shell of the claws so that the flesh can be taken out easily.

Make the sauce by heating up the oil in a wok or saucepan; toss in the finely chopped onions and root ginger; add salt, sugar, stock and ground pepper. Thicken with the cornflour mixed with a little water. Finally add the sesame seed oil; pour it all over the lobster and serve.

CRAB BALLS

SERVES 6–8

½lb (225g) crab meat
2oz (50g) pork fat
2oz (50g) water chestnuts, peeled
2 eggs
2tbsp rice wine or dry sherry
1tsp monosodium glutamate
1tsp salt
2tbsp cornflour
1 slice fresh root ginger, finely chopped
1 spring onion, finely chopped
4fl oz (100ml) chicken stock
1lb (450g) lard for deep-frying
1oz (25g) cooked ham

Finely chop the crab meat, pork fat and water chestnuts and add 2 eggs,

CRAB BALLS

DEEP-FRIED CONPOY AND SHREDDED KALE

1 tbsp of wine or sherry, ½ tsp of monosodium glutamate, ½ tsp of salt, and 1 tbsp of cornflour together with the finely chopped root ginger and onion. Blend well, then make into small balls about the size of walnuts.

Heat up the lard over high heat for about 3–4 minutes, then reduce the heat to moderate and deep-fry the crab balls for about 5 minutes until pale golden. Scoop them out with a perforated spoon and serve them hot or cold. Alternatively place them in a bowl with a little chicken stock — not quite enough to cover them — then place the bowl in a steamer and steam for 15 minutes.

Now mix the remaining wine or sherry, monosodium glutamate, salt and cornflour with the chicken stock and make a white sauce over a moderate heat, then pour it over the crab balls. Garnish with finely chopped ham and serve.

CRAB WITH EGGS

SERVES 4

4 eggs, beaten
4–6oz (100–175g) crab meat
1tsp sugar
1 small piece fresh root ginger, scraped and crushed in garlic press
2tsp light soy sauce
seasoning
a little oil for frying
4–6 spring onions, finely chopped

Set the beaten egg on one side, pick over the crab meat to remove any shell or cartilage. Stir in sugar, ginger and soy sauce and season to taste. Add this to the beaten eggs and scramble in fat in a pan for 1 minute. Add spring onions and serve at once.

DEEP-FRIED CONPOY AND SHREDDED KALE

SERVES 4–6

3½oz (80g) conpoy (dried scallops)
2 slices fresh root ginger
1tsp Chinese yellow wine
5oz (150g) Chinese kale leaves, or pickled snow cabbage leaves
¾pt (450ml) peanut oil
2tsp sugar
1tsp salt

Soak the conpoy in water for 30 minutes. Add the ginger and Chinese yellow wine and steam for 15 minutes. Remove the conpoy, tear it into fine shreds and pat dry. Set it aside.

Cut the Chinese kale leaves into fine shreds, pat it dry and set aside. (If you are using pickled snow cabbage, soak it in 1¾ pt [1 lt] hot water for 30 minutes. Change the water and soak for 30 minutes. Squeeze it dry, tear the leaves into small pieces and set them aside.)

Heat the peanut oil in a pan. Add the conpoy, stirring to separate, and fry until nicely golden in colour. Remove, dry and set aside.

Add the kale or cabbage, again stirring to separate, and fry for 1 minute. Remove. If the vegetable is not crispy enough return it to pan for a short time. Remove and pat dry with absorbent kitchen paper.

Sprinkle 2 tsp of sugar and 1 tsp of salt over the vegetables and mix well. (If you are using pickled snow cabbage, there is no need to add salt.) Place the crispy vegetables on a plate, arrange the conpoy on top and serve.

WINE-MARINATED SHRIMPS

SERVES 4–6

½lb (225g) fresh shrimps
3tbsp rice wine or dry sherry
2 spring onions, white parts only
2oz (50g) celery
2oz (50g) carrots
1tbsp peas

Sauce
2tbsp soy sauce
1tsp sesame seed oil

Wash the shrimps well, and place in a dish. Pour the wine or sherry over them, add the onion whites cut to 1 inch (2.5 cm) lengths; cover and marinate for 5 minutes.

Slice the celery and carrot; parboil with the peas for 5 minutes. Drain and add to the shrimps. Pour the sauce over and serve. Mix the sauce; pour it over the shrimps, serve.

◆ FISH AND CRUSTACEANS ◆

FRIED PRAWN BALLS WITH BABY CORNS

SERVES 4–6

½lb (225g) Pacific prawns
1 small can of baby corns
3–4 dried Chinese mushrooms, soaked
1 slice fresh root ginger
2 spring onions
½tbsp salt
1 egg white
1tbsp cornflour
1tbsp rice wine or dry sherry
1tsp sugar
1tsp sesame seed oil
oil for deep-frying
fresh coriander to garnish

Shell the prawns; use a sharp knife to make a deep incision down the back of each one, and pull out the black intestinal vein. Cut each prawn into two or three pieces. Mix with a little salt, egg white and cornflour.

Finely chop the root ginger and onions, cut large mushrooms into 2 or 3 pieces; smaller ones can be left whole. Drain the baby corns. Deep-fry the prawns in warm oil for 30 seconds; remove and drain.

Pour off the excess oil, leaving about 2 tbsp of oil in the wok, wait until it smokes, toss in the finely chopped root ginger and onions followed by mushrooms, baby corns and prawns; add salt, rice wine or sherry and sugar. Stir until well blended; add sesame seed oil just before serving. Garnish with fresh coriander.

STEAMED EEL

SERVES 4–6

2lb (1kg) white eel
6 slices fresh root ginger
2 spring onions
8tbsp peanut oil
1tsp Chinese yellow wine
½pt (300ml) chicken stock
1tsp salt
1tsp sugar
½tsp pepper
1tbsp cornflour

Put the eel in a basin and pour over it 4 pt (2 lt) of boiling water with 2 tbsp of salt added. Wash the fish thoroughly. Slit the eel open, remove the intestines and clean the inside carefully. Pat it dry with absorbent kitchen paper.

Make deep cuts (about three-quarters of the way through the flesh) at 1 inch (25 mm) intervals along the eel and place it on a plate, bending it into a ring form. Arrange the ginger and spring onion on top.

Steam the eel over a medium heat for 20 minutes. Remove the ginger and spring onions and discard them and drain away the liquid from the plate. Heat the oil and pour it over the eel, again draining any excess from the plate.

Add the remaining ingredients to the pan, stir and bring to the boil. Pour the sauce over the eel and serve.

STEAMED EEL

FRIED OYSTER

SERVES 4–6

12 large oysters
2tbsp cornflour (for cleaning oysters)
2tbsp salt (for cleaning oysters)
1tsp monosodium glutamate (optional)
1tsp salt

Sauce
2oz (50g) wheat flour
2tbsp cornflour
¾oz (20g) powdered yeast
1tsp oil
6fl oz (170ml) water
¾pt (450ml) peanut oil (for frying oysters)

Dips
1 small plate of ketchup
1 small plate of spiced salt

Rub the oysters thoroughly with cornflour and salt and then wash them in water. Drop the oysters into a pan of boiling water until they are half cooked (this takes about 20 seconds). Dry the oysters carefully with a towel then mix them well with the monosodium glutamate (if used) and 1 tsp of salt.

Mix the sauce ingredients, blending them together thoroughly.

Heat the peanut oil in a pan. Dip the oysters into the sauce and fry them until brown over low heat.

Serve with ketchup, or prepare a dish of spiced salt by putting 1–2 tbsp of salt and 1 tsp of peppercorns in a pan over low heat until they start to brown; remove the peppercorns and keep the salt.

SIZZLING EEL

SERVES 4–6

2lb (1kg) yellow eels
4pts (2lt) boiling water
2tbsp salt
4tbsp peanut oil
2tsp fresh root ginger, chopped
½tsp pepper
2tsp Chinese yellow wine
1tbsp sugar
2tbsp dark soy sauce
8tbsp chicken stock
1½tbsp cornflour dissolved in 1½tbsp water
2tsp spring onion, chopped
2tbsp sesame seed oil
2tsp minced ham
1½tsp chopped coriander

Place the eels in a basin. Pour over them the boiling water (to which has been added 2 tbsp of salt) and let them stand for 3 minutes. Take the eels out of the water and rinse them in cold water from the tap.

Separate the meat from the bone with the handle of a teaspoon, then cut the eel meat into ½ × 2 inch (1 × 5 cm) strips. Set aside. Heat the oil until very hot. Add the eel, stirring, and add the chopped ginger, pepper, yellow wine, sugar, soy sauce and chicken stock. Cook for 5 minutes. Stir in the cornflour and transfer to a plate. Make a small well in the centre of the eels and put into it the chopped spring onion.

Heat 2 tbsp of sesame seed oil until very hot and pour it into the 'well'. Add the minced ham, garnish with coriander and serve.

◆ FISH AND CRUSTACEANS ◆

OYSTER OMELETTE

SERVES 3–4

4 medium oysters
1tbsp cornflour
4 eggs
2 spring onions
1 stalk coriander
½tsp sesame seed oil
1tsp pepper
1tsp salt
2tbsp peanut oil

Clean the oysters, cut them into small ¼ inch (5 mm) pieces and mix them with 1 tbsp of cornflour. Set aside. Beat the eggs together lightly. Finely chop the spring onion and coriander and add to the egg.

Blanch the diced oyster in boiling water for 30 seconds. Drain and add the sesame seed oil, pepper and salt. Mix well.

Heat a pan over medium heat and add 2 tbsp of peanut oil. Pour half the egg mixture into the pan and half of the diced oyster. When the edge of the omelette browns slightly turn it over to complete cooking. Repeat with the rest of the egg and diced oyster. Serve on a well-heated dish.

STIR-FRIED CRAB IN CURRY SAUCE

DEEP-FRIED CRAB CLAWS

SERVES 5–6

10 large frozen crab claws
2 slices fresh root ginger
3 eggs
1tsp salt
8oz (225g) peeled prawns
3tbsp cornflour
8oz (225g) breadcrumbs
vegetable oil for deep-frying

Defrost the claws and chop into half lengthwise. Finely chop the ginger. Beat the eggs. Add the salt and ginger to the prawns and finely chop, mixing well. Divide the prawn mixture into 10 portions, and press each portion on to the meat of the crab claws. Sprinkle the prawn mixture with cornflour, dip each meat side of the claw into beaten egg, and coat with breadcrumbs. Place the prawn-filled claws on a plate and chill for 1 hour.

Heat the oil in a wok or deep-fryer. When hot, fry the claws in 2 batches for 3 minutes. Drain. Serve hot on a heated dish, garnished with wedges of lemon and sprigs of parsley.

ASPARAGUS TOPPED WITH CRAB MEAT SAUCE

SERVES 4–6

4oz (100g) crab meat
1¼lb (550g) fresh asparagus
4tbsp peanut oil
8tbsp chicken stock
4 slices fresh root ginger
1 clove garlic

Sauce
1 egg white
8tbsp chicken stock
1tsp sesame seed oil
2tsp Chinese yellow wine
½tsp sugar
¼tsp pepper
1½tsp cornflour

Steam a medium sized crab for 20 minutes. Scoop out the crab meat from the shells and set aside.

Clean the asparagus and cut the stalks into 1½ inch (3 cm) sections, discarding the part close to the roots.

Heat 1 tbsp oil and add the chicken stock to the pan. Cook the asparagus until the stock is almost absorbed.

Transfer to a plate and set aside to keep warm. Heat 3 tbsp oil in the pan, add the ginger and garlic and when browned, remove and discard.

Add the crab meat to the pan and sauté for 30 seconds. Mix the sauce ingredients, stir into the pan and bring to the boil. Pour the mixture over the asparagus and serve.

STIR-FRIED CRAB IN CURRY SAUCE

SERVES 5–6

2lb (1kg) crab
2tbsp cornflour
¾pt (450ml) peanut oil
6 slices fresh root ginger
2tsp garlic, chopped
4oz (100g) spring onions cut into 2inch (5cm) pieces
1tbsp curry paste
½pt (300ml) chicken stock
2tsp sugar
1tsp salt
1tsp Chinese yellow wine

Place the crab on a chopping board, belly side up, and cut through the middle with a cleaver, but avoid cutting into the top shell. Chop off the claws, lightly crush the shell and set them aside. Lift off the top shell and clean the crab, discarding the 'dead men's fingers'. Chop the body into 4 or 6 pieces, depending on the size, and lightly coat the crab meat with cornflour.

Heat the oil in a pan and fry the crab for 2 minutes over a very high heat. Remove, drain and set aside.

Heat 2 tbsp of oil in the pan. Add the ginger, garlic, spring onion and curry paste, stir and cook for 1½ minutes.

Return the crab to the pan, stirring, and add the chicken stock, sugar and salt. Cover the pan and cook over medium heat for 10 minutes, turning the contents once or twice to ensure that they are evenly cooked. Sprinkle with Chinese yellow wine and serve.

CRAB WITH FERMENTED BEANS AND PEPPERS

SERVES 4–6

2 crabs (approximately 1lb [450g] each)
2 red chilli peppers
1 green bell pepper
4 pieces ginger
3 spring onions
2 cloves garlic
¾pt (450ml) peanut oil (for frying crab)
3tsp salted, fermented soya beans
8tbsp stock or chicken soup

Seasoning
1tsp sugar
1tsp salt
2tsp oyster sauce
½tsp monosodium glutamate (optional)
2tsp rice wine or dry sherry

Clean the crabs and chop the flesh of each into 6 pieces. Mince the chilli and the green pepper. Slice the ginger and cut the spring onions into ¾ inch (2 cm) pieces. Crush and chop the garlic.

Heat the oil in a pan and add the crab, ginger and spring onions. Fry for 2 minutes and remove from the pan to drain. Reheat the pan to smoking point and add 1 tbsp of oil. Fry the garlic and beans for 10 seconds, then return the crab to the pan.

Mix the seasoning ingredients with the stock or chicken soup and add the mixture to the pan. Turn and stir contents for 30 seconds. Serve.

DEEP-FRIED CRISPY KING PRAWNS

CANTONESE FRESH POACHED PRAWNS WITH TWO DIPS

SERVES 4–5

1¼lb (550g) fresh unshelled prawns
1½tsp salt

Dip 1
2 spring onions
3 slices fresh root ginger
2 green chillies
3tbsp vegetable oil
3tbsp light soy sauce
1tbsp wine vinegar
½tbsp sesame seed oil

Dip 2
1tbsp fresh root ginger, shredded
3tbsp vinegar

Wash the prawns thoroughly under running water. Finely chop the spring onions, ginger and chillies, discarding the seeds, together. Place them in a small heatproof bowl.

Bring 2 pt (1.2 lt) water to the boil in a saucepan and add the salt. Simmer the prawns for 2 minutes, then leave to stand in the water, off the heat, for a further minute. Drain.

Place the prawns in a medium bowl. Heat the vegetable oil in a pan. When smoking hot, pour over the ginger, spring onions and chillies. Leave for 30 seconds, then add the soy sauce, vinegar and sesame oil; stir well. For the other dip, place the shredded ginger in a small bowl and spoon over the vinegar. To eat, peel each prawn up to the tail and then, holding the tail, dip into the dip sauces.

DEEP-FRIED CRISPY KING PRAWNS

SERVES 4–6

1 slice fresh root ginger
2 eggs
3oz (75g) plain flour
2tbsp self-raising flour
1½tsp salt
4tbsp water
1½lb (700g) king prawns, fresh or frozen, unshelled
vegetable oil for deep-frying

Finely chop the ginger. Beat the eggs for 15 seconds, then fold in both types of flour, salt, ginger and water. Beat for 1 minute to obtain a light batter. Shell the prawns, leaving the tail shells on. Clean, scraping away any dark or gritty bits.

Heat the oil in a wok or deep-fryer. When hot, hold each prawn by the tail and dip the flesh into the batter. Lower into the oil, frying 6 prawns at a time for 3 minutes. Remove with a perforated spoon and drain. When the first batch has been fried, keep hot and crispy in the oven while frying the remaining prawns.

SALT AND PEPPER PRAWNS

SERVES 6–7

1lb (450g) king prawns
8tbsp vegetable oil
2 spring onions
2 cloves garlic
2 dried chillies
1½tsp Sichuan peppercorns
1½tsp salt

Wash and shell the prawns. Sprinkle on 1½ tsp of the oil. Cut the spring onions into 1 inch (2.5 cm) sections. Thinly slice the garlic. Shred the chillies. Lightly pound the peppercorns and mix with the salt.

Heat the remaining oil in a wok or frying pan. When hot, stir-fry the prawns over a high heat for 1 minute. Remove the prawns and pour away the oil to use for other purposes, except for 1 tbsp. Reheat the oil in the wok or pan. When hot, quickly stir-fry the chilli, garlic and spring onion. Spread out the spring onion and chilli and return the prawns. Sprinkle on the salt and pepper mixture and stir-fry for another 45 seconds.

STEAMED SCALLOPS WITH BLACK BEAN SAUCE

SERVES 6–8

12 fresh scallops, with shells

Sauce
1½tbsp salted black beans
4tbsp vegetable oil
1tbsp fresh root ginger, finely chopped
½tbsp red chilli, finely chopped
½tbsp garlic, crushed
1tsp pounded Sichuan peppercorns
1tbsp spring onion, finely chopped
2tbsp soy sauce
1tbsp rice wine or dry sherry
2tbsp good stock (see recipe)
1tsp sesame seed oil

Scrub the scallops under running cold water, then remove the flat shell. Soak black beans in hot water for 5 minutes. Drain and crush.

Put the scallops on a large heat-proof dish, place in a steamer and steam for 8–9 minutes. Meanwhile, heat the vegetable oil in a small wok or saucepan. When hot, stir-fry the ginger, chilli, garlic, peppercorns, spring onion and black beans for 30 seconds. Add the soy sauce, sherry and stock and continue to stir-fry for another 15 seconds. Sprinkle on the sesame seed oil.

Drip about 2 tsp of the sauce over each scallop and serve them in the shells. The diners should be able to remove the scallops from their shells, then drink the remaining sauce from the shells.

STEAMED SCALLOPS WITH BLACK BEAN SAUCE

◆ FISH AND CRUSTACEANS ◆

STIR-FRIED PRAWNS IN GARLIC AND TOMATO SAUCE

SERVES 5–6

12oz (350g) peeled prawns, fresh or frozen
1tsp salt
¾tbsp cornflour
1 egg white
2 cloves garlic
2 spring onions
2 small firm tomatoes
6tbsp vegetable oil

Sauce
2tbsp tomato sauce or purée
¼tsp salt
1tbsp sugar
pinch of monosodium glutamate (optional)
6tbsp good stock (see recipe)
1½tbsp cornflour blended with 3tbsp water
1tsp sesame seed oil

Toss the prawns in the salt, dust with the cornflour and coat in the egg white. Crush the garlic. Cut the spring onions into shreds. Skin the tomatoes and cut into eighths.

Heat the oil in a wok or frying pan. When hot, stir-fry the prawns over high heat for 1½ minutes. Remove from the wok or pan. Pour away the excess oil and reheat the wok or pan. When hot, stir-fry the garlic, half the spring onions and tomatoes over high heat for 30 seconds. Add the tomato purée, salt, sugar, monosodium glutamate, if using, and stock and continue stir-frying for another 30 seconds. Stir in the blended cornflour until the sauce thickens. Sprinkle on the sesame seed oil and remaining spring onions. Return the prawns to the wok or pan, stir once more and serve.

FUKIEN CLAM SOUP

SERVES 4–5

3lb (1.5kg) clams
2tbsp salt
1½tbsp dried shrimps
2 slices fresh root ginger
3 spring onions
2 cloves garlic
2tsp salt
pepper to taste
1½ chicken stock cubes
1½pt (900ml) good stock (see recipe)
1½tbsp light soy sauce
1tbsp vinegar
½tsp sesame seed oil

Wash and clean the clams well with a stiff brush under running water. Bring 2pt (1.2lt) water to the boil in a saucepan and add the salt. Simmer the clams for 2 minutes then leave to stand in the water, off the heat, for a further minute. Drain. Discard any clams which are unopened. Soak the dried shrimps in hot water for 5 minutes, then drain. Finely shred the ginger and spring onions. Crush the garlic.

Place the poached clams in a saucepan. Add the dried shrimps, ginger, garlic, salt, pepper and crumbled stock cubes. Pour in the stock and bring to the boil. Reduce the heat and simmer for 10 minutes. Add the spring onions, soy sauce and vinegar, and continue to simmer for another 5 minutes.

Place the clams and soup in a large heated serving bowl and sprinkle over the sesame seed oil. Serve in individual bowls and eat like 'Moules Marinière', or the dish can be eaten from a large central bowl.

CANTONESE GINGER AND ONION CRAB OR LOBSTER

SERVES 5–6

3lb (1.5kg) crab or 2lb (1kg) live lobster
5 slices fresh root ginger
4 spring onions
1 medium red pepper
vegetable oil for deep-frying
½tsp salt
¼pt (150ml) good stock (see recipe)
2tbsp light soy sauce
3tbsp rice wine or dry sherry
1tsp sesame seed oil

Scrub the crab thoroughly under running water. Chop the crab into 4 pieces, discarding the grey 'dead men's fingers'. Alternatively, scrub the lobster under running cold water and chop into bite-sized pieces, discarding the hard stomach sac behind the head and the black intestinal vein. Crack the claws with the back of a chopper. Cut the ginger and spring onions into matchstick-sized shreds. Thinly slice the red pepper.

Heat the oil in a wok or deep-fryer. When very hot, add the crab or lobster pieces one by one to the oil. Fry over high heat for 2½ minutes. Remove and drain. Pour away the oil to use for other purposes, reserving about 2 tbsp. Reheat the wok or frying pan. When hot, stir-fry the ginger, spring onion, red pepper and salt over medium heat for 1 minute. Pour in the stock, soy sauce and rice wine or sherry. Bring to the boil and return the crab or lobster to the wok or pan. Toss a few times, then cover and cook for 3–4 minutes until the sauce is reduced by half. Sprinkle on the sesame seed oil, toss and transfer to a heated serving dish.

DEEP-FRIED OYSTERS

SERVES 4–6

20–25 medium oysters
1tsp salt
pepper to taste
2tsp fresh root ginger, finely chopped
vegetable oil for deep-frying
1½tbsp spring onions, finely chopped

Batter
1 egg
5tbsp plain flour
1tbsp cornflour
5tbsp water
½tsp baking powder

Shell and drain the oysters. Sprinkle with salt, pepper and ginger. Combine the ingredients for the batter until smooth. Heat the oil in a wok or deep-fryer. When very hot, dip the oysters individually into the batter. Fry in batches for 3 minutes until golden-brown. Drain. Transfer to a heated serving dish and sprinkle with spring onion.

CANTONESE GINGER AND ONION CRAB

BRAISED MUSSELS WITH BEAN CURD AND MUSHROOMS

SERVES 5–6

2½pt (1lt) mussels
4 slices fresh root ginger
6 medium dried Chinese mushrooms
2 cakes fresh bean curd
3 cloves garlic
3 spring onions
¾pt (450ml) good stock (see recipe)
4–5tbsp rice wine or dry sherry
½tsp salt
pepper to taste
1 chicken stock cube
1tbsp cornflour blended with 2tbsp water
1tsp sesame seed oil

Scrub the mussels thoroughly. Poach in a large saucepan of simmering water with the ginger for 1½ minutes, then drain. Discard any unopened ones. Transfer the mussels to a large pan or flameproof casserole. Soak the dried mushrooms in hot water to cover for 25 minutes. Drain and discard the tough stalks. Cut the mushroom caps into quarters. Cut the bean curd into cubes or rectangles. Finely chop the garlic. Shred the spring onions.

Place the pan of mussels over medium-high heat. Pour in the stock and wine or sherry, then add the bean curd, mushrooms, garlic, half the spring onion, salt and pepper. Bring to the boil and sprinkle in the crumbled stock cube. Stir, then simmer gently for 10 minutes. Stir in the blended cornflour. Sprinkle with the remaining spring onion and the sesame seed oil.

◆ FISH AND CRUSTACEANS ◆

'DRAGON AND PHOENIX' LEGS

SERVES 4–6

6oz (150g) lean pork
4oz (100g) chicken breast meat
6oz (150g) shelled shrimps uncooked
2oz (50g) onions
1tbsp rice wine or dry sherry
2tsp salt
5tbsp cornflour
freshly ground Sichuan pepper
2 eggs
A large sheet of cellophane paper
1tbsp sesame seed oil
oil for deep-frying

Coarsely chop the lean pork, chicken, shrimps and onions; mix with salt, rice wine or sherry and pepper and divide into 10 portions. Beat the eggs and mix with 2 tbsp of cornflour.

Cut the cellophane paper into 10 pieces roughly 2 × 4 inch (5 × 10 cm). On the middle of each piece place a portion of the filling, rub some egg and cornflour mixture all around it, then wrap the sheet round the filling to make the shape of a chicken leg, making 10 'legs' in all. Put them on a plate and steam for about 10 minutes, then take them out and place on a cold plate.

Mix the remaining 3 tbsp cornflour with 3 tbsp of water to make a batter; heat the oil in a wok or deep-fryer, deep-fry each of the 'legs' in the batter until golden and serve hot.

STEAMED EEL WITH PICKLED PLUM AND SOY BEAN PASTE

SERVES 4–6

2lb (1kg) freshwater eel
2tbsp salt
4–6 pickled plums (remove and discard the stones)
1tbsp sugar
2tbsp soya bean paste
2tsp dark soy sauce
2tsp garlic, chopped
1–2tsp red chilli, finely shredded
2tbsp peanut oil
1tbsp chopped coriander

Rub the eel with 2 tbsp of salt. Put it in a basin and pour over it approximately 1½ pt (900 ml) boiling water. Clean and pat dry. Cut off the back fin, slit it open from the back and remove the bones. Cut the eel into sections 2 inch (5 cm) long and place them on large plate.

Mix together the pickled plums, sugar, soy bean paste, dark soy sauce, chopped garlic and finely shredded red chilli and spread evenly over the eel. Steam over medium heat for 35 minutes. Pour 2 tbsp of very hot (boiling) peanut oil over the fish, sprinkle with the chopped coriander and serve.

DEEP-FRIED CRAB CLAWS

SERVES 5–6

10 large frozen crab claws
2 slices fresh root ginger
3 eggs
1tsp salt
8oz (225g) peeled prawns
3tbsp cornflour
8oz (225g) dry breadcrumbs
vegetable oil for deep-frying

Defrost the claws and chop into half lengthwise. Finely chop the ginger. Beat the eggs. Add the salt and ginger to the prawns and finely chop, mixing well. Divide the prawn mixture into 10 portions, and press each portion on to the meat of the crab claws. Sprinkle the prawn mixture with cornflour, dip each meat side of the claw into beaten egg, and coat with breadcrumbs. Place the prawn-filled claws on a plate and chill for 1 hour.

Heat the oil in a wok or deep-fryer. When hot, fry the claws in about 2 batches for 3 minutes. Drain.

Serve hot on a heated dish, garnished with wedges of lemon and sprigs of parsley.

'DRAGON AND PHOENIX' LEGS

◆ FISH AND CRUSTACEANS ◆

QUICK-FRIED CRYSTAL PRAWNS

SERVES 4–5

12oz (350g) king prawns, fresh or frozen, unshelled
1tsp salt
1½tbsp cornflour
1 egg white
½tsp sugar
pepper to taste
¼pt (150ml) vegetable oil
2 spring onions
2 slices fresh root ginger
3–4tbsp peas (optional)
2½tbsp good stock (see recipe)
1½tbsp dry sherry or white wine

Shell the prawns. Wash in salted water, then rinse under running cold water. Drain well. Place in a bowl. Add salt, cornflour, egg white, sugar, pepper and ½ tsp vegetable oil. Mix well. Finely chop the spring onions and ginger.

Heat the oil in a wok or deep frying pan. When hot, add the prawns, stir around and fry over medium heat for 1¾ minutes. Remove and drain. Pour away the oil to use for other purposes, leaving only 1–1½ tbsp. Reheat the wok or pan. When hot, stir-fry the ginger, spring onion and peas over high heat for 15 seconds. Add the stock and sherry or wine. As the sauce boils, return the prawns and adjust the seasoning. Fry for 1 minute.

PEPPERY SHRIMPS

SERVES 4–6

1½lb (700g) shrimps
¾pt (450ml) peanut oil
2tsp salt
½tsp sugar

PEPPERY SHRIMPS

1tsp garlic, chopped
1tsp red chilli, minced
1tsp Chinese yellow wine

Trim and devein the shrimps but leave the shells on. Pat them dry and set aside. Heat the peanut oil in a pan and add the shrimps to fry for 2 minutes. Turn off the heat and let them sit in the oil for another 2 minutes. Drain and set aside. Reheat the pan and add the salt, stirring over a low heat until it is slightly browned. Transfer the salt to a saucer and mix with ½ tsp of sugar. Set aside.

Heat 1 tbsp of oil in pan. Add the garlic and chilli and return the shrimps. Stir-fry them over a high heat for 1 minute and add the Chinese yellow wine, stirring for 20 seconds. Sprinkle the salt and sugar mixture over the shrimps, stir-fry for a further 30 seconds and serve.

STIR-FRIED SCALLOPS WITH EGG

SERVES 4–6

2 spring onions
2 eggs
3tbsp vegetable oil
8oz (225g) fresh shelled scallops
1tsp salt
½tsp sugar
1½tbsp rice wine or dry sherry
pepper to taste
¾oz (20g) lard
1½tbsp finely chopped ham

Coarsely chop the spring onions, dividing the white and green parts. Lightly beat the eggs.

Heat the oil in a wok or frying pan. When hot, stir-fry the scallops and white parts of the spring onions over medium heat for 1 minute. Add the salt, sugar, rice wine or sherry and pepper. Continue to stir-fry for 1 minute. Remove from the pan. Add the lard to the wok or pan. When hot, pour in the beaten eggs. Stir them around a couple of times and, before they have set, return the scallops to the pan. Turn and stir with the egg for 30 seconds. Sprinkle with the green parts of the spring onion. Stir once more, then transfer to a heated serving dish. Sprinkle with chopped ham.

QUICK-FRIED CHILLI PRAWNS

SERVES 5–6

1lb (450g) king prawns
1 small fresh green chilli
2 small dried red chillies
2 slices fresh root ginger
2 spring onions
1tsp salt
½tsp sesame seed oil
½tsp pepper
1tsp cornflour

½pt (225ml) water
¾pt (450ml) chicken stock
1 × 8oz (225g) can cream of sweet corn
1tbsp cornflour
2 eggs
1tbsp chopped coriander
2tbsp finely chopped ham, to garnish

Shell the prawns. Wash in salted water, then rinse under cold running water. Drain well. Finely chop the chillies, discarding the seeds. Coarsely chop the ginger and spring onions. Place the prawns in a bowl. Add 1 tsp of the salt, the cornflour, egg white and wine or sherry and mix well.

Heat the oil in a wok or frying pan. When hot, add the prawns, stir around and fry for 2 minutes. Remove and drain. Pour away the oil to use for other purposes, leaving only 2 tbsp. Reheat the wok or pan. When hot, stir-fry the chillies and ginger over medium heat for 30 seconds. Add the sugar, yellow bean paste, tomato purée, stock, remaining salt, vinegar and spring onions. Toss and stir for 15 seconds. Return the prawns to the pan. Stir and turn for 30 seconds. Pour in the blended cornflour. Sprinkle over the sesame seed oil. Stir and turn once more.

PRAWN FU-YUNG

SERVES 4–6

2 spring onions
2 slices fresh root ginger
5oz (150g) peeled prawns
2tsp cornflour
5 egg whites
1tsp salt
5tbsp vegetable oil
2tbsp rice wine or dry sherry
½oz (15g) lard

Finely chop the spring onions. Finely shred the ginger. Place the prawns in a bowl with the ginger and cornflour. Beat the egg whites in a bowl, with the salt and half of the chopped spring onion, for 15 seconds with a fork.

Heat 2 tbsp of the oil in a wok or frying pan. When hot, stir-fry the prawns with the wine or sherry over medium heat for 1½ minutes. Remove the prawns from the wok and place in the bowl with the egg whites. Mix together well. Heat the remaining oil in the wok or pan. When hot, pour in the egg white and prawn mixture. Stir quickly for 1 minute, then add the lard. Sprinkle on the remaining spring onion. Turn and scramble for a further minute. When the mixture has just set, transfer to a heated serving dish.

◆ ◆ ◆

◆ POULTRY ◆

CHICKEN AND BAMBOO SHOOTS ASSEMBLY

SERVES 4–6

6oz (175g) chicken breast meat
4oz (100g) bamboo shoots
1 egg white
12fl oz (350ml) chicken stock
2tbsp cornflour
1tbsp rice wine or dry sherry
1 slice fresh root ginger, peeled
2tbsp lard
1½tsp salt
oil for deep-frying

Cut the chicken into fine shreds about the size of matches and mix with the egg white and ½ tbsp of cornflour. Cut the bamboo shoots into shreds roughly the same size as the chicken. Finely chop the root ginger.

Heat up the oil in a deep-fryer, fry the chicken shreds in oil over a moderate heat for about 10 seconds only. Separate the shreds, scoop them out and drain.

Heat up the lard in a wok or frying pan, stir-fry the bamboo shoots, add root ginger, salt, wine or sherry and chicken stock. Bring it to the boil, then add the remaining cornflour mixed with a little cold water; stir until the ingredients are well blended. When the gravy starts to thicken, add the chicken shreds, blend well and serve.

DRUNKEN CHICKEN

SERVES 6–8

1 chicken weighing about 3lb (1.5kg)
¼pt (150ml) Chinese red wine, or port
3pt (1.8lt) chicken stock
6tbsp soy sauce
3tbsp rice wine or dry sherry
2–3 spring onions, cut to 2 inch (5cm) lengths
1tsp salt
oil for deep-frying

Clean and dry the chicken. Mix 2 tbsp each of soy sauce and rice wine or sherry and pour it all over the chicken both inside and out.

Heat up the oil in a deep-fryer, fry the chicken with onions until golden, then immerse the chicken (keeping the onions for later) in a large pot of boiling water for 3 minutes. Now transfer to another large pot or casserole, add the remaining soy sauce, rice wine or sherry, salt, Chinese red wine or port and the chicken stock, as well as the onions, and simmer gently for at least 2 hours, turning it over several times during cooking. Serve in a large bowl or in the casserole itself. You will find it very similar in flavour to the French *Coq au vin*.

CHICKEN IN 'BIRD'S NEST'

SERVES 4–6

½lb (225g) potatoes
1 lettuce heart
½lb (225g) chicken breast meat, boned
½lb (225g) celery
2 spring onions
1 slice fresh root ginger
½tbsp salt
1 egg white
½tbsp rice wine or dry sherry
2½tbsp cornflour
oil for deep-frying

Cut the potatoes into thin shreds; wash and rinse in cold water, drain and dry. Mix with a little salt and 2 tbsp of cornflour. Arrange the shreds in a criss-cross pattern against the side of a strainer, then place another strainer on top of it. Submerge both in hot oil and deep-fry for about 4 minutes until golden. This is the 'bird's nest'.

Drain and take the 'bird's nest' out of the strainer, place it in a serving dish on a bed of lettuce heart.

Shred the chicken breast meat. Marinate in a little salt, egg white and cornflour. Shred the celery to the same size as the chicken. Finely chop the onions and root ginger.

Warm up about 2 tbsp of oil; stir-fry the chicken meat for about 1 minute, remove; heat up a little more oil, toss in the onions and root ginger followed by celery. Add salt and rice wine or sherry, stir a few times then add chicken meat; cook together for about another minute, place it in the 'bird's nest' and serve.

BRIGHT MOON AND RED PINE CHICKEN

SERVES 4–6

1 chicken leg, boned but with skin attached
3oz (75g) pork
1 egg
3oz (75g) mange tout
½oz (15g) cooked ham
3tbsp lard
1½tbsp soy sauce
1tsp salt
1tbsp rice wine or dry sherry
1tbsp sugar
1tbsp cornflour
1 slice fresh root ginger, finely chopped

Break the egg into a bowl; cut the ends off a few mange tout and place them halfway round the egg to resemble the leaves of a flower. Finely shred the ham and arrange the shreds in the middle to make it look like a chrysanthemum. Warm up 1 tbsp of lard in a wok or frying pan and with one swift movement empty the bowl into the wok to be fried on one side until the egg just sets; lift the 'chrysanthemum' out.

Finely chop the pork and mix it with ½ tbsp of rice wine or sherry, ½ tsp of salt, 1 tsp of sugar and 1 tsp of cornflour.

Spread the chicken leg out flat with the skin side down, score the meat with a criss-cross pattern (not too deep), then press the minced pork hard on top. Make sure it is stuck firmly to the chicken, and add a little more cornflour to bind them together.

Heat another tbsp of lard; fry the chicken-pork piece on both sides until golden; add rice wine or sherry, 1 tsp of sugar, soy sauce, finely chopped root ginger and a little water. Bring it to the boil, then reduce heat and simmer for about 40 minutes. Remove and cut it into 3 strips with the pork side up; place them on a serving dish.

Now steam the egg 'chrysanthemum' for 2 minutes. In the meantime, stir-fry the rest of the mange tout with the remaining lard, salt and sugar. Arrange the mange tout around the chicken-pork pieces, and place the egg higher up in the middle. The egg is the 'bright moon' and the chicken-pork is the 'red pine'.

STIR-FRIED CHICKEN WITH GARLIC AND CUCUMBER CUBES

SERVES 5–6

about ½ chicken breast
1 medium cucumber
1tsp salt
pepper to taste
4tsp cornflour
½ egg white
2 cloves garlic
½oz (15g) lard
2tbsp good stock (see recipe)
2 spring onions
3tbsp vegetable oil
2 slices fresh root ginger
½tsp salt
1½tbsp rice wine or dry sherry
1tbsp light soy sauce
½tsp sesame seed oil

Cut the chicken into ½ inch (1 cm) cubes. Cut the cucumber into similar-sized cubes. Sprinkle and rub the chicken evenly with 1 tsp of salt, pepper and half the cornflour, then wet with egg white. Crush the garlic. Chop the lard. Blend the remaining cornflour with the 2 tbsp of stock. Cut the spring onions into 1½ inch (4 cm) sections.

Heat the vegetable oil in a wok or frying pan. When hot, stir in ginger slices for 15 seconds to flavour the oil. Remove and discard the ginger. Add the chicken cubes to the pan and stir-fry over medium to high heat for 45 seconds. Remove and drain. Add the lard and garlic to the wok or pan and stir over medium heat for 15 seconds. Add the cucumber cubes and sprinkle with the ½ tsp of salt and pepper. Stir-fry for 1 minute. Add the rice wine or sherry, soy sauce and spring onion. Return the chicken to the pan and stir-fry for 1 minute. Add the blended cornflour and sesame seed oil and stir-fry for 10 seconds. Serve.

DRUNKEN CHICKEN

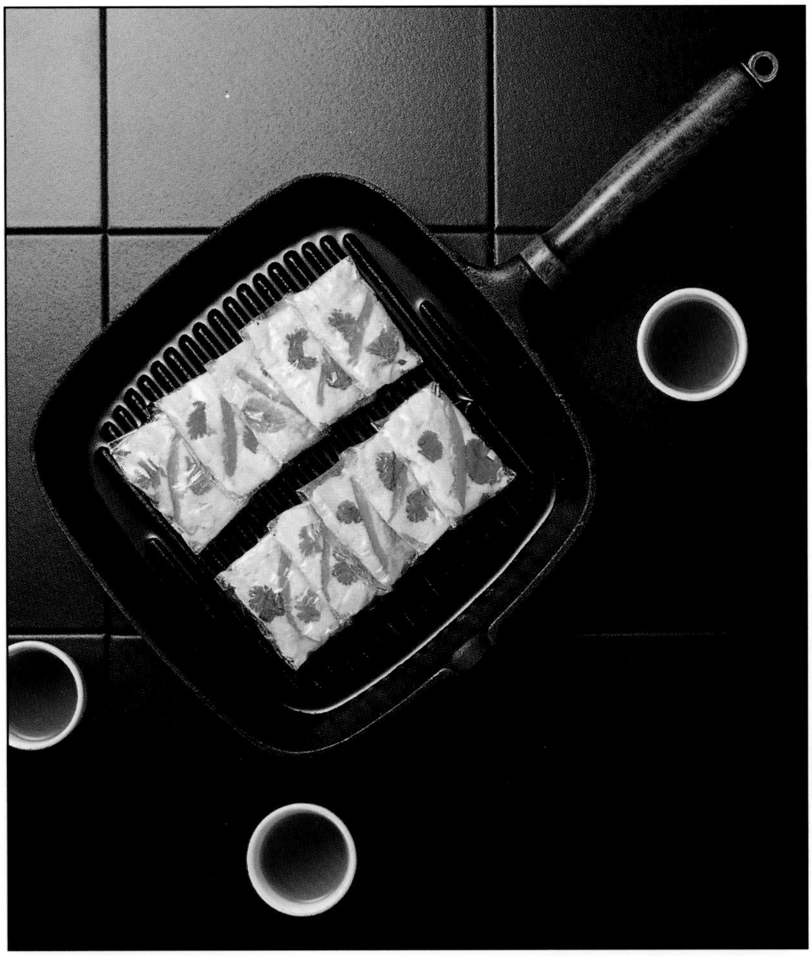

PAPER-WRAPPED, DEEP-FRIED CHICKEN

STIR-FRIED CHICKEN AND CELERY ON RICE

2–3 medium dried Chinese mushrooms
1 chicken breast
1 stalk celery
2oz (50g) drained, canned bamboo shoots
2 slices fresh root ginger
2 spring onions
3tbsp vegetable oil
salt and pepper to taste
2tbsp good stock (see recipe)
2tbsp rice wine or dry sherry
1tbsp light soy sauce
8oz (225g) boiled rice

Soak the dried mushrooms in hot water to cover for 25 minutes. Drain and discard the tough stalks. Cut the mushroom caps into small cubes. Dice the chicken into small cubes. Dice the celery and bamboo shoots into similar-sized cubes. Finely chop the ginger. Chop the spring onions.

Heat the oil in a wok or frying pan. When hot, stir-fry the ginger, spring onion, mushrooms, celery and bamboo shoots over high heat for 1 minute. Add the chicken and stir-fry for 1 minute. Sprinkle with salt and pepper to taste. Add the stock, rice wine or sherry and soy sauce, toss and turn for a further minute.

Serve on boiled rice. If liked, wrap spoonfuls of chicken and rice in lettuce leaves to eat with the fingers.

PAPER-WRAPPED DEEP-FRIED CHICKEN

SERVES 5–6

1lb (450g) chicken breasts
5 dried Chinese mushrooms
2 slices ham
2 spring onions
2 bunches parsley
15 sheets cellophane paper
2tbsp sesame seed oil
vegetable oil for deep-frying

Marinade
3tbsp light soy sauce
½tsp salt
1½tbsp rice wine or dry sherry
½tsp sugar
¼tsp pepper
2tsp sesame seed oil
2tsp cornflour

Cut the chicken into 2 × ½ inch (5 ×1 cm) strips. Place in a bowl and add all the ingredients for the marinade. Mix well and leave to marinate for 20 minutes. Soak the dried mushrooms in hot water to cover for 25 minutes. Drain and discard the tough stalks. Cut the mushroom caps into about 6 pieces each. Cut the ham and 2 inch (5 cm) strips. Cut the spring onions into 2 inch (5 cm) sections. Cut and divide the parsley into about 15 portions. Brush 1 sheet of cellophane paper with sesame seed oil and place a spray of parsley in the middle. Divide and place a little mushroom and ham on either side, lay some sliced chicken on top and a spring onion on top of that. Fold the cellophane to completely enclose the filling.

Heat the oil in a wok or deep-fryer. When hot, fry the envelopes for about 2 minutes. Remove. Reheat the oil and fry again for 2 minutes. Drain. Serve the envelopes arranged on a large heated plate.

SALT BURIED BAKED CHICKEN

SERVES 4–6

3½lb (1.5kg) chicken
sea salt

Wash the chicken and dry very carefully. Hang up overnight in a well-ventilated place to ensure it is perfectly dry. Heat the salt in a saucepan to ensure it too is dry.

SALT BURIED BAKED CHICKEN

Spoon a layer of salt in the bottom of a flameproof casserole. Put the chicken in the casserole and cover with the salt. Place a heavy lid on the casserole and cook over a low heat for about 15 minutes. Place in a preheated oven at 375°F/190°C Gas Mark 5, and cook for 30 minutes. Reduce the oven temperature to 350°F/180°C, Gas Mark 4, and continue to cook for another 40 minutes without lifting the lid.

Remove the chicken from the salt and chop it into small bite-sized pieces. Arrange on a heated platter. If liked, a mixture of 3 chopped spring onions fried in 3 tbsp of vegetable oil can be poured over the chicken.

◆ POULTRY ◆

HOT TOSSED SHREDDED CHICKEN IN RED CHILLI OIL

SERVES 4–6

½ medium chicken
1 medium onion
3tsp salt
3 slices fresh root ginger
1 medium cucumber

Sauce
1½tbsp chilli sauce or red chilli oil
1tbsp garlic, chopped
1tbsp fresh root ginger, chopped
1tbsp peanut butter
1tbsp spring onion, chopped
2tsp sesame seed oil
1½tbsp vegetable oil
4tbsp good stock (see recipe)
½tsp salt

Bring about 2 pt (1.2 lt) water to the boil in a pan. Add the chicken and simmer for about 10 minutes. Peel and slice the onion. Pour away a quarter of the water and add the salt, ginger and onion. Cook for another 35 minutes. Cut the cucumber into shreds, leaving the skin on. Remove the chicken and cool. Shred the meat into pieces of similar size to the cucumber shreds.

Place all the sauce ingredients in a bowl and mix well. Arrange the cucumber on a plate and pile the chicken on top. Pour over the sauce.

SHANGHAI QUICK-BRAISED CHICKEN ON THE BONE

SERVES 6–8

3–4lb (1.5–1.7kg) chicken
1tbsp cornflour
4tbsp vegetable oil
5 slices fresh root ginger

SHANGHAI QUICK-BRAISED CHICKEN ON THE BONE

2tbsp sugar
3tbsp light soy sauce
3tbsp dark soy sauce
1tbsp hoisin sauce
1tbsp oyster sauce
4tbsp rice wine or dry sherry
¾pt (450ml) good stock (see recipe)
spring onions

Chop the chicken through the bone into about 30 bite-sized pieces. Bring a large pan of water to the boil, add the chicken and simmer for about 5 minutes. Remove and drain thoroughly. Blend the cornflour with 3 tbsp of water.

Heat the oil in a wok or pan. When hot, stir in the ginger for about 1½ minutes. Add the chicken pieces and stir-fry for about 3 minutes. Put in the sugar, soy sauces, hoisin sauce, oyster sauce, wine or sherry and stock. Bring to the boil and continue to stir over the highest heat until the sauce begins to thicken and reduce. Add the blended cornflour and stir until the sauce is thick and coats the chicken pieces. Garnish with chopped spring onions.

MELON CHICKEN

SERVES 6–8

3 large dried Chinese mushrooms
1oz (25g) dried shrimps
1 large melon, approximately 8in (20cm) in diameter
3oz (75g) ham
3oz (75g) drained, canned bamboo shoots
2½–3lb (1.25–1.5kg) chicken
2tbsp vegetable oil
2 slices fresh root ginger
3oz (75g) button mushrooms
1tsp salt
pepper to taste
½pt (300ml) good stock (see recipe)
2tbsp dry sherry

Soak the dried mushrooms and dried shrimps separately in hot water to cover for 25 minutes. Slice the top of the melon off and reserve for a lid. Scrape out most of the flesh and reserve about a quarter for cooking with the chicken. Drain and discard the tough mushroom stalks. Cut the mushroom caps into quarters. Cut the ham and bamboo shoots into cubes.

Place the chicken in a steamer and steam for about 1 hour. Leave to cool. When cool enough to handle, remove the meat from the bones and cut into cubes. Heat the oil in a wok or large frying pan. When hot, stir-fry the ginger, dried shrimps and dried mushrooms over high heat for about 2 minutes. Add the ham, half of the chicken, the bamboo shoots, reserved melon, fresh mushrooms, salt and pepper. Stir-fry for a further 3 minutes. Pack all the stir-fried ingredients into the melon. Add any excess to the remaining chicken. Mix the crumbled stock cube with the stock and sherry and pour on to the melon to the brim. Replace melon lid and fasten with a few wooden cocktail sticks. Place on a heatproof plate, steam for 30 minutes.

Bring the whole melon to the table to serve. This is a pretty dish and the different savoury flavours in the chicken-ham-mushroom stuffing and the sweetness of the melon give it a unique appeal.

MELON CHICKEN

CRISPY 'FIVE SPICED' CHICKEN LEGS

SERVES 4–6

8 chicken drumsticks
2½tsp salt
pepper to taste
1tsp ground ginger
vegetable oil for deep-frying

Sauce
½pt (300ml) good stock (see recipe)
1½tbsp hoisin sauce
1½tbsp yellow bean paste
¾tsp pepper
1½tbsp mixed five-spice pieces

Rub the chicken drumsticks with a mixture of the salt, pepper and ground ginger. Leave to season for 30 minutes. Bring a pan of water to the boil, add the drumsticks and cook for 3 minutes. Drain and cool.

Place the cooking sauce ingredients in a wok or pan and bring to the boil. Add the drumsticks and simmer for about 15 minutes. Leave the drumsticks to cool in the sauce for 15 minutes, then remove and drain thoroughly. Heat the oil in a wok or deep-fryer. When hot, gently fry the chicken for about 5 minutes until golden-brown.

Remove the knuckle from the drumstick and put a cutlet frill on the exposed bone. Arrange on a heated plate and serve.

CHICKEN FU YUNG

SERVES 6–8

12oz (350g) chicken breasts
1½tbsp cornflour
8 egg whites
2½tsp cornflour
½pt (300ml) vegetable oil for deep-frying
¼pt (150ml) good stock (see recipe)
1tsp salt
3tbsp green peas

Cut chicken meat into 1½ × 2½ inch (4 × 6.5 cm) thin slices. Place them in a bowl. Add the 1½ tbsp of cornflour and coat the chicken pieces evenly. Beat the egg whites lightly in another bowl. Blend the 2½ tsp of cornflour with 2 tbsp of water.

Heat the oil in a wok or deep-fryer. When hot, gently fry the chicken pieces over low to medium heat for 1½ minutes. Pour in the egg white slowly and evenly over the contents of the pan. When the egg white rises, turn them around once with the chicken pieces. Transfer with a perforated spoon to a bowl. Pour away the oil to use for other purposes. Return the wok or pan to the heat. Add the stock, salt and peas. Bring to the boil and stir in the blended cornflour until thickened. Return the chicken and egg white pieces to the pan. Bring back to the boil and serve. If liked, sprinkle with presoaked, chopped dried shrimps.

RED-COOKED CHICKEN

SERVES 6–8

3–4lb (1.5–1.75kg) chicken
½pt (300ml) good stock (see recipe)
1 chicken stock cube
4 slices fresh root ginger
¼tsp salt
1½tbsp sugar
pepper to taste
5–6tbsp light soy sauce
2 pieces star anise

Bring a large pan of water to the boil, add the chicken and simmer for about 8 minutes. Remove and drain thoroughly. Place the bird in a flameproof casserole, add the stock, crumbled stock cube, ginger, salt, sugar, pepper, soy sauce and star anise. Bring to the boil.

Cover and place the casserole in a preheated oven at 400°F/200°C/Gas Mark 6, and cook for 30 minutes. Turn the bird over, reduce the oven temperature to 350°F/180°C/Gas Mark 4, and cook for a further 25 minutes. Turn the bird over again and continue to cook for a final 25 minutes.

QUICK-BRAISED CHICKEN WITH HONEY

SERVES 6–8

3½–4lb (1.5–1.75kg) chicken
1½tsp salt
6tbsp vegetable oil
6 slices fresh root ginger
½pt (300ml) good stock (see recipe)
2tbsp light soy sauce
2tbsp dark soy sauce
2tbsp yellow bean paste
1½tbsp sugar
4tbsp rice wine or dry sherry
5tbsp honey

Chop the chicken through the bone into 28–30 bite-sized pieces. Sprinkle and rub with salt.

Heat the oil in a wok or flameproof casserole. When hot, add the ginger and stir over high heat for 30 seconds. Add the chicken, stir and turn in the flavoured oil over high heat for 5 minutes. Drain away any excess oil. Pour the stock, soy sauces, yellow bean paste, sugar and wine or sherry evenly over the chicken. When the contents begin to boil, turn and stir the chicken in the sauce for 2 minutes over high heat. Cover the wok or casserole and continue to boil for a further 10 minutes. Remove the lid and turn the chicken so that all the pieces are coated in the sauce. Continue to boil rapidly until the sauce is reduced to less than 10 per cent of its original volume, stirring now and then. The consistency will be very sticky and rich. Stir the chicken pieces to coat in the thickened sauce. Pour the honey evenly over the chicken. Turn the contents once more, then serve.

CHICKEN WITH CHILLIES AND RED PEPPER

SERVES 5–6

1lb (450g) chicken breasts
1tsp salt
1½tbsp cornflour
1½tbsp rice wine
1 egg white
2 slices fresh root ginger
1 clove garlic
1 fresh chilli
1 dried chilli
2 spring onions
1 red pepper
¼pt (150ml) vegetable oil
2tbsp good stock (see recipe)
1tsp sugar
1tbsp light soy sauce
1¼tbsp wine vinegar

Skin the chicken and cut into cubes. Add the salt, cornflour, wine and egg white. Mix together thoroughly. Finely chop the ginger, garlic and fresh and dried chillies, discarding the seeds, together. Shred the spring onions. Cut the red pepper into cubes.

Heat the oil in a wok or frying pan. When hot, stir-fry the chicken cubes over high heat for about 45 seconds. Drain and pour away the oil to use for other purposes. Reheat the wok or pan. Stir-fry the chillies, ginger and garlic over high heat for a few seconds until the fragrance begins to rise. Add the spring onion and red pepper and stir-fry for 30 seconds. Return the chicken to the wok or pan and add the stock, sugar, soy sauce and vinegar. Turn all the ingredients together for 15 seconds.

SIMULATED BEGGARS' CHICKEN

SERVES 6–8

3½–4lb (1.5–1.75kg) chicken
2 slices fresh root ginger
2tsp salt

1tbsp hoisin sauce
1½tbsp oyster sauce
3½tbsp rice wine or dry sherry
2½tbsp soy sauce
2tsp sugar

Stuffing
6 medium dried Chinese mushrooms
1lb (450g) pork
10oz (275g) drained, canned bamboo shoots
4oz (100g) drained, canned Sichuan hot Ja Chai pickles
2tbsp vegetable oil

Wrapping
2 large lotus leaves
1 large sheet of suet
1¼lb (550g) plain flour
¾pt (450ml) water

Bring a large pan of water to the boil. Add the chicken and simmer for about 5 minutes. Remove, drain and dry very thoroughly. Finely chop the ginger. Mix together the salt, hoisin sauce, oyster sauce, wine or sherry, soy sauce, sugar and ginger. Rub about three-quarters of this mixture both inside and outside the chicken. Leave the chicken to season for 30 minutes.

For the stuffing, soak the dried mushrooms in hot water to cover for 25 minutes. Drain and discard the tough stalks. Finely slice the mushroom caps. Cut the pork, bamboo shoots and pickles into similar-sized shreds. Place the pork into the remaining marinade and leave to marinate. Heat the oil in a small frying pan. When hot, stir-fry the mushrooms and pork for about 2 minutes. Add the pickle and bamboo shoots and stir-fry for 1 minute. Stuff all these ingredients into the chicken cavity. Soak the lotus leaves in water for 10 minutes until soft.

CHICKEN FU YUNG

Wrap the chicken in the suet, then the lotus leaves. Mix together the flour and water to form a thick dough and wrap the chicken in the dough. Finally cover the chicken completely in foil.

Place the foil parcel in a preheated oven at 400°F/200°C/Gas Mark 6, and cook for 45 minutes. Reduce the oven temperature to 375°F/190°C/ Gas Mark 5, and cook for a further 45 minutes. Reduce the heat again to 350°F/180°C/Gas Mark 4, and cook for a final 45 minutes.

Remove the foil and crack the tough casing with a hammer. Lift out the lotus-wrapped chicken and serve on a heated platter straight from the leaves.

STEAMED CHICKEN IN AROMATIC GROUND RICE

SERVES 6–8

2 slices fresh root ginger
3½–4lb (1.5–1.75kg) chicken
2tsp salt
pepper to taste
1 egg white
6tbsp roasted ground rice

Sauce
1tbsp chicken fat
2tbsp light soy sauce
½tsp salt
3tbsp good stock (see recipe)
1tbsp malt vinegar
1½tbsp rice wine or dry sherry
1tbsp spring onion, chopped
2 cloves garlic, crushed

Chop the ginger. Chop the chicken into 20 bite-sized pieces. Sprinkle with salt, pepper and ginger and leave to season for 10 minutes. Dip in the egg white and coat with the ground rice.

Place the coated pieces of chicken on to a heatproof dish, place in a steamer and steam for 1 hour. Drain off the liquid which has collected in the dish into a small pan. Add the chicken fat and bring to the boil. Add the rest of the sauce ingredients and stir together for about 15 seconds. Arrange the chicken pieces on a heated plate and pour over the sauce.

STEAMED CHICKEN AND FROGS' LEGS IN LOTUS LEAVES

PEKING SLICED EGG-BATTERED CHICKEN

SERVES 4–6

1lb (450g) chicken breasts
salt and pepper to taste
2 eggs
2 spring onions
2 cloves garlic
4–5tbsp vegetable oil
5tbsp good stock (see recipe)
2tsp wine vinegar
1½tbsp rice wine or dry sherry

Cut chicken meat into approximately 2 × 4 × ¼ inch (5 × 10 × 0.5 cm) thick slices. Sprinkle and rub with salt and pepper. Break the eggs in a bowl, add the chicken slices and coat thoroughly. Finely chop the spring onions and garlic.

Heat the oil in a wok or frying pan over medium heat. Add the battered chicken slices, one by one, and spread them out evenly over the surface of the wok or pan. Shake the pan and reduce the heat to low. Cook the chicken pieces for 1½ minutes. Once the egg has set, turn the chicken slices over to cook for 30 seconds. Sprinkle the chicken with garlic and onion. Mix the stock with 1½ tsp of salt, vinegar and rice wine or sherry in a bowl. Pour half this mixture evenly over the chicken pieces. Simmer gently for 1¾ minutes.

Remove the chicken slices with perforated spoon and place them on a chopping board. Cut into ¼ inch (0.5 cm) wide strips. Arrange them on a heated serving dish. Add ¼ tsp of salt and remaining stock to the pan. Bring to the boil and pour it evenly over the chicken pieces.

STEAMED CHICKEN AND FROGS' LEGS WRAPPED IN LOTUS LEAVES

SERVES 4–6

1lb (450g) chicken legs
8oz (225g) frogs' legs

Marinade
1 egg white
1tsp salt
1tbsp light soy sauce
1tsp dark soy sauce
1tsp sugar
2tsp Chinese yellow wine
1tbsp cornflour
½tsp sesame seed oil

4oz (100g) fresh straw mushrooms
2 spring onions
1–2 lotus leaves (depending on their size)
1oz (25g) ham, sliced
6 slices fresh root ginger

Chop the chicken legs into bite-sized pieces and cut the frogs' legs in half, discarding the lower leg. Marinate the chicken and frogs' legs and set aside. Cut the straw mushrooms in half and cut the spring onions into 1½ inch (3 cm) sections.

Blanch the dry lotus leaves in 2 pt (1 lt) boiling water until they are soft, remove, rinse under the tap and pat dry. Put all the ingredients in an even layer on the lotus leaves, wrapping them up firmly and neatly. Place the parcel on a heatproof plate and steam over medium heat for 35 minutes. Unwrap the parcel and trim the lotus leaves to fit the plate. Serve.

TANGERINE PEEL CHICKEN

SERVES 4–6

1lb (450g) chicken meat, boned
2 slices fresh root ginger
1 spring onion
1½tbsp rice wine or dry sherry
1tsp salt
2tsp soy sauce
1tbsp sugar
1tbsp vinegar
3–4 dried chillies
½tsp Sichuan pepper
1tsp dried tangerine peel
oil for deep-frying
½tsp sesame seed oil

Cut the chicken meat into small pieces and crush the root ginger and onion; add them to the chicken meat together with salt, rice wine or sherry and 1 tbsp of soy sauce. Let it marinate for a while.

Mix the remaining soy sauce with the sugar and vinegar in a bowl to make sweet and sour sauce.

Heat up the oil; discard the root ginger and onion; deep-fry the chicken until golden; remove and drain.

Pour off the excess oil leaving about 2 tbsp in the wok; put in the dried red chillies, Sichuan pepper and tangerine peel. Add chicken, stir a few times, then add the sweet and sour sauce; blend well and serve hot.

When eating, savour each mouthful slowly. After the initial hot taste is passed, you will be able to distinguish all the other different flavours, with the subtle fragrance of tangerine peel.

CHICKEN CUBES IN BEAN SAUCE

SERVES 4–6

½lb (225g) chicken breast meat
1 egg white
2tsp cornflour
1pt (600ml) oil for deep-frying
2tbsp lard
2tbsp crushed yellow bean sauce
1tsp sugar
1tbsp rice wine or dry sherry
1 slice fresh root ginger, finely chopped

Soak the chicken meat in cold water for 1 hour, separate the meat from the white tendon and membrane, then dice it into ⅓ inch (7 mm) cubes. Mix them with the egg white and cornflour together with a little water — say, 2 tsp.

Heat up the oil in a deep-fryer, lower the chicken cubes in and separate them with chopsticks or a fork. As soon as they start to turn golden, scoop them out with a perforated spoon and drain.

Meanwhile heat the lard in a wok or frying pan, add the crushed bean sauce, stir until the sizzling noise dies down, then add the sugar followed by wine or sherry and finely chopped root ginger. After about 10–15 seconds, it should have a smooth consistency. Now add the chicken cubes and stir well for 5 seconds so that each cube is coated with this bright reddish sauce. Serve.

CHICKEN FEET IN BEAN PASTE SAUCE

SERVES 6

2lb (900g) chicken feet (24 approx)
1tsp oyster sauce
1tsp light soy sauce
1tsp dark soy sauce
1tsp sesame seed oil
½tsp five-spice powder
freshly ground pepper
oil for deep frying
1½in (4cm) piece fresh root ginger
3 cloves garlic
1tbsp bean paste
2tbsp oil
1oz (25g) dried Chinese mushrooms, washed and soaked in 1pt (600ml) cold water for 30 minutes
salt to taste
1tbsp cornflour

Wash the chicken feet well — trimming off the nails. Put the feet into a pan of boiling, salted water until they become stiff; drain. Mix the oyster and both soy sauces, sesame seed oil, five-spice powder and pepper together. Pour this over the feet and mix well. Set aside for as long as possible, at least 1 hour.

Heat the oil in a wok, fry the feet until they are golden-brown and crisp. If the fat splutters and splashes a lot you can cover the wok with a lid. Lift out and pop into cold water.

Meanwhile peel and slice the ginger and garlic. Set aside one-third of each for frying and finely pound the rest with the bean paste. First fry the ginger and garlic in oil to bring out the flavour. Add the pounded ingredients and fry over a brisk heat. Stir in ¾ pt (450 ml) of the juice drained from the mushrooms and taste for salt. Place the drained chicken feet in an ovenproof casserole. Pop in the mushrooms and pour over the sauce. Cover and cook in a moderate oven (350°F/180°C/Gas Mark 4) for 30 minutes then reduce the heat to 300°F/150°C/Gas Mark 2, and cook for 3–4 hours or until the feet are tender. Mix the cornflour into a paste with a little water, stir into the sauce to thicken just before serving.

GOLDEN CHICKEN WITH SHRIMP PASTE

SERVES 6–8

3–3½lb (1.5kg) fresh chicken
2–3tbsp shrimp paste (fresh shrimps finely minced)
1¼pt (½lt) peanut oil

Marinade
3tbsp cornflour
1tbsp rice wine or dry sherry
2tsp ginger juice
1tsp sugar
few drops sesame seed oil

Chop the chicken into large, bite-sized pieces and pat them dry.

Mix the shrimp paste with the marinade ingredients, and marinate

the chicken with the mixture for 20 minutes.

Heat the peanut oil in a pan until it is very hot. Put in the chicken pieces and fry them for 2 minutes over a low heat. Remove the chicken and set the pieces aside while you reheat the oil to boiling point. Fry them again for 1½ minutes and serve.

ROAST GOOSE

SERVES 6–8

1 young goose (approximately 6lb [3kg])
1tbsp soya bean paste
1tsp five-spice powder
1 piece star anise
1tbsp sugar
2tbsp light soy sauce
2tsp garlic, chopped
1tbsp Chinese yellow wine
2½pt (1.25lt) boiling water
2tbsp malt sugar
4tbsp honey or corn syrup
4tbsp vinegar
8fl oz (225ml) water

Cut off the feet and wing tips of the goose. (If a young goose is not available, use a duck.)

Blend together the soya bean paste, five-spice powder, star anise, sugar, soy sauce, chopped garlic and yellow wine and rub the mixture all over the inside of the goose. Tightly fasten the neck and tail openings with skewers or string to ensure that the mixture does not run out when the goose is hung.

Place the goose on a rack, breast up, and pour half the boiling water over it. Turn the goose over and pour the remaining boiling water over it. Pat the goose dry and set it aside.

Heat the malt sugar, honey, vinegar and 8 fl oz (225 ml) water together, stirring to mix well, and brush the mixture all over the goose. Tie a piece of string around the neck of the goose and hang it up in a draughty place for 1 hour to dry.

Pre-heat the oven to 450°F/230°C/Gas Mark 8. Place the goose on a rack in a deep 2 inch (5 cm) roasting pan and roast the goose, breast side up, for 12 minutes until golden. Turn the goose over with a towel (avoid using a fork) and roast for another 12 minutes.

Reduce the heat to 350°F/180°C/Gas Mark 4 and, with the goose breast side up again, roast for 20 minutes. Reduce the heat to 300°F/150°C/Gas Mark 2 and roast for a further 10 minutes, then reduce the heat to 250°F/130°C/Gas Mark ½ and roast for a further 10 minutes. Finally, increase the heat to 450°F/230°C/Gas Mark 8 again and roast for 10 minutes. You have to watch closely at this point to avoid burning the goose. Chop the goose into bite-sized pieces and serve.

ROAST GOOSE CASSEROLE WITH BAMBOO SHOOTS

SERVES 4–6

12oz (350g) roast goose
7oz (200g) bamboo shoots
6 medium black mushrooms
⅓ whole piece of aged dried orange peel
1tbsp peanut oil
6 slices fresh root ginger
2–3 garlic cloves, crushed
1tbsp cornflour
spring onion cut into 1½in (3cm) lengths
1tbsp fresh coriander, chopped

Sauce
1tbsp oyster sauce
1tbsp light soy sauce
1tbsp dark soy sauce
½tsp sesame seed oil
2tsp Chinese yellow wine
8fl oz (225ml) chicken stock

Cut the roast goose into bite-sized pieces and the bamboo shoots into wedge shapes. Soak the black mushrooms and dried orange peel in hot water for 30 minutes. Remove and discard the mushroom stems. Finely shred orange peel. Set aside.

Blanch the bamboo shoots in 20 fl oz (½ lt) of boiling water for 5 minutes. Remove, rinse under the tap, drain and set aside.

Heat the peanut oil in a clay pot and add the ginger and garlic. When the aroma rises add the roast goose, bamboo shoots, black mushrooms and orange peel, stir and cook for

ROAST GOOSE CASSEROLE WITH BAMBOO SHOOTS

1 minute.

Add the sauce ingredients to the pan and enough water to cover the ingredients. Bring to the boil, reduce the heat and simmer for 45 minutes. Thicken the sauce with 1 tbsp of cornflour mixed with an equal amount of water. Add the spring onion and coriander and serve.

STIR-FRIED MINCED GOOSE WITH LETTUCE

SERVES 4–6

4 medium dried Chinese mushrooms
1lb (450g) roast goose meat
4oz (100g) bamboo shoots
2 cloves garlic
2 slices fresh root-ginger
4 water chestnuts
1 spring onion
4tbsp peanut oil
1tsp salt
¼tsp pepper
1tbsp light soy sauce
½tbsp yellow bean paste
½tbsp hoisin sauce
½tbsp sugar
1tbsp rice wine or dry sherry
1½tsp sesame seed oil
2 sprigs of parsley to garnish
12 lettuce leaves

Soak the mushrooms in hot water for 30 minutes. Remove and discard the stems and coarsely mince the caps.

Chop the duck into small pieces; arrange on a dish and garnish with coriander. Mix a little salt and freshly ground pepper as a dip.

This duck has gone through four the oil is hot, add the ginger and mushrooms. Stir them in the hot oil for 30 seconds before adding the bamboo shoots, garlic and water chestnuts. Continue to stir and fry for 1 minute, then add the spring onion and goose meat, together with the salt and pepper. Continue to stir all the ingredients for 2 minutes, turning them over to ensure that they are all thoroughly cooked.

Sprinkle the soy sauce, yellow bean paste, hoisin sauce, sugar and rice wine or sherry over the pan, and continue to stir, turn and fry, over a medium heat, for 3 minutes. Add the sesame seed oil and serve, garnished with sprigs of parsley.

TEA-SMOKED DUCK

SERVES 6–8

1 duckling weighing about 3½–4lb (1.5–1.75kg)

Marinade
½tbsp salt
2 Sichuan peppercorns
½tsp ground pepper
3tbsp rice wine or dry sherry
2tbsp hoisin sauce

Smoking material
2oz (50g) tea leaves
2oz (50g) camphor leaves
¼lb (100g) saw dust
¼lb (100g) cypress tree branch
oil for deep-frying

Garnish
fresh coriander and salt and pepper, to garnish

Make the marinade; rub it all over the duck both inside and out; leave to marinate for 12 hours, then let it dry in an airy place.

Mix the smoking materials together, then divide into 3 portions and put 1 portion in an earthenware bowl; place the bowl inside a large container such as a wine barrel sawn in half. Light a piece of charcoal until red; put it inside the bowl and place a sheet of wire netting on top. Lay the duck on the wire netting and place the other half of the wine barrel on top so that it keeps the smoke in. After 10 minutes, add the second portion of the smoking material to the bowl together with a new piece of burning charcoal, then turn the duck over and replace the lid. After 7 minutes add the last portion of the smoking material with another piece of burning charcoal, turn the duck over again and smoke for another 5 minutes. The duck should be nice and brown all over. Take it out and steam it for about 3 hours; remove to cool.

Heat up the oil and deep-fry the duck for 5 minutes, turning it over once or twice to ensure the skin is crispy.

Chop the duck into small pieces; arrange on a dish and garnish with Chinese parsley. Mix a little salt and freshly ground pepper as a dip.

This duck has gone through four processes: marinating, smoking, steaming and frying. It should be aromatic, crisp, tender and delicious — an ideal accompaniment for wine.

FRIED DUCK LIVER AND GIZZARD

SERVES 4–6

giblets from one duck (the liver and gizzard)
1lb (450g) duck fat (or lard) for deep-frying
salt and Sichuan pepper

Clean and trim off all excess fat on the gizzard. Remove the gall bladder from the liver, making sure that it is not broken, otherwise it will leave a sharp, bitter taste. Now cut the gizzard into 6 small pieces, and the liver into 6 triangular pieces. Parboil the liver first — testing it by pressing with your finger to see it is still soft to the touch — remove and drain; parboil the gizzard for roughly the same length of time, then also remove and drain.

Heat up the fat until you can see blue smoke appearing, then fry the gizzard first for 3 minutes; remove and drain. Wait for the fat to produce more blue smoke, put both the liver and the gizzard into it and fry for another 3 minutes, then remove and drain. Serve with salt-pepper mixture as a dip (one part ground pepper mixed with 2 parts salt).

BRAISED DUCK

BRAISED DUCK

SERVES 6–8

1 duckling weighing about 4½lb (2kg)
5½tbsp red fermented rice
2fl oz (50ml) soy sauce
1tsp salt
2tbsp rice wine or dry sherry
5½ tbsp crystal sugar, crushed
2tsp Chinese cinnamon bark
1tsp fennel seeds
2 spring onions
2 slices fresh root ginger
5½tbsp sugar
1½tbsp cornflour

Clean the duck thoroughly; place it in a large pot with its back facing upwards; add enough water to cover it, then add red fermented rice, soy sauce, salt, rice wine or sherry, crystal sugar, cinnamon bark, fennel seeds, spring onions and ginger root. Bring it to a rapid boil and keep the heat fairly high for 1 hour; turn the duck over and simmer gently for ½ hour; take it out to cool.

Leave about half the juice in the pan (keep the other half for future use), add sugar and when it is dissolved, strain through a sieve to get rid of the spices; mix the cornflour with a little cold water to thicken the gravy, then leave to cool. Chop the duck into small pieces, pour the gravy over it and serve.

◆ POULTRY ◆

DUCK WEBS IN OYSTER SAUCE

SERVES 4–6

5–6 duck webs
½lb (225g) broccoli or other greens
2–3 dried Chinese mushrooms, soaked
2 slices fresh root ginger
2 spring onions
2tbsp rice wine or dry sherry
1tbsp soy sauce
½tbsp sugar
1tsp salt
1 star anise
2tbsp oyster sauce
1tsp sesame seed oil
1tbsp cornflour
4tbsp oil

Remove the outer skin of the duck webs; wash and clean well. Crush the root ginger and onions.

Heat up 2 tbsp of oil; toss in the crushed root ginger and onions followed by the duck webs; stir a few times; add rice wine or sherry and soy sauce. After 5 minutes or so, transfer the entire contents to a sand-pot or casserole. Add sugar, a little salt, star anise and a little stock or water. Simmer gently for 3 hours.

Just before serving, stir-fry the broccoli or greens with the dried Chinese mushrooms, a little salt and sugar. Place them on a serving dish, then arrange the duck webs on top of that. Meanwhile heat a little oil in a saucepan, add oyster sauce and sesame seed oil. Thicken with cornflour mixed with a little cold water; when it is smooth, pour it over the duck webs and serve.

DUCK WEBS IN OYSTER SAUCE

BRAISED FOUR TREASURES

SERVES 4–6

6 duck webs
4 duck wings
10 duck tongues
5–6 duck kidneys
½lb (225g) lard for deep-frying
1 spring onion, finely chopped
1 slice fresh root ginger, finely chopped
½pt (300ml) chicken stock
2tbsp rice wine or dry sherry
½tsp monosodium glutamate
1tbsp crushed bean sauce
2tsp soy sauce

Clean the duck webs in warm water and remove the outer coat of skin, then parboil for 20 minutes. Cool them in cold water and cut into small pieces about ½ inch (1 cm) in length.

Parboil the wings for 20 minutes. Cool them in cold water and cut into small pieces about ½ inch (1 cm) in length.

Clean the tongues in warm water and remove the outer layer of skin; parboil for 10 minutes, then cool in cold water.

Parboil the kidneys for 15 minutes and remove the outer layer of fat. Split each in half, cut each half in 2, then marinate in a little soy sauce. Heat up the lard in a wok or pan until smoking; fry the kidney pieces for 5 minutes or until golden, then remove and drain.

Leaving about 2 tbsp of lard in the pan, first fry the finely chopped onion and root ginger; add the chicken stock with wine or sherry, monosodium glutamate, crushed bean sauce and the remaining soy sauce, stir and add the 'four treasures'. Bring to the boil, then reduce the heat and simmer for about 15 minutes. When the stock is reduced by half, increase the heat to high to thicken the gravy, and serve.

MINCED DUCK WITH CROÛTONS

SERVES 4–6

4oz (100g) cooked duck meat
2oz (50g) peas
3 slices white bread
1pt (600ml) stock
1tsp salt
½tsp monosodium glutamate
2tsp rice wine or dry sherry
1tbsp cornflour mixed with 1tbsp water
1tsp chicken fat for frying the bread

Finely mince the duck meat. Add it to the stock together with the peas, rice wine or sherry, salt and monosodium glutamate. Bring it to the boil over a high flame, then slowly pour in the cornflour and water mixture. When it boils again, stir in the chicken fat, and remove.

Fry the bread cut into small cubes until they become golden and crispy; drain and place them on a soup plate, pour the minced duck all over them so they make a sizzling noise and serve at once before the fried bread croûtons become soggy.

PEKING DUCK

SERVES 6–8

3–4lb (1.5–1.75kg) duck
1 medium cucumber
1 bunch spring onions

Sauce
2–3tbsp vegetable oil
7–8tbsp yellow bean paste
3tbsp sugar
1tsp sesame seed oil
Chinese pancakes

Wash and dry the duck thoroughly. Hang it up in a well-ventilated place overnight to dry the skin. Cut the cucumber into matchstick-sized shreds. Cut the spring onions into similar-sized shreds.

Place the duck on a wire rack over a roasting dish. Place in a preheated oven at 400°F/200°C/Gas Mark 6, for 1 hour 10 minutes. It is important to make sure the oven is correctly pre-

heated for a good result. Do not open the oven door during the roasting, the duck requires no basting.

Meanwhile, to make the sauce, heat the oil in a small saucepan. When hot, add the yellow bean paste and stir over low heat for 2–3 minutes. Add the sugar and 3 tbsp of water and stir for another 2–3 minutes. Finally, add the sesame seed oil and stir for a further 30 seconds.

Slice off the crispy skin with a sharp knife into 1½ × 2 inch (4 × 5 cm) pieces and arrange on a heated plate. Carve the meat into similar-sized pieces and arrange on a separate heated plate. Brush each pancake with 1–1½ tsp of sauce, and add a little shredded cucumber and spring onion. Place a little duck skin and meat overlapping on each pan-cake. Roll up, turning up one end of the pancake to stop the filling falling out. Eat using the fingers.

AROMATIC AND CRISPY DUCK

SERVES 6–8

4–5lb (1.75–2.25kg) duck
vegetable oil for deep-frying

Cooking sauce
2½pt (1.5lt) good stock (see recipe)
6tbsp sugar
6 slices fresh root ginger
10tbsp soy sauce
4tbsp yellow bean paste
6tbsp rice wine or dry sherry
6 pieces star anise
½tsp five-spice powder
¼tsp pepper

AROMATIC AND CRISPY DUCK

Mix the ingredients for the cooking sauce together in a large saucepan. Clean the duck thoroughly and cut in half down the backbone. Place into the liquid and submerge.

Simmer the duck gently for 2 hours. Remove from the cooking liquid and leave to cool. When required, heat the oil in a wok or deep-fryer. When hot, place the duck gently in the oil and fry for 10–11 minutes. Drain well and serve.

RED-COOKED DUCK

SERVES 6–8

4–5lb (1.75–2.25kg) duck
3 spring onions
4 slices fresh root ginger

Sauce
½tsp salt
6tbsp soy sauce
2tbsp yellow bean paste
2½tsp sugar
4tbsp rice wine or dry sherry

Wipe the duck inside and out with a damp cloth. Place breast side up in a flameproof casserole and cover with water. Bring to the boil for 10 minutes, then pour out about a quarter of the water. Cut the spring onions into 1½ inch (4 cm) sections.

Add the ginger, spring onions, salt, soy sauce and yellow bean paste to the casserole. Bring to the boil, cover and simmer for about 1 hour, turning the duck over a couple of times during the cooking. Add the sugar and sherry and continue to cook, covered, for another 45 minutes.

Serve the duck whole, or chopped through the bone into bite-sized pieces. The remaining sauce can be reduced over high heat and thickened with a small amount of cornflour mixed with a little water, if liked. Two tsp of sesame seed oil can also be added. Pour the sauce over the whole duck or pieces of duck arranged on a large heated plate.

DUCK CARCASS SOUP

SERVES 6–8

1 duck carcass
2–3pt (1.2–1.75lt) water
2lb (1kg) Chinese white cabbage
salt and pepper to taste

This soup is cooked and prepared in a short time. Simply boil the duck carcass in the water for 15 minutes. Cut the white cabbage into 3 inch (7.5 cm) sections and add to the soup. Continue to cook for another 15 minutes. The only seasoning required is salt and pepper added to taste. If liked 1 tbsp dried shrimps, 2 tbsp of wine vinegar and a crumbled chicken stock cube can be included. During the cooking, keep the soup boiling. The resulting soup will be very white. If not white enough, add a couple of tbsp of milk. This soup is relatively light and is much appreciated after a rich meal.

CANTONESE ROAST DUCK

SERVES 6–8

1 duck, about 3½lb (1.5kg)
3tsp salt

Filling
3 slices fresh root ginger
3 cloves garlic
2 spring onions
3tbsp soy sauce
¾tbsp sugar
½tbsp pounded Sichuan peppercorns
¼pt (150ml) good stock (see recipe)
1tbsp yellow bean paste
2 pieces star anise
1tbsp broken dried tangerine peel

Baste
¼pt (150ml) boiling water
2tbsp vinegar
2tbsp soy sauce
2tbsp honey

Wash and dry the duck. Rub the duck inside and out with the salt. Hang it up to dry for 2½–3 hours. Shred the ginger. Chop the garlic. Coarsely chop the spring onions. Mix the ginger, garlic and spring onion together with the remaining filling ingredients. Tie the neck of the duck securely so that there is no leakage. Place the duck in a large bowl, back side up, and pour in the

ROAST DUCK WITH GARLIC

filling mixture. Sew the skin up securely. Mix the basting ingredients together.

Place the duck on a wire rack over a roasting tin filled with 1½ inches (4 cm) of water. Brush the duck with the basting mixture and roast in a preheated oven at 400°F/200°C/Gas Mark 6, for 30 minutes. Brush again with the basting mixture, reduce the oven temperature to 375°F/190°C/Gas Mark 5 and roast for 30 minutes. Brush the duck once more, reduce the oven temperature to 350°F/180°C/Gas Mark 4 and roast for a further 20 minutes.

Drain the liquid from the duck into a large bowl. Place the duck on a chopping board and chop through the bones into 3 × 2 inch (7.5 × 5 cm) pieces. Reassemble the duck on a heated serving dish. Boil the liquid from inside the duck in a small pan until reduced by a quarter. Pour this sauce over the duck. Serve hot or cold.

KOU SHOA DEEP-FRIED BONELESS DUCK

SERVES 6–8

1 duck, about 4–5lb (1.75–2.25kg)
2½pt (1.5lt) cooking sauce (see Aromatic and Crispy Duck recipe)
vegetable oil for deep-frying

Batter
1 egg
5tbsp cornflour
2tbsp self-raising flour

Parboil the duck in a pan of boiling water for about 5 minutes, then drain. Mix the ingredients for the batter in a bowl until smooth.

Heat the cooking sauce in a heavy pan. Add the duck and simmer gently for about 45 minutes. Remove the duck and drain thoroughly. Allow the duck to cool for 30 minutes, then remove the meat from the bones, leaving the meat in large pieces if possible. Turn the meat in the batter mixture until evenly coated. Heat the oil in a wok or deep-fryer. When hot, fry the battered duck for about 5 minutes. Drain.

Place the large duck pieces on a chopping board, cutting each piece into 3–4 pieces, and serve.

ROAST DUCK WITH GARLIC

SERVES 4–6

5–6 dried scallops
3oz (75g) garlic
9oz (250g) roast duck breast
5oz (150g) spinach
½tsp salt
2tbsp oil

Seasoning
1tbsp soy sauce
¼tsp sugar
1tbsp oyster sauce
few drops sesame seed oil
1tsp cornflour
2tsp rice wine or dry sherry

Soak the scallops for 3–4 hours and steam for 30 minutes. Fry the garlic until brown. Cut the duck breast into 12 slices (each slice with skin attached) and arrange the meat in a big bowl (the skin to the bottom of the bowl), add a layer of scallops and finally the garlic. Steam for 45 minutes.

Fry the spinach with a little salt and oil and spread it out on a plate. Put the roast duck, scallops and garlic on top of the spinach and reserve the gravy. Boil the gravy from the bottom of the bowl in a pan. Add the seasonings and stir into a sauce. Pour the sauce over the dish and serve.

PIGEONS IN DARK SOY SAUCE

SERVES 4–6

2 pigeons
1¾pt (1lt) water
1 piece of stick cinnamon
2–3 slices liquorice root
3 slices fresh root ginger
4 shallots
8fl oz (225ml) dark soy sauce
6fl oz (170ml) light soy sauce
¾pt (450ml) stock
2tbsp Chinese yellow wine
1oz (25g) rock sugar

Clean the pigeons. Boil 40 fl oz (1 lt) of water and blanch the pigeons for 2 minutes. Remove the pigeons from the boiling water, drain and pat dry.

Place all the remaining ingredients in a clay pot and bring to the boil. Allow to simmer over a low heat for 15 minutes before putting the pigeons into the pot to simmer in the sauce for a further 15 minutes. Let the pigeons colour evenly by turning them over from time to time.

Cover the pot and turn off the heat, leaving the contents to sit for 30 minutes. Dismember the pigeons and serve with the sauce from the cooking pot.

SALT-BAKED PIGEON

SERVES 4–6

2 pigeons

Marinade
1 crushed star anise
2 cloves shallot
1tbsp spring onion, shredded
1tsp fresh root ginger, shredded
2 slices liquorice root
1tsp Chinese yellow wine
1tbsp dark soy sauce
1tsp ginger juice

½tsp sesame seed oil
5–6lb (2½kg) coarse salt
2 sheets greaseproof paper
2 sheets tin foil

Clean the pigeons and dry them with absorbent kitchen paper. Mix together the star anise, shallots, spring onion, ginger and liquorice and rub the skin and the inside of the pigeons with the mixture. Blend the yellow wine, soy sauce, ginger juice and sesame seed oil together, divide it and put it into the cavities of the pigeons.

Stir-fry the coarse salt over high heat for 2 minutes. Insert about one-third of the salt into the pigeon cavities, and cover the outside of the birds with the remaining salt. Wrap each pigeon first with a piece of greaseproof paper and then with foil. Bake the wrapped pigeons in an oven at 350°F/180°C/Gas Mark 4 for 40 minutes.

Remove the paper and foil from the pigeons and shake them free of salt. To serve, cut the pigeons into bite-sized pieces.

SALT-BAKED PIGEON

FRIED CRISPY PIGEON

SERVES 4–6

2 young pigeons

Spicy stock
½tsp dried orange peel
2 star anise
1tsp peppercorns
3 slices fresh root ginger
1 spring onion
2tbsp dark soy sauce
1tsp salt
1tbsp sugar
1¾pt (1lt) water

½tsp white vinegar
2tsp malt sugar, molasses or honey
1tsp cornflour
2tsp water

¾pt (450ml) peanut oil

Clean the pigeons. Prepare the ingredients for the spicy stock. Bring the mixture to the boil. Reduce the temperature and put the pigeons into the stock to simmer for 7 minutes. Remove and drain the pigeons and pat them dry.

Mix the vinegar, malt sugar and cornflour with 2 tsp of water and rub the pigeons with the mixture. Hang the pigeons up to dry for 3–4 hours.

Heat the oil and fry the pigeons, turning them from side to side and basting them with the hot oil all the time to fry them evenly until the pigeons become brown, which takes about 5 minutes. Remove the pigeons and drain. Chop the pigeon in bite-sized pieces to serve.

DOUBLE-BOILED PIGEON, HAM AND BLACK MUSHROOM SOUP

SERVES 4–6

2 pigeons
8oz (225g) lean pork
6 medium black mushrooms
1½oz (40g) ham
3 slices fresh root ginger
1tbsp Chinese yellow wine
20fl oz (½lt) chicken stock
2–3tbsp oil

Clean the pigeons thoroughly. Cut out the breast meat and save it. Blanch the lean pork and pigeons in boiling water for 2 minutes and rinse under the tap for 1 minute.

Soak the black mushrooms in warm water for about 30 minutes until they have softened. Discard the stems and cut the caps into evenly sized pieces.

Put all ingredients in a heavy pot or casserole with a lid, add the stock and an equal amount of water, and cover and steam over medium heat for 3 hours.

STIR-FRIED SUPREME OF PIGEON, BLACK MUSHROOMS AND BAMBOO SHOOTS

STIR-FRIED SUPREME OF PIGEON, BLACK MUSHROOMS AND BAMBOO SHOOTS

SERVES 4–6

5oz (150g) supreme of pigeon (breast meat)

Marinade
1tsp light soy sauce
½tsp salt
½tsp sesame seed oil
¼tsp pepper
1tsp Chinese yellow wine
1tbsp cornflour

5–6 medium black mushrooms
5oz (150g) bamboo shoots
¾pt (450ml) peanut oil
1tsp salt
1tbsp stock
½tsp garlic, minced
½tsp fresh root ginger, minced

Sauce
1tbsp oyster sauce
1tsp dark soy sauce
1tbsp light soy sauce
2tbsp stock
1tsp sugar
½tsp sesame seed oil
1tbsp cornflour
1tsp Chinese yellow wine

Cut the pigeon breasts into thin slices. Mix together the marinade ingredients and marinate the pigeon slices. Set them on one side.

Soak the black mushrooms in hot water for about 30 minutes, remove and discard the stalks and cut the caps into thin slices. Cut the bamboo shoots into slices 1½ × ¾ × 2 inch (30 × 20 × 4 mm) thick.

Heat a pan until very hot, add the oil and after 1 minute add the pigeon pieces. Stir to separate. Remove them from the oil and set aside. Reheat the pan and add the bamboo shoot and mushroom slices. Sauté for 1 minute. Add 1 tsp of salt and 1 tbsp of stock, cook for 2 minutes and set aside.

Heat 2 tbsp of oil in the pan. Add the garlic and ginger and when the fragrance rises add all the cooked ingredients. Stir-fry for 1 minute over high heat before adding the sauce ingredients. Stir rapidly for 15 seconds. Serve.

◆ ◆ ◆

'THREE FAIRIES' IN THEIR OWN JUICE

SERVES 4–6

1 young chicken (poussin) weighing about 1½lb (700g)
1 duckling weighing about 2½lb (1.25kg)
½ leg of pork weighing about 2lb (1kg)
1oz (25g) dried Chinese mushrooms, soaked
8oz (225g) bamboo shoots, sliced
1½tbsp salt
2pt (1.2lt) duck, chicken and pork stock

Clean the chicken, duck and pork well; parboil them together in the stock (which is made from duck, chicken and pork in the first place, thus the term 'in their own juice' in the name of this dish).

Place the chicken, duck and pork in a large bowl or deep dish; add soaked mushrooms, bamboo shoot slices and salt; steam vigorously for at least 2½ hours.

Obviously you will need a very large steamer for this dish. Those who would like to try it out at home can reduce the quantity of the ingredients by three-quarters.

◆ MEAT ◆

ANTS CLIMBING TREES

SERVES 4–6

½lb (225g) pork
2tbsp soy sauce
1tbsp sugar
1tsp cornflour
½tsp chilli paste
1 small red chilli
2 spring onions, chopped
4oz (100g) transparent noodles
3tbsp oil
¼pt (150ml) stock or water.

The ground pork forms the 'ants'; the transparent noodles the 'trees'.

Mince the pork; mix it with the soy sauce, sugar, cornflour and chilli paste. Soak the noodles in warm water for 10 minutes.

Heat up the oil; first fry the chilli and onions, then the pork. When the colour of the meat starts to change, drain the noodles and add them to the pan. Blend well, then add the stock or water; continue cooking. When all the liquid is absorbed, it is ready to serve.

SWEET AND SOUR SPARERIBS

SERVES 4–6

1lb (450g) pork spareribs
2tbsp soy sauce
1tbsp rice wine or dry sherry
½tsp monosodium glutamate
2tbsp cornflour
2tbsp sugar
1½tbsp vinegar
lard for deep-frying
salt and Sichuan pepper for dipping

Clean the spareribs into small bits using a cleaver. Mix ½ tbsp of soy sauce with the rice wine or sherry and monosodium glutamate. When they are all well blended together, add 1 tablespoon cornflour. Coat each bit of the sparerib with this mixture.

In a bowl mix the remaining soy sauce with sugar and vinegar. Warm up the lard in a wok or deep-fryer, put in about half of the spareribs, fry for 30 seconds, scoop them out. Wait for a while to let the lard heat up again, then fry the rest of the spareribs for 30 seconds, scoop out. Now wait for the lard to get hot before returning all the spareribs to the wok to fry for another 50 seconds or so; scoop them out when they turn golden and place them on a serving dish.

Pour off the excess lard, leaving about 1 tbsp in the pan; add the sauce mixture. When it starts to bubble, add the remaining cornflour mixed in a little cold water; stir to make a smooth sauce, then pour it over the spareribs.

Serve with salt and pepper mixed as a dip.

CRYSTAL-SUGAR PORK

SERVES 4–6

1 leg or picnic shoulder (hand) of pork weighing about 2½–3lb (1.25–1.5kg)
5tbsp soy sauce
2oz (50g) crystal sugar
4tbsp rice wine or dry sherry
2 spring onions
2 slices fresh root ginger
2–2½pt (1lt) water

Clean the skin or rind of pork well, making sure it is smooth and free of hairs; score an X mark down the middle as far as the bone; this will prevent the skin sticking to the pan.

Place the pork in a large pot with the skin side down, cover it with cold water, bring it to a rapid boil, skim off the scum; add all the other ingredients, place the lid on tightly, reduce heat and simmer for 30 minutes. Then turn the pork over, replace the lid and continue cooking for about 2 hours. The juice should by now be reduced to less than 1¼ pt (150 ml). Turn the heat up for 5 minutes to thicken the gravy, then take the pork out and place it on a bowl or deep dish. Pour the gravy over it and serve. Like many casseroles this is even more delicious cooked in advance and then reheated and served the following day.

'LYCHEE' PORK

SERVES 4–6

10oz (275g) lean pork
1tbsp cornflour
1tbsp sugar
1½tsp vinegar
1tbsp soy sauce
2 spring onions, white parts only
1tsp sesame seed oil
2tbsp stock
oil for deep-frying

First cut the pork into large slices of ¼ inch (1 cm) thickness; score a criss-cross pattern on each slice, then cut them into diamond-shaped pieces; coat each piece with cornflour. Cut the onion whites into short lengths.

Heat up the oil, put in the pork piece by piece and deep-fry for 3 minutes. The pieces should curl up slightly to look like lychee. Scoop them out and drain.

Pour off the excess oil; put in onions, sugar, vinegar, soy sauce and stock. When it starts to bubble, add the pork and sesame seed oil; blend well. Serve.

STIR-FRIED PORK SLICES WITH FRESH VEGETABLES

SERVES 4–6

½lb (225g) pork fillet
½lb (225g) fresh mushrooms
1 small Chinese cabbage
1tbsp soy sauce
1tbsp rice wine or dry sherry
1tsp sugar
½tbsp cornflour
1 spring onion
1tsp salt
3tbsp oil

Cut the pork into small slices, about the size of an oblong stamp; mix with soy sauce, rice wine or sherry, sugar and cornflour. Wash the mushrooms and cut them into thin slices. Cut the cabbage into pieces about the same size as the pork. Finely chop the onion.

Heat up about 1 tbsp of oil; before it gets too hot, stir-fry the pork about

ANTS CLIMBING TREES

1 minute or until the colour of the meat changes; then dish out and keep it aside.

Wash and dry the wok; heat up the remaining oil. When it smokes, toss in the finely chopped onion followed by the mushrooms and cabbage; add salt and stir constantly for about ½ minute, then return the pork to the wok and mix it well with the vegetables; add a little stock or water if necessary. As soon as the gravy starts to bubble it is ready to serve.

SLICED PORK WITH GARLIC SAUCE

SERVES 4–6

2 spring onions
6 slices fresh root ginger
1¼lb (550g) shoulder of pork
2tbsp peanut oil
1tsp Sichuan peppercorns
1tbsp garlic, chopped
1tsp spring onions, chopped
1tbsp dark soy sauce
4tbsp chicken stock
1tsp sesame seed oil
1tsp sugar
1tsp chilli oil

Bring 4 pt (2 lt) water to the boil. Add one of the spring onions and the ginger and pork and cook for 30 minutes. Remove the pork from the pan and rinse under the tap. Return to the water and cook over medium heat for another 30 minutes.

Take out the pork again, rinse it under the tap, pat dry and cut into wafer thin slices. Arrange on a plate and set aside.

Heat 2 tbsp oil in a pan and add the peppercorns. When they change colour, take them out of the pan and discard. Add the garlic and remaining spring onion (cut into ½ inch (1 cm) sections) and sauté for 15 seconds. Add all the other ingredients, stir and mix well. Pour the mixture into a bowl and serve the pork with the sauce so that diners may dip the slices of meat into it.

SPARERIB OF PORK, CARP AND SALTED PLUM IN A CLAY POT

SERVES 4–6

1¼lb (550g) sparerib of pork
2lb (1kg) carp or any other freshwater fish
1pt (½lt) chicken stock
1pt (½lt) water
3–4 salted plums
6 slices fresh root ginger
2 spring onions

Chop the sparerib across the bones into bite-sized pieces and blanch them in boiling water for 2 minutes. Remove and set aside.

Clean the carp thoroughly, paying particular attention to the inside of the cavity. Set aside.

Bring the chicken stock and water to the boil in a clay pot. Add all the ingredients and when the mixture boils again, lower the heat to medium. Cook for 5 minutes. Leave the heat further and simmer gently for 15 minutes. Serve.

◆ MEAT ◆

TWICE-COOKED PORK

SERVES 6

2lb (900g) belly of pork, rind and bones removed after weighing
4tbsp canned black beans, rinsed
1tbsp soya bean paste
2tbsp soy sauce
1tbsp tomato purée
1tbsp hoisin sauce
2tsp chilli sauce
1tbsp sugar
a little oil for frying
2 garlic cloves, peeled and finely crushed
½in (1cm) fresh root ginger, finely chopped
2fl oz (50ml) chicken stock
2tbsp sherry
few drops sesame seed oil
few pieces bamboo shoot, finely sliced
spring onion curls to garnish

Place the pork into a pan of boiling water and cook for just over 30 minutes, or until tender. Lift out, drain, cool a little and cut into slices, a finger width, and then each slice into 4 pieces, and set aside. Drain the beans. Blend the soya bean paste with soy sauce, tomato purée, hoisin and chilli sauce. Stir in sugar. Mash the black beans to a paste. Heat the oil in a wok, and fry the garlic and ginger, add the mashed beans, stir well, then add the meat and the mixture of sauces. Toss the meat well to coat each piece with the sauce. Add stock and extra water if the sauce is too thick. Cook for 5 minutes. Increase the heat, add the bamboo shoot slices, sherry and the sesame seed oil. Serve on a warm platter garnished with spring onion curls.

STEAMED PORK LIVER AND SPARERIB OF PORK

SERVES 4–6

9oz (250g) pork liver
1¼lb (550g) spare rib of pork
1tbsp ground bean paste
1tbsp shallot, chopped

Marinade
1tbsp light soy sauce
1tsp dark soy sauce
1tsp sesame seed oil
1tsp Chinese yellow wine
1tsp sugar
1tbsp cornflour

Cut the pork liver into slices ⅛ inch (3 mm), soak the pieces in water and set aside. Chop the spare rib of pork into bite-sized pieces. Blend together the ingredients for the marinade and add three-quarters of the mixture to the spare rib and the remaining quarter to the liver. Add the bean paste and chopped shallot to the spare rib and mix well. Lay the spare rib in the bottom of small dishes and place two or three pieces of liver on top.

Bring 6 pt (3 lt) water to the boil in a large wok with a bamboo steamer in it. Put the small dishes of spare rib and liver in the steamer, cover and steam over a high heat for 12–15 minutes. Serve.

STIR-FRIED MINCED PORK, CHILLI, MUSHROOMS AND BLACK OLIVES

SERVES 4–6

9oz (250g) minced pork
4oz (100g) button mushrooms
1 red chilli
1tbsp black olives in sesame seed oil
1tbsp peanut oil
1tsp garlic, chopped

Marinade
1tsp cornflour
2tsp light soy sauce
1tsp sugar
1tsp Chinese yellow wine
2tbsp peanut oil

Prepare the marinade and marinate the minced pork. Set aside. Slice the button mushrooms and finely shred the red chilli. Chop the black olives into small pieces.

Heat 1 tbsp of oil in pan. Add the garlic and when the aroma rises, add the minced pork. Stir and cook over medium heat for 3 minutes. Add the black olives, button mushrooms and red chilli and stir-fry over medium heat for 2 minutes.

STEAMED MINCED PORK WITH CHINESE SAUSAGES

SERVES 6–8

2 Chinese wind-dried sausages
1lb (450g) minced pork
1tsp salt
pepper to taste
1½tbsp light soy sauce
1½tbsp cornflour
1 egg
1 cauliflower

Cut the sausages slantwise into 1½ inch (4 cm) sections. Mix the pork with the salt, pepper, soy sauce, cornflour and egg. Blend thoroughly until smooth. Cut the cauliflower into 2 inch (5 cm) florets. Space the cauliflower evenly on the bottom of a deep heatproof dish. Cover with a thick layer of minced pork. Stud the top of the pork evenly with pieces of sausage. Place the dish in a steamer and steam for 30 minutes.

LION'S HEAD MEAT BALLS IN CLEAR BROTH

SERVES 6–8

6 medium dried Chinese mushrooms
4oz (100g) pork fat
4oz (100g) pork skin
5 water chestnuts
2 spring onions
1½lb (700g) minced lean pork
2tbsp cornflour
1 egg
1½tsp salt
1½tbsp dark soy sauce
1tbsp yellow bean paste
5tbsp finely chopped shrimps
vegetable oil for deep-frying
1 Chinese white cabbage
1½pt (900ml) good stock (see recipe)

Soak the dried mushrooms in hot water to cover for 25 minutes. Drain. Discard the tough stalks and finely chop half the mushroom caps. Mince the pork fat and skin. Chop the water chestnuts and spring onions. Mix all the ingredients for the meat balls together in a large bowl, except the whole mushroom caps. Form the

mixture into 3–5 large meat balls. Heat the oil in a wok or deep-fryer. When hot, add the meat balls, one by one, and fry gently for 6–7 minutes until brown all over. Drain on absorbent kitchen paper. Cut the Chinese cabbage into large sections.

Heat the stock and whole mushroom caps in a flameproof casserole or Chinese clay-pot. When boiling, add the meat balls. Cover and simmer gently for 1 hour. Add the Chinese cabbage sections, cover and continue to simmer for about 20 minutes.

Place the meat balls on a large heated serving dish and serve the soup separately. They are too large to eat whole and need to be eaten broken into quarters or pieces, then accompanied by rice.

STEAMED MINCED PORK WITH CHINESE SAUSAGES

◆ MEAT ◆

STEAMED GROUND RICE-PORK WRAPPED IN LOTUS LEAVES

SERVES 6–7

3–4 lotus leaves
1½lb (700g) belly of pork, thick end
2tbsp light soy sauce
vegetable oil for deep-frying
2 slices fresh root ginger
2 spring onions
1½tbsp oyster sauce
½tsp salt
1½tsp sugar
2 cloves garlic
3tbsp ground rice
1½tsp sesame seed oil

Immerse the lotus leaves in warm water for 3–4 minutes to soften. Bring a large pan of water to the boil, add the pork and simmer for 10 minutes. Remove and drain. Rub the pork with the soy sauce. Heat the oil in a wok or deep-fryer. When hot, fry the pork for about 3 minutes. Drain. Cut the pork into ½ inch (1 cm) slices. Finely chop the ginger and spring onions. Mix together the oyster sauce, salt, sugar, ginger, garlic and spring onions. Add the ground rice and sesame seed oil. Mix in the pork slices and make sure they are evenly coated. Pile the slices neatly into a stack, then wrap in the softened lotus leaves. Tie securely with string.

Place the parcel in a heatproof dish, put in a steamer and steam for 3 hours. When ready, drain away any excess water and serve straight from the lotus leaves. The pork will be tender and the ground rice will have soaked up any fattiness.

SICHUAN YU-HSIANG SHREDDED PORK

SERVES 4–6

8oz (225g) pork fillet
2 spring onions
2 slices fresh root ginger
2 fresh chillies
1 clove garlic, crushed
3–4 dried Chinese mushrooms
1oz (25g) drained, canned bamboo shoots
2 egg whites
2tsp cornflour
vegetable oil for deep-frying
½tsp salt
1tbsp yellow bean paste
1tbsp good stock (see recipe)
1tbsp rice wine or dry sherry
1½tbsp soy sauce
1½tbsp vinegar
½tsp white pepper
2tsp cornflour blended with 2tbsp cold stock
1tsp sesame seed oil
2tsp red chilli oil or chilli sauce
1tsp crushed Sichuan peppercorns

Shred the pork fillet finely. Chop the spring onions, ginger, chillies, discarding the seeds, and garlic. Soak the dried mushrooms in boiling water to cover for 25 minutes. Drain and discard the tough stalks. Shred the mushroom caps. Shred the bamboo shoots. Put the pork in a bowl with the egg whites, cornflour and 1 tbsp of oil. Toss together very well.

Heat the oil in a wok or deep-fryer. When medium hot, fry the pork for about 1½ minutes. Add the bamboo shoots and mushrooms and stir for about 1½ minutes. Drain and pour away the oil. Reheat the wok or a pan with about 1 tbsp of oil. When

hot, stir-fry the ginger, garlic, spring onions, salt and chillies for 1 minute. Add the bean paste, stock, sherry or wine, soy sauce, vinegar and white pepper. Stir and bring to the boil. Add the shredded pork and vegetables to the wok. Thicken the sauce with the blended cornflour. At the last minute, drizzle over the sesame seed oil and toss together. Transfer to a heated plate and sprinkle on the red chilli oil and crushed peppercorns.

DEEP-FRIED CRISPY FINGERS OF PORK

SERVES 5–6

1½lb (700g) lean pork
1tsp salt
¼tsp pepper
½tsp ground ginger
1tbsp rice wine or dry sherry
1tsp sesame seed oil
vegetable oil for deep-frying

Batter
1 egg
5tbsp plain flour
1½tbsp cornflour

Sauce
1½tbsp vegetable oil
1½tbsp spring onion, chopped
2tsp garlic, crushed
2tsp fresh chillies, chopped
1½tbsp fresh root ginger, chopped
5tbsp good stock (see recipe)
2tbsp vinegar
2tbsp light soy sauce
1tsp salt
1tsp sugar
radish rose and halved lemon slices, to garnish

Cut the pork into finger-sized strips. Mix the salt, pepper, ginger, wine or sherry and sesame seed oil together. Add the pork and mix thoroughly. Leave to marinate for 10 minutes. To make the batter, mix the egg, flour and cornflour together. To make the dip sauce, heat the oil in a wok or pan. When hot, add the onion, garlic, chilli and ginger and stir for a few seconds. Add the rest of the dip sauce ingredients. Bring to the boil, then pour into a small heatproof bowl.

Heat the oil in a wok or deep-fryer. When very hot, dip the pork fingers in the batter and put gently into the oil. Fry for about 3 minutes. Drain. Allow the oil to reheat, then fry the pork again for 30 seconds. Drain. Arrange the pork fingers on a heated plate and serve with the dip sauce.

DEEP-FRIED CRISPY FINGERS OF PORK

BARBECUE SPARERIBS

SERVES 5–6

3–3½lb (1.5kg) spareribs
1½tsp salt
pepper to taste
6tbsp vegetable oil
3–4 slices fresh root ginger
3 spring onions

Sauce
1pt (600ml) good stock (see recipe)
1 chicken stock cube
3tbsp soy sauce
1tbsp yellow bean sauce
3 pieces star anise
6tbsp rice wine or dry sherry
2tbsp sugar

Separate the spareribs. Parboil them in a pan of boiling water for 5 minutes. Drain, sprinkle and rub them with the salt and pepper. Heat the oil in a flameproof casserole. When hot, stir in the ginger for 1½ minutes, then add the ribs. Turn and stir the ribs for 4–5 minutes. Drain away all the excess oil. Cut the spring onions into ¼ inch (5 mm) sections.

Add the sauce ingredients to the casserole, partly submerging the ribs. Bring to the boil, stir and turn the ribs in the sauce over high heat for 5 minutes. Reduce the heat to low, cover and cook for 40 minutes, turning the ribs over after 20 minutes. If there is a fair quantity of the sauce left in the casserole, raise the

heat to high and turn the ribs in the thickening sauce until the sauce is well reduced. Sprinkle the ribs with the spring onions and serve.

QUICK-FRIED SHREDDED PORK IN CAPITAL SAUCE

SERVES 4–6

12oz (350g) pork fillet
½tsp salt
3tbsp cornflour
1 egg white
2 spring onion
vegetable oil for deep-frying

Capital sauce
3tbsp vegetable oil
1½tbsp yellow bean paste
1tbsp sugar
½tbsp dark soy sauce
1tbsp rice wine or dry sherry
½tbsp cornflour blended with 2tbsp water
1tsp sesame seed oil

Cut the pork into matchstick-sized shreds. Mix the pork with the salt, cornflour and egg white. Cut the spring onion into ½ inch (1 cm) sections.

Heat the oil in a wok or deep-fryer. When hot, add the pork, separating all the shreds, and stir-fry for about 2 minutes. Drain and pour off the oil to use for other purposes. Meanwhile, heat the 3 tbsp of oil in a wok or pan. When hot, add the yellow bean paste, sugar, soy sauce and rice wine or sherry. Stir until smooth and glossy, then stir in the blended cornflour. Bring back to the boil and add the pork. Stir in the spring onions and sprinkle over the sesame seed oil.

Serve on crispy rice-flour noodles. If liked, wrap spoonfuls of pork and rice in lettuce leaves to eat with the fingers.

PEARL-STUDDED PORK BALLS

PEARL-STUDDED PORK BALLS

SERVES 4–6

8oz (225g) glutinous rice
2tbsp dried shrimps
1lb (450g) minced pork
1tsp salt
1½tbsp onion, finely chopped
1tbsp fresh root ginger, finely chopped
1tbsp light soy sauce
1 egg
2tbsp cornflour

Soak the rice in cold water to cover for at least 8 hours. Drain well. Soak the dried shrimps in hot water to cover for 25 minutes. Drain and finely chop. Place the pork in a bowl and add the dried shrimps, salt, onion, ginger, soy sauce, egg and 1½ tbsp of water. Combine thoroughly. Mix the soaked rice with the cornflour. Form the pork mixture into even-sized balls and wet each ball lightly with water. Roll the balls in the rice mixture and pat on lightly to get an even covering.

Arrange the balls on a steaming tray in a steamer and steam vigorously for about 25 minutes. Serve on a heated dish and accompany with either soy or tomato sauce.

SOYA-BRAISED PORK — LONG-COOKED VERSION

SERVES 4–6

1½–2lb (700–900g) belly of pork
½pt (300ml) good stock (see recipe)
1½tbsp sugar
4tbsp soy sauce

Cut the pork through the skin into 1 × 1½ × 2 inch (2.5 × 4 × 5 cm) pieces. Bring 2 pt (1.2 lt) of water to the boil in a flameproof casserole. Blanch the pork for 3 minutes. Pour away the water. Add the stock, sugar and soy sauce to the casserole and bring to the boil. Cover and place the casserole in a preheated oven at 400°F/200°C/Gas Mark 6, for 15 minutes. Remove the lid and stir the contents. Cover and cook for another 15 minutes, then stir again. Add a little more liquid if the sauce seems too thick. Reduce the oven temperature to 350°F/180°C/Gas Mark 4 and continue to cook for a further 1½ hours.

◆ MEAT ◆

CAPITAL SPARERIBS

SERVES 5–6

1½lb (700g) meaty pork spareribs
1½tsp salt
pepper to taste
vegetable oil for deep-frying

Sauce
2tsp fresh root ginger, chopped
2tsp garlic, chopped
3tbsp yellow bean paste
2tsp sugar
2tbsp good stock (see recipe)
1½tbsp dark soy sauce
2tbsp rice wine or dry sherry
1½tbsp hoisin sauce
1tbsp cornflour blended with 2tbsp stock

Chop the spareribs into 1–1½ inch (2.5–4 cm) pieces. Place in a large pan of water and bring to the boil. Simmer for 2 minutes, then drain. Sprinkle with the salt and pepper.

Heat the oil in a wok or deep-fryer. When hot, fry the spareribs over medium heat for about 8 minutes. Drain thoroughly and pour away the oil to use for other purposes, leaving 2 tbsp. Heat the oil in the wok or pan. When hot, stir in the ginger and garlic for about 15 seconds. Stir in the yellow bean paste and sugar. Add the stock, soy sauce, wine or sherry and hoisin sauce and stir until smooth. Bring to the boil, return the spareribs to the sauce and simmer for about 1 minute. Pour on the blended cornflour and stir until the sauce thickens.

SWEET AND SOUR PORK

SERVES 4–6

2lb (1kg) lean and fat pork
cornflour for coating
2 slices canned pineapple or bamboo shoots
1 small green pepper
1 small red pepper
vegetable oil for deep-frying

Batter
3tbsp cornflour
3tbsp self-raising flour
1tsp salt
1 egg

Sweet and sour sauce
2tbsp sugar
3tbsp vinegar
3tbsp tomato purée
3tbsp orange juice
1½tbsp soy sauce
1½tbsp cornflour blended with 4tbsp water

Cut the pork into 1 inch (2.5 cm) pieces and coat in cornflour. Coarsely chop the pineapple or bamboo shoots, green and red peppers. Mix the cornflour, flour, salt and egg into a smooth batter. Mix the sauce ingredients together until smooth. Add the pork pieces to the batter and coat evenly.

Heat the oil in a wok or deep-fryer. When hot, fry the battered pork pieces for 3½ minutes. Remove and drain. Heat 2 tbsp of oil in another wok or frying pan. When hot, stir-fry the pineapple and peppers for a few seconds. Add the sauce and stir over medium heat until the sauce thickens and becomes translucent. Transfer the fried pork to the wok or pan containing the sweet and sour sauce. Stir and turn the pork in sauce over medium heat for 1 minute.

LONG-STEAMED KNUCKLE OF PORK

SERVES 8–10

1 knuckle of pork with skin on, about 5lb (2.25kg) before boning, ask the butcher to remove the bone
2tbsp dark soy sauce
vegetable oil for deep-frying
4tbsp light soy sauce
3–4 slices fresh root ginger
1pt (600ml) good stock (see recipe)
½tsp salt
3tbsp sugar
3 pieces star anise

Bring a large pan of water to the boil. Add the knuckle of pork and boil for about 5 minutes, then remove and drain. Rub the skin and flesh with the dark soy sauce. Heat the oil in a wok or deep-fryer. When hot, fry the pork for about 5 minutes. Drain.

Place the knuckle of pork in a flameproof casserole and add the light soy sauce, ginger, stock, salt, sugar and star anise. Bring to the boil and simmer for about 5 minutes. Turn the knuckle over and put on the lid. Place the casserole into a steamer and cook for 2½ hours, turning the knuckle over every 30 minutes.

Serve the knuckle in a heated deep bowl with the sauce poured over the top. If liked, stir-fry about 1 lb (450 g) spinach, then arrange it around the knuckle. A knife may be used to carve off the meat into bite-sized pieces but usually the meat is tender enough to remove with a pair of chopsticks.

CRISPY FIVE-SPICE PORK

SERVES 5–6

1lb (450g) lean pork
1tsp salt
½tsp five-spice powder
1½tbsp cornflour
2 slices fresh root ginger
2 cloves garlic
vegetable oil for deep-frying
1½tbsp soy sauce
1tsp caster sugar
2tsp sea salt
1½tsp pounded Sichuan peppercorns

Cut the pork into thick strips. Sprinkle and rub with the salt, five-spice powder and cornflour. Leave to season for 30 minutes. Finely chop the ginger and garlic.

Heat the oil in a wok or deep-fryer. When hot, fry half the pork strips over medium heat for 3½ minutes. Drain and place in a bowl. Fry the remaining pork strips for 3½ minutes, then drain and add to the bowl. Add the soy sauce and sugar to the pork, mixing well. Pour away the oil to use for other purposes, leaving 2 tbsp. Reheat the wok or pan. When hot, stir in the ginger, garlic, sea salt and pepper over medium heat for 25 seconds. Pour the once-fried and seasoned pork into the pan. Turn

and stir around quickly so that the pork is evenly coated by the spicy ingredients. Turn, toss and stir for 1 minute. Transfer to a heated serving dish.

STIR-FRIED SHREDDED LAMB, BAMBOO SHOOTS, BLACK MUSHROOMS AND GREEN PEPPER ON CRISPY FRIED RICE NOODLES

SERVES 4–6

1¼lb (550g) lamb fillet
4 medium black mushrooms
11oz (300g) fresh bamboo shoots
1 green pepper
¾pt (450ml) peanut oil
1oz (25g) dried rice vermicelli noodles
1½tsp garlic, chopped
1½tsp fresh root ginger, chopped

Marinade
1 egg white
2tsp cornflour
1tbsp light soy sauce
1tsp sugar
1tsp Chinese yellow wine
1tsp sesame seed oil

Sauce
1tbsp oyster sauce
1tbsp light soy sauce
½tsp sugar
½tsp sesame seed oil
1tbsp Chinese yellow wine
½ cup chicken stock
1tbsp cornflour

1tbsp lime leaves, finely shredded
1tbsp fresh coriander, chopped

Shred the lamb into matchstick-sized pieces and mix well with the marinade. Set aside.

Soak the black mushrooms in hot water for 30 minutes. Cut away and discard the stems and squeeze the mushrooms to remove any excess water. Shred the caps and set aside.

Finely chop the bamboo shoots and green pepper. Blanch the bamboo shoots in 1½ pt (900 ml) boiling water for 2 minutes. Remove and rinse under tap. Drain and set aside.

Heat the oil in a pan. Add the lamb and, after 75 seconds, stir to separate. Remove and set aside.

Add the dried rice noodles to the hot oil, removing them as soon as they fluff up (it takes only an instant). Place them as a bed on a large platter and keep warm.

Heat 3–4 tbsp of oil in the pan and add the garlic and ginger. When the aroma rises, add the black mushrooms, green pepper and bamboo shoots and sauté for 1 minute. Return the lamb and stir rapidly over a very high heat for 30 seconds.

Add the sauce ingredients and continue to stir over a very high heat for another 30 seconds. Transfer to the platter and place on top of the noodles. Add the lime leaves and coriander and serve.

STIR-FRIED SHREDDED LAMB, BAMBOO SHOOTS, BLACK MUSHROOMS AND GREEN PEPPER ON CRISPY FRIED RICE NOODLES

STIR-FRIED ASSORTED MEATS WITH THIN RICE-FLOUR NOODLES IN CURRY SAUCE

TUNG-PO PORK

SERVES 4–6

10oz (275g) fresh belly of pork
1tbsp crystal sugar
2tbsp soy sauce
2tbsp rice wine or dry sherry
2 spring onions
2 slices fresh root ginger

Cut the pork into 4 equal squares. Put enough cold water in a sand-pot (or casserole) to cover the meat; bring it to the boil, then blanch the meat for 5 minutes. Take it out and rinse in cold water.

Discard the water in which the meat has been blanched; place a bamboo rack at the bottom of the pot, then place the meat skin side down in it; add crystal sugar, soy sauce and rice wine or sherry. Place the onions and root ginger on top; seal the lid tightly with flour and water paste and cook gently for at least 2 hours or until tender. Discard the root ginger and onions and transfer the meat into a bowl, skin side up this time, with 3 pieces on the bottom layer and 1 piece on top. Pour the juice over them, cover and steam vigorously for at least 2 hours before serving.

HAM AND BROAD BEANS

SERVES 4–6

4oz (100g) best ham
½lb (225g) fresh broad beans, peeled
2tbsp lard
1tsp salt
¼tsp monosodium glutamate
1tsp sugar
½tsp cornflour
4tbsp stock

Use the young, tender broad beans when in season. Peel off the skin. Dice the ham into small cubes.

Warm up the lard and stir-fry the broad beans and ham at the same time. Add sugar, salt and stock, continue cooking for a while, then add monosodium glutamate and the cornflour mixed with a little cold water; blend well and serve.

STIR-FRIED ASSORTED MEATS WITH THIN RICE-FLOUR NOODLES IN CURRY SAUCE

15oz (425g) dried rice-flour noodles (rice vermicelli)
2 eggs
4oz (100g) pork fillet
4oz (100g) shrimps, shelled and deveined
1 green pepper
1 red chilli
7tbsp peanut oil
1tbsp spring onion, chopped
1tbsp fresh coriander, chopped

Marinade
1tbsp egg white (from main recipe)
1tsp salt
2tsp cornflour
½tsp sesame seed oil

Curry sauce
1tbsp curry paste
1tsp garlic, chopped
1tsp sugar
2tbsp light soy sauce
6fl oz (170ml) chicken stock

Soak the dried rice-flour noodles in 3 pt (1.25 lt) cold water for 15 minutes. Drain and set aside.

Break 2 eggs into a mixing bowl, taking 1 tbsp of egg white for the marinade. Beat the remainder lightly and set aside. Make the marinade in a separate bowl. Cut the fillet of pork into matchstick-sized shreds and mix with half of the marinade. Set aside.

Clean the shrimps, pat them dry and mix with the other half of the marinade. Keep refrigerated for 30 minutes. Cut the green pepper and red chilli into thin shreds. Set aside.

Heat 2 tbsp of oil. Stir-fry the chopped spring onions until nicely browned; remove and set aside. Add the shrimps and pork, stir-frying them for 1 minute. Remove and set aside.

Make the curry sauce by heating 1½ tbsp of oil in a pan. Add the garlic and curry paste. When the aroma rises, add the sugar, soy sauce and chicken stock. Bring to the boil, transfer to a bowl and set aside.

Heat 3 tbsp of oil in a pan until very hot. Add the rice noodles and stir, turning the noodles over with the help of chopsticks. Stir-fry over a high heat for 3 minutes. Transfer to a plate and set aside.

Add 1 tbsp of oil to the pan. Fry the beaten egg until partly set and add the green pepper and red chilli. Keep stirring.

Return the shrimps and pork, and stir. Add the rice noodles to the pan and the curry sauce, stirring vigorously over a high heat for 3 minutes. Transfer to a plate, place the fried spring onion and chopped coriander on top and serve.

BEEF AND BLACK MUSHROOMS

SERVES 4–6

4oz (100g) pork fat
1¼lb (550g) minced beef
8tbsp stock
1tbsp cornflour
1tsp sesame seed oil
2½tsp salt
12 small black mushrooms
1tsp sugar
1tbsp peanut oil

Cut the pork fat into tiny cubes and blanch the pieces in boiling water for 1 minute. Rinse under the tap. Put the pork fat, minced beef, stock, cornflour, sesame seed oil and 1½ tsp of salt in a mixing bowl and stir in one direction only, with a fork until the mixture becomes sticky.

Soak the black mushrooms in hot water for 30 minutes, remove and discard the stems and place the caps in a bowl. Add 1 tsp of salt, the sugar and peanut oil and mix well. Steam the mushrooms over a medium heat for 5 minutes and set aside.

Divide the beef into 12 portions, moulding each portion into an egg shape and place 1 mushroom on top of each 'egg'. Use 6 small dishes and place 2 of the beef and mushroom 'eggs' in each dish. Steam over a high heat for 5 minutes and serve.

SHREDDED BEEF WITH CELERY

SERVES 4–6

½lb (225g) beef steak
2oz (50g) celery
2oz (50g) leek or spring onion
2 slices fresh root ginger
1tbsp chilli paste
2tbsp soy sauce
½tsp salt
1tsp sugar
1tbsp rice wine or dry sherry
1tsp vinegar
3tbsp oil

Shred the beef into thin matchstick-sized strips. Shred the celery and leeks the same size (Chinese leeks are a cross between the Western leek and spring onion with thin skin and green foliage). Peel the root ginger and cut it into thin shreds.

Heat up the wok or pan and put in the oil. When it starts to smoke, stir-fry the beef for a short while, add the chilli paste, blend well, then add the celery, leek and root ginger, followed by the soy sauce, salt, sugar and wine. Stir for 1–2 minutes, then add vinegar and serve.

SESAME BEEF

SERVES 4–6

11oz (300g) rump steak
1tbsp white sesame seeds
20fl oz (½lt) peanut oil

Marinade
1tbsp light soy sauce
1tsp dark soy sauce
1tsp sugar
1tsp sesame seed oil
1tsp Chinese yellow wine

Cut the steak into thin slices 1 × 2 × ⅛ inch (30 × 50 × 2 mm). Prepare the marinade and mix the beef slices with it. Set aside. Sauté sesame seeds in a pan over a low heat until nicely golden in colour. Set aside.

Heat the peanut oil. Add the beef, reduce the heat to medium and fry for 3 minutes. Remove the meat and bring the oil back to a high temperature. Return the beef to the oil and fry for a further 30 seconds.

Drain the beef and pat it with absorbent kitchen paper before transferring it to a serving dish. Sprinkle it with sesame seeds and serve.

SHREDDED BEEF WITH CELERY

◆ MEAT ◆

DRY-FRIED BEEF, FLAVOURED WITH AGED ORANGE PEEL

SERVES 4–6

1½lb (700g) lean beef (topside, tenderloin, etc)
1 dried, aged orange or tangerine peel
3 slices fresh root ginger
2 green chilli peppers
2 dried red chilli peppers
2 spring onions
6tbsp cornflour
1 egg, lightly beaten
20fl oz (½lt) peanut oil
½tsp salt
1½tbsp sugar
1½tbsp dark soy sauce
1tbsp hoisin sauce
2tbsp good stock (see recipe)
2tbsp rice wine or dry sherry
1½tsp sesame seed oil

Shred the beef into 'double matchstick-sized' pieces. Wash and drain the pieces thoroughly.

Soak the dried orange or tangerine peel in warm water for 20 minutes and cut it into matchstick-sized shreds. Cut the ginger and the green and red chilli peppers into similar-sized pieces and the spring onion into 2 inch (5 cm) sections.

Mix together the cornflour and lightly beaten egg and coat the shredded beef, making sure that each piece is evenly covered.

Heat the oil in a pan or wok and, when a crumb dropped into the oil sizzles, add the beef. Using a fork or wooden chopstick to separate the shreds, stir-fry the beef over a medium heat for 6–7 minutes. Remove the beef from the pan with a perforated spoon and set it aside to drain. Meanwhile, allow the oil in the pan to increase in temperature until it is smoking. Return the beef and stir-fry for a further 2 minutes. Remove the beef with a perforated spoon and drain thoroughly.

In a separate pan or wok heat 3 tbsp of oil. When the oil is hot, add the shredded ginger, orange or tangerine peel and green and red chilli peppers and the spring onion pieces. Stir-fry them together for 1 minute before adding the salt, sugar, soy sauce, hoisin sauce, stock and wine or sherry. Continue to stir and cook for another minute, by which time the liquid should have reduced by about half. Return the beef to the pan and stir well to mix the ingredients together for 1 minute. Sprinkle the sesame seed oil over the mixture and serve.

DRY-FRIED CRISPY BEEF

SERVES 4–6

1lb (450g) rump steak
4oz (100g) carrot
1 Chinese celery
4tbsp peanut oil
3tsp Chinese yellow wine
1tbsp sugar
1tbsp spring onion, chopped
1tsp fresh root ginger, chopped
½tsp Sichuan peppercorn powder

Seasoning
2tsp chilli bean paste
1tbsp hoisin sauce
2tsp garlic, chopped
2tsp spring onion, chopped
1tsp sesame seed oil
1tsp salt

Cutting across the grain, thinly slice the beef and then further cut it into ⅛ inch (2 mm) shreds. Set aside. Cut the carrot and celery into similar tiny pieces and set aside.

Heat a pan until it is very hot and add the oil. When the oil is hot, add the beef, stirring gently to separate, and 2 tsp of Chinese yellow wine. Keep on stirring until the beef shreds are 'bouncing' in the pan.

Thoroughly mix together the seasonings and add them to the beef. Stir-fry over a high heat for 45 seconds. Add 1 tbsp of sugar and 1 tsp of Chinese yellow wine. Stir-fry for 15 seconds. Add the celery and carrot, stir-fry for 30 seconds before adding the ginger, spring onion and peppercorn powder. Stir and serve.

DRY-FRIED BEEF FLAVOURED WITH AGED ORANGE PEEL

STIR-FRIED SHREDDED BEEF FILLET IN A BIRD'S NEST

SERVES 4–6

6oz (175g) beef fillet, shredded
2 potatoes, finely shredded
¾pt (450ml) peanut oil
1 clove garlic, chopped
4oz (100g) pickled cabbage or bamboo shoots
1 red chilli
1 green pepper
1tbsp flour
½tsp salt

Marinade
½tsp sugar
1tsp rice wine or dry sherry
2tsp cornflour
¼tsp sesame seed oil
1tbsp soy sauce

Sauce
½tsp salt
½tsp sugar
2½tsp oyster sauce
2tbsp water

Prepare the marinade, omitting the soy sauce, and steep the shredded beef fillet for 20 minutes. Just before cooking, add the soy sauce and mix well.

To make the bird's nest, lay potato shreds in a large, perforated metal spoon or ladle, making a bowl shape by pressing the shredded potato down with another spoon. Deep-fry in the perforated spoon until golden-brown and crisp. Arrange on a dish.

Heat ¾ pt (450 ml) oil in a pan. Add the beef and stir to separate. Turn the heat off as soon as the beef changes colour. Remove the beef and drain. Mix the sauce ingredients and set aside.

Put 1 tbsp of oil in a pan. When it is hot, stir-fry the garlic first, then add the pickled cabbage or bamboo shoots, red chilli and green pepper (all shredded) and continue to fry for 1 minute.

Add the shredded beef and mixed sauce and stir-fry all the ingredients together for 30 seconds. Serve in the bird's nest.

STIR-FRIED SLICED BEEF, SQUID, FRESH MUSHROOM AND BABY CORN

SERVES 6–8

5oz (150g) beef fillet
5oz (150g) squid
7oz (200g) straw mushrooms, fresh or canned
7oz (200g) baby corn
8fl oz (225ml) peanut oil
1tsp salt
½tsp garlic, minced
3–4 slices fresh root ginger
2–3 slices spring onion cut into 1½in (3cm) lengths
1½tbsp Chinese yellow wine

Sauce
2tsp oyster sauce
2tsp soy sauce
½tsp salt
1tsp sugar
¼tsp pepper
1tbsp cornflour
6tbsp stock
few drops sesame seed oil
1tsp Chinese yellow wine
4tbsp peanut oil

STIR-FRIED SLICED BEEF, SQUID, FRESH MUSHROOMS AND BABY CORN

Seasoning for beef
2tsp light soy sauce
½tsp sesame seed oil
½tsp pepper
½tsp sugar
1tbsp cornflour

Seasoning for squid
1tsp ginger juice
1tsp Chinese yellow wine
½tsp salt
½tsp sesame seed oil
1tbsp cornflour

Cut the beef fillet into very thin slices 2 × 3 inch (5 × 7 cm).

Divide the squid into pieces ¾ × 2 inch (2 × 5 cm), scoring the flesh on one side to form a diamond pattern. Cut the straw mushrooms and baby corns into halves.

Separately prepare the individual seasonings for the beef and the squid. Heat a pan, add 8 fl oz (225 ml) of oil and heat for 1 minute over medium heat. Add the seasoned beef, stir to separate and remove with a perforated spoon after 75 seconds.

Add the seasoned squid to the oil, removing it with a strainer when it curls up. Keep 1 tbsp of oil in the pan. Add the baby corns, straw mushrooms, 1 tsp of salt and stir well over a high heat for 30 seconds. Remove and set aside.

Heat the pan, this time over a very high heat and add 2 tbsp of oil, the minced garlic and ginger slices. When the aroma rises, add the beef, squid and spring onions, sprinkle 1 tbsp of Chinese yellow wine over them and stir rapidly for 30 seconds. Add the baby corns and straw mushrooms. Stir for 30 seconds.

Blend together the sauce ingredients and add them to the pan. Stir for 10 seconds, sprinkle with ½ tbsp of wine and serve.

STEWED BRISKET OF BEEF WITH TURNIPS

SERVES 4–6

2lb (1kg) brisket of beef
2lb (1kg) turnips
6tbsp peanut oil
2 star anise
1tsp peppercorns
2oz (50g) fresh root ginger slices
2–3 cloves garlic
2tbsp soya bean paste

Sauce
1tbsp oyster sauce
2tsp dark soy sauce
2tbsp light soy sauce
2tbsp cornflour
1tbsp Chinese yellow wine
1tsp sugar

Blanch the brisket of beef in 1¾pt (1 lt) of boiling water for 5 minutes. Remove from the water, cut into 1½ inch (3 cm) cubes.

Peel the turnips, and cut them into 2 inch (5 cm) wedges. Cook them in 20 fl oz (½ lt) of boiling water for 15 minutes stirring all the time. Set aside.

Heat a pan over high heat and add 2 tbsp of oil. When the oil is hot, add the beef, star anise and peppercorns and cook for 3–5 minutes, stirring all the time. Set aside.

Heat 4 tbsp of oil in a clay-pot, heavy saucepan or casserole. Add the ginger, garlic and soya bean paste and, when the aroma rises, add the beef and cook, stirring, for 1 minute over very high heat.

Add enough water to cover meat. Bring to the boil, lower the heat and simmer for 1 hour. Turn off heat and allow to stand for 1 hour.

Bring to the boil again and simmer for 30 seconds. Add the turnips and sauce ingredients. Mix well and simmer for 15 minutes before serving.

STIR-FRIED SHREDDED BEEF WITH PICKLED MUSTARD GREEN, GREEN PEPPER AND RED CHILIES

SERVES 4–6

11oz (300g) beef fillet
11oz (300g) pickled mustard green
11oz (300g) green pepper
2 red chillies
2tsp sugar
3tbsp peanut oil
1tsp salt
8fl oz (225ml) peanut oil
1oz (25g) rice vermicelli
1tsp fresh root ginger, chopped
1tsp garlic, chopped

Marinade
½ egg white
1tsp cornflour
½tsp sesame seed oil
1tsp Chinese yellow wine
1tbsp light soy sauce
½tsp sugar

Sauce
1tbsp oyster sauce
1tbsp light soy sauce
1tsp dark soy sauce
1tsp sesame seed oil
1tsp sugar
1tbsp cornflour
8tbsp chicken stock

Prepare the marinade ingredients in a separate bowl. Cut the beef fillet into matchstick-sized shreds and marinate. Set aside.

Soak the pickled mustard green in water for 30 minutes. Chop into shreds and set aside. Shred the green pepper and red chilli into 'double matchstick-sized' pieces.

Heat a pan and add the chopped pickled mustard green, stirring to cook over a medium heat until quite dry. Add 2 tsp of sugar and 1 tbsp of oil, stir and cook for 30 seconds. Remove and set aside.

Heat 1 tbsp of oil in the pan and add the green pepper and 1 tsp of salt. Stir-fry for 2 minutes. Remove and set aside.

Heat 8 fl oz (225 ml) of oil in a pan and add the beef, stirring to separate. Remove with a perforated spoon and set aside.

Heat the same oil for 15 seconds and add the rice vermicelli. It should expand and froth up immediately. Remove straight away and put on a plate to keep warm.

Heat 1 tbsp of oil. Add the chopped ginger, garlic and red chillies and, when the aroma rises, return the beef, pickled mustard green and green pepper to the pan. Blend and add the sauce ingredients. Stir-fry over very high heat for 1 minute, place on top of the crispy rice vermicelli on the serving dish and serve.

STEWED BRISKET OF BEEF WITH TURNIPS

◆ MEAT ◆

RED-COOKED OXTAIL

SERVES 4–6

2 cloves garlic
5–6lb (2.25–2.75kg) oxtail (ask butcher to cut into sections)
2–3 young carrots
3 slices fresh root ginger
1tsp salt
6tbsp soy sauce
1½tbsp hoisin sauce
4tbsp rice wine or dry sherry
¼pt (150ml) good stock (see recipe)
2tsp sugar
2tbsp peas (optional)

Crush the garlic. Clean the oxtail. Cut the carrots slantwise into ¼ inch (0.5 cm) slices. Blanch the oxtail for 3–4 minutes in a pan of boiling water. Drain and place in a heavy saucepan or flameproof casserole with the garlic, ginger, salt, soy sauce, hoisin sauce and carrots. Add 1½ pt (900 ml) of water.

Bring the contents of the pan to the boil, cover and simmer very gently for 1½ hours. Turn the contents every 30 minutes. Add the wine or sherry, stock and sugar and continue to simmer gently for a further 1 hour, turning the contents after 30 minutes. Add the peas 10 minutes before the end of the cooking time. (If cooked in the oven, cook at 300°F/150°C/Gas Mark 2 for 3 hours.

QUICK-FRIED SHREDDED BEEF WITH GINGER AND ONIONS

SERVES 5–6

1lb (450g) beef steak, eg, rump or fillet
1tsp salt
pepper to taste
1½tbsp cornflour
1 egg white
3 medium onions
3 slices fresh root ginger
4tbsp vegetable oil
1oz (25g) lard
2tbsp soy sauce
1tbsp sugar
3tbsp good stock (see recipe)
1½tbsp rice wine or dry sherry
2tsp cornflour blended with 2tbsp water

Using a very sharp knife, cut the beef into thin slices, then cut again into matchstick-sized shreds. Sprinkle with the salt and pepper. Toss in the 1½ tbsp of cornflour and coat in the egg white. Peel and thinly slice the onions. Shred the ginger.

Heat the oil in a wok or frying pan. When hot, stir-fry the beef over high heat for 1½ minutes. Remove and set aside. Add the lard to the pan. When hot, stir-fry the ginger and onions over high heat for 1½ minutes. Add the soy sauce, sugar and stock and stir together for 30 seconds. Return the beef, add the wine or sherry and blended cornflour and continue to stir-fry for 30 seconds.

SLICED BEEF IN BLACK BEAN AND CHILLI SAUCE

SERVES 4–6

1lb (450g) beef steak, eg, rump, fillet or sirloin
¼tsp salt
pepper to taste
2tbsp cornflour
1 egg white
4tbsp vegetable oil

Sauce
1 medium onion
2 dried chillies
1 small red pepper
1 small green pepper
1½tbsp salted black beans
½oz (15g) lard
3tbsp good stock (see recipe)
1tbsp rice wine or dry sherry
1tbsp soy sauce
½tbsp cornflour blended with 2tbsp water

Cut the beef into thin slices and rub evenly with salt and pepper. Toss in the cornflour and coat in the egg white. Peel and thinly slice the onion. Finely chop the chillies. Cut the red and green peppers into 1 inch (2.5 cm) pieces. Soak the black beans in 4 tbsp of cold water for 3 minutes, then drain.

Heat the oil in a wok or frying pan. When hot, stir-fry the beef over high heat for 1 minute. Remove and set aside. Add the lard to the pan. When hot, stir-fry the onion, black beans, chillies and peppers. Mash the softened black beans with a metal spoon against the edge of the wok or pan. Stir in the stock, rice wine or sherry and soy sauce over high heat. Return the beef to the pan and mix well. Finally, add the blended cornflour to thicken the sauce. Stir all the ingredients for a further 30 seconds.

CANTONESE STIR-FRIED BEEF IN OYSTER SAUCE

SERVES 4–6

1lb (450g) beef steak, eg, rump or fillet
1tsp salt
pepper to taste
2tbsp cornflour
1 egg white
3 slices fresh root ginger
4oz (100g) mange tout or 3–4 spring onions
4tbsp vegetable oil
1tsp lard
1½tbsp good stock (see recipe)
1tbsp soy sauce
1½tbsp oyster sauce
1tbsp rice wine or dry sherry

Cut the beef into thin strips and mix with the salt and pepper. Toss in the cornflour and coat in the egg white. Shred the ginger. Cut each mange tout slantwise in half or cut the spring onions slantwise in 1½ inch (4 cm) sections.

Heat the oil in a wok or frying pan. When hot, stir-fry the ginger in the oil to flavour. Add the beef and stir-fry over high heat for about 1 minute. Remove and set aside. Add the lard to the pan. When hot, stir-fry the mange tout or spring onions for 1–2 minutes. Add the stock and soy sauce, and continue to stir-fry for 30 seconds. Return the beef to the pan, add the oyster sauce and wine or sherry and stir-fry over high heat for 30 seconds.

CANTONESE STIR-FRIED BEEF IN OYSTER SAUCE

◆ MEAT ◆

MANGO BEEF

SERVES 4–6

1 large sheet bean curd skin
8oz (225g) beef fillet
½tsp salt
pepper to taste
1tbsp cornflour
1 large rice mango
2 slices fresh root ginger
1tbsp oyster sauce
½tbsp light soy sauce
2tsp sugar
1 egg, beaten
vegetable oil for deep-frying
6tbsp hoisin sauce
12 iceberg lettuce leaves

Soak the bean curd skin in hot water for 10 minutes. Cut the beef into 12 pieces and rub with the salt and pepper. Toss in the cornflour. Slice the mango flesh into 12 pieces. Shred the ginger. Place a few pieces of ginger over the top of the beef, then brush the beef with oyster sauce, soy sauce and sprinkle with sugar. Cover with a piece of mango. Cut the bean curd sheet into 12 pieces and use to wrap each mango, ginger and beef parcel up tightly. Seal the bean curd firmly with the beaten egg.

Heat the oil in a wok or deep-fryer. When hot, fry the beef and mango parcels in batches for 2 minutes, then turn and fry for another 1 minute. Drain and keep the parcels warm as you fry the others. Heap the parcels on a heated dish. Serve with a spoonful of hoisin sauce and wrap in a lettuce leaf.

MUSTARD AND RED CHILLI OIL BEEF WITH LEEKS

SERVES 4–6

1lb (450g) beef steak, eg, rump, fillet or sirloin
1tsp salt
1½tbsp cornflour
1 egg white
3 slices fresh root ginger
3 leeks, about 8oz (225g)
4tbsp vegetable oil
1oz (25g) lard
1tbsp light soy sauce
2tbsp good stock (see recipe)
1tbsp prepared English mustard
2tsp red chilli oil

Cut the beef into very thin slices and rub with salt. Toss in the cornflour and coat in the egg white. Shred the ginger. Clean the leeks thoroughly and cut slantwise into 1 inch (2.5 cm) pieces.

Heat the vegetable oil in a wok or frying pan. When hot, fry half the ginger for 30 seconds to flavour the oil. Add the leeks and stir-fry for 1½ minutes. Remove and set aside. Add the lard to the pan. When hot, stir-fry the beef for 1½ minutes. Add the soy sauce and remaining ginger, then return the leeks and stock to the pan. Toss together for another 30 seconds.

Transfer to a heated serving dish. Drizzle the mustard and red oil evenly over the dish.

SICHUAN PEPPERED BEEF MEDALLIONS

SERVES 4–6

1¾lb (800g) beef steak, eg, fillet, sirloin or topside
2 slices fresh root ginger
1½tbsp soy sauce
1½tbsp hoisin sauce
1tbsp Worcestershire sauce
½tsp salt
1½tsp lightly pounded Sichuan peppercorns
1 green pepper
5tbsp vegetable oil

Cut the beef at an angle into ⅙ inch (4 mm) thickness, then trim into medallion round shapes. Finely chop the ginger. Mix the soy, hoisin and Worcestershire sauces together and use as a marinade for the beef. Stir the salt, peppercorns and ginger into the marinade and leave the beef to season for about 30 minutes. Turn the beef over and marinate for a further 30 minutes. Cut the pepper into 1 inch (2.5 cm) squares.

Heat the oil in a wok or frying pan. When hot, add the beef pieces and space them evenly on the surface of the pan. Cook for 2 minutes, then turn them over and fry for another minute. Add pepper and any leftover marinade. Stir-fry for 30 seconds.

SICHUAN HOT CRISPY FRIED SHREDDED BEEF

SERVES 4–6

1lb (450g) beef, eg, rump, topside or fillet
3 eggs
1tsp salt
4oz (100g) cornflour
vegetable oil for deep-frying

Sauce
3 medium carrots
4 slices fresh root ginger
3 spring onions
3 cloves garlic
2 fresh chillies
1 dried chilli
2tbsp sugar
1½tbsp soy sauce
3tbsp vinegar

Using a very sharp knife, cut the beef into thin slices, then cut again into matchstick-sized shreds. Whisk the eggs, salt and cornflour to make a batter. Add the shredded beef and coat evenly. Cut the carrots and ginger into similar-sized shreds as the beef. Divide each spring onion into quarters lengthwise, then cut into 1½ inch (4 cm) sections. Coarsely chop the garlic. Shred the chillies, discarding the seeds.

Heat the oil in a wok or deep-fryer. When hot, fry the beef, stirring to keep the shreds separate, for 4 minutes. Remove with a perforated spoon and set aside. Reheat the oil, then fry the beef again to ensure it is crispy. Drain the beef on absorbent kitchen paper. Pour away the oil from the wok to use for other purposes, leaving 1 tbsp. Heat the wok with the oil. When hot, stir-fry the carrots, spring onions, garlic, ginger and chillies over medium heat for 2½ minutes. Add the sugar, soy sauce, vinegar and finally the beef. Turn the ingredients around quickly over high heat for 15 seconds.

MONGOLIAN BARBECUE OF LAMB

SERVES 5–6

3–4lb (1.5–1.75kg) leg of lamb
4 slices fresh root ginger
5 spring onions
1tbsp pounded Sichuan peppercorns
1tbsp salt
3tbsp soy sauce
1½tbsp yellow bean paste
1½tbsp hoisin sauce
¼tsp five-spice powder
2tbsp rice wine or dry sherry
vegetable oil for deep-frying

Wrapping and eating
12 lettuce leaves
2 small bowls of Peking Duck sauce (see recipe)
3 saucers of matchstick-sized pieces of cucumber
3 saucers of shredded spring onions

Cut the lamb along the grain into 6 long strips. Shred the ginger and spring onions. Mix with the peppercorns and salt and use to rub into the lamb. Mix the soy sauce, yellow bean paste, hoisin sauce, five-spice powder and wine or sherry and place in a bowl with the lamb. Marinate for 1–2 hours.

Pack the seasoned lamb strips in a heatproof bowl, cover the top with foil. Place in a steamer and steam for about 2 hours or place the bowl in a

pan containing 2 inches (5 cm) of water and double boil for 2 hours. Remove from the bowl and leave to cool until required. When required, heat the oil in a wok or deep-fryer. When hot, fry the lamb for 4 minutes.

Place the lamb on a chopping board and chop into bite-sized pieces while still hot. Serve the dish in the same way as Peking Duck. Spoon some duck sauce on to a pancake or lettuce, then place on a few slices of lamb, followed by a little cucumber and spring onion. Form into a roll and turn up the end so nothing falls out, then eat.

◆ MEAT ◆

LAMB IN SWEET AND SOUR SAUCE

SERVES 4–6

½lb (225g) lamb fillet
2 slices fresh root ginger,
1tbsp crushed yellow bean sauce
2tbsp cornflour
1½tbsp soy sauce
1tbsp rice wine or dry sherry
1tbsp vinegar
2tbsp sugar
oil for deep-frying
½tbsp chicken fat or sesame seed oil

Thinly slice the lamb fillet and finely chop the root ginger. Mix the lamb with ½ tbsp of cornflour with soy sauce, rice wine or sherry, vinegar, sugar and the finely chopped root ginger.

Heat up the oil in a wok or pan, fry the lamb slices for about 15 seconds and stir to separate them. When they turn pale, scoop them out and return the lamb slices to the wok over a high heat. Add the sauce mixture, stir and blend well for about 1 minute; add chicken fat or sesame seed oil, stir a few more times, then serve.

RINSED LAMB IN FIREPOT

If you cannot obtain a Chinese firepot, sometimes known as a chafing pot, then use a fondue or an electrically heated pan on the table.

SERVES 4–6

3–3½lb (1.5kg) boned shoulder, loin or leg of lamb
1lb (450g) Chinese cabbage
1lb (450g) spinach
2 cakes bean curd (fresh or frozen)
4oz (100g) transparent noodles
4–5pt (2lt) water or stock

Sauce
spring onions, finely chopped
garlic and fresh root ginger
soy sauce
rice wine or dry sherry
hoisin sauce
vinegar
sugar
chilli sauce and sesame seed oil

Cut the lamb into fairly large but very, very thin slices — you will find that it is much easier to do this if the meat is half-frozen.

Wash and cut the cabbage and spinach into biggish pieces; cut each cake of the bean curd into 10 to 12 slices; soak the transparent noodles in warm water for a few minutes, then drain.

Arrange the cabbage, spinach, bean curd, transparent noodles and the meat in separate serving dishes and place them on the table with the firepot in the middle.

While waiting for the water or stock to boil in the moat of the firepot, each diner prepares his or her sauce by mixing a little of the various ingredients in individual sauce

dishes according to his or her own taste.

When the water or stock is boiling vigorously, pick up a piece of lamb with chopsticks and dip it in the water to cook it, occasionally dunking it as if rinsing — hence the name of the dish.

Depending on the thickness and cut of the meat, it should not take more than 20–30 seconds to cook, otherwise it will be too tough. Then dip the cooked meat in the sauce mixture and eat it.

Start adding the vegetables to the moat and eat them with the meat. As the cooking progresses, the pot is recharged with charcoal; the remaining water or stock is put in the moat, and the contents get tastier and tastier.

When all the meat is eaten, put the rest of the vegetables into the moat, to make a delicious soup.

DICED LAMB WITH SPRING ONIONS

SERVES 4–6

½lb (225g) lamb fillet
½lb (225g) spring onions
1½tbsp cornflour
1tsp salt
2tsp soy sauce
1 eggwhite
½tbsp rice wine or dry sherry
oil for deep-frying
1tsp sesame seed oil

Dice the lamb into ½ inch (1 cm) cubes, marinate with ½ tsp of salt, egg white and ¾ tbsp of cornflour. Cut the onions into ½ inch (1 cm) lengths.

Heat about 1 pt (600 ml) of oil in a wok. Before the oil gets too hot, add the lamb cubes, separate them with chopsticks or a fork, then scoop them out and drain.

Pour off the excess oil and leave about 2 tbsp in the wok. Put in the onions followed by the lamb cubes, salt, soy sauce, rice wine or sherry and remaining cornflour; stir for 1–2 minutes; add the sesame seed oil, stir a few more times, then serve.

LEFT AND BELOW: RINSED LAMB IN FIREPOT. DIP PIECES OF LAMB INTO THE FIREPOT WITH CHOPSTICKS.

◆ MEAT ◆

CASSIA LAMB

The cassia is a tiny, yellow four-petaled flower that blooms in late September; the dish is named from the similar colour of the eggs.

SERVES 4–6

4oz (100g) lamb fillet
3 eggs
½tsp monosodium glutamate
2tsp rice wine or dry sherry
1tsp salt
1 slice fresh root ginger
2tbsp chicken fat

Cut the lamb into thin shreds. Finely chop the root ginger. Beat up the eggs and mix them with the lamb shreds and root ginger.

Heat up the chicken fat in a wok or pan, put in the egg mixture, stir and scramble for about 10 seconds and add salt, monosodium glutamate and rice wine or sherry. Stir and scramble for another 10 seconds. Serve.

TRIPLE LAMB QUICK-FRY

SERVES 6–7

12oz (350g) leg of lamb
2 spring onions
2 slices fresh root ginger
3 cloves garlic
4½tbsp soy sauce
¾tbsp yellow bean paste
7tbsp vegetable oil
pepper to taste
3tbsp rice wine or dry sherry
12oz (350g) lambs' liver
3 lambs' kidney
1½tbsp sesame seed oil

Cut the lamb meat into thin slices or cubes. Coarsely shred the spring onions, coarsely chop the ginger and garlic. Place the lamb in a bowl with 1½ tbsp of the soy sauce, the yellow bean paste, 1 tsp of the oil, pepper to taste, 1 tbsp of the rice wine or sherry and the spring onions. Marinate for about 30 minutes. Cut the liver into similar-sized pieces as the lamb and place in another bowl with 1½ tbsp of soy sauce, 1 tbsp of rice wine or sherry, 1 tsp of oil, half the ginger and the garlic. Cut each kidney into 4 pieces and score the smooth side with a criss-cross pattern, if liked. Marinate in another bowl with 1½ tbsp of soy sauce, 1 tbsp of rice wine or sherry, 1 tsp of oil and the remaining ginger. Marinate the 3 types of lamb for 30 minutes.

Place 3 tbsp of the oil in a wok or frying pan. When hot, stir-fry the marinated lamb meat over high heat for 1½ minutes. Remove and set aside. Reheat the wok or pan with 1½ tbsp of oil. When hot, stir-fry the marinated liver over high heat for 1½ minutes. Remove and set aside. Finally, heat the remaining oil in the wok or pan. When hot, stir-fry the kidneys over high heat for 1 minute, then push them to the side of the pan. Add the sesame seed oil and return the lamb meat and liver to the pan. Mix together with the kidneys and stir-fry for another 30 seconds. Serve immediately.

PEKING JELLY OF LAMB

SERVES 6–8

1½lb (700g) leg of lamb
8oz (225g) pork skin
2 spring onions
3 cloves garlic
3 slices fresh root ginger
1½tsp salt
pepper to taste
1pt (600ml) good stock (see recipe)
3tbsp white wine
1tbsp light soy sauce

Sauce
4tbsp soy sauce
1tbsp fresh root ginger, finely chopped
1tbsp garlic, finely chopped
1tbsp spring onion, finely chopped

Cut the lamb into 1½ × 2 × 1 inch (4 × 2.5 cm) pieces. Cut the pork skin into smaller pieces. Parboil the lamb and pork skin in a pan of water for 2 minutes, then drain. Cut the spring onions into 1 inch (2.5 cm) sections, keeping the green and white pieces separate. Thinly slice the garlic. Shred the ginger.

Place the pork skin on the bottom of a heavy casserole and cover with the lamb. Add the salt, pepper, white parts of spring onions and the ginger. Pour in the stock and about ½ pt (300 ml) of water to cover the contents and bring to the boil. Reduce the heat to low, cover and simmer for 1¼ hours. Cool, then place in the refrigerator to encourage setting. The contents should be set after 3 hours. Remove the casserole from the refrigerator and peel away the pork fat and skin. Heat briefly to melt the jelly and then stir in the wine, soy sauce, garlic and green parts of the spring onions. Pour the lamb mixture into a rectangular mould and leave in the refrigerator to set again. Mix the dip sauce ingredients together. Turn the mould out on to a serving dish and cut into ¼ inch (0.5 cm) slices. Serve with the dip sauce.

STIR-FRIED LAMB AND LIVER

SERVES 4–6

2oz (50g) dried Chinese mushrooms or canned straw mushrooms, drained
12oz (350g) leg of lamb
8oz (225g) lambs' liver
1tsp salt
1½tbsp cornflour
1 egg white
3oz (75g) drained, canned bamboo shoots
4 cloves garlic
2oz (50g) lotus seeds
4tbsp vegetable oil
¾oz (20g) lard
3oz (75g) peas
3tbsp good stock (see recipe)
1½tbsp light soy sauce
1½tbsp rice wine or dry sherry

Soak the dried mushrooms, if using, in hot water to cover for 25 minutes. Drain and discard the tough stalks. Cut the lamb into small cubes. Cut the liver into similar-sized cubes. Rub the salt into the lamb and liver. Toss in the cornflour. Coat in the egg white. Cut the bamboo shoots into cubes. Thinly slice the garlic. Blanch the lotus seeds in a pan of boiling water for 3 minutes, then drain.

Heat 3 tbsp of oil in a wok or frying pan. When hot, stir-fry the lamb cubes over high heat for 1 minute. Remove and set aside. Heat the remaining tbsp of oil in the wok or pan. When hot, stir-fry the cubed liver for 1 minute. Remove and set aside. Melt the lard in the wok or pan. When hot, stir in the garlic for 10 seconds, then add the bamboo shoots, peas, lotus seeds and mushrooms. Stir-fry over high heat for 2 minutes. Add the stock, soy sauce and rice wine or sherry and continue to stir and turn for 1 minute. Return the lamb cubes and liver to the pan and stir-fry gently for 1 minute.

MARINATED LAMB

SERVES 4–6

1½lb (700g) leg of lamb
½tsp salt
pepper to taste
½tbsp yellow bean paste
1tbsp soy sauce
1tbsp hoisin sauce
1½tbsp rice wine or dry sherry
2 medium onions
6 slices fresh root ginger
2 spring onions
2–3 cloves garlic
4tbsp vegetable oil

Cut the lamb into 2 × 1 × ¼ inch (5 × 2.5 × 0.5 cm) thick slices. Sprinkle and rub with the salt and pepper. Mix the yellow bean paste, soy sauce, hoisin sauce and rice wine or sherry together. Add this marinade to the lamb and leave to season for 30 minutes. Peel and thinly slice the onions. Shred the ginger. Cut the spring onions into 1 inch (2.5 cm) sections. Coarsely chop the garlic.

Heat the oil in a wok or frying pan. When hot, stir-fry the onion and ginger over high heat for 45 seconds, then push them to the sides of the wok or pan. Spread out the marinated slices of lamb in one layer at the centre of the pan and fry over high heat for 1¼ minutes on each side. Sprinkle with the spring onion and garlic. Bring in the onion and ginger from the sides and stir-fry for 1 minute.

QUICK-FRIED SHREDDED LAMB AND LEEKS

QUICK-FRIED SHREDDED LAMB AND LEEKS

SERVES 4–6

8oz (225g) leg of lamb
1tsp salt
pepper to taste
3 slices fresh root ginger
8oz (225g) young leeks
5oz (150g) transparent pea starched noodles or ribbon noodles
2tsp dried shrimps
3tbsp vegetable oil
½pt (300ml) good stock (see recipe)
½ chicken stock cube
2tbsp light soy sauce
1½tbsp rice wine or dry sherry
1½tbsp vinegar
1tsp sesame seed oil

Cut the lamb into matchstick-sized shreds and sprinkle with salt and pepper. Cut the ginger into similar shreds. Wash the leeks and shred. Soak the noodles in hot water for about 5 minutes, then drain. Soak the dried shrimps in hot water to cover for 10 minutes, then drain.

Heat the oil in a wok or frying pan. When hot, stir-fry the ginger and leeks over high heat for 1 minute. Add the lamb and continue to stir-fry for 1 minute. Pour in the stock and add the crumbled stock cube, soy sauce, rice wine or sherry, shrimps and vinegar. Bring to the boil, stirring. Simmer for 5 minutes, then add the noodles and simmer for a further 5 minutes. Sprinkle with sesame seed oil.

◆ MEAT ◆

LONG-STEAMED WINE-SOAKED LAMB

SERVES 7–8

1½lb (700g) leg of lamb
12oz (350g) turnips
1 dried tangerine peel
¾pt (450ml) white wine
¼pt (150ml) rice wine or dry sherry
½pt (300ml) water
5 slices fresh root ginger
1½tsp salt

Cut the lamb into 1 inch (2.5 cm) cubes. Cut the turnips into similar-sized cubes. Parboil the lamb and turnips in a pan of water for about 3 minutes, then drain. Soak the tangerine peel in hot water for 5 minutes, then drain and break into small pieces.

Put the lamb and turnip into a large heavy flameproof casserole with the white wine, rice wine or sherry, water, ginger, salt and tangerine peel. Bring to the boil, then place the casserole, covered, in a steamer and steam for 3 hours. If you do not have a large enough steamer, it is possible to cook the dish by placing the casserole into a pan containing 2 inches (5 cm) of water (a roasting tin will do) and then double boil the casserole for the same amount of time. The dish is brought to the table and diners serve themselves.

MUSLIM LONG-SIMMERED LAMB

SERVES 8–10

4–5lb (1.75–2.25kg) neck of lamb
3 medium onions
2 dried chillies
4 slices fresh root ginger
4 cloves garlic
3pt (1.75lt) water
3tsp salt

Dip sauce
9tbsp soy sauce
2tbsp garlic, finely chopped
2tbsp fresh root ginger, finely chopped
2tbsp spring onions, finely chopped
2tbsp fresh coriander, finely chopped
1½tbsp prepared English mustard
1½tbsp wine vinegar
3tbsp rice wine or dry sherry
1tbsp sesame seed oil
1tbsp vegetable oil

Cut the lamb into 2 × 1 × ¼ inch (5 × 2.5 × 0.5 cm) thick slices. Parboil in a pan of water for 3 minutes, then drain. Peel and slice the onions. Shred the chillies, discarding the seeds. Shred the ginger. Crush the garlic.

Place the lamb in a heavy flameproof casserole with a lid. Add the water, salt, onion, ginger, garlic and chilli. Bring to the boil, reduce the heat and simmer slowly for 3 hours, turning the contents every 30 minutes. Add more water if the sauce becomes too thick. Meanwhile, mix the dip sauce ingredients together. Serve the casserole at the table. Eat the lamb with the dip sauce.

AROMATIC MUTTON

SERVES 4–6

1½lb (675g) mutton fillet
11oz (300g) leeks
¾pt (450ml) peanut oil
1tsp garlic, chopped
1tsp Chinese yellow wine

Marinade
1tbsp light soy sauce
1tsp dark soy sauce
1tsp sesame seed oil
2tsp Chinese yellow wine
1tbsp cornflour

Cut the mutton fillet into thin slices. Mix together the marinade ingredients, add the mutton slices and set to one side. Cut the leek into thin slices and set aside.

Heat a pan until it is very hot and add the oil. Heat the oil until it is warm and add the mutton (reserving the marinade in a separate bowl) and stir to separate. Remove, drain and set aside.

Heat 2 tbsp of oil in the pan and add the chopped garlic and leek, stir and cook over a very high heat for 1 minute.

Return the mutton to the pan, stirring well. Add the reserved marinade, stirring vigorously over a very high heat for 15 seconds. Finally, add the Chinese yellow wine, stir for another 10 seconds and serve.

TUNG-PO MUTTON

SERVES 4–6

½lb (225g) stewing mutton
4oz (100g) potato
4oz (100g) carrot
2tbsp soy sauce
1tbsp sugar
2 spring onions
1 slice fresh root ginger
1 clove garlic, crushed
1tsp five-spice powder
3tbsp rice wine or dry sherry
½tsp Sichuan pepper
oil for deep-frying

Cut the mutton into 1 inch (2.5 cm) cubes, then score one side of each square halfway down. Peel the potato and carrot and cut them the same size and shape as the mutton.

Heat up quite a lot of oil in a wok or deep-fryer. When it is smoking, deep-fry the mutton for 5–6 seconds or until it turns golden; scoop out and drain, then fry the potato and carrot, also until golden.

Place the mutton in a pot or casserole, cover the meat with cold water, add soy sauce, sugar, onions, root ginger, garlic, pepper, five-spice powder and rice wine or sherry, and bring it to the boil. Then reduce the heat and simmer for 2–3 hours; add potato and carrot, cook together for about 5 minutes and serve.

PORK VARIETY MEATS (OFFAL) IN CASSEROLE

SERVES 6–8

pigs' heart, liver, tripe, kidneys and tongue
½lb (225g) Chinese cabbage (or spinach)
4oz (100g) bamboo shoots
3–4 dried Chinese mushrooms

1 slice fresh root ginger
1 spring onion
1tbsp rice wine or dry sherry
salt to taste

The tripe should be cleaned thoroughly, parboiled for about 10 minutes, and then marinated in a little salt and vinegar for 2 minutes. After that, rinse well in clean, cold water.

First place the tripe on the bottom of a big pot or casserole, followed by the tongue and heart, and finally the kidneys and liver. Add enough cold water to cover, then bring it to a rapid boil. Skim off the impurities floating on the surface, then reduce the heat and let it simmer with a lid on.

After simmering for 30 minutes, remove the liver and kidneys; next remove the tongue and heart, after about an hour's cooking. The tripe will have to be cooked for 2 hours or more, so take it out when it is well done. Reserve the stock in which the meat has been cooked.

Cut the tripe and heart into small chunks, the tongue, kidneys and liver into slices.

Wash the cabbage or spinach in cold water and cut it into small pieces. Soak the dried mushrooms in warm water for about 20 minutes, then remove the hard stalks and cut them into small pieces together with the bamboo shoots.

Place the cabbage or spinach on the bottom of a pot or casserole, then put the tripe, heart, tongue, kidneys and liver over it, followed by the bamboo shoots and dried Chinese mushrooms; finally, add the root ginger and onions, salt and rice wine or sherry. Add enough of the stock in which the meats have been cooked to cover the entire contents, cover with a tightly fitting lid and bring to a rapid boil. To serve, bring the casserole or pot to the table.

TUNG-PO MUTTON

◆ MEAT ◆

BRAISED TRIPE

SERVES 4–6

2lb (1kg) tripe
salt
2 slices fresh root ginger
2 spring onions
2tbsp rice wine or dry sherry
4tbsp soy sauce
1tbsp sugar
1tsp five-spice powder
2tbsp oil
1tsp sesame seed oil

Wash the tripe thoroughly, rub both sides with the salt several times and rinse well. Blanch it in boiling water for 20 minutes. Drain and discard the water.

Heat oil, brown the tripe lightly, add root ginger, onions, rice wine or sherry, soy sauce, sugar and five-spice powder. Add 2 pt (1.2 lt) of water and bring it to the boil, reduce heat and simmer gently under cover for 2 hours.

Remove the tripe and cut into small slices; garnish with sesame seed oil and serve hot or cold.

SHREDDED KIDNEYS IN WINE SAUCE

SERVES 4–6

1lb (450g) pigs' kidneys
5–6 dried Chinese mushrooms
2oz (50g) bamboo shoots
2oz (50g) green cabbage heart or broccoli
1½tbsp rice wine or dry sherry
1tsp salt
1tbsp soy sauce
½tsp monosodium glutamate
1 slice fresh root ginger, 1 spring onion, chopped and freshly ground pepper, to garnish

Peel off the thin white skin covering the kidneys, split them in half lengthwise and discard the white parts in the middle. Shred each half into thin slices and soak them in cold water for an hour or so.

Soak the mushrooms in warm water for 20 minutes, squeeze dry and discard the hard stalks, then cut them into thin shreds. Cut the bamboo shoots and greens into thin shreds, blanch them in boiling water for a few minutes (if using canned bamboo shoots this will be unnecessary as they have already been cooked), then drain and mix them with 1 tsp of salt.

POACHED KIDNEY AND LIVER WITH SPRING ONION AND GINGER

Parboil the kidneys in about 1¾ pt (1 lt) of boiling water for a few minutes, scoop them out, rinse in cold water and drain. Place them in a bowl, add the bamboo shoots, mushrooms, greens, soy sauce, rice wine or sherry and monosodium glutamate; mix well and marinate for 20 minutes or so. Arrange the contents on a serving plate and garnish.

POACHED KIDNEY AND LIVER WITH SPRING ONION AND GINGER

SERVES 4–6

8oz (225g) pigs' kidney
8oz (225g) pigs' liver
4tbsp peanut oil
¾pt (450ml) boiling water
1tbsp salt
2tbsp fresh root ginger, shredded
4tbsp spring onion, shredded

Sauce
8tbsp chicken stock
2tsp dark soy sauce
2tbsp light soy sauce
1tsp sugar
1tsp sesame seed oil
2tsp Chinese yellow wine

Slit open the kidney and remove the membrane and gristle. Cut the kidney into slices ⅛ inch (3 mm) thick and soak in cold water. Set aside.

Cut the liver into slices ⅛ in (3 mm) thick. Soak in cold water and set aside. Heat 2 tbsp of oil in a pan, add the boiling water, bring to the boil and add the salt. Add the kidney to the boiling water. Poach for 2 minutes, remove and drain. Bring the water to the boil again and add the liver. Poach for 2 minutes, remove and drain. Bring the water to the boil for the third time. Return the kidney and liver and add the shredded ginger and spring onion. Turn off the heat and allow the ingredients to stand in the hot water for 4–5 minutes. Remove and drain.

In the meantime prepare the sauce. Heat 2 tbsp of oil in a pan, add the sauce ingredients and bring to the boil.

Transfer the poached kidney, liver, ginger and spring onion to a serving dish, pour the sauce on top and serve.

FIVE-FRAGRANT KIDNEY SLICES

SERVES 4–6

½lb (225g) pigs' kidneys
1tsp red colouring
12fl oz (350ml) chicken stock
1tbsp soy sauce
1tbsp rice wine or dry sherry
1 slice fresh root ginger
1tsp salt
1tsp five-spice powder
1 spring onion (scallion)

Place the kidneys in cold water in a pan; bring to the boil; skim off any impurities floating on the surface; reduce heat and simmer for 30 minutes. Remove and drain.

Place the kidneys in fresh cold water (just enough to cover), add

the red colouring (if Chinese red-powder is unobtainable, then use a little cochineal). Bring to the boil, then remove and rinse in cold water and drain.

Put the chicken stock in a pot or pan; add the soy sauce, wine or sherry, root ginger, onion, salt, five-spice powder and the kidneys. Boil for 5 minutes, then place the kidneys with the stock in a large bowl to cool. This will take 5–6 hours.

Take the kidneys out and cut them into as thin slices as you possibly can. Place the unevenly cut slices in the middle of a plate to make a pile, then neatly arrange the rest of the slices all the way around it in 2 or 3 layers like the petals of an opened flower. Then through a sieve pour a little of the juice in which the kidneys have been cooking over the 'flower', but be careful not to disturb the beautiful 'petals'. Serve cold as an hors d'oeuvre.

HAPPY FAMILY (ASSORTED MEATS AND SEAFOOD STEW)

SERVES 6–8

4oz (100g) Bêche-de-Mer (soaked)
2oz (50g) fish maw (soaked)
2oz (50g) cooked tripe
1 pigs' kidney
4oz (100g) shrimps, peeled
2oz (50g) cooked chicken meat
1 egg
8 fish balls, can be bought pre-prepared
6 meat balls, can be bought pre-prepared
2oz (50g) bamboo shoots
4oz (100g) cauliflower
4oz (100g) broccoli
2 slices fresh root ginger
2 spring onions
1½tbsp dried shrimps
3tbsp lard
1tbsp sugar
2tbsp rice wine or dry sherry
3tbsp soy sauce
2tbsp cornflour
½pt (300ml) chicken stock
vinegar and salt

HAPPY FAMILY (ASSORTED MEATS AND SEAFOOD STEW)

Bêche-de-Mer, also known as sea-cucumber or sea-slug, is regarded by the Chinese as a delicacy. It must be soaked overnight to become gelatinous. Cut it diagonally into thin slices.

Fish maw is bought already fried. It has a puffy, spongy, yet crispy texture. It too should be soaked in water overnight before being cut into small pieces about the same size as the Bêche-de-Mer. Cut the tripe into similar-sized pieces.

Split the kidney in half lengthwise and discard the fat and white parts in the middle. Score the surface of the kidney diagonally in a criss-cross pattern and then cut into medium-sized pieces; marinate in a little salt and vinegar; blanch in boiling water for a few seconds until the kidney pieces curl up; remove and drain.

Marinate the peeled shrimps in a little salt and cornflour. Cut the cooked chicken meat into thin slices. Wash the cauliflower and broccoli and cut them into small pieces; blanch in boiling water for a while, remove and drain. Slice the bamboo shoots; finely chop the root ginger and onions.

Beat up the egg with a little salt and 2–3 tsp water. Rub some lard on the bottom of a bowl, pour the beaten egg into it and steam for 2–3 minutes, then open the lid of the steamer for a few seconds to let out some hot air; replace the lid and steam for 5–6 minutes more. When the steamed egg is cooled, remove from the bowl and cut it into thin slices.

Parboil all the ingredients together for a few seconds; remove and drain. Heat up the lard in a large pot; fry the finely chopped root ginger and onions; add dried shrimps and rice wine or sherry followed by the rest of the ingredients. Now add soy sauce, sugar and chicken stock; bring it to the boil, then reduce heat and simmer for a few minutes.

Finally mix the remaining cornflour with a little water and add to the pot to thicken the gravy. Serve in a large bowl with rice.

THREE-LAYER SHREDS

SERVES 4–6

2oz (50g) cooked ham
2oz (50g) cooked chicken meat
4oz (100g) cooked pork
2oz (50g) bamboo shoots
1 large dried Chinese mushroom
2tsp salt
½tsp monosodium glutamate
1tbsp lard
1pt (600ml) stock

Cut the ham, chicken, pork and bamboo shoots into matchstick-sized shreds, but keep them separate. Discard the stalk of the mushroom after soaking it in warm water for 20 minutes. Place the mushroom smooth side down in the middle of a large bowl, and arrange the ham shreds around it in 3 neat rows, forming a triangle. Now arrange the chicken shreds on one of the outer edges and the bamboo shoots on the second edge with the pork on the third. Spread 1 tsp of salt all over it, add about 4 tbsp of stock and steam vigorously for 30 minutes. Remove and turn the bowl out into a deep serving dish without disarranging the contents. The success of this dish depends on the cutting and arranging, which must be done with skill and care.

Bring the remaining stock to the boil, add salt, monosodium glutamate and lard; let it bubble for a second or 2, then pour it all over the three-layer shreds and serve.

◆ ◆ ◆

◆ DESSERTS AND SNACKS ◆

SPRING ROLL WRAPPERS

MAKES APPROXIMATELY 12

1 egg
8oz (225g) plain flour
½tsp salt
4fl oz (120ml) water
cornflour

Lightly beat the egg. Sift the flour and salt into a large bowl. Make a well in the centre and mix the beaten egg and water into the flour. Stir with a wooden spoon to form a smooth dough. Place the dough on a floured board and knead it for 10 minutes until smooth. Cover with a damp cloth and leave to rest for about 30 minutes. Roll the dough into a 12 inch (30 cm) sausage, then cut into 1½ inch (4 cm) pieces. Dust with cornflour and flatten with the palm of your hand. Roll as thinly as possible, then trim to 6 × 7 inch (15 × 18 cm) rectangles. Dust with cornflour and stack them up.

SPRING ROLL FILLINGS

SERVES 6–8

12oz (350g) lean pork or chicken meat
2 slices fresh root ginger
3oz (75g) drained, canned bamboo shoots
8 medium dried Chinese mushrooms
2 spring onions
3tbsp vegetable oil
1tsp salt
2tbsp soy sauce
4–5oz (100–150g) bean sprouts
1tbsp cornflour blended with 2tbsp water
beaten egg for sealing
vegetable oil for deep-frying

Cut the pork or chicken into matchstick-sized shreds. Cut the ginger and bamboo shoots into similar or finer shreds. Soak the dried mushrooms in hot water to cover for 25 minutes. Drain and discard the tough stalks. Cut the mushroom caps into fine shreds. Divide the spring onions lengthwise in half, then cut into ½ inch (1 cm) sections.

Heat the 3 tbsp of oil in a wok or frying pan. When hot, stir-fry the ginger, salt, mushrooms and shredded meat over high heat for 1¼ minutes. Add all the other ingredients, except the cornflour, and stir-fry for 1 minute. Pour in the blended cornflour, stir and turn for another 30 seconds. Remove from the heat and leave to cool before using as a filling.

Take 2 tbsp of filling and spread across each pancake just below the centre. Fold the pancake up from the bottom by raising the lower corner to fold over the filling. Roll the filling over once, and bring in the 2 corners from the side to overlap each other. Finally fold the top flap down, sealing with a little beaten egg. Stack the spring rolls as you make them, placing them so that the weight of the pancake rests on the flap that has just been sealed.

Fry the pancakes soon after they have been made, as otherwise they may become soggy. Heat the oil in a wok or deep-fryer. When hot, fry not more than 5–6 pancakes at a time for 3¾–4½ minutes until golden-brown and crispy. Once fried, they can be kept crispy in the oven for up to 30 minutes. Or store them in the refrigerator for a day after an initial frying of 2½ minutes, then re-fry them for 3 minutes when required.

SESAME PRAWNS ON TOAST

SERVES 7–8

8oz (225g) peeled prawns
2oz (50g) pork fat
1tsp salt
pepper to taste
½tsp ground ginger
1tbsp dry sherry or white wine
1½tbsp spring onion, finely chopped
1 egg white
2tsp cornflour
6 slices bread
4oz (100g) sesame seeds
vegetable oil for deep-frying

Chop and mix the prawns and pork fat into a paste in a bowl. Add the salt, pepper, ginger, sherry or wine, spring onion, egg white and cornflour. Mix together thoroughly. Spread the mixture very thickly on the top of the slices of bread. Spread the sesame seeds evenly over the surface of a large plate or a small tray. Place each piece of bread, spread side down, on the sesame seeds. Press gently so that each slice has a good coating of seeds.

Heat the oil in a wok or deep-fryer. When hot, fry the slices of bread, spread-side down (only 2–3 slices of bread can be fried at a time) for 2½ minutes. Turn over and fry for a further 1½ minutes. Drain on absorbent kitchen paper.

When all the slices of bread have been fried and drained, place each piece of bread on a chopping board, cut off and discard the crusts. Cut the coated and fried bread slices into 6 rectangular pieces (the size of fish fingers) or into 4 triangles. Arrange them on a heated serving dish and serve hot.

SA CHI MA

4oz (125g) flour
2tsp baking powder
3 eggs
8oz (225g) sugar
6oz (175g) maltose or honey
1 cup water
oil for deep-frying

Sift flour and baking powder onto a pastry board. Spread to form a hollow in the centre; add eggs, blend well. Then knead the dough thoroughly until it is smooth.

Roll the dough with a rolling pin until it is like a big pancake about ⅛ inch (3 mm) in thickness. Cut it into 2 inch (5 cm) long thin strips; dust strips with flour so they won't stick.

Heat up the oil and deep-fry the thin strips in batches for 45 seconds until light golden. Remove. Drain.

Place the sugar, maltose or honey and water in a saucepan; bring it to the boil over a high heat; simmer and stir until the mixture is like syrup. Add the thin strips and mix thoroughly until each strip is coated with syrup. Turn it out into a pre-greased cake tin and press to form one big piece. When cool, cut it into squares with a sharp knife.

SPRING ONION PANCAKES

SERVES 5–6

3 large spring onions
12oz (350g) plain flour
½pt (300ml) boiling water
2½oz (65g) lard
5tbsp cold water
1¼tbsp large grain sea salt

Coarsely chop the spring onions. Sift the flour into a large bowl. Slowly add the boiling water and ½ oz (15 g) of the lard. Stir with a fork or a pair of chopsticks for 3 minutes. Mix in the cold water and knead for 2 minutes. Leave the dough to stand for 30 minutes. Form and roll the dough into a long roll and cut into 10 equal sections. Roll each piece into a ball and press the ball into a flat pancake. Sprinkle the pancake evenly with salt and chopped spring onion. Fold it up from the sides to form a ball again, then press again into a pancake.

Heat the remaining lard in a wok or frying pan. When hot, spread the pancake evenly over the pan and fry over low heat for 2½ minutes on either side, until golden-brown.

TOFFEE BANANAS

SERVES 4

4 bananas, peeled
1 egg
2tbsp plain flour
oil for deep-frying
4tbsp sugar
1tbsp cold water

Cut the bananas in half lengthwise and then cut each half into 2 crosswise.

Beat the egg, add the flour and mix well to make a smooth batter.

Heat the oil in a wok or deep-fryer. Coat each piece of banana with batter and deep-fry until golden. Remove and drain.

Pour off excess oil leaving about 1 tbsp of oil in the wok. Add sugar and water and stir over a medium heat. When the sugar has caramelized, add the hot banana pieces. Coat well and remove. Dip hot bananas in cold water to harden the toffee and serve.

PLUM-BLOSSOM AND SNOW COMPETING FOR SPRING

SERVES 4

2 apples
2 bananas
2 eggs
4oz (100g) sugar
3tbsp milk
3tbsp cornflour
2tbsp water

Skin and remove the cores of the apples, then cut the apples and bananas into thin slices. Arrange them in alternate layers on an ovenproof dish. Separate the yolks from the whites and mix the yolks with the sugar, milk, water and cornflour. Heat this mixture over a gentle heat until smooth, then pour it over the apple and banana.

Beat the egg whites, pour on top of the yolk mixture and bake in a hot oven (425°F/220°C/Gas Mark 7) for about 5 minutes. Serve hot or cold.

SPRING ROLLS

◆ DESSERTS AND SNACKS ◆

LOTUS-LEAF PANCAKES

SERVES 4–6

1lb (450g) plain flour
½pt (300ml) boiling water
3tsp vegetable oil

Sift the flour into a mixing bowl and very slowly pour in the boiling water, mixed with 1 tsp of oil, while stirring with a pair of chopsticks or a wooden spoon. Do not be tempted to add any more water than the amount given, otherwise the mixture will get too wet and become messy.

Knead the mixture into a firm dough, then divide it into 3 equal portions. Now roll out each portion into a long 'sausage', and cut each sausage into 8 equal parts; then, using the palm of your hand, press each piece into a flat pancake. Brush one of the pancakes with a little oil, and place another one on top to form a 'sandwich', so that you end up with 12 sandwiches. Now use a rolling pin to flatten each sandwich into a 6 inch (15 cm) circle by rolling gently on each side on a lightly floured surface.

To cook, place a frying pan over a high heat, and when it is hot reduce the heat to moderate. Put one pancake sandwich at a time into the ungreased pan, and turn it over when it starts to puff up with bubbles. It is done when little brown spots appear on the underside. Remove from the pan and very gently peel apart the 2 layers and fold each one in half.

If the pancakes are not to be served as soon as they are cooked, they can be stored and warmed up, either in a steamer, or the oven for 5–10 minutes.

PEARS IN HONEY SAUCE

SERVES 6

6 firm, ripe pears
4tbsp runny honey
4tbsp sweet liqueur, eg, Chinese Rose Dew, kirsch, cherry brandy
4tbsp sugar

Peel the pears, leaving on the stalks and a little of the surrounding skin. Blend the honey with the liqueur, 1 tbsp of the sugar and 2 tbsp of water.

Stand the pears in a flat-bottomed pan and barely cover with water. Bring slowly to the boil. Add the remaining sugar and simmer gently for 20 minutes. Refrigerate the pears with a quarter of the sugar water for 2 hours, discarding the remaining sugar water.

Stand each pear in a small bowl. Spoon over a little sugar water, then pour about 2 tbsp of the honey sauce over each pear. Chill for another 30 minutes before serving.

WATER CHESTNUT 'CAKE'

SERVES 5–6

8oz (225g) canned water chestnuts, drained
6–8oz (175–225g) caster sugar
6–8oz (175–225g) water chestnut flour
4tbsp corn oil
3tbsp vegetable oil

Cut the water chestnuts into matchstick-sized shreds. Place them in a saucepan, add the sugar and ¾ pt (450 ml) of water. Bring to the boil. Stir in the water chestnut flour and add another ¾ pt (450 ml) of water. Stir and mix well, then simmer for 5 minutes. Add the corn oil, stir and bring once more to the boil. Reduce heat to very low and simmer gently for 5 minutes. Pour the mixture into a square cake tin or Swiss roll tin. Place the tin in a steamer and steam for 30 minutes. Remove from the steamer and leave to cool.

When cold the 'cake' is like a firm jelly with streaks of water chestnut inside. Cut into pieces about the thickness of bread slices. Heat the vegetable oil in a frying pan. When hot, fry each slice of chestnut 'cake' for 2½ minutes on each side. Serve hot or cold.

EIGHT TREASURE PUDDING

EIGHT TREASURE PUDDING

SERVES 6–8

1¼lb (550g) glutinous rice
2½oz (65g) lard
3oz (75g) sugar

◆ DESSERTS AND SNACKS ◆

about 1oz (25g) nuts, eg, almonds, walnuts, chestnuts or lotus seeds
6tbsp candied and dried fruits (optional)
about 3oz (75g) sweet bean paste

Wash the rice and place in a saucepan. Cover with ½ inch (1 cm) of water. Bring to the boil and simmer gently for 11–12 minutes. Add half the lard and all the sugar, turn and stir until well mixed. Grease the sides of a large heatproof basin or bowl heavily with the remaining lard (lard must be cold). Stick the nuts and candied or dried fruits of your choice in a pattern on the sides of the basin in the lard, arranging the remainder at the bottom of the basin. Place a layer of sweetened rice in the basin, then spread a thinner layer of sweet bean paste on top of the rice. Repeat the layers, finishing with a rice layer. Cover the basin with foil, leaving a little room for expansion.

Place the basin into a steamer and steam steadily for 1 hour 10 minutes until cooked. Invert the basin on to a large round heated serving dish to turn out the pudding. Decorate with extra candied fruits, if liked.

PEARS IN HONEY SAUCE

RED BEAN PASTE PANCAKES

8oz (225g) plain flour
4fl oz (125ml) boiling water
1 egg
3tbsp oil
4–5tbsp sweetened red bean paste or chestnut purée

Sift the flour into a mixing bowl and very gently pour in the boiling water. Add about 1 tsp of oil and the beaten egg. Knead the mixture into a firm dough and then divide it into 2 equal portions. Roll out each portion into a long 'sausage' on a lightly floured surface and cut it into 4–6 pieces. Using the palm of your hand, press each piece into a flat pancake. On a lightly floured surface, flatten each pancake into a 6 inch (15 cm) circle with a rolling pin and roll gently.

Place an ungreased frying pan on a high heat. When hot, reduce the heat to low and place one pancake at a time in the pan. Turn it over when little brown spots appear on the underside. Remove and keep under a damp cloth until you have finished making all the pancakes.

Spread about 2 tbsp of red bean paste or chestnut purée over about 80 per cent of the pancake surface and roll it over 3 or 4 times to form a flattened roll.

Heat the oil in a frying pan and shallow-fry the pancakes until golden-brown, turning over once. Cut each pancake into 3–4 pieces and serve hot or cold.

THOUSAND-LAYER CAKES

WON'T STICK THREE WAYS

SERVES 4–6

5 egg yolks
2tbsp cornflour
5tbsp water
4oz (100g) sugar
3tbsp lard

Beat the egg yolks, add sugar, cornflour and water, blend well.

Heat the lard in a frying pan over a high heat, tilt the pan so that the entire surface is covered by lard, then pour the excess lard (about half) into a jug for later use. Reduce the heat to moderate, pour the egg mixture into the pan, stir and scramble for about 2 minutes and add the remaining lard from the jug little by little, stirring and scrambling all the time until the eggs become bright golden, then serve.

THOUSAND-LAYER CAKES

1½lb (700g) flour
2tsp dried yeast
12fl oz (350ml) warm water
6oz (150g) sugar
4oz (100g) lard
3tbsp walnuts, crushed

Sift the flour into a mixing bowl and add the sugar; dissolve the yeast in warm water and slowly pour it in, then knead it well for 5 minutes. Cover the dough with a damp cloth and let it stand for 3 hours or until it doubles in volume.

Now divide the dough into 3 equal portions, then roll out each portion into a thin rectangle measuring about 1 ft × 8 inch (30 × 20 cm). Spread some lard and sprinkle a few chopped walnut pieces on the surface of one portion, and place another one on top to make a 'sandwich'. Then spread some lard and walnut pieces on top of the sandwich, and place the third portion on top to form a double-decker sandwich.

Now roll this sandwich flat until it measures roughly 2½ × 1 ft (75 × 30 cm). Spread some lard and walnuts over two-thirds of the surface of the dough, then fold one-third over to cover the middle section and spread lard and walnuts on top of that, then fold the other one-third over.

Turn the dough around so that the folded edge faces you. Repeat the rolling, spreading and folding twice more so that you end up with the dough measuring roughly 1 ft × 8 inch (30 × 20 cm) again but with 81 layers.

Let it stand for 30 minutes, then place it on a wet cloth in a steamer and steam over boiling water for 50–60 minutes.

Remove and let it cool a little, then cut the cake into squares or diamonds before serving.

TOFFEE APPLES

TOFFEE APPLES

SERVES 4

3 apples
1tbsp lemon juice
4oz (100g) cornflour
2tbsp sesame seeds
1 cup ice cubes
20fl oz (½lt) iced water
¾pt (450ml) peanut oil
12oz (350g) sugar
1tsp vinegar

Peel and core the apples and cut each into 6 pieces. Cut each piece into 3. Sprinkle lemon juice over the apples immediately to prevent discolouration. Coat the apple pieces with cornflour and set them aside. Sauté the sesame seeds in a pan over a low heat. Set aside.

Rub a serving plate with oil and set it aside. Place the ice cubes and iced water in a bowl and set them aside.

Heat the oil and fry the apple for 10 minutes until nicely golden. Remove, drain and set aside. In another pan bring 12 fl oz (340 ml) of water to a vigorous boil. Add the sugar, stirring until it starts to caramelize, then add the vinegar and stir. Add the apple pieces until they are evenly coated with syrup. Sprinkle sesame seeds over the apple and transfer them to a plate.

Dip the syrup-coated apple pieces into the iced water. Remove immediately or when the syrup hardens and becomes brittle. It is worth practising this recipe a few times to achieve the correct contrast between the brittle, ice-cold coating of caramelized sugar and the hot, tender apple centre.

◆ ◆ ◆

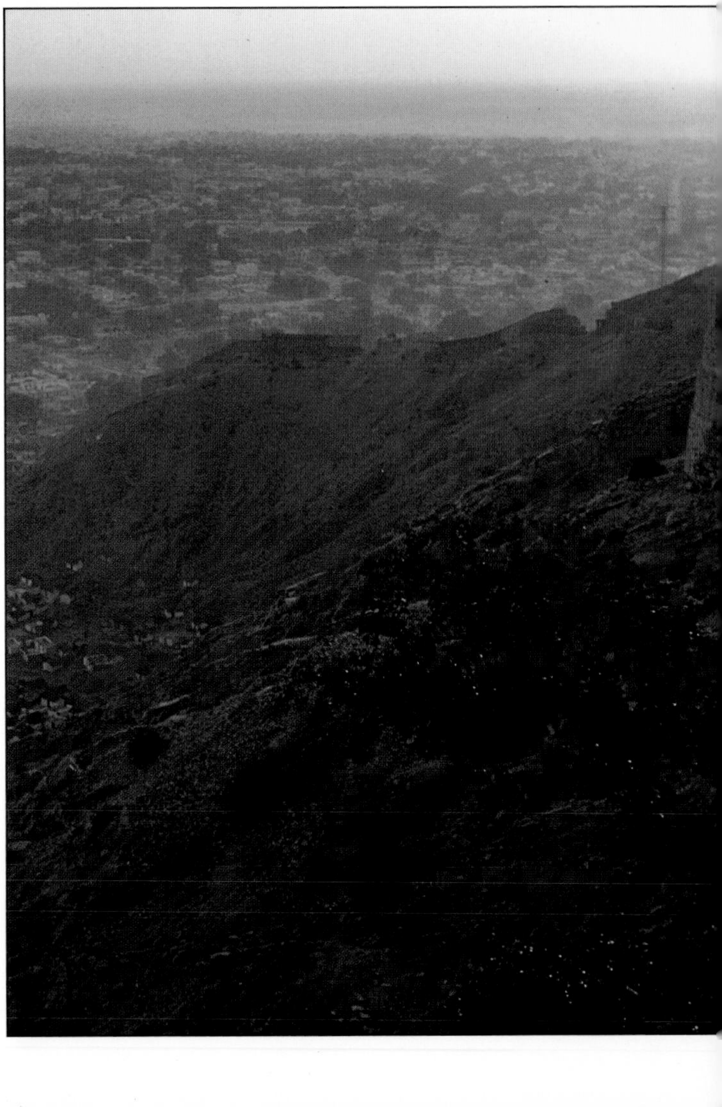

Top: *the tropical landscape of Southern India.*
Top right: *fishermen at work on the Arabian Sea off the west coast of India. People in this area love fish to such an extent that they store it in airtight containers so they can eat it all year round as no fishing takes place during the harsh monsoon season.*
Above: *Assam, in eastern India, lies at the foothills of the Himalayas, and is renowned for its tea.*
Right: *the sun rises over Jaipur, the capital of Central India.*

INDIA

To many people outside India, Indian food means just curry. Indeed, many of the dishes now popular in the West are delicious and fiery curries such as the Goan favourite, vindaloo. Food is, however, a celebrated item all over India and you do not need to delve too deeply into the subject to discover that there is a stunning array of dishes, some steamed, some fried, some grilled; some subtle and delicate, some full-bodied and rich to reflect the great diversity of the country.

There is no one India and no one Indian cuisine. It is a vast country of more than one and a half million square miles of changing topography and more than seven hundred million people of various faiths.

There are about 25 spices on the shelf in the Indian pantry. Many of them will have come from the back garden along with fresh herbs and bulbs – onions, garlic and shallots. With this huge treasury of flavours the Indian cook can create an infinite number of different dishes. Spices can be used individually or combined, roasted or ground with water into a paste to produce flavours anywhere in the spectrum from sweet to sour, fiery to bland and fragrant to pungent.

The traditional way to serve Indian food is on a *thali* or large tray, often of beautifully wrought metal. Each different dish will be in a small metal or earthenware bowl perched around the edge of the tray, or laid out on a low communal brass table. The diners sit on the floor or on very low stools. The carpet is spread with coloured cloth to protect it and the guests are given giant coloured napkins. The dishes can be wrapped in cotton or silk, which is loosely folded back over the food after it has been served. Often banana leaves will serve as disposable plates.

Indians eat with their hands. The right hand only is used; the left is thought unclean. In some parts of India the whole hand is used, in others just the fingertips. Generally, food is scooped up with a piece of flat bread in the north and mopped up with rice in the south. This means that cleanliness is very important, so hands are washed before and after eating and water for washing is provided even on barrows selling snacks in the streets.

◆ SPECIAL INGREDIENTS ◆

Left: *panch phoron is a combination of five spices:* ***clockwise from top:*** *cumin, fennel, mustard, fenugreek and kalongi (onion seeds).*

◆ SPECIAL INGREDIENTS ◆

***Above:** fragrant mountains of vibrant colour characterize the spice merchant's store.*

Spices

Spices are the main ingredient for Indian cookery. Whole spices have a different taste from ground spices, and when the spices are dry roasted, they taste entirely different again. Simple dishes may have just one or two spices, whereas more elaborate dishes might involve ten or twelve. By adding different spices, the entire taste of the dish can be changed.

In India, spices are normally bought whole and then ground for daily use on a grinding stone with a little water. If spices are required to be ground dry, a mortar and pestle is used. In the modern kitchen, the spices can easily be ground in an electric coffee grinder, so long as you make sure that you do not overheat it.

Spices can be bought ready ground but these have to be stored in airtight jars as they lose their flavour very quickly.

As Indian cookery has become popular, more and more spices are easily available. Supermarkets sell many of the spices you will need, but for a few special ones you will have to make a trip to an Indian grocery store.

In Indian cooking, onions, coconut, poppy seeds and almonds are some of the thickening agents. Normally the spices are cooked a little before the meat, fish or vegetables are added so that you get all the flavour.

Asafetida: A strong smelling gum resin. It is sold in pieces or in ground form. It is popular in India as a digestive and is used in small amounts only. A pinch is added to hot oil and allowed to sizzle for a few seconds before the other ingredients are added.

Black cumin seeds: These are smaller than the ordinary cumin seeds and dark in colour.

Black salt: This is a rock salt with a distinctive flavour. It is used in small quantities in chutneys, pickles and snacks.

Cardamom: When the recipe calls for cardamoms, take the whole, small cardamom pods and, just before using, press the cardamom on a hard surface with your thumb and forefinger to break the skin, so that the flavour mixes with the other ingredients while cooking.

Ground cardamom is available in Indian grocery stores or supermarkets, but cardamoms can be ground easily in an electric coffee grinder.

Chilli, dried red: Available in whole or ground form. The whole chillies, when added to hot oil and fried for a few seconds, turn darker and give a lovely flavour to the dish.

Cinnamon: This is the dried inner bark of the cinnamon tree. It is mainly used whole in rice, meat and fish dishes for its aroma and flavour.

Cloves: This is the flower bud of the clove tree and when dried it is used as a spice. Cloves also contain essential oils. They are used whole in rice and meat dishes for their aroma and flavour.

Coriander, fresh: This is also known as Chinese parsley or cilantro. It is used in small amounts to garnish or added towards the end of the cooking time for its aroma; it is also used for making chutney.

◆ SPECIAL INGREDIENTS ◆

Coriander seeds: The seeds are small and round in shape and beige in colour. Ground coriander is used a great deal in cooking vegetables and meats.

Cumin: Like caraway seeds, but with a lightly pungent flavour. Whole and ground forms are used greatly in Indian cooking.

Curry leaves: Used mainly in South Indian cooking.

Fennel: Light green, oval shaped seeds with a liquorice flavour – used a great deal in Kashmiri cooking.

Fenugreek: Used in small amounts only, either whole or ground after dry roasting.

Ginger: The rhizome of a plant with a pungent flavour; it can be stored in the refrigerator for about one month. To use, peel the skin and use either grated or cut into strips.

Kalonji (Onion seeds): Small, black seeds that are an important spice for pickling.

Mango powder: This is made by peeling and slicing the unripe mango and drying it in the sun until it shrivels up. It is then powdered.

Mustard: White and dark purple mustard seeds are available. In Indian cooking the darker variety is used. They are tiny and round in shape. When added to hot oil they start to splutter. At this stage, either the oil is poured over a cooked dish or vegetables are added to the oil.

Panch phoron: A combination of five spices mixed in equal proportions: cumin, kalonji (onion seeds), fennel, fenugreek and mustard. Used for lentil or vegetable preparations and normally used whole.

Pistachio nuts: The kernel is green with a reddish brown skin, and the flavour is delicate. They are used as a garnish on desserts either chopped or slivered.

Poppy seed: Tiny, white, round seeds with a nutty taste, used in both sweet and salt dishes. Sometimes used as a thickening agent.

Saffron: These threads are orangey red and are the dried stems of a flower of the crocus family. A small amount of good quality saffron is enough to colour and flavour a dish. It is usually soaked in warm milk and kept aside for 15–20 minutes before using.

Sesame: Tiny, beige seeds with a nutty flavour. The sesame seed oil is used for cooking.

Tamarind: Tamarind trees grow in tropical climates. The pods are 5–7 inches in length and become dark brown when ripe. The pulp is dried in the sun and sold in packets at Indian grocery stores. A little tamarind pulp is soaked in hot water for 30 minutes and then squeezed to drain out all the juice. It has a sour taste.

Turmeric: Mainly found in ground form at Indian grocery stores or supermarkets. It is the root of a plant of the ginger family. Pungent in taste and yellow in colour.

Cumin seed

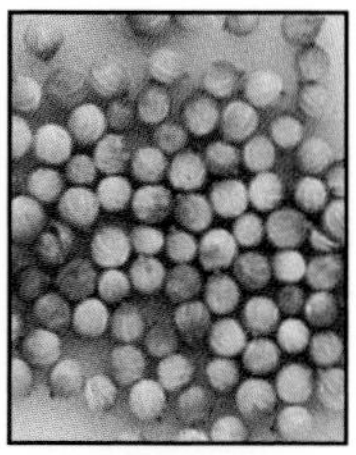

Coriander seed

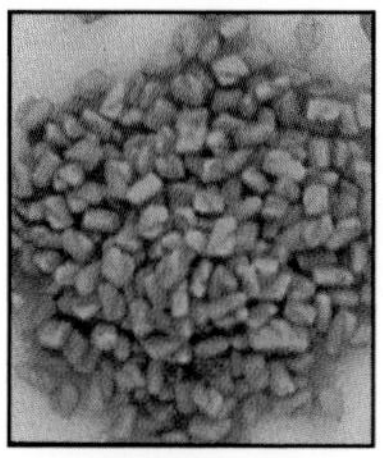

Fenugreek

Mustard seed

Onion seed

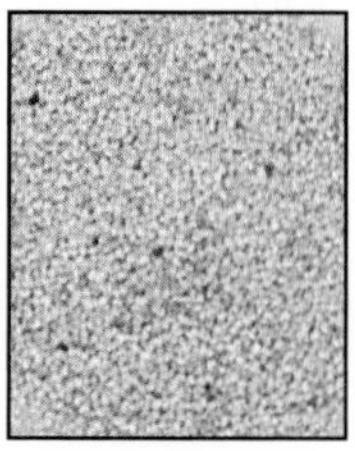

Poppy seed

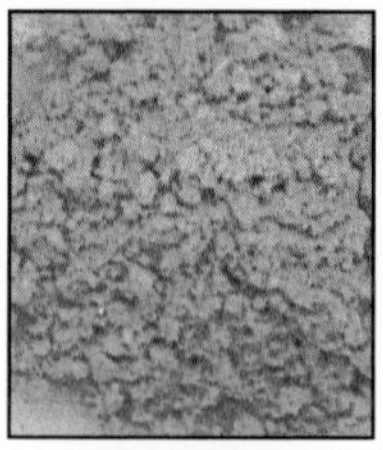

Ground tumeric

Ground asafetida

Small cardamons

Bay leaves

Stick cinnamon

◆ SPECIAL INGREDIENTS ◆

Moong dal

Masoor dal

Chole

Channa dal

Rajma

Urid dal

Lobia

Matar

Oils

Many different kinds of oil are used for cooking in India. Some of the vegetable and fish dishes from Eastern India are normally cooked in mustard oil, but you can use vegetable oil.

Coconut oil: Has a delicate flavour and solidifies at low temperatures.

Groundnut oil: This is the oil from peanuts. It is used for cooking in Southern India and has a nutty flavour.

Mustard oil: Yellow, with a strong smell. Fish cooked in mustard oil has a distinctive flavour.

Sesame seed oil: Has a strong, distinct flavour and is dark.

Dals

There are many varieties available in India and a great many of these can be found in North America at Indian grocery stores. They are available whole or split.

Black-eyed beans: *(Lobia)* White, kidney-shaped beans with a black 'eye'.

Channa dal: These are similar to split peas, but slightly smaller.

Chole: *(Chickpeas or garbanzos)* Beige, round, dried peas. Should be soaked overnight to reduce the cooking time. Chickpea flour is called gram, and is widely used in cooking.

Masoor dal: *(Split red lentils)* Salmon-coloured, small, flat, round lentils which cook easily.

Matar: *(Split peas)* Round, yellow lentils which are uniform in size.

Moong dal: Small, yellow, split lentils. Bean sprouts are made by sprouting these beans.

Rajma: *(Red kidney beans)* Large, dark red kidney-shaped beans. Should be soaked overnight to reduce cooking time.

Toovar dal: Also called arhar dal, this is the main dal used in southern India.

Urid dal: *(Black gram)* The bean is reddish black, is very small in size and takes a long time to cook. The split urid dal is pale cream. It is usually soaked and ground to a paste.

◆ EQUIPMENT AND TECHNIQUES ◆

Equipment

A degchi: A pan without handles, made of polished brass, stainless steel or other metals. The lid of the degchi is slightly dipped so that sometimes live coal can be placed on it to cook food slowly or to keep food warm. Ordinary saucepans with lids can be used in the same way and the oven can be used to cook food slowly or to keep it warm.

A karai: This is found in every Indian kitchen. It is a deep concave metallic dish with two handles – one on each side. It looks like a Chinese wok but it is a little more rounded. It is used for deep frying.

A tava: Made from cast iron, it is slightly concave, and is about 10 inches (25cm) in diameter. It is ideal for making chappatis or parathas because it distributes the heat evenly. A griddle or heavy skillet will serve the same purpose.

Tongs: These are used to remove a karai from the fire, or to remove the hot lid from the degchi. To remove the degchi from the fire it is normally held at either side with a cloth.

Metallic stirrers: These are used in India because the pans are not nonstick. Use wooden spoons when using nonstick pans. Wooden spoons are easier to use as they do not get hot, although if left in hot oil they tend to burn.

A thick stone slab: This is used with a round stone roller like a rolling pin for grinding. Whole spices are ground with a little water; if dry ground spice is required a mortar and pestle is used. Lentils are also ground on the slab.

Below: *traditional Kitchen equipment includes the Karai, shown on the left with tongs to lift it from the heat and a wooden stirrer. The heavy frying pan and saucepan on the right are suitable modern substitutes for the tava and the degchi. Also shown rolling pin, wooden spatula and sieve.*

◆ EQUIPMENT AND TECHNIQUES ◆

A tandoor: This is a clay oven used in northern India. Tandoori chicken, whole or in pieces, different kinds of breads and kebabs are baked in this oven. It is about 3–4 ft (90 cm–1.2 m) deep and about 2 ft (60 cm) wide on top with a hole of 12 inches (30 cm) diameter through which the food is put for cooking. It is fuelled by wood and coal and intensive heat builds up inside.

Tandoori chicken can be cooked easily in the modern oven, and then put under a very hot grill for a few minutes to dry out. It can also taste excellent barbecued.

Techniques

Adding spices to hot oil: Oil is heated until it is very hot, and whole spices, crushed garlic or green chillies are added until the spices swell up or splutter or change colour. This is then added to a cooked dish, or vegetables, or other spices are added and cooking continues.

Dry roasting: Place whole spices in a small, heavy-based frying pan and heat gently, stirring the spices constantly so that they do not burn. Soon the spices will turn a few shades darker and a lovely aroma will emerge.

Frying onions: Place the oil in a frying pan over a medium high heat. When hot add the onions, and, stirring occasionally, fry until the onions start to change colour. Lower the heat and continue to fry until they are reddish brown.

Adding yoghurt while cooking: When a recipe calls for yoghurt, always whisk the yoghurt until smooth, and add slowly, otherwise it curdles.

Peeling tomatoes: Place the tomatoes in boiling water for 30 seconds. Drain and cool under running cold water. Peel, chop and use as required.

Cleaning chillies: Pull out the stalks of the chillies and, holding them under cold running water, slit them open with a sharp knife and remove the seeds. The seeds are the hottest part of the chillies and most Indians do not remove them. Be very careful, when handling chillies, not to put your hands near your eyes as the oil will make your eyes burn.

◆ RICE DISHES ◆

CREAMED RICE

SERVES 4–6

2 tbsp basmati rice
2pt (1.2lt) milk
3oz (75g) sugar
1oz (25g) peeled almonds
¼tsp ground cardamom
1tsp rose water

Wash the rice in several changes of water and soak in plenty of water for 30 minutes. Drain.

Bring the milk to a boil over a high heat, stirring constantly. Lower the heat and simmer for 30 minutes, stirring occasionally. Add the drained rice and sugar and continue to cook for a further 30–40 minutes until the milk has thickened and the rice is very soft and disintegrated. Add the almonds and continue to cook for a further 10 minutes, stirring constantly.

Remove from the heat and stir in the cardamom and rose water. Place in a serving dish and refrigerate. Serve chilled.

TAMARIND RICE

SERVES 4–6

8oz (225g) basmati rice
¾pt (450ml) water
2tbsp oil
1tbsp channa dal (split yellow peas)
2tsp mustard seeds
¼tsp fenugreek seeds
2tbsp unsalted peanuts
pinch of asafetida
½tsp turmeric
4fl oz (100ml) tamarind juice
1½tsp salt

Wash the rice in several changes of water and soak for 20 minutes. Drain. Place the rice and measured amount of water in a saucepan and bring to a boil over a high heat. Lower the heat to very low, cover and cook for about 20 minutes until all the water has evaporated and the rice is cooked. Remove from the heat and fluff with a fork.

Heat 1 tbsp of the oil in a large skillet and fry the channa dal and 1 tsp of the mustard seeds until the dal turns golden. Add the cooked rice, mix well and remove from the fire.

Dry roast the fenugreek seeds and grind to a fine powder. Dry roast the peanuts and put aside.

In a large saucepan, heat the remaining oil, add the mustard seeds, peanuts, asafetida and turmeric and fry for a few seconds, taking care that the spices do not burn. Add the tamarind juice and salt and cook until the mixture becomes thick. Add the powdered fenugreek, and stir to mix.

Add the rice and mix gently, cover and cook on a very low heat for 5 minutes. Serve hot or cold.

CREAMED RICE

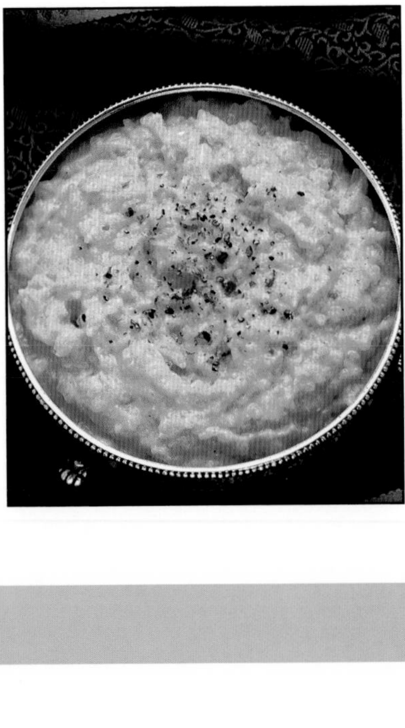

BROWN RICE

SERVES 4–6

12oz (350g) basmati rice
1tsp sugar
1½pt (900ml) cold water
½tsp cumin seeds
1inch (2.5cm) piece of stick cinnamon

Wash the rice in several changes of water. Drain. Brown the sugar in a small pan over a medium heat. When dark brown, add ½ pt (300 ml) of the water, cumin and cinnamon and cook for 5 minutes.

Place the cleaned rice in a large saucepan, add the browned water and the remaining water and bring to a boil over a high heat. Lower the heat to very low, cover tightly and cook for about 20 minutes until all the water has evaporated. Fluff the rice gently with a fork.

SAFFRON RICE

SERVES 4–6

12oz (350g) basmati rice
½tsp saffron
about 1½pt (900ml) boiling water
5tbsp butter or ghee
2–3 cardamom pods
4tbsp almonds, slivered
5tbsp sugar
1tbsp pistachio nuts, chopped

Wash the rice in several changes of water and soak in water for 15 minutes. Place the rice in a sieve to drain thoroughly.

Soak the saffron in 2 tbsp of boiling water for 15 minutes.

Heat the butter or ghee in a large saucepan over a medium high heat; add the cardamom and let it sizzle for 3–4 seconds. Add the drained rice and almonds and, stirring constantly, fry for 3–4 minutes until lightly golden.

Add the boiling water, saffron and sugar and stir to mix. Lower the heat to very low, cover and cook for about 20 minutes until all the water has been absorbed and the rice is tender. Fluff with a fork, garnish with pistachio nuts and serve.

LIME RICE

SERVES 4–6

8oz (225g) rice
1tbsp channa dal (split yellow peas)
1tbsp urid dal (black gram)
¾pt (450ml) water
¼tsp turmeric
½tsp fenugreek seeds
4tsp asafetida
2tbsp oil
1tbsp unsalted cashew nuts
¾tsp mustard seeds

2 green chillies, chopped
6–8 curry leaves
1tsp salt
juice of 1 lime

Wash the rice in several changes of water and soak in plenty of water for 30 minutes. Drain.

Wash the channa and urid dals and soak in plenty of water for 30 minutes. Drain. Place the rice and the measured amount of water in a saucepan with the turmeric and bring to a boil. Lower the heat to very low, cover and cook for about 20 minutes until the rice is cooked.

Dry roast the fenugreek and asafetida and grind to a fine powder. Heat the oil in a large frying pan, add the cashew nuts, mustard, chillies, curry leaves and the drained dals; fry until the dals are golden in colour. Add the cooked rice, salt and lime juice and, stirring gently, mix well. Sprinkle with ground spices.

PEA PILAF

SERVES 4–6

12oz (350g) basmati rice
2 large onions
6tbsp oil
1tbsp unsalted cashew nuts
3 cardamom pods
4 peppercorns
2 cloves
½tsp cumin seeds
½inch (1.25cm) fresh root ginger, grated
1 clove garlic, crushed
4oz (100g) peas (fresh or frozen)
1pt (600ml) water
1tsp salt

Wash the rice in several changes of water and leave to soak in plenty of water for 30 minutes. Drain and leave the rice in a sieve for 30 minutes.

Peel the onions and finely slice 1½ onions and chop the remaining half. Heat the oil, and fry the sliced onions until brown and crisp. Drain on absorbent kitchen paper and put aside. In the remaining oil, fry the cashew nuts until golden-brown. Drain on absorbent kitchen paper and put aside. Add the cardamom, peppercorns, cloves and cumin, and let them sizzle for 5–6 seconds.

Add the ginger, garlic and chopped onion and stir-fry until the onions are soft and transparent. Add the peas and rice and sauté for 5 minutes. Add the water and salt and bring to a boil. Lower the heat to very low, cover and cook for 20 minutes until the water has been absorbed.

Fluff the rice gently with a fork and serve on a platter garnished with the fried onions and cashew nuts.

SAFFRON RICE

◆ RICE DISHES ◆

HYDERABADI BIRIYANI

SERVES 4–6

2lb (900g) lamb, cut into large pieces
2lb (900g) basmati rice
1inch (2.5cm) fresh root ginger
4 cloves garlic
1oz (25g) coriander leaves
1tbsp mint leaves
4 green chillies
8 cloves
2×1inch (2.5cm) pieces of cinnamon stick
1tsp black cumin seeds
¼ nutmeg
6 cardamom pods, skinned
6–8tbsp milk
1tsp saffron
5oz (125g) butter or ghee
3 large onions, halved and finely sliced
2tsp chilli powder
juice of 2 lemons
¾pt (450ml) yoghurt
3tsp salt
5pt (2.5lt) water
3 hard-boiled eggs (optional) cut into quarters

Wash the meat and leave in a colander to allow all the water to drain out.

Wash the rice in several changes of water. Soak for 15 minutes in water and then leave in a sieve to drain.

Blend the ginger, garlic, coriander, mint and green chillies to a fine paste. Grind together 4 cloves, 1 piece of stick cinnamon, ½ tsp black cumin seeds, nutmeg and 3 cardamom pods to a fine powder. Warm 2 tbsp of milk and soak the saffron in it. Put aside.

Heat the butter or ghee and fry the onions until golden-brown. Drain and put aside.

Place the meat in a large bowl, add the coriander paste and, with the back of a wooden spoon, beat the meat for 15–20 minutes, turning the meat frequently. To the meat add the chilli powder, lemon juice, yoghurt, 2 tsp of salt, the powdered spices and half the fried onions, mix and put aside for 3–4 hours.

In a saucepan, melt the butter or ghee again over a medium high heat and add the meat and the marinade. When it starts to boil, lower the heat, cover and, stirring occasionally, cook for about 1 hour until the meat is tender and the gravy thickened. While the meat is being cooked, bring the water to a boil in a large saucepan. Add the remaining spices and 1 tsp of salt. When the water is boiling rapidly, add the drained rice, bring it back to a boil and boil the rice for 3–4 minutes until the rice is nearly cooked. Remove and drain the rice.

Lightly grease a large casserole dish big enough to hold all the rice and meat, and place half the cooked rice evenly at the bottom. Put the meat and gravy evenly on the rice and the remaining rice on top.

Sprinke the saffron milk, the remaining milk and the rest of the fried onions on top. Cover tightly with tin foil and then the lid and place in a preheated oven at 375°F/190°C/Gas Mark 5 for about 45 minutes until the rice is cooked.

HYDERABADI BIRIYANI

VEGETABLE PILAF

SERVES 4–6

12oz (350g) basmati rice
5tbsp butter or ghee
2tbsp unsalted cashew nuts
1 medium onion, finely chopped
½inch (1.25cm) fresh root ginger, cut into very thin strips
4oz (100g) green beans, cut into 1½inch (4cm) lengths
2 small carrots, scraped and diced
4oz (100g) peas
1 small red pepper, seeded and thinly sliced
1¾pt (1lt) water
1½tsp salt
1tbsp coriander leaves

Wash the rice in several changes of water and leave in a sieve to drain thoroughly.

Heat the butter or ghee in a large saucepan and fry the cashew nuts until golden. Drain and put aside. In the remaining ghee, add the onion and ginger and fry until the onion is soft and transparent. Add the rice and stir-fry for 1–2 minutes. Add all the vegetables and mix with the onion and rice.

Add the water and salt and bring to a boil. Give it a good stir, lower the heat to very low, cover and cook for about 20 minutes until the rice and vegetables are tender and all the water is absorbed. Garnish with the fried cashew nuts and coriander leaves.

SAVOURY PUFFED RICE

SERVES 4–6

4oz (100g) puffed rice
1 medium potato, boiled and diced into ¼inch (0.5cm) cubes
1 small onion, finely chopped
2tbsp coriander leaves, chopped
½tsp salt

Tamarind chutney
about 4fl oz (100ml) thick tamarind juice
½tsp salt
½tsp chilli powder
1½tsp sugar

Green chutney
4 sprigs of coriander, washed
2 green chillies
½tsp salt
2–3tbsp lemon juice
a little water

Mix together the puffed rice, potato, onion, coriander leaves and salt and put aside. Make the tamarind chutney by mixing together the tamarind juice, salt, chilli powder and sugar; put aside. Make the green chutney by first chopping the coriander leaves and throwing away the lower stalks and roots.

Blend together the coriander leaves, green chillies, salt and lemon juice until smooth. Add a little water if necessary. This sauce should not be too thick.

SAVOURY PUFFED RICE

When ready to serve, add the chutneys to the puffed rice mixture (the amount can vary to suit individual taste). Serve immediately as a snack.

◆ RICE DISHES ◆

RICE AND LENTIL PANCAKE WITH A POTATO STUFFING

SERVES 4–6

9oz (250g) rice, washed
3oz (75g) urid dal (black gram), washed
1tsp salt
about 6oz (175ml) water
a little oil for frying

Filling
4tbsp oil
½tsp mustard seeds
1tbsp channa dal (split yellow peas)
⅓tsp asafetida
2tbsp cashew nuts, chopped (optional)
8–10 curry leaves
¾ inch (2.5cm) fresh root ginger, grated
3–4 green chillies, chopped
1 large onion, finely sliced
1lb (450g) potatoes, peeled and diced into ¼inch (2.5cm) cubes and then boiled
½tsp turmeric
1tsp salt
4fl oz (100ml) water

Soak the rice and urid dal separately in plenty of water and put aside for 6–8 hours. Drain. In a blender or food processor, blend the rice and dal separately to a fine paste. During the blending add a little water, if required. Mix the two pastes together, add the salt and beat for 1–2 minutes. Cover and keep aside on a warm plate overnight to let it ferment.

Next morning, give the mixture a good stir and add enough water to give a thin pouring consistency.

To make the filling, heat 4 tbsp of oil in a saucepan over a medium high heat, add the mustard seeds, channa dal, asafetida, cashew nuts, curry leaves, ginger and green chillies and let them sizzle for 6–8 seconds. Add the onion and fry until transparent. Add the potatoes, turmeric and salt and mix with the other spices. Add the water, bring to a boil, cover and simmer over a medium heat for about 10 minutes until well mixed and all the water has evaporated. Put aside.

To make the pancakes, heat a non-stick frying pan over a medium heat and brush with a little oil. Pour in a ladleful of the mixture and spread it like a pancake. Put a little more oil around the edges and a little on top. Cook for a couple of minutes until lightly golden. Turn the pancake and cook for a further couple of minutes.

Put on a plate, place a heaped tablespoon of the hot filling on one end of the pancake, fold in half and serve hot with coconut chutney and (It can also be folded to make a triangle.)

LEMON RICE

SPICED RICE

SERVES 4–6

12oz (350g) basmati rice
3tsp coriander seeds
2tsp cumin seeds
½inch (1.25cm) piece of stick cinnamon
3 cardamom pods, shelled
2 cloves
3tbsp oil
¾tsp mustard seeds
good pinch of asafetida
½tsp turmeric
1tsp chilli powder
1 small cauliflower, broken into large florets
1¼pt (650ml) water
1½tsp salt
3tbsp coriander leaves, chopped
3tbsp coconut, grated

Wash the rice in several changes of water and soak for 1 hour in plenty of water. Drain the rice and leave in a sieve for about 20 minutes. While the rice is soaking, dry roast the coriander, cumin, cinnamon, cardamom and cloves over a medium heat, until they are a few shades darker and emit a rich aroma. Grind the spices to a fine powder and put aside.

In a large saucepan, heat the oil, add the mustard seeds and let them sizzle for 5–6 seconds. Add the asafetida, turmeric, chilli powder and cauliflower and, taking care not to burn the spices, stir-fry for 1–2 minutes. Add the rice and sauté for a few minutes, making sure that the rice does not become brown.

Add the water, bring it to the boil, stir well and lower the heat to very low, cover and cook for 8 minutes. Add the powdered spices and salt, mix, cover again and cook for a further 10 minutes until all the water is absorbed. Fluff gently with a fork.

◆ RICE DISHES ◆

Garnish with the coriander leaves and coconut. Serve hot with butter or ghee.

RICE AND LENTIL CURRY

SERVES 4–6

8oz (225g) basmati rice, washed and drained
2oz (50g) moong dal (split yellow lentils) washed and drained
1¼pt (750ml) water
1½tbsp butter or ghee

Mix the rice and dal and soak in plenty of water for 1 hour. Drain. Add the rice and dal mixture to the measured water in a large saucepan and bring it to the boil over a high heat. Turn heat down to very low, cover and cook for about 20 minutes until all the water has been absorbed. Remove from heat.

In a small pan heat the butter or ghee until very hot and pour it over the cooked rice and dal. Mix. Serve hot.

MUSHROOM PILAF

SERVES 4–6

2tbsp oil
2 bay leaves
2inch (5cm) piece of cinnamon stick
4 cardamom pods
1 large onion, finely chopped
6oz (175g) mushrooms, sliced
12oz (325g) basmati rice, washed and drained
1tsp salt
1½pt (900ml) water

Heat oil in a large saucepan over medium high heat. Add the bay leaves, cinnamon and cardamoms and let them sizzle for a few seconds. Add the onion and fry until soft. Add the mushrooms and fry for about 5 minutes until all the moisture has been absorbed. Add the rice and salt and stir-fry for 2–3 minutes. Add the water and bring to the boil.

Cover tightly, lower heat to very low and cook for about 20 minutes until all the water has been absorbed. Fluff the pilaf with a fork and serve.

TOMATO RICE

SERVES 4

2tbsp oil
½tsp mustard seeds
2tbsp channa dal (split yellow peas), soaked in water for 20 minutes, then drained
6 curry leaves
1 red chilli pepper, cut into pieces
1 onion, chopped
1tbsp fresh root ginger, finely grated
2 cloves garlic, sliced
1 green chilli pepper, chopped
10oz (275g) tomatoes, peeled and chopped
1tsp sugar
10oz (275g) cooked basmati rice
1tsp butter or ghee
salt

Heat the oil in a pan, add the mustard seeds, dal, curry leaves and red chilli and fry until all the mustard seeds have popped and the dal is golden-brown. Add the onion, ginger, garlic and green chilli and fry for 3–5 minutes, stirring.

Add the tomato and sugar and cook, mashing the tomato with the back of a wooden spoon to make a thick paste. Stir in the rice and butter or ghee and heat through, stirring for about 5 minutes. Add extra salt to taste.

LEMON RICE

SERVES 4

10oz (275g) cooked basmati rice
2tbsp lemon juice
½tsp asafetida
½tsp turmeric
salt
2tbsp oil
½tsp mustard seeds
1tsp urid dal (black gram)
6 curry leaves
2tbsp chana dal (split yellow peas), soaked in water for 20 minutes, then drained
1tbsp fresh root ginger, finely grated
1 green chilli pepper, chopped

Mix the rice with the lemon juice, asafetida, turmeric and salt to taste.

Heat the oil in a pan, add the mustard seeds, dal, curry leaves and dal and fry until all the mustard seeds have popped. Add the ginger, green chilli and rice and heat through, stirring, for about 5 minutes, until hot. Add extra salt to taste.

TOMATO RICE

◆ RICE DISHES ◆

POTATO PILAF

SERVES 4–6

4oz (100g) creamed coconut
1pt (600ml) hot water
1½oz (40g) coriander leaves
1tbsp shredded coconut
2 green chillies
2tbsp lemon juice
½tsp sugar
1½tsp salt
½tsp garam masala
¼tsp ground turmeric
10–12 small new potatoes, washed and peeled
3tbsp oil
2 cloves
1 medium onion, finely sliced
1 clove garlic, crushed
10oz (275g) basmati rice, washed and drained

Make the coconut milk by blending together the creamed coconut and hot water. Put aside.

Chop the coriander leaves and throw away the lower stalks and roots. Wash them thoroughly. Blend together the coriander leaves, shredded coconut, chillies, lemon juice, sugar, ½ tsp of salt, garam masala and turmeric until you have a fine paste.

Parboil the potatoes. Drain and cool. Take a potato and make 2 cuts like a cross about three-quarters of the way down the length. Take care not to cut right through the potato. Cut all the potatoes in this way. Fill each potato with a little of the coriander paste. If you have any paste left, rub it on to the potatoes.

Heat the oil over a medium high heat in a large saucepan. Add the cloves, and, after 3–4 seconds, add the onion and garlic and fry until the onion is lightly golden. Add the rice and sauté for 2–3 minutes, stirring constantly.

Add the coconut milk and 1 tsp of salt and bring to a boil. Add the potatoes, and when it comes to the boil again, lower the heat to very low, cover and cook for about 20 minutes until all the water has been absorbed. Fluff the rice with a fork before serving.

FRIED RICE

SERVES 4–6

12oz (350g) basmati rice, cooked and cooled
3tbsp butter or ghee
2 bay leaves
2inch (5cm) piece of stick cinnamon
4 cardamom pods
3 large onions, finely sliced
3 green chillies, cut lengthwise
1tsp salt
½tsp sugar
2tbsp raisins (optional)

Heat the butter or ghee in a large frying pan over a medium high heat. Add the bay leaves, cinnamon and cardamom and let them sizzle for a few seconds. Add the onions and chillies and fry until the onions are golden-brown. Add the rice, sugar and raisins and continue frying until the rice is thoroughly heated. This dish tastes even better if you use rice that was cooked a day earlier.

PILAF WITH COCONUT AND MILK

SERVES 4–6

12oz (325g) basmati rice, rinsed and drained
2tbsp desiccated coconut
2–3 green chillies
1tsp salt
½tsp sugar
2tbsp raisins
1tbsp pistachio nuts, skinned and cut into thin strips
2 bay leaves
2inch (5cm) piece of cinnamon stick
4 cardamom pods
3tbsp butter or ghee
1pt (600ml) milk
½pt (300ml) water

Mix the rice with the coconut, chillies, salt, sugar, raisins, pistachios, bay leaves, cinnamon and cardamoms.

Heat the butter or ghee in a large saucepan over medium heat. Add the rice mixture and sauté for 5 minutes, stirring constantly. Add the milk and water, increase the heat to high and bring it to the boil. Stir.

Lower heat to very low, cover and cook for about 20 minutes until all the liquid has evaporated. Fluff the pilaf with a fork and serve hot.

RICE WITH YOGHURT

SERVES 4

8oz (225g) yoghurt
10oz (275g) cooked basmati rice
2tbsp oil
2tsp urid dal (black gram)
1tsp mustard seeds
4–6 curry leaves
2 red or green chilli peppers, chopped
salt

Mix the yoghurt into the rice, without mashing the grains. Heat the oil in a pan, add the lentils and fry until light brown. Add the mustard seeds, curry leaves and chilli and fry until all the seeds have popped.

Stir contents of the pan into the rice, mix, and add salt to taste.

◆ ◆ ◆

FRIED EGG CURRY

SERVES 4–6

3 medium onions
5 cloves garlic
1 inch (2.5cm) fresh root ginger
1tbsp white vinegar
8tbsp mustard oil
8 eggs
3 bay leaves
2 inch (5cm) piece of stick cinnamon
6 cardamom pods
2–3 green chilli powder
1½tsp turmeric
½tsp chilli powder
1tsp salt
¼tsp sugar

Blend the onions, garlic, ginger and vinegar in a blender until you have a fine paste.

Heat the oil in a large frying pan over a medium heat, fry the eggs one at a time and set aside.

To the remaining oil add the bay leaves, cinnamon and cardamom pods and let them sizzle for a few seconds. Add the blended paste and the green chillies and fry for 6–8 minutes, stirring constantly. Add the turmeric, chilli powder, salt and sugar and continue frying for another minute. Carefully add the eggs and, stirring gently, cover them with some of the spices. Cover and cook for 5 minutes. Serve hot.

HARD-BOILED EGGS WRAPPED IN SPICY MEAT

SERVES 4–6

¾lb (350g) finely minced lamb
2tbsp coriander leaves, finely chopped
1tsp salt
2–3 green chillies, finely chopped
3 cloves garlic, crushed
3tbsp onions, finely chopped
3tbsp lemon juice
1 egg, beaten
4 hard-boiled eggs
oil for deep-frying

Mix the minced meat well with the coriander, salt, chillies, garlic, onion, lemon juice and the beaten egg. Divide into 4 portions. Take 1 portion and wrap it around a hard-boiled egg, making sure no holes appear.

Deep-fry over a medium high heat for about 4-5 minutes until nicely browned. Cut in half lengthwise to serve.

SPICED SCRAMBLED EGG

SERVES 2

2 eggs
1 small onion, finely chopped
1 green chilli pepper, finely chopped
2 curry leaves
1tbsp fresh root ginger, finely grated
2tbsp oil
salt

Beat the eggs well. Stir together the onion, chilli, curry leaves and ginger. Heat the oil in a pan, add the onion mixture and fry for 3 minutes, stirring.

Add the egg and cook gently, stirring, for about 2 minutes, until scrambled. (The egg will continue cooking after you take it from the heat, so be careful not to overcook.) Add salt to taste.

HARD-BOILED EGGS WRAPPED IN SPICY MEAT

◆ EGGS, LEGUMES AND VEGETABLES ◆

FISH WITH EGGS

SERVES 4–6

2–3 medium tomatoes
1½lb (700g) white fish
8tbsp oil
3 medium onions, finely chopped
3 cloves garlic, crushed
1½tsp chilli powder
1½tsp ground cumin
1½tsp salt
6 eggs
3fl oz (75ml) vinegar
1tbsp sugar
2oz (50g) coriander leaves, chopped
3–4 green chillies, chopped

Skin the tomatoes and purée them in a food processor or blender.

Wash the fish and cut into 8–10 pieces. Pat dry with absorbent kitchen paper.

Heat the oil in a large skillet and fry the onions and garlic until the onions are golden. Add the chilli powder, cumin and salt and fry with the onions for about 1 minute. Add the pieces of fish and the tomato purée. Stir gently. When it starts to boil, lower the heat, cover and cook for about 10–12 minutes until the fish is tender. Carefully remove the pieces of fish and put aside. Let the sauce cool down completely.

Beat the eggs with the vinegar and sugar and pour into the cold sauce. Heat the sauce again over a very gentle heat, stirring constantly, until the sauce is thickened. Add the pieces of fish and cook for 1–2 minutes more. Remove from the heat and garnish with the coriander leaves and green chillies. Serve immediately.

EGGS ON OKRA

SERVES 4–6

1lb (450g) okra
4tbsp oil
2 medium onions, finely sliced
2 green chillies, chopped
1tsp salt
4 eggs

DEVILLED EGGS

Wash the okra and dry thoroughly. Cut off the stalk end and slice the okra into 1 inch (2.5cm) pieces. Heat the oil in a frying pan and add the onions, okra, chillies and salt and fry for about 10 minutes until the okra is tender.

Place in an ovenproof dish. Break the eggs on top of the okra so that it is completely covered and bake in a preheated oven at 350°F/180°C/Gas Mark 4 for about 15 minutes until the eggs are set.

OMELETTE CURRY

SERVES 4–6

6 eggs
½tsp salt
6tbsp oil
1 large potato, cut into 1inch (2.5cm) pieces
1tsp turmeric
½tsp chilli powder
¾tsp salt
12fl oz (350ml) water

Whisk the eggs and the salt together. Heat 1tbsp of the oil in a large frying pan and make an omelette with half the beaten eggs. Set aside and cut into 4 pieces. Similarly, make another omelette.

Heat the rest of the oil and fry the potatoes until lightly browned. Set aside. Add the onion mixture and fry for 2–3 minutes. Add the turmeric, chilli and salt, and stir well with the onion mixture.

Add the water and bring it to the boil. Put in the potatoes, cover, lower heat and simmer for 10 minutes. Place the pieces of omelette in the pan, cover again and cook until the potatoes are tender.

SCRAMBLED EGGS WITH MUSHROOMS AND SHRIMP

SERVES 2

2tbsp oil
1 small onion, finely chopped
3oz (75g) sliced mushrooms

SCRAMBLED EGGS WITH MUSHROOMS AND SHRIMPS

3oz (75g) shelled shrimp
1tbsp fresh root ginger, finely grated
1 green chilli pepper, finely chopped
3oz (75g) tomatoes, peeled and chopped
2 curry leaves
3 eggs, beaten
salt

Heat the oil in a pan, add the onion and fry until golden. Add the mushrooms, shrimp, ginger, green chilli, tomato and curry leaves and fry, stirring, for 5 minutes.

Add the egg with ½ tsp of salt and cook gently, stirring, for about 3 minutes to scramble. (The egg will continue to cook after you take it from the heat, so be careful not to overcook.)

DEVILLED EGGS

SERVES 4–6

4 hard-boiled eggs, cut in half lengthwise
1½tbsp onions, finely chopped
2 green chillies, finely chopped
1tbsp coriander leaves, chopped
½tsp salt
2tbsp mashed potatoes
oil for deep-frying
1tbsp plain flour
2fl oz (50ml) water

Remove the yolks and mix with the onions, chillies, coriander leaves, salt and mashed potatoes. Put the mixture back into the egg whites. Chill for 30 minutes.

Heat the oil in a karai or saucepan over high heat. While the oil is heating up make a batter with the flour and water. Be careful not to allow the oil to catch fire. Dip eggs into the batter and gently put into the hot oil. Fry until golden, turning once.

◆ EGGS, LEGUMES AND VEGETABLES ◆

WHOLE EGGS FRIED WITH SPICE

SERVES 4–6

6 hard-boiled eggs
2tbsp oil
2tsp ground coriander
1tsp chilli powder
¼tsp ground pepper
salt
2tbsp lemon juice

Make several cuts into the eggs with the point of a sharp knife to allow the spices to enter.

Heat the oil in a pan, add the coriander, chilli powder, pepper and salt and fry for about 3 minutes. Add the lemon juice and stir to make a paste.

Add the eggs to the pan and turn in the paste to coat. Continue cooking, turning occasionally, for 4–5 minutes.

YELLOW RICE WITH HARD-BOILED EGGS

SERVES 4–6

10oz (300g) basmati rice
4oz (100g) butter or ghee
1 small onion, chopped
2 cloves garlic, chopped
1 green chilli pepper, chopped
seeds from 2 cardamom pods
2 bay leaves
3 cloves
salt
½tsp turmeric
1 chicken bouillon cube, optional
10–15 cashew nuts
2oz (50g) butter or ghee
2tbsp sultanas
4–6 hard-boiled eggs
1tsp lemon juice

Wash the rice thoroughly in 2 or 3 changes of water, then soak for 10–15 minutes.

Heat the butter or ghee in a saucepan, add the onion, garlic, green chilli, cardamom pods, bay leaves and cloves, and fry until the onion is golden.

Drain the rice, pour it into the saucepan, stir and fry for 10 minutes, until it turns translucent. Pour in 1 pt (500 ml) of boiling water, add ½ tsp of salt, the turmeric and the bouillon cube, and simmer over low heat for 10 minutes. Turn off heat and let stand, covered, for 5 minutes until all the moisture has been absorbed and the grains of rice are separate and tender.

Fry the cashew nuts for a couple of minutes in the butter or ghee, adding the sultanas for the last few seconds. Cut the eggs in half, sprinkle with lemon juice and rub with salt.

Spread the rice in a serving dish,

WHOLE EGGS FRIED WITH SPICE

sprinkle with salt to taste and arrange the eggs, cashew nuts and sultanas on top.

SCRAMBLED EGGS WITH ONION

SERVES 2

1 small onion, finely chopped
1tsp chilli powder
2 curry leaves
2 eggs, beaten
salt
1–2tbsp oil

Pound, grind, or blend in a blender or food processor the onion, chilli powder and curry leaves, then mix with the beaten egg and ½ tsp salt.

Heat the oil in a pan, add the eggs and cook gently, stirring, until scrambled, about 2 minutes. (The eggs will continue to cook after you have removed them from the heat, so be careful not to overcook.)

YELLOW RICE WITH HARD-BOILED EGGS

SPLIT PEA AND YAM CURRY

SERVES 4

8oz (225g) channa dal (yellow split peas)
½tsp turmeric
½tsp chilli powder
1lb (450g) yams, peeled and cubed
8oz (225g) white pumpkin or green plantain, peeled and cubed
4oz (100g) coconut grated fresh or dried unsweetened
1tsp cumin seeds
1tsp mustard seeds
2–3tbsp oil
1 red chilli pepper, cut into pieces
6–8 curry leaves
salt

Soak the split peas in water with the turmeric and chilli powder for about 2 hours. Drain and cook in about 2 pt (1.2 lt) of water for 15–20 minutes, until the peas can be crushed with the back of a wooden spoon and most of the water has evaporated.

Cook the yam and pumpkin or plantain in water to cover for about 15 minutes, until tender but not soft. Add the cooked peas to the vegetables over low heat, stirring occasionally. Blend three-quarters of the coconut with the cumin seeds in a blender or food processor for a few seconds. Add to the curry.

Fry the mustard seeds in the oil until they have all popped. Add the red chilli, curry leaves and remaining coconut. Fry for a further 3–4 minutes, stirring, then add to the curry.

Take the curry off the heat, cover and let stand for 3–4 minutes, then add salt to taste.

◆ EGGS, LEGUMES AND VEGETABLES ◆

CURRIED EGGS

SERVES 4–6

3–4tbsp oil
2 small onions, grated
1tbsp fresh root ginger, finely grated
2 cloves garlic, crushed
1 inch (2.5cm) piece of cinnamon stick
1 bay leaf
½tsp chilli powder
2tbsp ground coriander
2 cashew nuts, ground
8oz (225g) tomatoes, peeled and chopped
salt
6 hard-boiled eggs
½tsp garam masala
leaves from 1 sprig of coriander
1tsp lemon juice
4 peppercorns, crushed

Heat the oil in a pan, add the onion, ginger, garlic, cinnamon and bay leaf and fry until the onion is golden. Add the chilli powder, ground coriander, cashews and tomato and continue to cook, mashing the tomato with the back of a wooden spoon to make a thick paste. Pour in ¼ pt (150 ml) water with ½ tsp of salt, bring to the boil and add the eggs. Cook over low heat for 5 minutes.

Take the curry off the heat and sprinkle on the garam masala, coriander leaves, lemon juice and pepper. Add extra salt to taste.

DAL AND MUSHROOM CURRY

SERVES 4

8oz (225g) masoor dal (red split lentils)
1½tsp turmeric
8oz (225g) button mushrooms, halved
1tbsp fresh root ginger, finely grated
1 green chilli pepper, sliced
8oz (225g) onion, chopped
1tbsp sambar powder
2tbsp coconut, grated fresh or dried unsweetened
8oz (225g) tomatoes, peeled and chopped
2 tbsp oil
1tsp mustard seeds
4–6 curry leaves
salt

Pick over the dal and wash it thoroughly. Cook in about 1½ pt (900 ml) of water with the turmeric, for 10–15 minutes, until it can be crushed with the back of a wooden spoon. Add the mushrooms, ginger, chilli and half of the onion, and cook for 10 minutes longer.

Meanwhile, blend the sambar powder with the coconut in a blender or food processor, add to the curry with the tomato and cook for a further 6–8 minutes, until the sauce is thick and smooth.

Heat the oil in a pan, add the

DAL AND MUSHROOM CURRY

mustard seeds and let them sizzle for a few seconds until they have all popped. Add the curry leaves and remaining onion and fry until the onion is golden. Add to the curry with salt to taste.

CURRIED PUMPKIN AND BLACK-EYED BEANS

SERVES 4

8oz (225g) dried black-eyed beans, soaked overnight
8oz (225g) unripe red pumpkin, peeled and thinly sliced
2 green chilli pepper, cut into 4 pieces
2tbsp coconut oil
4 curry leaves
salt

Drain the beans and cook in fresh water for about 10 minutes, until barely tender. Add the pumpkin and green chilli and cook for a further 5–7 minutes, until tender.

Mix the coconut oil with 1 tbsp of water to release its aroma, then add to the curry with the curry leaves and salt to taste.

BLACK-EYED BEANS WITH ONIONS

SERVES 4–6

7oz (200g) black-eyed beans, washed
2 pt (1.2lt) water
2tbsp oil
1 large onion, finely chopped
2 cloves garlic, crushed
¼inch (0.5cm) fresh root ginger, grated
1–2 green chillies, finely chopped
½tsp salt
1tsp molasses

Soak the beans in the water overnight. Boil the beans in the water and then cover and simmer for 1 hour until tender. Drain.

Heat the oil in a large saucepan and fry the onion, garlic, ginger and chilli until the onions are soft. Add the beans, salt and molasses and cook until all the moisture is absorbed, for about 15 minutes.

SPICED CHICK PEAS

SERVES 4

8oz (225g) chick peas
4oz (100g) butter or ghee
1 onion, finely chopped
2 cloves garlic, finely chopped
1tbsp fresh root ginger, finely grated
8oz (225g) tomatoes, peeled and chopped
½tsp ground coriander
½tsp chilli powder
1tbsp (anchur) mango powder
½tsp ground cumin
1tsp garam masala
leaves from 1 sprig of coriander
salt

Pick over the chick peas, wash thoroughly and soak in water for at least 10 hours. Drain and cook in fresh water for 1–1½ hours, depending on the age of the chick peas, until tender but not soft.

Heat the butter or ghee in a pan, add the onion, garlic and ginger and fry until the onion is golden. Add the tomato, ground coriander, chilli, anchur, cumin, garam masala and half of the coriander leaves. Cook, stirring briskly to mash the tomato with the back of the spoon into a paste.

Drain the chick peas, reserving the cooking liquor, and add to the pan with 2 tbsp of the liquor. Cover and cook over low heat, stirring occasionally, for about 10 minutes, until the chick peas have absorbed the flavours of the spices. Sprinkle on the remaining coriander leaves and add salt to taste.

CURRIED PUMPKIN AND BLACK-EYED BEANS

CHICK PEAS WITH MANGO AND COCONUT

SERVES 2

4oz (100g) chick peas
flesh of ½ coconut
8oz (225g) green mango, peeled
2tbsp butter or ghee
½tsp ground cumin
salt

Pick over the chick peas, wash thoroughly and soak in water for at least 10 hours. Drain. Cook in fresh water for 1–1½ hours, depending on the age of the chick peas, until tender but not soft.

Chop the coconut flesh and mango into small even pieces and mix with the chick peas. Heat through in a frying pan for 3–4 minutes, stirring briskly.

In a separate pan, heat the butter or ghee and fry the cumin for a few seconds until the fragrance emerges. Add to the vegetables. Add salt to taste.

CHICK PEAS WITH MANGO AND COCONUT

LENTIL CURRY

SERVES 4–6

7oz (200g) moong dal (split yellow lentils)
2½pt (1.4lt) water
¼tsp turmeric
1tsp ground cumin
2 tomatoes, chopped
1tsp salt
1tbsp butter or ghee
¾tsp whole cumin seeds
2 dried red chillies
2 bay leaves
1inch (2.5cm) piece of stick cinnamon
4 cardamom pods

Heat a saucepan and dry roast the lentils, stirring constantly until all the lentils turn light brown. Wash the lentils in several changes of water and bring to the boil in the measured amount of water in a large saucepan. Skim off any scum that forms.

Lower the heat, add the turmeric, cumin, tomatoes and salt and partially cover and simmer for about 1¼ hours until the lentils are soft.

In a small pan heat the butter or ghee over medium heat, add the cumin seeds, red chillies, bay leaves, stick cinnamon and cardamom pods and let them sizzle for a few seconds. Add the hot butter or ghee and spices to the lentils and stir. Serve with rice.

RED LENTILS WITH FRIED ONIONS

SERVES 4–6

7oz (200g) masoor dal (split red lentils), washed
1¾ pt (1 lt) water
¼tsp turmeric
1½tsp ground cumin
2 tomatoes, chopped
½tsp salt
2–3 green chillies
1tbsp coriander leaves, chopped
3tbsp butter or ghee
3 cloves garlic, crushed
1 onion, finely sliced

Bring the dal to the boil in the measured amount of water in a large saucepan. Remove any scum that forms. Add the turmeric, cumin and tomatoes, and mix with the lentils.

Lower the heat, partially cover and simmer the dal for about 40 minutes until tender. Add the salt, chillies and coriander leaves and mix with the dal. Remove from heat.

In a small pan, heat the butter or ghee. Add the garlic and onion and fry until golden-brown. Pour over the dal and serve with rice.

STUFFED VEGETABLES

SERVES 4–6

2 long aubergines
6 small potatoes, peeled
6 onions, peeled
5 green chillies
½inch (1cm) fresh root ginger
3oz (75g) gram flour
1tbsp ground coriander
½tsp ground cumin
pinch of turmeric
1tsp salt
¾tsp sugar
about 10tbsp oil
2tbsp lime juice
¾tsp mustard seeds
good pinch of asafetida
2tbsp coconut, grated
2tbsp coriander leaves, chopped

Wash the vegetables and dry thoroughly. Cut the aubergine into 1½ inch (3.5 cm) slices.

Make 2 cuts crosswise on each vegetable; cut about three-quarters of the way down the length, but do not cut right through. Grind together 2 green chillies and the ginger to a paste. Make a paste by mixing the gram flour, coriander, cumin, turmeric, salt, sugar, 2½ tbsp of oil, lime juice and the chilli and ginger paste.

Carefully open the slits in the vegetables and stuff them with this paste. If you have any paste left over after stuffing add it to the vegetables while they are being fried.

In a large, heavy-based frying pan, heat the remaining oil, add 3 green chillies, broken in half, mustard and asafetida and let them sizzle for 8–10 seconds. Add the vegetables carefully, cover and fry over a low heat, occasionally stirring gently. When one side is done, turn the vegetables over, and cover and cook the second side. Add a little more oil if necessary. Serve hot, garnished with the coconut and coriander.

LENTIL CURRY

◆ EGGS, LEGUMES AND VEGETABLES ◆

CHEESE WITH PEAS

SERVES 4–6

10oz (275g) panir (cottage cheese), drained
1 medium onion, quartered
2 cloves garlic
½inch (1cm) fresh root ginger
2 tomatoes
6tbsp oil
1tsp turmeric
½tsp chilli powder
1tsp ground coriander
1tsp salt
6oz (175g) peas (fresh or frozen)
½pt (300ml) water
1tbsp coriander leaves, chopped

Cut the panir into ½ inch (1 cm) cubes. Blend the onion, garlic, ginger and tomatoes to a purée.

Heat the oil in a karai or saucepan over a medium high heat and fry the panir cubes, a few at a time, turning frequently, until golden-brown. Remove and drain on absorbent kitchen paper and put to one side.

In the remaining oil add the blended mixture and fry for 3–4 minutes, stirring constantly, until the oil comes to the top. Add the turmeric, chilli, coriander and salt and continue to fry for another 1–2 minutes. Add the peas and stir to mix with the spices. Add the water and bring to the boil. Cover, lower the heat to medium low and simmer for 5 minutes. Add the fried panir and simmer for a further 10 minutes. Garnish with the coriander leaves.

CURRIED RED KIDNEY BEANS

SERVES 4–6

7oz (200g) red kidney beans, washed
2 pt (1.2lt) water
6tbsp oil
2 bay leaves
2inch (5cm) piece of stick cinnamon
3 cardamom pods
1 large onion, finely sliced
2 cloves garlic, crushed
½inch (1cm) fresh root ginger, grated
¾tsp turmeric
½tsp chilli powder
½tsp salt
2 tomatoes, chopped
4floz (100ml) water

Soak the beans in the water overnight. Boil the beans in the water and then cover and simmer for 1 hour until tender. Drain.

Heat the oil in a large saucepan over medium high heat and put in the bay leaves, cinnamon and cardamoms and let them sizzle for a few seconds. Add the onion, garlic and ginger and fry until the onions are golden-brown.

Add the turmeric, chilli, salt and tomatoes and fry for 1 minute. Add the drained beans and fry with the spices for 2–3 minutes. Add 4 fl oz (100 ml) of water and bring to the boil, stirring occasionally. Cover, lower heat and cook for 10–15 minutes.

LAMB AND LENTIL KEBAB

SERVES 4–6

1lb (450g) lean minced lamb
3oz (75g) channa dal (yellow split peas), washed and drained
2 large black cardamom pods, skinned
6 black peppercorns
1 medium onion, chopped
3 cloves garlic, crushed
1inch (2.5cm) fresh root ginger, grated
½tsp chilli powder
1tsp salt
about ¼pt (125ml) water
1 egg, lightly beaten

Stuffing
1 medium onion, finely chopped
3 green chillies, chopped
3tbsp coriander leaves, chopped
oil for frying

In a saucepan, place the minced lamb, channa dal, cardamom, peppercorns, onions, garlic, ginger, chilli powder, salt and water; bring to the boil over a medium high heat. Cover, lower the heat and simmer until the dal is tender and all the water absorbed. Place the mixture in a food processor or liquidizer and blend until smooth. Mix in the beaten egg, divide into small balls.

Combine the ingredients for the filling and put aside. Take a minced lamb and dal ball, and, with your thumb, make a depression in the middle to form a cup shape. Fill the centre with a little filling and re-form into a smooth ball. Flatten slightly.

Heat the oil in a large frying pan and fry the kebabs, turning once until nicely browned. Drain. Serve hot with onion salad and wedges of lemon.

STUFFED, SPICED PASTRIES

SERVES 4–6

Filling
4oz (100g) urid dal (black gram), washed
1tsp butter or ghee
1tsp salt
¼tsp fennel seeds
½inch (1cm) piece of stick cinnamon
½ cardamom pod, skinned
6 peppercorns
pinch of asafetida
pinch of ground ginger
¼tsp ground cumin
½tsp chilli powder

Dough
8oz (225g) wholewheat flour
1tsp salt
2tsp melted butter or ghee
4fl oz (100ml) hot water
oil for deep-frying

To prepare the filling, soak the dal in plenty of cold water overnight. Drain and blend to a smooth paste, adding a little water if necessry. Heat the butter or ghee in a karai, add the dal paste and salt and, stirring constantly, fry until the mixture leaves the side and forms a lump. Keep on one side. Grind together the fennel, cinnamon, black cardamom and peppercorns to a fine powder. Add this and all the remaining spices to the dal and mix.

To make the dough, mix the wholewheat flour and salt. Rub the butter or ghee into the flour/salt mixture. Add enough hot water to make a soft, pliable dough. Knead for about 10 minutes.

Divide the dough into 12–14 balls. Take one ball, flatten slightly and make a depression in the middle with your thumb, to form a cup shape. Fill the centre with the spiced dal mixture and re-form the pastry ball, making sure that the edges are well gathered. Flatten the ball slightly between the palms of your hands.

Heat the oil in a karai over a medium heat and fry the pastries a few at a time for 7–8 minutes until they are lightly browned. Serve with pickle.

LAMB AND LENTIL KEBAB

LENTIL CAKES IN YOGHURT

SERVES 4–6

8oz (225g) urid dal, (black gram) washed
3/4pt (425ml) water
3 green chillies
1/2tsp salt
1/4tsp asafetida
oil for deep-frying
1 1/2pt (900ml) yoghurt
1tsp ground roasted cumin
1/4tsp garam masala
1/2tsp chilli powder

Wash the dal and soak in the water overnight. Put the dal, green chillies, salt and asafetida and enough of the soaking liquid into a blender or food processor and blend until you have a thick paste.

In a karai or saucepan, heat the oil over a medium high heat. Put tablespoonfuls of the mixture into the hot oil and fry for 3–4 minutes until they are reddish brown, turning once. Drain them on absorbent kitchen paper.

When all the cakes have been fried, put them in a bowl of warm water for 1 minute. Squeeze out the water gently and put in a large dish. Combine the yoghurt, roasted cumin, garam masala and chilli powder and mix until smooth. Pour over the cakes. Chill and serve when needed.

◆ EGGS, LEGUMES AND VEGETABLES ◆

LENTILS WITH SPICY DUMPLINGS

SERVES 4–6

2 green chillies
½inch (2.5cm) fresh root ginger
7oz (200g) toovar dal (glossy split yellow pea), washed
1½pt (900ml) water
½tsp turmeric
1tsp salt
½tsp sugar
2–3tbsp lime juice
½tsp mustard seeds
½tsp whole cumin seeds
pinch of asafetida
good pinch of cinnamon
2tbsp coconut, grated
2tbsp coriander leaves, chopped
2tbsp butter or ghee

Dough
4oz (100g) wholewheat flour
1tbsp gram flour
½tsp chilli powder
pinch of turmeric
pinch of asafetida
½tsp salt
1tbsp oil
2fl oz (50ml) hot water
1tbsp butter or ghee

Grind the chillies and ginger together into a paste. Place the toovar dal, water, turmeric, salt, and chilli and ginger paste in a large saucepan and bring to the boil. Cover, leaving the lid slightly open, and simmer for 40–45 minutes until the dal is tender. Add the sugar and lime juice and mix thoroughly. Remove from the heat and put aside.

To make the dough, sift together the wholewheat flour, gram flour, chilli powder, turmeric, asafetida and salt. Rub in the oil. Add enough water to make a stiff dough. Knead for 8–10 minutes until soft and smooth. Divide into 4 portions. Take one, flatten slightly and roll into a round 8 inches (20 cm) across. Cut into small diamond shapes; do the same with the other portions.

In a small saucepan, heat the oil, add the mustard and cumin seeds and, as soon as the seeds start to splutter, add the asafetida and cinnamon and fry for 2–3 seconds. Add to the dal.

Add the small diamond pieces of dough to the dal, bring to the boil again and boil for 12–15 minutes, stirring occasionally. (Add a little water if the dal gets too thick.) Garnish with the coconut, coriander and butter or ghee. Serve hot.

FLAT BREAD STUFFED WITH SWEETENED LENTILS

SERVES 4–6

Filling
7oz (100g) channa dal (split yellow peas)
1¼pt (750ml) water
8oz (225g) sugar
½tsp ground cardamom
½tsp saffron

Dough
8oz (225g) wholewheat flour
1tbsp oil
about 4fl oz (100ml) hot water
butter or ghee

To make the filling, wash the channa dal in several changes of water. In a large saucepan, bring the dal and water to the boil over a medium high heat. Lower the heat, cover, leaving the lid slightly open, and simmer for about 1¼ hours until soft and thick. Remove from the heat. Add the sugar, cardamom and saffron and stir well to mix thoroughly. Return the pan to the heat and, stirring constantly, cook until thick and dry. Cool.

To make the dough, sift the flour and rub in the oil. Add enough water to make a stiff dough. Knead for about 8–10 minutes until soft and smooth.

Divide the dough into 10–12 balls. Take a ball, flatten it on a slightly floured surface and roll into a round of 3 inches (7.5 cm) across. Place 1 tbsp of the filling in the centre and fold up the edges, enclosing the filling completely. Gently roll into a round 7 inches (18 cm) across.

Place in a hot frying pan and cook over a medium heat for 1–2 minutes on each side until brown spots appear. Brush with melted butter or ghee and serve hot.

SOURED CHICK PEAS

SERVES 4–6

7oz (200g) chick peas, washed
1½ pt (900ml) water
1 teabag
3 tbsp oil
8oz (225g) potatoes, boiled and diced into ½ inch (1cm) cubes
2 medium onions, finely chopped
1 clove garlic, crushed
½inch (1cm) fresh root ginger, grated
2tsp ground coriander
2 green chillies, chopped
1½tbsp anchoor (mango powder)
1½tsp chilli powder
¾tsp salt
6fl oz (175ml) water

Soak the chick peas in the water with the teabag overnight. Discard the teabag and place the chick peas and the water in a saucepan and bring to the boil. Cover and simmer for about 1 hour until tender. Drain.

Heat the oil in a saucepan over medium heat and fry the diced potatoes until lightly browned. Set aside.

In the remaining oil fry the onions until golden-brown. Add the garlic and ginger and fry a further 2 minutes. Add the chick peas, coriander, green chillies, amchoor, chilli, salt and potatoes and stir-fry for about 2 minutes until well mixed. Add the water and cook for about 15 minutes. Serve hot.

FRIED LENTIL CAKES

SERVES 4–6

7oz (200g) channa dal (split yellow peas), washed
1–2 green chillies, chopped
1 small onion, finely chopped
pinch of asafetida
½tsp chilli powder (optional)
½tsp salt
oil for deep-frying

Soak the dal in plenty of cold water for 4–5 hours. Drain. Grind the dal coarsely in a food processor or blender. (If using a blender, add a little water only if necessary). To the ground dal, add the green chillies, onions, asafetida, chilli powder and salt and mix well. Heat oil over a medium high heat. Take a tablespoon of the mixture in your palm and flatten it slightly and deep-fry for 1–2 minutes until golden-brown. Serve hot.

LENTILS COOKED WITH FISH HEADS

SERVES 4–6

7oz (200g) moong dal (split yellow lentils)
about 2½pt (1.4lt) water
¼tsp turmeric
1tsp salt
4tbsp oil
2 fish heads, quartered
3 green chillies
2 dried red chillies
1 medium onion, chopped
¼tsp chilli powder
4 cardamom pods
2inch (5cm) piece of stick cinnamon
2 bay leaves
good pinch of sugar

Dry roast the dal, stirring constantly, until golden-brown. Wash the dal in several changes of water. Bring the dal to the boil in the measured amount of water with the turmeric and salt. Throw away the scum, lower the heat, cover, leaving the lid slightly open, and simmer for about 1 hour. Put aside.

Heat the oil in a pan, and fry the fish heads until golden-brown. Drain the fish heads and add to the dal. Put the remaining oil aside. Bring the dal to the boil again, add the green chillies, lower the heat and simmer for about 15 minutes.

In a small pan, heat the remaining oil again until very hot. Add the dried red chillies and fry for 4–5 seconds. Add the onion and stir-fry until golden-brown.

Add the chilli powder, cardamom, cinnamon, bay leaves and sugar and fry for a few seconds. Add to the dal and stir thoroughly.

SOURED CHICK PEAS

PEAS AND CAULIFLOWER WITH GINGER

SERVES 4–6

3tbsp oil
3oz (75g) fresh root ginger, cut into very thin strips
1 small cauliflower, broken into large florets
12oz (350g) peas
1tsp turmeric
1tsp salt
2tbsp coriander leaves, chopped

Heat the oil in a karai or saucepan over a medium high heat. Add the ginger and fry, stirring constantly, until slightly browned. Add the cauliflower, peas, turmeric and salt and mix with the ginger.

Lower the heat, cover and, stirring occasionally, cook for about 20–25 minutes until the vegetables are tender. Garnish with the coriander leaves.

DRY PEAS

SERVES 4–6

2tbsp oil
2inch (5cm) fresh root ginger, cut into very thin strips
1½lb (700g) peas (fresh or frozen)
1tsp salt
½tsp amchoor (mango powder)

Heat the oil in a karai or saucepan over a medium high heat and fry the ginger, stirring constantly, until slightly browned. Add the peas and salt and mix with the ginger.

Lower the heat, cover and cook for about 15 minutes until the peas are tender. Add the amchoor, mix and remove from the heat.

STUFFED BITTER GOURD

SERVES 4–6

1lb (450g) bitter gourds
2–3tsp salt
½lb (225g) potatoes, peeled and diced
6oz (175g) peas
6tbsp oil
¼inch (0.5cm) fresh root ginger, grated
2 cloves garlic, crushed
1 large onion, finely chopped
2–3 green chillies, chopped
2tbsp coconut, grated
1tbsp coriander leaves, chopped

BITTER VEGETABLE CURRY

Peel the bitter gourds and slit them lengthwise along one side. Carefully remove the seeds and pulp. Wash the gourds and sprinkle on 2 tsp of the salt and leave them in a sieve for 3–4 hours to get rid of the bitter taste.

Boil the potatoes and peas. Heat 2 tbsp of the oil in a saucepan. Add the ginger, garlic and onion and fry until the onion is lightly golden. Add the chillies, boiled vegetables and ¾ tsp of salt and stir-fry with the onion for 1 minute. Remove from the heat and mix in the coconut and coriander leaves. Cool.

Wash the bitter gourds once again and dry thoroughly. Stuff them carefully with the vegetable mixture. Secure with toothpicks.

Heat the remaining oil in a large frying pan. Add the stuffed bitter gourds carefully, and fry for 4–5 minutes, stirring occasionally. Cover, lower the heat and cook for about 15 minutes until tender.

PUMPKIN WITH SPICES

BITTER VEGETABLE CURRY

SERVES 4–6

6oz (175g) white radish, scraped
4oz (100g) potatoes, peeled
4oz (100g) beans
3oz (75g) bitter gourd
1 medium green banana, peeled
1tbsp oil
½tsp whole mustard seeds
½inch (1cm) fresh root ginger, grated
1tsp salt
¼tsp sugar
¾pt (450ml) water

Wash all the vegetables. Quarter the white radish lengthwise and then cut into ¼ inch (½ cm) slices.

Quarter the potatoes lengthwise and then cut into ½ inch (1 cm) slices. Cut the beans into 1 inch (2.5 cm) pieces. Cut the bitter gourd into ¼ inch (0.5 cm) slices.

The green banana should be halved lengthwise and then cut into ½ inch (1 cm) slices.

Heat the oil in a karai or saucepan over a medium high heat. Add the mustard seeds and, as soon as they start to splutter, add the ginger and fry for 5–6 seconds. Add all the vegetables, salt and sugar and stir-fry for 5–6 minutes. Add the water, bring it to a boil, cover, lower the heat and cook until all the vegetables are tender.

PUMPKIN WITH SPICES

SERVES 4–6

1½lb (700g) pumpkin
3tbsp oil
1tsp fenugreek seeds
½tsp turmeric
1tsp chilli powder
1tsp salt
2tsp sugar
1½tsp amchoor (mango powder)
½tsp garam masala

Peel the pumpkin and cut into 1 inch (2.5 cm) cubes. Wash and drain.

Heat the oil in a saucepan over a medium high heat. Add the fenugreek and, as soon as it starts to splutter, add the pumpkin, turmeric, chilli and salt. Stir-fry for 1 minute. Lower the heat, cover and cook for about 15–20 minutes, stirring occasionally, until the pumpkin is soft and pulpy. Add the sugar and amchoor, mix into the pumpkin and cook a further 1–2 minutes. Sprinkle on the garam masala and serve hot.

ROASTED AUBERGINE

SERVES 4–6

1 large aubergine
1 small onion, finely chopped
1–2 green chillies, finely chopped
½tsp salt
2–3tbsp mustard oil

Place the aubergine under a preheated grill for about 15 minutes, turning frequently, until the skin becomes black and the flesh soft. Peel the skin and mash the flesh. Add the rest of the ingredients to the mashed aubergine and mix thoroughly.

CABBAGE WITH COCONUT

SERVES 4–6

2tbsp oil
2 bay leaves
¾tsp whole cumin seeds
1–2 green chillies, chopped
1½lb (700g) cabbage, shredded
¾tsp salt
⅓tsp sugar
3tbsp desiccated coconut
½tsp ground cumin

Heat the oil in a karai or saucepan over a medium high heat and add the bay leaves, cumin seeds and the green chillies and let them sizzle for a few seconds.

Add the cabbage, salt and sugar and mix. Cover, lower the heat to medium and cook for about 15 minutes until half done. Add the coconut and ground cumin and fry, stirring constantly for 10–15 minutes until all the moisture has evaporated.

SPICY POTATOES

SERVES 4–6

1½lb (700g) small potatoes
2–3 medium tomatoes
4tbsp oil
1tsp cumin seeds
pinch of asafetida
¾tsp turmeric
1tsp ground coriander
¾tsp chilli powder
1tsp paprika
1tsp salt
½pt (300ml) water
½tsp garam masala
2 tbsp coriander leaves, chopped

Peel the potatoes and wash them. Place the tomatoes in boiling water for 10 seconds. Carefully peel and chop them.

Heat the oil over a medium high heat in a karai or saucepan. Add the cumin seeds and asafetida and let them sizzle for 5–6 seconds. Add the chopped tomatoes, turmeric, coriander, chilli, paprika and salt and, stirring constantly, fry for 30 seconds. (If it starts to stick to the bottom, sprinkle on a little water.)

Add the potatoes and fry for 2–3 minutes, stirring constantly. Add

POTATOES WITH GREEN PEPPERS AND COCONUT

the water and bring to the boil. Lower the heat, cover and cook for about 15 minutes until the potatoes are tender. Add the garam masala and mix. Remove and garnish with the coriander leaves.

VEGETABLE FRITTERS

SERVES 4–6

Batter
4tbsp gram flour
2tsp oil
1tsp baking powder
½tsp salt
3fl oz (75ml) water

Use any of the following vegetables
aubergines: cut into very thin rounds
onion: cut into rings
potato: cut into very thin rounds
cauliflower: cut into florets
chilli: leave whole
pumpkin: cut into thin slices
green pepper or capsicum: cut into thin strips
You can use a few slices of 3–4 different vegetables or one type only.
oil for deep-frying

Mix all the batter ingredients together to make a smooth paste. Wash the slices of vegetables and pat dry. Heat the oil in a karai or saucepan until very hot.

Dip a slice of vegetable in the batter and put into the hot oil. Place as many slices as you can into the oil. Fry until crisp and golden. Drain and serve with mint or coriander chutney.

CABBAGE WITH COCONUT

POTATOES WITH GREEN PEPPERS AND COCONUT

SERVES 4–6

3tbsp oil
½tsp whole mustard seeds
pinch of asafetida
6–8 curry leaves
1lb (450g) potatoes, boiled, peeled and diced into ½inch (1cm) cubes
1 green pepper, seeded and cut into ½inch (1cm) pieces
3tbsp desiccated coconut
½tsp salt
2 green chillies, chopped
1tbsp coriander leaves, chopped

Heat the oil in a karai or saucepan over a medium heat, add the mustard seeds, asafetida and curry leaves and let them sizzle for 3–4 seconds. Add the potatoes and green pepper and stir-fry for 5 minutes.

Add the coconut and salt and, stirring occasionally, cook for another 5–7 minutes. Before removing from the heat, sprinkle with the chillies and coriander leaves.

CABBAGE ROLLS

SERVES 4–6

8 large cabbage leaves, parboiled for 5 minutes and drained
3tbsp oil
2 medium onions, finely chopped
7oz (200g) panir (cottage cheese), drained
½tsp turmeric
½tsp chilli powder
½tsp garam masala
1–2 green chillies, chopped
½tsp salt
1tbsp coriander leaves, chopped
string for tying rolls
oil for shallow frying

Heat the 3 tbsp of oil in a frying pan over medium high heat and fry the onions until lightly browned. Add the panir, turmeric, chilli, garam masala, green chillies and salt and stir-fry for 5–6 minutes. Sprinkle with the coriander leaves and remove from the heat.

Place 2 tbsp of the mixture on a cabbage leaf and roll up, folding the 2 sides in. Tie with the string. Make all the rolls in the same way.

Heat the oil for shallow-frying over medium heat and fry the rolls, turning once, until browned.

SPINACH WITH COTTAGE CHEESE

SERVES 4–6

4tbsp oil
6oz (175g) panir (cottage cheese), drained and cut into ½inch (1cm) cubes
1 large onion, finely sliced
4 cloves garlic, crushed
½inch (1cm) fresh root ginger, grated
12oz (350g) frozen spinach, chopped
½tsp turmeric
⅓tsp chilli powder
1tsp ground coriander
¾tsp salt

Heat oil in a karai or saucepan over a medium/high heat and fry the panir until brown. Set aside.

Add the onion, garlic and ginger in the remaining oil and fry until golden. Add the spinach, turmeric, chilli, coriander and salt and fry for 2–3 minutes. Lower the heat to medium, cover and cook a further 10 minutes. Add the fried panir and, stirring constantly, cook until dry.

DRY SPICED CABBAGE

SERVES 4

1lb (450g) cabbage
8oz (225g) potatoes
2tbsp oil
½tsp ground cumin
½tsp ground coriander
½tsp turmeric
¼tsp asafetida
½tsp chilli powder
salt

Cut the cabbage into strips; peel and finely chop the potatoes.

Heat the oil and fry the cumin, coriander, turmeric, asafetida and chilli powder for 3–4 minutes, until the fragrance of the spices emerges.

Add the cabbage and potato, sprinkle on 1–2 tbsp of water and ½ tsp of salt, cover the pan tightly and cook on a low heat for 5–6 minutes, until the potato is cooked.

Take the pot off the heat and let it stand, covered, for 3–4 minutes. Add extra salt to taste.

DRY SPICED CABBAGE

STUFFED OKRA

SERVES 2

8oz (225g) okra
½tsp paprika
½tsp chilli powder
1tbsp amchoor (mango powder)
½tsp ground ginger
salt
5 tbsp oil

Wash the okra and dry on absorbent kitchen paper. Cut off the stems and cut the okra in half lengthwise.

Mix together the spices and salt. Stuff the okra with the spice mix and let them stand in a cool place for at least 30 minutes.

Heat the oil and fry the okra for about 4 minutes, turning carefully to cook on all sides.

MASHED AUBERGINE

SERVES 2

1 aubergine
2oz (50g) butter or ghee
1 onion, finely chopped
leaves from 1 sprig of coriander
1 clove garlic, chopped
1tbsp fresh root ginger, finely grated
½tsp garam masala
1 green chilli pepper, sliced
½tsp turmeric
½tsp cumin
½tsp chilli powder
8oz (225g) tomatoes, peeled and chopped
salt
1tbsp lemon juice

Put the aubergine in a roasting pan and bake in a preheated 400°F/200°C/ Gas Mark 6 oven for 40 minutes or until cooked through. Allow it to cool, then peel off the skin and immerse the vegetable in cold water.

Heat the butter or ghee in a pan and add the onion, half the coriander leaves, the garlic, ginger, garam masala, green chilli, turmeric, cumin and chilli powder. Stir and fry until the onion is golden.

Add the tomatoes, mashing well with the back of a wooden spoon to make a paste. Meanwhile, drain the aubergine and mash with a fork.

When the butter runs out of the spice paste, add the aubergine and ½ tsp of salt, stir thoroughly and cook for 3–4 minutes to heat through.

Sprinkle on the remaining coriander leaves and the lemon juice. Add more salt to taste if desired.

STUFFED OKRA

OKRA WITH MUSTARD

SERVES 4–6

1½tsp ground mustard
½tsp turmeric
¼tsp chilli powder
¾tsp salt
2tbsp hot water
1lb (450g) okra
4tbsp oil
½tsp kalonji (onion seeds)
2–3 green chillies, cut lengthwise
1½tbsp yoghurt
3fl oz (75ml) water

Mix the mustard, turmeric, chilli and salt with the hot water, cover and set aside for 20 minutes.

Wash the okra, pat dry with absorbent kitchen paper. Cut off the tops and leave whole.

Heat oil in a karai or saucepan over a medium high heat, add the kalonji and green chillies and let them sizzle for a few seconds. Add the okra and, stirring gently, fry for 5 minutes.

Add the spice mixture and yoghurt and mix with the okra; add the water and bring it to the boil. Lower the heat, cover and simmer until the okra is tender.

DRY SPICED POTATO

SERVES 4

1lb (450g) new potatoes
4oz (100g) butter or ghee
1 onion, chopped
1tbsp fresh root ginger, finely grated
2 cloves garlic, finely chopped
leaves from 1 sprig of coriander
6oz (175g) tomatoes, peeled and chopped
½tsp garam masala
½tsp chilli powder
½tsp amchoor (mango powder)
salt
½tsp ground cumin

Scrub the potatoes and cut into quarters. Put them in a pan of cold water to prevent discoloration.

Heat three-quarters of the butter or ghee in a pan and add the onion, ginger, garlic and half the coriander leaves. Fry until the onion turns golden. Add the tomato, garam masala, chilli powder and amchoor, stirring well to mix and crushing the tomato with the back of a wooden spoon to make a paste.

Drain the potatoes and add to the pan with 1–2 tbsp of water. Cover and cook over low heat for about 20 minutes, until the potato is tender but not soft, and all the water has been absorbed. Add salt to taste.

Heat the remaining butter or ghee in a separate pan and fry the cumin for 3–4 minutes until the fragrance emerges. Add to the cooked potato and garnish with the remaining coriander leaves.

VEGETABLE CURRY, KERALA STYLE

VEGETABLE CURRY, KERALA STYLE

SERVES 4–6

12oz (350g) toovar dal (glossy split yellow pea)
½tsp turmeric
4–6oz (100–150g) okra, trimmed and cut into 1inch (2.5cm) lengths
4tbsp oil
1 medium onion, quartered and sliced
8oz (225g) potatoes, cubed
2 tomatoes, peeled and chopped
2tbsp tamarind juice
3oz (75g) fresh coconut, grated
4–6 curry leaves
2tbsp sambar powder
1tsp mustard seeds
1 red chilli pepper, cut into 4 pieces
salt
coriander leaves, to garnish

Pick over the dal, wash thoroughly and cook in about 2 pt (1.2 lt) of water with the turmeric for about 15 minutes, until you can mash it with the back of a wooden spoon. Meanwhile, fry the okra in 1 tbsp of oil, turning gently, until all the oil is absorbed. This seals the okra and helps it keep its shape. Set aside.

When the dal is ready, stir in the onion and potato and continue to cook gently over low heat for about 8 minutes, until the vegetables are half-cooked.

Add the tomato and okra and cook for a further 10 minutes, until the vegetables are tender, adding a little extra water if the pot threatens to boil dry. Stir in the tamarind juice, cover and keep hot.

Fry the coconut and half the curry leaves in 1 tbsp of oil, then blend with the sambar powder and add to the vegetables. Heat the remaining oil, add the mustard seeds and the red chilli and let them sizzle for a few seconds until all the mustard seeds have popped. Add to the curry. Stir in salt to taste and garnish with coriander leaves.

MIXED VEGETABLE CURRY

SERVES 4–6

1 hard green banana, unpeeled
4oz (100g) green beans, trimmed
8oz (200g) yam or potato, peeled
4oz (100g) white pumpkin or green papaya, peeled
½tsp chilli powder
salt
1tbsp tamarind juice
2 green chilli peppers
3tbsp fresh coconut, grated
6–8 curry leaves
1 cup yoghurt
2tbsp coconut oil
a little sugar, optional

Cook the banana and vegetables in water to cover with the chilli powder and ½ tsp of salt for about 15 minutes, until tender but not soft, stirring occasionally with a wooden spoon. Add the tamarind juice and set aside, covered.

Cut the chillies into 4 pieces and crush them with the grated coconut and curry leaves. Stir in the yoghurt and add to the vegetables, mixing well.

Mix the coconut oil with a little water to release its fragrance. Pour over the vegetables and add salt to taste. Mix again and add a little sugar, if desired.

◆ ◆ ◆

◆ FISH AND CRUSTACEANS ◆

FISH WITH MUSTARD

SERVES 4–6

1½lb (700g) white fish, cleaned
1½tsp turmeric
1½tsp salt
½tsp chilli powder
1tsp black mustard seeds, ground
3tbsp hot water
8tbsp oil
½tsp Kalonji (onion seeds)
2–3 green chillies, slit in half lengthwise
½pt (300ml) water

Cut the fish into 8–10 pieces of equal size. Rub ½ tsp each of turmeric and salt into the pieces of fish.

Mix together the remaining turmeric, salt, chilli powder and ground mustard with the 3 tbsp of hot water in a small bowl. Cover with a saucer and set aside for 15–20 minutes for the mustard to become stronger.

Heat the oil in a karai or saucepan over a medium high heat, and fry the pieces of fish, a few at a time, until lightly browned. Put aside.

In the remaining oil, add the onion seed and green chillies and let them sizzle for 4–5 seconds. Add the spices and stir-fry for 1–2 minutes. Add the water and bring to the boil. Put the pieces of fish in gently. Cover, lower the heat to medium and cook for about 15 minutes until the fish is tender and the gravy thickened.

FISH IN A HOT SAUCE

SERVES 4–6

1½lb (700g) white fish, cleaned
1½tsp turmeric
1½tsp salt
8tbsp oil
1 large onion, finely sliced
½tsp chilli powder
½pt (300ml) water
2–3 green chillies

Cut the fish into 8–10 pieces of equal size. Rub ½ tsp each of turmeric and salt into the fish.

Heat the oil in a karai or saucepan over a medium high heat and fry the pieces of fish, a few at a time, until lightly browned. Put aside.

In the remaining oil, fry the onion until brown. Add the remaining turmeric, salt and chilli powder and stir-fry for a further minute. Add the water and bring to the boil; gently add the pieces of fish and the green chillies. Cover, lower the heat to medium and cook for about 15 minutes until the fish is cooked and the gravy thickened.

FISH COOKED IN BANANA LEAVES

SERVES 4–6

1½lb (700g) hilsa (herring), cleaned and cut in 1inch (2.5cm) slices
1tsp turmeric
½tsp chilli powder
1tsp black mustard seeds, ground
2–3 green chillies
1tsp salt
4tbsp oil
8 banana leaves

Gently mix the turmeric, chilli powder, ground mustard, green chillies, salt and 2 tbsp of oil with the fish.

Place 4 banana leaves in a large frying pan. Place 1 tbsp of oil on the

FISH COOKED IN BANANA LEAVES

top leaf and put the pieces of fish in, making sure they do not overlap. Now place the other banana leaves on top. (Grease the leaf in contact with the fish with 1 tbsp of oil.)

Cook over a medium heat for 20 minutes. Turn over and cook for a further 20 minutes. (Place a plate over the leaves when you want to turn it over.)

FISH WRAPPED IN BANANA LEAVES

SERVES 4–6

1½lb (700g) pomfret or any white fish, cleaned
½tsp salt
14–16 sprigs of coriander leaves
2oz (50g) fresh coconut, grated
4 green chillies
¾tsp cumin seeds
¾tsp sugar
½tsp salt
juice of 1 lime
2–3 banana leaves, washed and dried
string for tying parcels
oil for shallow-frying

Wash the fish and cut into 8–10 pieces. Rub in the salt and put aside.

Wash and chop the coriander leaves discarding the lower stalks and roots. In a food processor or blender, blend together the coriander leaves, coconut, chillies, cumin seeds, sugar, salt and lime juice into a fine paste. (If necessary, add a little water.)

Spread the chutney on both sides of the pieces of fish. Cut the banana leaves into sizes suitable for wrapping a piece of fish. Tie with some string.

Heat the oil in a large frying pan and fry the parcels over a medium low heat until the leaves turn brownish-black. Turn the parcels over carefully and fry until the leaves turn dark brown.

Drain, remove the string and place the parcels on a flat dish. The parcels should be unwrapped at the table (the leaves should not be eaten).

FISH CURRY WITH YOGHURT

SERVES 2

4tbsp oil
6 cloves garlic, finely chopped
½tsp fenugreek seeds
1 onion, finely chopped
2tsp chilli powder
1tsp ground coriander
salt
1lb (450g) white fish, boned, skinned and cubed
8oz (225g) tomatoes, peeled and chopped
5oz (125g) yoghurt
4–6 curry leaves

Heat the oil in a pan, add the garlic and fry until golden. Add the fenugreek seeds and continue to cook until lightly browned. Remove the garlic and fenugreek with a slotted spoon and set aside.

Add the onion to the pan and fry until golden, then return the garlic and fenugreek to the pan and cook for a further 3–4 minutes. Add the chilli powder and coriander and cook for 3–4 minutes until their fragrance emerges. Pour in about ½ pt (300 ml) of water and bring to the boil. Add ½ tsp of salt, then add the fish and tomato and cook gently for 10–15 minutes, until the fish is tender and the sauce is thick. Stir in the yoghurt and curry leaves, taking care not to break up the fish. Heat through for 2–3 minutes and then add extra salt to taste.

FRIED FISH

SERVES 4–6

1lb (450g) fish fillets
2 cloves garlic, crushed
½inch (1cm) fresh root ginger, grated
1tsp poppy seeds, roasted and ground
½tsp garam masala
1tsp ground mustard
½tsp chilli powder
2oz (50g) plain flour
2oz (50g) gram flour
8fl oz (225ml) yoghurt
1tsp salt
oil for deep-frying

Cut the fish into 2 inch (5 cm) wide pieces. Wash and pat dry.

Mix the garlic, ginger, poppy seeds, garam masala, mustard and chilli thoroughly.

Make a smooth, thick batter with the plain flour, gram flour and yoghurt. Add the spices and salt. Add the pieces of fish and coat well with the batter. Put to one side for 3–4 hours.

Heat oil over a medium high heat and fry the fish for about 8 minutes, until golden.

FISH CURRY WITH YOGHURT

DRY FISH HEAD CURRY

SERVES 4–6

6tbsp oil
2 fish heads, quartered
3 cardamom pods
2inch (5cm) pieces of stick cinnamon
2 bay leaves
2 medium onions, chopped
¾inch (1.5cm) fresh root ginger, grated
1tsp ground turmeric
½tsp chilli powder
1tsp salt
¼tsp sugar
1tbsp raisins (optional)
2oz (50g) rice, washed and dried
½pt (300ml) water

Heat the oil in a karai or saucepan over a medium high heat and fry the fish heads until browned. Put aside.

In the remaining oil, add the cardamom, cinnamon and bay leaves and let them sizzle for 3–4 seconds. Add the onions and ginger and stir-fry until the onions are slightly brown.

Add the turmeric, chilli, salt, sugar and raisins and, stirring constantly, fry for 1–2 minutes. Add the rice and continue to fry for a further 2 minutes. Add the fish heads and mix with the rice and spices. Add the water and bring to the boil. Cover, lower the heat and, stirring occasionally, cook for about 20 minutes until the rice is cooked.

LIGHT FISH CURRY

SERVES 4–6

1½lb (700g) rui (or any white fish), cleaned
1¼tsp turmeric
1½tsp salt
½tsp chilli powder
1tsp ground cumin
3tbsp hot water
6tbsp oil
1 large potato, peeled and cut into 8 pieces
½tsp onion seed
2–3 green chillies, slit in half
12fl oz (350ml) water
1tbsp coriander leaves, chopped

Cut the fish into 10 equal-sized pieces. Sprinkle ½ tsp each of turmeric and salt on the fish and rub into the pieces.

In a small bowl, mix together the remaining turmeric, salt, chilli powder and cumin with the 3 tbsp of water and set aside.

In a karai or saucepan, heat the oil over a medium high heat and fry the potatoes until evenly browned. Put aside.

In the remaining oil, add the

FISH CURRY

pieces of fish, a few at a time, and fry until light brown in colour. Put aside.

Add the onion seed and green chillies to the remaining oil and let them sizzle for 3–4 seconds. Add the spices and stir-fry for 1–2 minutes. Add the water and bring to the boil; gently add the pieces of fish and potatoes. Cover, lower the heat and cook for about 15 minutes until the fish is cooked and the potatoes are tender. Sprinkle with the coriander leaves.

FRIED SPICED FISH

SERVES 2

1 onion, finely chopped
1tbsp fresh root ginger, finely grated
6 curry leaves
salt
¼tsp turmeric
1tsp chilli powder
1lb (450g) white fish, boned, skinned and cubed
5tbsp oil

Pound, grind or blend in a blender or food processor the onion, ginger, curry leaves, ½ tsp of salt, the turmeric and chilli powder. Spread the paste over the fish and let marinate for about 2 hours.

Heat the oil in a large pan that will hold the fish in one layer, add the fish and fry for about 10 minutes, until tender. Add extra salt to taste.

FISH MOLIE

SERVES 2

1lb (450g) white fish, boned and skinned
salt
flesh of 1 coconut, grated
4tbsp oil
1 onion, finely chopped
1tbsp fresh root ginger, finely grated
2 green chilli peppers, chopped
¼tsp turmeric
2tsp ground coriander
1tsp cornflour
2tbsp white wine vinegar
4–6 curry leaves

FRIED SPICED FISH

Rub the fish with salt, let stand for 5 minutes and then rinse under cold running water. Cut into large chunks and set aside.

Blend the coconut in a blender or food processor with 1–2 tbsp of boiling water. Transfer to a square of cheesecloth and squeeze the milk into a bowl. Return the coconut to the blender and repeat the process.

Heat the oil in a pan, add the onion, ginger, green chilli, turmeric and coriander and fry until the onion is golden.

Mix the cornflour with the coconut milk, add to the pan and bring to the boil. Add the fish and ½ tsp of salt and cook gently for 10 minutes, until the fish is tender. Add the vinegar, cook for a further minute, then take the curry from the heat and sprinkle on the curry leaves.

FISH CURRY

SERVES 2

1lb (450g) white fish, boned and skinned
5tbsp oil
1 onion, finely chopped
½tsp fennel seeds
2oz (50g) fresh coconut, grated
1tsp chilli powder
¼tsp turmeric
4tbsp tamarind juice
1tbsp fresh root ginger, finely grated
2oz (50g) tomatoes, peeled and chopped
1 green chilli pepper, chopped
salt
4–6 curry leaves

Cut the fish into 2 inch (5 cm) squares and wash well. Heat 4 tbsp of oil in a pan, add three-quarters of the onion, the fennel seeds and coconut and fry until the onion is golden.

Add the chilli powder and turmeric and continue to cook for 4–5 minutes, then pound, grind or blend in a blender or food processor.

Heat the tamarind juice in a small saucepan over low heat and mix in the blended spices, ginger, tomato and green chilli. Heat until the mixture bubbles, then add the fish and ½ tsp of salt and cook gently for 10 minutes, until the fish is tender.

Meanwhile, fry the remaining onion in the remaining oil until golden. Add to the curry when the fish is cooked. Sprinkle on the curry leaves and add extra salt to taste.

BAKED FISH STUFFED WITH MUSHROOMS

SERVES 4

4tbsp oil
1 onion, sliced and separated into rings
1tbsp fresh root ginger, finely grated
1tsp mint leaves, chopped
8oz (225g) tomatoes, peeled and chopped
½tsp chilli powder
salt
12oz (350g) sliced mushrooms
1–1½lb (450–700g) whole fish, such as cod, cleaned
2tbsp lemon juice

Heat 2 tbsp of oil in a pan, add the onion, ginger and mint and fry until the onion is golden. Add the tomato, chilli powder and ½ tsp of salt and cook, mashing the tomato into a thick paste with the back of a wooden spoon. Add the mushrooms and continue to cook for 6–7 minutes.

Use this mixture to stuff the fish. Lay it in a greased ovenproof dish, sprinkle with the remaining oil and the lemon juice, cover with foil and bake in a preheated 350°F/180°C/Gas Mark 4 oven for 30–35 minutes, until tender. Remove skin and serve.

SARDINES IN A THICK, SPICY SAUCE

SERVES 4

4tbsp oil
2tbsp coriander seeds
3 red chilli peppers, cut into pieces
2oz (50g) fresh coconut, grated
1–2tbsp tamarind juice
1 green chilli pepper, chopped
1tbsp fresh root ginger, finely grated
1 onion, finely chopped
¼tsp turmeric
1lb (450g) fresh sardines, cleaned
salt
4–6 curry leaves

Heat half the oil in a pan, add the coriander seeds and red chilli and fry for 3–4 minutes until the fragrance rises, then grind, pound or blend with the coconut.

Return to the pan and continue to fry, adding the tamarind, green chilli, ginger, half the onion and the turmeric, for a further 5–7 minutes, until they make a thick paste.

Lay the sardines on a plate, smother them in the paste and let marinate for 15 minutes. Meanwhile, heat the remaining oil and fry the remaining onion until golden.

Add the marinated sardines to the pan with 2 tbsp of water, cover and cook over low heat for 5–8 minutes, until tender. Add salt to taste and sprinkle on the curry leaves.

BAKED FISH STUFFED WITH MUSHROOMS

◆ FISH AND CRUSTACEANS ◆

BENGALI FRIED FISH

SERVES 4–6

1lb (450g) medium-sized herring, cleaned and washed
1tsp salt
½tsp turmeric
oil for shallow-frying

Rub the salt and turmeric into the fish and leave aside for 15–20 minutes. Heat the oil over a medium high heat and fry the fish for about 3–4 minutes on each side.

MADRAS PEPPER CRAB

SERVES 4–6

10tbsp oil
3 medium onions, finely sliced
1 large cooked crab, cut into pieces
1½tbsp coarsely ground black pepper
1½tsp salt

Heat the oil and fry the onions until soft and transparent. Add the pieces of crab and fry with the onions for 3–4 minutes. Add the pepper and salt and continue to fry for 8–10 minutes until cooked. Serve with plain rice.

SARDINES IN A THICK SPICY SAUCE

PORTUGUESE SHRIMP VINDALOO

SERVES 4–6

1lb (450g) shrimps
4 dried red chillies
6 black peppercorns
1tsp coriander seeds
1tsp cumin seeds
¾inch (1.5cm) fresh root ginger, grated
3 cloves garlic, crushed
4tbsp white vinegar
1tsp salt
4tbsp oil
2 medium onions, finely sliced

Shell the shrimp, leaving the tails on. Make a little incision along the back and remove the black vein. Wash and pat dry.

Dry roast the chilllies, peppercorns, coriander and cumin until they turn a few shades darker and emit a pleasant aroma. Grind to a fine powder. Mix the powder to a paste with the ginger, garlic, vinegar and salt. Rub the paste into the shrimp.

Heat the oil and fry the onions until golden. Let the oil and onions become cold together. Add the onions and oil to the shrimp. Mix well and marinate for 3–4 hours.

Place the shrimp with all the marinade in a large saucepan over a medium high heat. When it starts to boil, lower the heat to very low, cover and cook for 30–40 minutes, stirring occasionally, until the shrimp are tender. (If necessary, add a little water to make a thickish gravy.)

SHRIMP IN A COCONUT SAUCE

SERVES 4–6

1lb (450g) jumbo shrimp
1½tsp turmeric
1½tsp salt
2oz (50g) creamed coconut
½pt (300ml) hot water
8tbsp oil
2 medium potatoes, peeled and quartered
1 large onion, finely sliced
½tsp chilli powder
½tsp sugar
2–3 green chillies

Shell the shrimp, leaving the tails on. Make a small cut along the back to remove the black vein. Wash and pat dry. Rub ½ tsp each of turmeric and salt into the shrimp.

In a food processor or liquidizer, blend together the creamed coconut and water. Put aside.

Heat the oil in a saucepan and fry the potatoes until evenly browned. Put aside. Add the shrimp and fry until golden. Put aside.

Add the onion to the remaining oil and fry until golden-brown. Add the remaining turmeric, salt, chilli powder and sugar and fry for 1–2

STEAMED SHRIMP

minutes with the onion. Add the blended coconut milk and bring to the boil. Add the shrimp and chillies.

Cover, lower the heat and cook for 10 minutes. Add the potatoes, cover again and cook for a further 20–25 minutes, until the shrimp are cooked and the gravy is thickened.

STEAMED SHRIMP

SERVES 4–6

1lb (450g) jumbo shrimp
1tsp turmeric
½tsp chilli powder
1tsp black mustard seeds, ground
2–3 green chillies
1tsp salt
2tbsp oil

Shell the shrimp, leaving the tails on. Make a small cut down the back to remove the black vein. Wash and pat dry.

Thoroughly mix all the ingredients with the shrimp. Place the mixture in a bowl (half fill it only), and tie a double thickness of tin foil around the top of the bowl.

In a large saucepan, boil some water and place the bowl of shrimp in the saucepan, so that the water reaches a quarter of the way up the bowl. Cover the saucepan, lower the heat and keep boiling, topping up the boiling water during cooking as necessary. Steam for about 30–40 minutes.

FRIED SPICED SHRIMP

SERVES 2

2tsp ground coriander
1tsp chilli powder
½tsp turmeric
2oz (50g) fresh coconut, grated
4oz (100g) tomatoes, peeled and chopped
1 onion, finely chopped
1tbsp fresh root ginger, finely grated
8oz (225g) shelled shrimp
5tbsp oil
4–6 curry leaves
1tbsp lemon juice
leaves from 1 sprig of coriander

Grind, pound or blend the ground coriander, chilli powder, turmeric and coconut. Mix with the tomato, half the onion, the ginger and ½ tsp of salt. Coat the shrimp in this mixture and let marinate for 10–15 minutes.

Heat the oil in a pan, add the remaining onion and the curry leaves and fry until the onion is golden. Add the shrimp and cook gently for 10 minutes. Remove the curry from the heat, add extra salt to taste and sprinkle with the lemon juice and coriander leaves.

GOAN SHRIMP CURRY

SERVES 4–6

3oz (75g) dried tamarind
1pt (600ml) hot water
2oz (50g) creamed coconut
1lb (450g) jumbo shrimp
1½tsp ground cumin
good pinch turmeric
4 cloves garlic, crushed
½inch (1cm) fresh root ginger, grated
6 dried red chillies, ground
1 onion, finely sliced

FRIED SPICED SHRIMP

1tsp salt
3 green chillies, slit lengthwise

Soak the tamarind in ½ pt (300 ml) of the hot water and leave aside for 30 minutes. Make the coconut milk by blending the creamed coconut and the remaining water in a blender or food processor.

Shell the shrimp, leaving the tails on. Make a small cut on the back and remove the black vein. Wash and dry.

Mix the cumin, turmeric, garlic, ginger and red chillies into a paste. Squeeze the soaked tamarind well to draw out all the pulp. Strain. Mix the juice with the coconut milk, the onion, salt, green chillies and the paste. Place the mixture in a saucepan over a medium high heat and bring to the boil. Boil for about 10 minutes.

Add the shrimp. Bring to the boil once more. Lower the heat to medium and cover and cook for about 30 minutes, until the shrimp are tender and the gravy has thickened.

◆ FISH AND CRUSTACEANS ◆

SHRIMP BIRIYANI

SERVES 4

For the shrimp
1 green chilli pepper
1tbsp fresh root ginger, finely grated
1 clove garlic, chopped
2oz (50g) coconut, grated fresh or dried unsweetened
4 cashew nuts
2tsp biriyani masala
2oz (50g) butter or ghee
1 small onion, chopped
1lb (450g) shelled shrimp
salt
1tbsp lemon juice
cashew nuts and sultanas, fried in a little butter or ghee, for decoration

For the rice
2oz (50g) butter or ghee
1 small onion, chopped
2 bay leaves
8oz (225g) basmati rice, washed, soaked in water for 20 minutes and drained
salt
4oz (100g) fresh peas

Grind, pound or blend in a blender or food processor the chilli, ginger, garlic, coconut, cashews and biriyani masala to make a thick paste.

Heat the butter or ghee in a pan,

add the onion and fry until golden. Add the blended spice paste and fry for a further 5–8 minutes, stirring. Add the shrimp and ½ tsp of salt and cook over low heat for 3–4 minutes, stirring, until the shrimp are heated through and coated in the spice mixture.

For the rice, heat the butter or ghee in another pan, add the onion and bay leaves and fry until the onion turns golden. Pour in the rice, stir and fry for about 10 minutes, until translucent. Add ½ tsp of salt, the peas and enough water to cover and simmer over low heat for 10–15 minutes, until the rice is almost cooked. Stir in the shrimp and rice together in an ovenproof casserole, cover with a lid or foil and cook in a preheated 300°F/150°C/Gas Mark 2 oven for 10–15 minutes. Sprinkle with the lemon juice, cashews and sultanas and add extra salt to taste.

CHILLI FRIED SHRIMP

SERVES 2

8oz (225g) shelled shrimp
½tsp turmeric
1tsp chilli powder
salt
2tbsp oil
1 lemon, sliced, for garnish

Wash the shrimp well and dry them on absorbent kitchen paper. Mix them with the turmeric, chilli powder and ½ tsp of salt in a bowl, and let marinate for 10 minutes.

Heat the oil in a pan, add the shrimp and fry gently for 5 minutes. Transfer the shrimp to a serving dish and decorate with lemon slices.

SHRIMP VINDALOO

SERVES 4

½tsp cumin seeds
2tbsp fresh root ginger, finely grated
1–2 cloves garlic, finely chopped
1tsp mustard seeds
4tbsp oil
2 onions, finely chopped
6 curry leaves
4oz (100g) tomatoes, peeled and chopped
2tsp chilli powder
½tsp turmeric
1lb (450g) shelled jumbo shrimp (or crawfish)
4tbsp white wine vinegar
1tsp cornflour, optional
salt
½tsp sugar, optional

Crush the cumin seeds with the ginger, garlic and mustard seeds.

Heat the oil in a pan, add the onion and curry leaves and fry until the onion is golden. Add the tomato, chilli powder, turmeric and 1–2 tbsp of water and cook, mashing the tomato with the back of a wooden spoon to make a thick paste. Add the crushed spices and continue to fry for 5 minutes, then add the shrimp and 5 tbsp of water and simmer for 10 minutes.

Pour in the vinegar. The sauce may be thickened, if necessary, by adding the cornflour mixed with 1 tsp of water. Add salt to taste and sugar, if desired.

◆ ◆ ◆

MEAT CURRY IN A THICK SAUCE

SERVES 4

1 small onion, finely chopped
2tbsp oil
1tbsp plain flour
2lb (1kg) meat, trimmed and cubed
1tbsp lemon juice
½tsp ground pepper
salt
2oz (50g) butter or ghee
8oz (225g) tomatoes, chopped
1 green chilli pepper, sliced
leaves from 1 sprig of coriander
½tsp garam masala

Fry the onion in the oil until golden. Add the flour and continue to fry, stirring, until the flour is coloured and has formed a paste. Add the meat, lemon juice, pepper and ½ tsp of salt, stir and pour in 1½ pt (900ml) of water. Bring to the boil and simmer, covered, for 1 hour, stirring occasionally, until the meat is tender and the sauce is thick.

Heat the butter or ghee in a pan, add the tomato and green chilli and fry gently, stirring, for 3–4 minutes, then add to the meat. Add the coriander leaves and garam masala.

MEAT CURRY WITH YOGHURT

SERVES 4

4–6tbsp oil
2 onions, coarsely chopped
2tbsp fresh root ginger, chopped
2 cloves garlic, chopped
1 green chilli pepper, chopped
seeds from 2 cardamom pods
1 inch (2.5cm) piece of stick cinnamon
3 cloves
½tsp fennel seeds
1tbsp ground coriander
1tsp ground cumin
leaves from 2 sprigs of coriander
½tsp turmeric
1tsp chilli powder
8 oz (225g) yoghurt
2lb (1kg) meat, trimmed and cubed
4–6 curry leaves
salt

Heat half the oil in a pan, add half the onion, the ginger, garlic, green chilli, cardamom seeds, cinnamon, cloves, fennel seeds, ground coriander, cumin, half the coriander leaves, the turmeric and chilli powder and fry gently, stirring, for 10 minutes.

Take the pan off the heat and stir in the yoghurt. Mix well and set aside.

Chop the remaining onion finely and fry in the remaining oil until golden. Add the meat and fry for about 15 minutes, stirring occasionally. Stir in the spiced yoghurt and cook gently for 8–10 minutes, stirring.

Pour on about 1 pt (600 ml) of boiling water, turn down the heat and cook, covered, for about 1 hour or until the meat is tender. Cook uncovered and stir frequently if a thicker sauce is required. Sprinkle on the curry leaves and remaining coriander leaves and add salt to taste.

MEAT CURRY IN A THICK SAUCE

PLAIN MEAT CURRY

SERVES 4

2lb (1kg) meat, trimmed and cubed
1tbsp lemon juice
salt
2tbsp ground coriander
2tsp chilli powder
½tsp ground pepper
1tsp ground cumin
½tsp turmeric
2oz (5og) butter or ghee
1tbsp oil
1 small onion, finely chopped
2tbsp fresh root ginger, chopped
2 cloves garlic, chopped
1tsp garam masala
4–6 curry leaves

Wash the meat thoroughly in hot water. Drain and cook, covered, in 1 pt (600 ml) of fresh water with the lemon juice and a pinch of salt for about an hour or until the meat is tender and most of the liquid has evaporated.

Meanwhile, mix the coriander, chilli powder, pepper, cumin and turmeric with 2 tbsp of water to make a smooth paste. Heat the butter or ghee in a pan with the oil, add the onion, ginger and garlic and fry until the onion is golden.

Add the spice paste and continue to fry for 10 minutes. Add the paste to the cooked meat with ½ tsp of salt and cook, covered, over low heat for 10–15 minutes, until the sauce is thick. Sprinkle on the garam masala and the curry leaves and add extra salt to taste.

MEAT AND TOMATO CURRY

SERVES 4

2oz (50g) butter or ghee
1 small onion, finely chopped
1tbsp fresh root ginger, finely grated
3 cloves garlic, finely chopped
8oz (225g) tomatoes, peeled and chopped
½tsp turmeric
2tsp chilli powder
1tbsp ground coriander
½tbsp ground cumin
salt
1tsp garam masala
2lb (1kg) meat, trimmed and cubed
8oz (225g) potatoes, peeled and diced
leaves from 1 sprig of coriander

Heat the butter or ghee in a large saucepan, add the onion, ginger and garlic and fry until the onion is golden. Add the tomato, turmeric, chilli powder, ground coriander, cumin, ½ tsp of salt and garam masala. Stir and continue to fry until the fat runs clear of the spices, then add 1 pt (600 ml) of boiling water and mix well.

Add the meat and cook, covered, over a low heat for about 1 hour, until tender and the sauce is thick. Add the potato and a little extra water, if necessary, and cook for a further 10–15 minutes until tender but not soft. Sprinkle on the coriander leaves and extra salt to taste.

SPICED MEAT BIRIYANI

SERVES 4

2oz (50g) fresh coconut, grated
2oz (50g) whole cashew nuts
1tbsp mint leaves, chopped
leaves from 2 sprigs coriander
2tbsp fresh root ginger, thinly sliced
4 cloves garlic, thinly sliced
1 green chilli pepper, sliced
1 small onion, thinly sliced
5oz (125g) yoghurt
1tbsp lemon juice
2tsp biriyani masala
1tsp ground coriander
salt
2lb (1kg) meat, trimmed and cubed
6oz (175g) basmati rice, washed and soaked in water for 2 hours
2tbsp butter or ghee
2tbsp milk
cashew nuts, almonds and sultanas to decorate

In a blender or food processor, blend the coconut, cashews, mint and coriander leaves to make a smooth paste. Transfer to a large bowl. Stir in the ginger, garlic, green chilli, onion, yoghurt, lemon juice, biriyani masala, ground coriander and ½ tsp of salt. Turn the meat in this mixture to coat and let marinate for about 5 minutes.

Put the meat in a heavy-bottomed pan, pour in 1 pt (600 ml) of boiling water, cover and cook over low heat for about an hour, until tender.

Meanwhile drain the rice and cook in 1½ pt (900 ml) of boiling water for 10 minutes, until half-cooked. Drain.

In a large ovenproof casserole, heat the butter or ghee, then add the meat and rice and mix thoroughly. Cook, covered with foil or a lid, in a preheated 300°F/150°C/Gas Mark 2 oven for 10 minutes.

Sprinkle on the milk and decorate with cashews, almonds and sultanas.

SWEET AND SOUR MEAT CURRY

SERVES 4

2tbsp oil
2oz (50g) butter or ghee
2 onions, finely chopped
1 green chilli pepper, chopped
1tbsp fresh root ginger, finely grated
2 cloves garlic, crushed
8oz (225g) tomatoes, peeled and chopped
leaves from 2 sprigs of coriander
½tsp garam masala
½tsp turmeric
1tsp chilli powder
2lb (1kg) meat, trimmed and cubed
8oz (225g) potatoes, peeled and chopped
½tsp ground pepper
1tbsp sugar
5oz (125g) yoghurt
2tbsp lemon juice

Heat the oil and butter or ghee in a saucepan, add the onion, green chilli, ginger and garlic and fry until the onion turns golden.

Add the tomato, half the coriander leaves, the garam masala, turmeric and chilli powder and cook, stirring and mashing the tomato with the back of a wooden spoon until it makes a paste and the fat has run clear of the spices.

Add the meat and 1 pt (600 ml) of boiling water and cook over low heat for about 1 hour, until tender. Add the potato and cook for a further 10–15 minutes until tender but not soft.

Mix the remaining coriander leaves, the pepper and sugar with the yoghurt, add to the curry and cook for 2–3 minutes, stirring, to heat through. Sprinkle on the lemon juice and add salt to taste.

MEAT CURRY WITH ROASTED SPICES

SERVES 4

4tbsp oil
2tbsp coriander seeds
2 red chilli peppers, cut into pieces
1 inch (2.5cm) piece of stick cinnamon
3 cloves
2oz (50g) fresh coconut, grated
1lb (500g) meat, trimmed and cubed
½tsp turmeric
salt
2 green chilli peppers, sliced
1tbsp fresh root ginger, grated
1 small onion, chopped
8oz (225g) potatoes, peeled and diced
8oz (225g) tomatoes, peeled and chopped
6 curry leaves

Heat half the oil in a pan and fry the coriander seeds, red chilli, cinnamon, cloves and coconut for about 5 minutes, then transfer to a blender or mortar and reduce to a smooth paste.

Put the meat in a bowl with the turmeric, ½ tsp of salt, green chilli, ginger and half the onion, add the spice paste and mix well. Let it marinate for 15 minutes.

Heat the remaining oil in a large saucepan and fry the remaining onion until golden. Add the marinated meat, the potato and tomato. Pour in 1½ pt (900 ml) of boiling water, cover and cook over low heat for about 1 hour, until the meat is tender and the sauce is thick. Add extra salt to taste and sprinkle on the curry leaves.

MEAT CURRY WITH ROASTED SPICES

FRIED SPICED MEAT KEEMA

SERVES 4

4oz (100g) butter or ghee
1 onion, finely chopped
2 cloves garlic, finely chopped
1tbsp fresh root ginger, finely grated
leaves from 1 sprig of coriander
6oz (175g) tomatoes, peeled and chopped
seeds from 2 cardamom pods, crushed
1 inch (2.5cm) piece of stick cinnamon
3 cloves
1 bay leaf
½tsp ground coriander
½tsp turmeric
½tsp ground cumin
½tsp chilli powder
salt
1lb (450g) lean minced meat
8oz (225g) potatoes, peeled and diced

Heat the butter or ghee in a pan, add the onion and fry until golden. Add the garlic, ginger, half the coriander leaves, the tomato, cardamom, cinnamon, cloves and bay leaf and fry for 3–4 minutes, stirring.

Add the coriander, turmeric, cumin, chilli powder and ½ tsp of salt and stir to make a thick paste. Add the meat and potato and fry for about 15 minutes, stirring occasionally, then pour in ½ pt (300 ml) of boiling water, cover and cook over low heat for a further 15 minutes, until the meat and potato are cooked and the sauce is thick. Add salt to taste and sprinkle on the remaining coriander leaves.

MEAT CURRY WITH NUTS AND COCONUT MILK

SERVES 4

flesh of 1 coconut, grated
2oz (50g) cashew nuts
2 cloves garlic, chopped
½tsp chilli powder
1tsp fresh root ginger, grated
½tsp ground coriander
½tsp turmeric
leaves from 1 sprig of coriander
½tsp garam masala
½tsp ground pepper
4oz (100g) butter or ghee
1 small onion, chopped
2lb (1kg) meat, trimmed and cubed
¼tsp saffron
2tbsp sultanas
2oz (50g) almonds
salt
4–6 curry leaves

Purée the coconut in a blender or food processor with 1 tbsp of boiling water. Transfer to a square of cheesecloth and squeeze out the milk into a bowl. Return the coconut to the blender or food processor and repeat the process.

Grind, pound or blend in a blender or food processor the cashew nuts, garlic, chilli powder, ginger, ground coriander, turmeric, coriander leaves, garam masala and pepper.

Heat the butter or ghee in a pan, add the onion and fry until golden, then add the blended spices and fry for a further 5 minutes.

Add the meat, stir and fry for 5 minutes, then add the coconut milk, saffron, sultanas, almonds and ½ tsp of salt and cook, covered, over low heat for about 1 hour, until the meat is tender and the sauce has thickened. Sprinkle on the curry leaves.

MEATBALL AND CAULIFLOWER CURRY

SERVES 4

Meat and Cauliflower
1 egg, beaten
1lb (450g) lean minced meat
1tbsp fresh root ginger, grated
2 cloves garlic, chopped
½tsp garam masala
½tsp ground cumin
leaves from 1 sprig of coriander
salt
1 small cauliflower, cut into florets, tough stems discarded

LEFT: MEAT CURRY WITH NUTS AND COCONUT MILK

Sauce
3oz (75g) butter or ghee
1 small onion, finely chopped
seeds from 2 cardamom pods, crushed
2 cloves
1inch (2.5cm) piece of stick cinnamon
1tbsp fresh root ginger, grated
2 cloves garlic, crushed
½tsp turmeric
1tsp chilli powder
½tsp ground cumin
½tsp ground coriander
8oz (225g) tomatoes, peeled and chopped or 2tsp tomato purée
5oz (125g) yoghurt
salt
leaves from 1 sprig of coriander

Mix the egg with the minced meat. Grind, pound or purée in a blender or food processor the ginger, garlic, garam masala, cumin, coriander leaves and ½ tsp salt.

Mix the spice paste with the meat, form it into small balls and set aside.

For the sauce, heat the butter or ghee in a pan, add the onion and fry until golden. Add the cardamom seeds, cloves, cinnamon, ginger, garlic, turmeric, chilli powder, cumin and coriander and fry for 3-4 minutes, stirring. Add the tomato or tomato purée and cook, stirring, until the fat runs clear of the spices.

Stir in the yoghurt with a pinch of salt and 1–2 tbsp of water and bring gently to the boil. Carefully slide in the meatballs and cauliflower florets and cook for about 20 minutes over low heat, stirring occasionally and taking care not to break the meatballs. Sprinkle on the coriander leaves and add salt to taste.

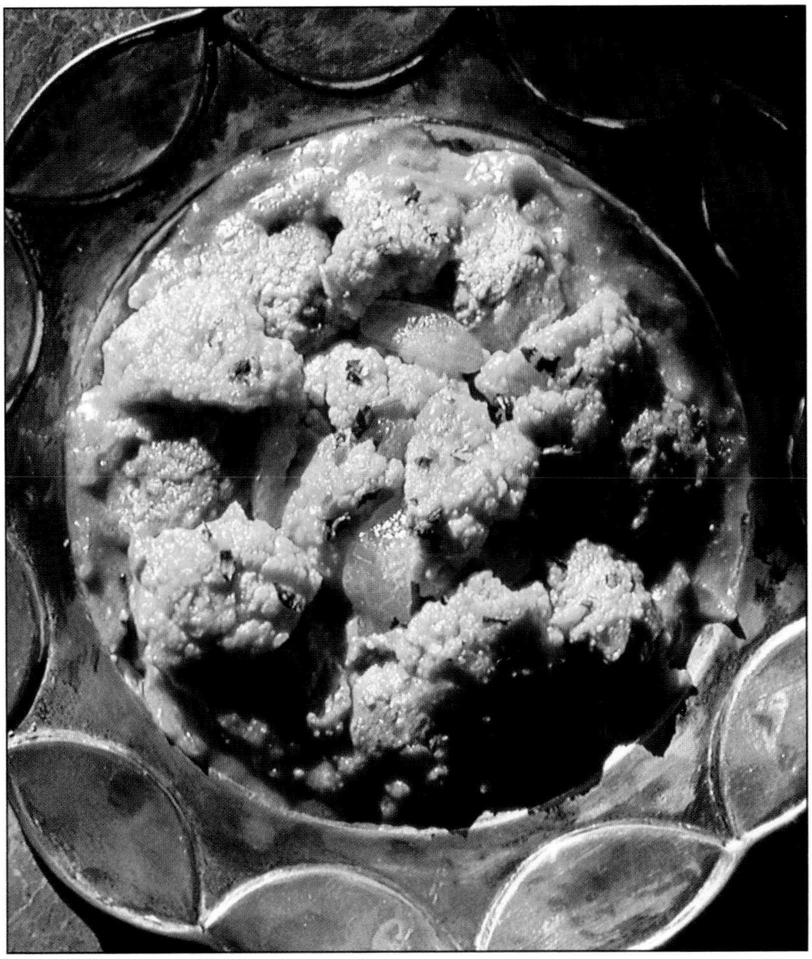

MEATBALL AND CAULIFLOWER CURRY

KOFTA (MEATBALL) CURRY

SERVES 4–6

Kofta
1½lb (700g) minced lamb
1 large onion
¾inch (2cm) fresh root ginger
8 cloves garlic
2tsp ground poppy seeds
¾tsp ground coriander
¾tsp ground cumin
2–3 green chillies
1tsp salt
2 eggs, lightly beaten

Curry
6tbsp oil
1 large onion, finely chopped
¾tsp turmeric
½tsp chilli powder
1tsp ground coriander
1tsp ground cumin
1tsp salt
3 tomatoes, chopped
12fl oz (350ml) water
6fl oz (175ml) yoghurt
2–3tbsp coriander leaves, chopped

Place all the kofta ingredients, except the eggs, in a food processor or blender and blend until well mixed. Add the eggs and mix in thoroughly. Using your hands, divide the mixture into 12–14 portions and form into balls between the palms of your hands. Put to one side.

Heat the oil in a large saucepan over a medium high heat and fry the onion until brown. Add the turmeric, chilli, coriander, cumin and salt and fry for about 30 seconds. Add the tomatoes, mix with the spices and cook until soft. Add the water and bring to the boil. Add the meatballs gently and boil rapidly for 10 minutes.

Lower the heat, cover and cook for 15 minutes, turning the koftas gently every 5–6 minutes. Add the yoghurt, stir gently, cover again and cook for a further 15–20 minutes until all the water has been absorbed and a thick, rich gravy remains. Garnish with the coriander leaves.

MEAT WITH SPINACH

SERVES 4–6

6tbsp oil
4 cardamom pods
2inch (5cm) piece of stick cinnamon
3 bay leaves
2 medium onions, finely sliced
2 cloves garlic, crushed
¾inch (1.5cm) fresh root ginger, grated
½tsp turmeric
1tsp chilli powder
1½lb (700g) lamb, cut into 1inch (2.5cm) cubes
1tsp salt
1½lb (700g) frozen spinach, chopped

Heat the oil in a large saucepan, add the cardamom, cinnamon and bay leaves and let them sizzle for 4–5 seconds. Add the onions, garlic and ginger and fry until the onions are golden-brown; add the turmeric and chilli and fry for another minute. Add the lamb and salt and mix well with the spices.

Cover, lower the heat to very low and cook for about 30 minutes, stirring occasionally. Add the spinach and continue to cook until all the liquid has evaporated.

MEAT STEW

SERVES 4–6

4oz (100g) creamed coconut
1pt (600ml) hot water
2lb (1kg) lamb, cut into 1inch (2.5cm) cubes
2–3 green chillies
1inch (2.5cm) fresh root ginger, cut into thin strips
2 large onions, sliced
2inch (5cm) piece of stick cinnamon
6 cloves
2 cardamom pods
6–7 curry leaves
1½tsp salt
2tbsp butter or ghee
1 small onion, finely chopped
½tsp freshly ground pepper
1tbsp flour

Blend together the coconut and water until smooth. In a large saucepan, put the lamb, chillies, ginger, onions, cinnamon, cloves, cardamom, curry leaves, salt and 16 fl oz (450 ml) of the coconut milk and bring to the boil. Cover, lower heat and simmer for 45 minutes. Add the remaining coconut milk and cook for a further 10 minutes. Remove from the heat.

In a small pan, heat the butter or ghee and fry the onion until lightly browned. Add the pepper and the flour and, stirring constantly, mix the flour with the fried onion and butter or ghee. Add a little of the meat gravy and mix until smooth. Add this to the stew and, stirring constantly, bring it to the boil. Serve hot with rice.

MEAT COOKED WITH WHEAT GRAINS

SERVES 4–6

1lb (450g) whole wheat grains
5 cardamom pods
1inch (2.5cm) piece of stick cinnamon
6 cloves
1inch (2.5cm) fresh root ginger
4 cloves garlic
6oz (175g) butter or ghee
4 medium onions, finely sliced
1½lb (700g) boneless lamb, cut into 1inch (2.5cm) cubes
1tsp turmeric
2tsp chilli powder
1tbsp ground poppy seeds
3tbsp dry coconut, grated
2tbsp coriander leaves, chopped
1tbsp mint leaves, chopped
2tsp salt
6fl oz (175ml) yoghurt
juice of 2 limes

Soak the wheat in plenty of water overnight. Drain. Place the wheat and some water in a large saucepan and bring to the boil. Cook until it is tender and mushy.

Grind the cardamom, cinnamon and cloves to a fine powder. Grind the ginger and garlic to a fine paste.

In a large saucepan, heat the butter or ghee and fry the onions until golden. Remove one-third of the fried onions and put aside.

Add the ginger and garlic paste, the lamb, turmeric, chilli powder, poppy seeds, dry coconut, coriander and mint leaves, the salt and half the ground spices and stir-fry for 5 minutes. Add the yoghurt and mix thoroughly. Lower the heat. Cover and cook for about 30 minutes. Add the remaining ground spices and continue to cook for about another 30 minutes until the meat is tender. Remove from the heat.

Add the boiled wheat and beat with the back of a wooden spoon until the meat disintegrates. Add the lime juice and stir well. Bring to the boil again and boil for 5 minutes. Serve garnished with fried onions.

MEAT AND VEGETABLE CURRY

SERVES 4

3oz (75g) butter or ghee
1 small onion, finely chopped
1tbsp fresh root ginger, grated
2 cloves garlic, chopped
½tsp turmeric
½tsp chilli powder
½tsp ground coriander
½tsp garam masala
½tsp ground cumin
1 green chilli pepper, chopped
4–6 curry leaves
1lb (450g) meat, trimmed and cubed
6oz (175g) tomatoes, peeled and chopped
4oz (100g) okra, trimmed and cut into 2 or 3 pieces
4oz (100g) carrots, peeled and diced
8oz (225g) potatoes, peeled and cubed
6oz (175g) aubergine, peeled and cubed
2oz (50g) fresh peas
salt

Heat the butter or ghee in a pan, add the onion and fry until golden. Add the ginger, garlic, turmeric, chilli powder, coriander, garam masala, cumin, green chilli and curry leaves, stir and fry for a further 5 minutes.

Add the meat and fry for 5 minutes, then add the tomato, okra, carrot, potato, aubergine and peas, pour in 1½ pt (900 ml) of water, add ½ tsp of salt and cook over low heat for 1 hour.

MEAT KEBABS

SERVES 4

1tbsp fresh root ginger, finely grated
1 green chilli pepper, chopped
salt
½tsp garam masala
1lb (450g) lean minced meat
1 onion, finely chopped
½tsp chilli powder
½tsp ground pepper
½tsp ground cumin
leaves from 1 sprig of coriander
1 egg, beaten
7tbsp oil

Grind, pound or purée in a blender or food processor the ginger, green chilli, ½ tsp of salt and the garam masala with 1–2 tbsp of water to make a paste.

In a bowl, mix the spice paste with the meat and onion, sprinkle on the chilli powder, pepper, cumin and coriander leaves, add the egg and 1–2 tsp oil and combine well.

Roll the mixture into small sausages and thread on skewers. Grill the kebabs, basting with a little oil and turning frequently until cooked through.

Remove the kebabs from the skewers and fry in the remaining oil for about 10 minutes, turning gently.

LIGHT MEAT CURRY

SERVES 4–6

6tbsp oil
3 medium potatoes, peeled and halved
4 cardamom pods
2inch (5cm) piece of stick cinnamon
2 bay leaves
1 large onion, finely sliced
2 cloves garlic, crushed
1inch (2.5cm) fresh root ginger, grated
1tsp turmeric
½tsp chilli powder
1tsp salt
good pinch of sugar
1tbsp vinegar

MEAT KEBABS

2lb (1kg) lamb, cut into 1inch (2.5cm) cubes
1½pt (900ml) water

Heat the oil in a large saucepan over a medium high heat, and fry the pieces of potato until evenly browned. Put aside.

Put the cardamom, cinnamon and bay leaves in the hot oil and let them sizzle for 4–5 seconds. Add the onions, garlic and ginger and fry until the onions are golden-brown. Add the turmeric, chilli, salt, sugar and vinegar and fry for another minute. Add the lamb, mix with the spices and fry, stirring constantly, for 10–15 minutes, until all the meat juices have evaporated.

Add the water and bring to the boil. Cover, lower the heat and cook for 40 minutes, stirring occasionally. Add the potatoes, cover again and cook for a further 20 minutes until the meat and potatoes are tender.

◆ POULTRY AND MEAT ◆

PORK VINDALOO

SERVES 4

6 cloves garlic
1oz (25g) fresh root ginger
4 red chilli peppers, seeded
1tsp mustard seeds
½tsp fenugreek seeds
½tsp turmeric
½tsp ground cumin
5tbsp white wine vinegar
2–3tbsp oil
2 onions, finely chopped
8oz (225g) tomatoes, peeled and chopped
2–3lb (1–1.5kg) shoulder of pork, trimmed and cubed
salt
4–6 curry leaves
4 cloves
1inch (2.5cm) piece of stick cinnamon
1tsp sugar

Chop 4 cloves garlic with half the ginger, then grind, pound or blend in a blender or food processor with the chillies, mustard seeds, fenugreek seeds, turmeric, cumin and half the vinegar.

Heat the oil in a pan, add the onion and fry until golden. Add the spice paste, stir and fry gently for 15 minutes.

Add the tomato and continue to cook, mashing it with the back of a wooden spoon to make a paste. When the oil has run clear of the spices, add the pork and fry for 5 minutes, turning the pieces in the spice mixture.

Add ½ tsp of salt and pour in 1 pt (600 ml) of boiling water. Simmer, covered, for 40 minutes, until the pork is tender.

Slice the remaining garlic and ginger and add with the curry leaves, cloves and stick cinnamon. Cook for a further 5 minutes. Add the sugar and remaining vinegar. Add salt to taste.

PORK VINDALOO

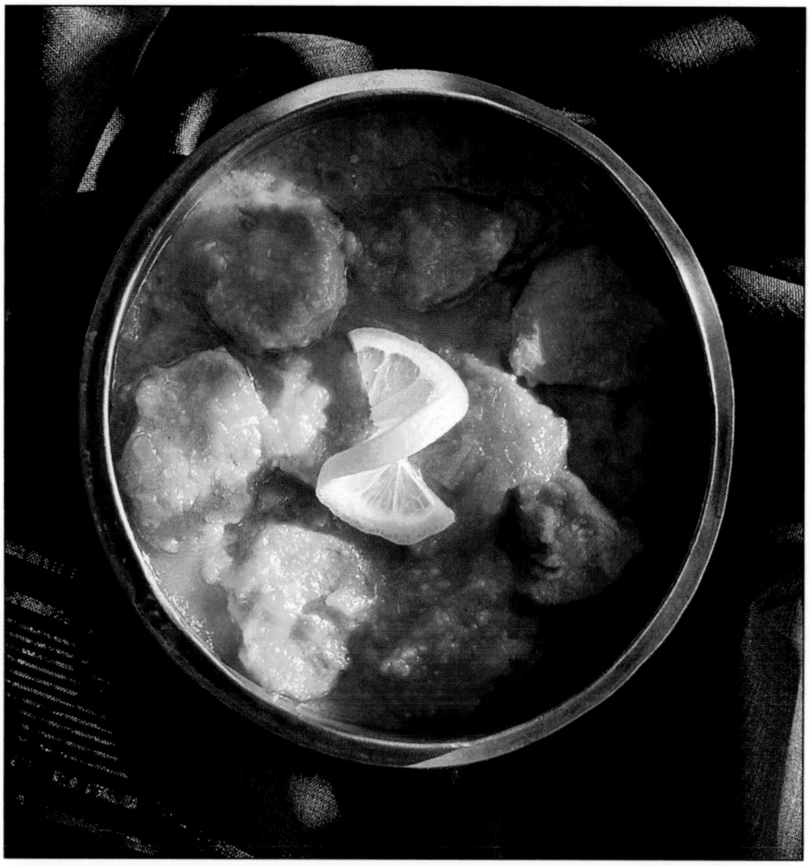

SPICY PORK

SERVES 4–6

10 dried red chillies
½tsp coriander seeds
1tsp cumin seeds
1tsp mustard seeds
½tsp peppercorns
4 cloves
1inch (2.5cm) piece of stick cinnamon
1 large onion, finely sliced
3 green chillies, chopped
½inch (1cm) fresh root ginger, grated
6 cloves garlic, crushed
6tbsp vinegar
1½lb (700g) pork, cut into very small cubes
½lb (225g) liver, cut into ½inch (1cm) pieces
6tbsp oil
½tsp turmeric
1tsp salt
½pt (300ml) water
4fl oz (100ml) tamarind juice

Grind together the chillies, coriander, cumin, mustard, peppercorns, cloves and cinnamon until finely ground. Mix the ground spices with the onion, chillies, ginger, garlic and vinegar. Add to the meat and liver and mix well. Put aside for 1 hour.

Heat the oil in a large saucepan over a medium high heat. Add the meat mixture, turmeric and salt and sauté for about 15 minutes until the oil floats on top. Add the water and tamarind juice. Bring to the boil, cover and cook on a gentle heat for about 1 hour, until the pork is tender. Serve with rice.

LAMB WITH ONIONS

SERVES 4–6

2lb (1kg) lamb, cut into 1inch (2.5cm) cubes
½tsp turmeric
½tsp chilli powder
1tsp ground cumin seeds
1tsp ground coriander seeds
1inch (2.5cm) fresh root ginger, grated
2 cloves garlic, crushed
12fl oz (350ml) yoghurt
1tsp salt

4 large onions
10 tbsp oil
4 cardamom pods
2inch (5cm) piece of stick cinnamon
3 cloves

Marinate the lamb with the turmeric, chilli, cumin, coriander, ginger, garlic, yoghurt and salt and set aside for 3–4 hours.

Cut 3 of the the onions in half and finely slice them. Chop the remaining onion.

Heat the oil in a large saucepan over a medium high heat and fry the sliced onions, stirring occasionally, until golden-brown. Drain on absorbent kitchen paper and put aside.

In the remaining oil add the cardamom, cinnamon and cloves and let them sizzle for 4–5 seconds. Add the chopped onion and fry until lightly browned. Add the meat and spices and fry, stirring constantly, for about 5–7 minutes. Cover, lower the heat to very low and simmer for about 1 hour until tender.

Add two-thirds of the fried onions and mix with the meat and cook for another minute. Garnish with the remaining onions.

LAMB CHOP KEBABS

SERVES 4–6

1½lb (700g) lamb chops
16fl oz (450ml) yoghurt
1½tsp salt
1inch (2.5cm) fresh root ginger, grated
8 cloves garlic, crushed
¾tsp garam masala
1tbsp ground poppy seeds
2–3 green chillies, finely chopped
2tbsp oil

Remove excess fat from the chops. Wash and pat dry. Lightly beat the yoghurt and mix in all the ingredients. Add the lamb chops and marinate for at least 6 hours.

Preheat the grill. Take the chops out of the marinade and place on a baking tray. Grill for 8–10 minutes on each side. Serve with onion salad.

LAMB CHOP KEBABS

LAMB WITH COCONUT

SERVES 4–6

1 fresh coconut, grated
1pt (600ml) hot water
1tsp cumin seeds
1tbsp coriander seeds
8 peppercorns
10 dried red chillies
1½tbsp poppy seeds
1inch (2.5cm) piece of stick cinnamon
3 cardamom pods, skinned
3 cloves
4 cloves garlic
¾inch (2cm) fresh root ginger
6tbsp oil
2 large onions, halved and then finely sliced
1lb (450g) lamb, cut into 1inch (2.5cm) cubes
1tsp turmeric
1½tsp salt
2fl oz (50ml) tamarind juice
2tbsp coriander leaves, chopped

Take three-quarters of the grated coconut and blend with ½ pt (300 ml) of the hot water. Strain and keep the thick milk aside. Blend the pulp again with the remaining water, and strain again to extract the thin milk.

Dry roast the remaining coconut with the cumin, coriander, peppercorns, red chillies, poppy seeds, cinnamon, cardamom and cloves over a medium heat, stirring constantly until the coconut is golden.

Grind the roasted coconut and spices with the garlic and ginger to a fine paste. (If you need to add any liquid during grinding, add a little of the thin coconut milk.)

Heat the oil in a large saucepan over a medium high heat. Add the onions and fry, stirring constantly, until lightly golden. Add the lamb and brown all over, turning it frequently and reducing the heat if necessary. Add the turmeric, salt and ground paste and mix thoroughly with the meat.

Carefully add the thin milk and bring to the boil. Cover, lower the heat and cook for about 45 minutes. Add the tamarind juice and simmer for a further 10 minutes. Add the thick coconut milk and simmer for 5 minutes more. Garnish with the coriander leaves and serve hot.

LAMB WITH ALMONDS AND YOGHURT

SERVES 4–6

2lb (1kg) onions
2lb (1kg) lamb, cut into 1inch (2.5cm) cubes
1tsp ground coriander
1tsp ground cumin
1tsp chilli powder
1½tsp salt
8fl oz (225ml) oil
16fl oz (450ml) yoghurt
½tsp garam masala
2tsp ground poppy seeds
7 cloves garlic, crushed
1inch (2.5cm) fresh root ginger, grated
6 cardamom pods, slightly crushed
4oz (100g) almonds, blanched and slivered
8fl oz (225ml) single cream

Peel all the onions and finely chop half of them. Finely slice the other half.

Put the lamb in a large bowl, add the chopped onions, coriander, cumin, chilli and salt, mix with the meat and marinate for 4–5 hours.

Heat the oil in a large frying pan and fry the sliced onions until brown. Drain them on absorbent kitchen paper and blend to a fine paste in a liquidizer or food processor without adding any water. (Keep the oil for making the curry.)

Place the yoghurt, garam masala and poppy seeds in a bowl, add the onion paste, mix thoroughly and put aside.

Heat 6 tbsp of the oil in a large saucepan over a medium high heat; add the garlic and ginger and fry until very lightly golden. Add the lamb and the spices and mix with the oil. Lower the heat and, stirring occasionally, cook until all the water that came out of the lamb has been absorbed.

Add the yoghurt paste, cardamom and almonds and mix with the meat. Cover and cook for about 30 minutes until the lamb is tender and the gravy very thick. Add the cream and stir gently to mix. Cook for a further 10 minutes.

SPICY MINCED LAMB WRAPPED WITH POTATOES

LAMB WITH CARDAMON

SPICY MINCED LAMB WRAPPED WITH POTATOES

SERVES 4–6

1tsp salt
2tbsp oil
1 large onion, finely sliced
2 cloves garlic, crushed
½inch (1cm) fresh root ginger, grated
¾tsp turmeric
½tsp chilli powder
1tsp salt
good pinch of sugar
1tbsp raisins (optional)
2tsp vinegar
1lb (450g) minced lamb
1tsp garam masala
1 egg, slightly beaten
breadcrumbs
oil for shallow-frying
1¾lb (800g) potatoes, peeled and boiled
1tsp ground, roasted cumin seeds
½tsp dried red chillies, ground and roasted (optional)

For the filling, heat the oil in a large frying pan over a medium high heat. Add the onion, garlic and ginger and fry for 4–5 minutes, stirring constantly, until the onion becomes pale gold.

Add the turmeric, chilli, salt, sugar, raisins and vinegar, mix thoroughly with the onion and fry for 1 minute. Add the minced lamb and mix with the spices.

Cover, lower the heat, and, stirring occasionally, cook for about 20 minutes. Remove the cover, turn the heat up and, stirring constantly, cook until all the liquid has evaporated and the minced lamb is dry. Mix in the garam masala and remove from the heat and set aside to cool.

To prepare the potato, mash with the cumin, chilli and salt. Divide into 20–22 balls.

Take a ball and make a depression in the middle with your thumb, to form a cup shape. Fill the centre with the minced meat and re-form the potato ball, making sure no cracks appear.

Place the balls in the egg, one at a time, and roll in the breadcrumbs. Heat the oil over a very high heat in a large frying pan and fry the balls until golden-brown, turning once (about 1 minute).

LAMB WITH CARDAMOM

SERVES 4–6

30 black peppercorns
25 cardamom pods, skinned
5 medium tomatoes
1inch (2.5cm) fresh root ginger, cut into small pieces
8tbsp oil
2 large onions, finely chopped
2lb (1kg) lamb, cut into 1inch (2.5cm) cubes
2tsp paprika
1½tsp salt
½pt (300ml) water
3tbsp coriander leaves, chopped

Grind the peppercorns and cardamom pods finely. In a blender or food processor, blend the tomatoes and ginger.

Heat the oil in a saucepan and fry the onions until golden. Add the meat and the ground spices. Stir constantly and fry for 5 minutes. Add the blended mixture, paprika and salt, mix with the meat and fry for a further 2–3 minutes. Add the water, bring to the boil, cover, lower the heat to very low and cook for about 1 hour until tender. Garnish with coriander leaves and serve with rice.

SWEET AND SOUR LAMB

SERVES 4–6

8tbsp oil
1½lb (700g) onions, halved and sliced
½tsp chilli powder
¼tsp turmeric
1inch (2.5cm) fresh root ginger, grated
1½lb (700g) lamb, cut into 1inch (2.5cm) cubes
3 medium tomatoes, chopped
¾pt (425ml) water
3tbsp vinegar
2tsp sugar
1tsp salt

Heat the oil in a saucepan over a medium high heat and fry the onion until golden-brown. Add the chilli, turmeric and ginger, and, stirring constantly, fry for 1–2 minutes. Add the lamb and tomatoes and continue to fry for another 8–10 minutes, until the meat is browned.

Add the water, stir well and bring to the boil. Lower the heat, cover and cook for about 45 minutes. Add the vinegar, sugar and salt and cook for another 15 minutes.

CHICKEN BIRIYANI

SERVES 4–6

Chicken

1tbsp biriyani masala
1 green chilli pepper
1tbsp fresh root ginger, finely grated
2 cloves garlic, chopped
leaves from 2 sprigs of coriander
1tbsp mint leaves, chopped
2oz (50g) cashew nuts
3lb (1.5kg) chicken
7tbsp oil
2oz (50g) butter or ghee
1 small onion, chopped
8oz (225g) tomatoes, peeled and chopped
salt

Rice

4oz (100g) butter or ghee
2 bay leaves
1 small onion, chopped
8oz (225g) basmati rice, washed, soaked in water for 20 minutes and drained
10 cashew nuts
2oz (50g) sultanas

Pound, grind or purée in a blender or food processor the biriyani masala, green chilli, ginger, garlic, coriander leaves, mint and cashews, adding about 2 tbsp of water to make a paste.

Skin the chicken and cut into 8 pieces. Wash in hot water and dry on absorbent kitchen paper.

Heat 5 tbsp of oil in a pan, add the chicken and fry for about 10 minutes, turning once. Remove the chicken. Add the remaining oil and the butter or ghee to the pan and, when hot, add the onion and fry until golden. Add the spice mixture and cook, stirring, until the fat runs clear of the spices.

Add the tomato, mashing it with the back of a wooden spoon to make a paste.

Add the chicken pieces and salt and pour in 1 pt (600 ml) of boiling water. Cook for about 1 hour, until the chicken is tender and the sauce has thickened.

Meanwhile, for the rice, heat three-quarters of the butter or ghee in a heavy-bottomed saucepan, add the bay leaves and onion and fry until the onion is golden. Pour in the rice and stir well over low heat for about 10 minutes, until the rice is translucent. Add 1 pt (600 ml) of boiling water, bring back to the boil and cook over low heat, covered, for 8–10 minutes. Drain off the water.

Mix the rice, chicken and sauce together in an ovenproof casserole, cover with a lid or foil and cook in a preheated 300°F/150°C/Gas Mark 2 oven for 10–15 minutes, until the rice is completely cooked. This dish should be moist but not too wet.

Fry the cashews and sultanas briefly in the remaining butter or ghee and sprinkle on top of the curry.

CHICKEN WITH HONEY

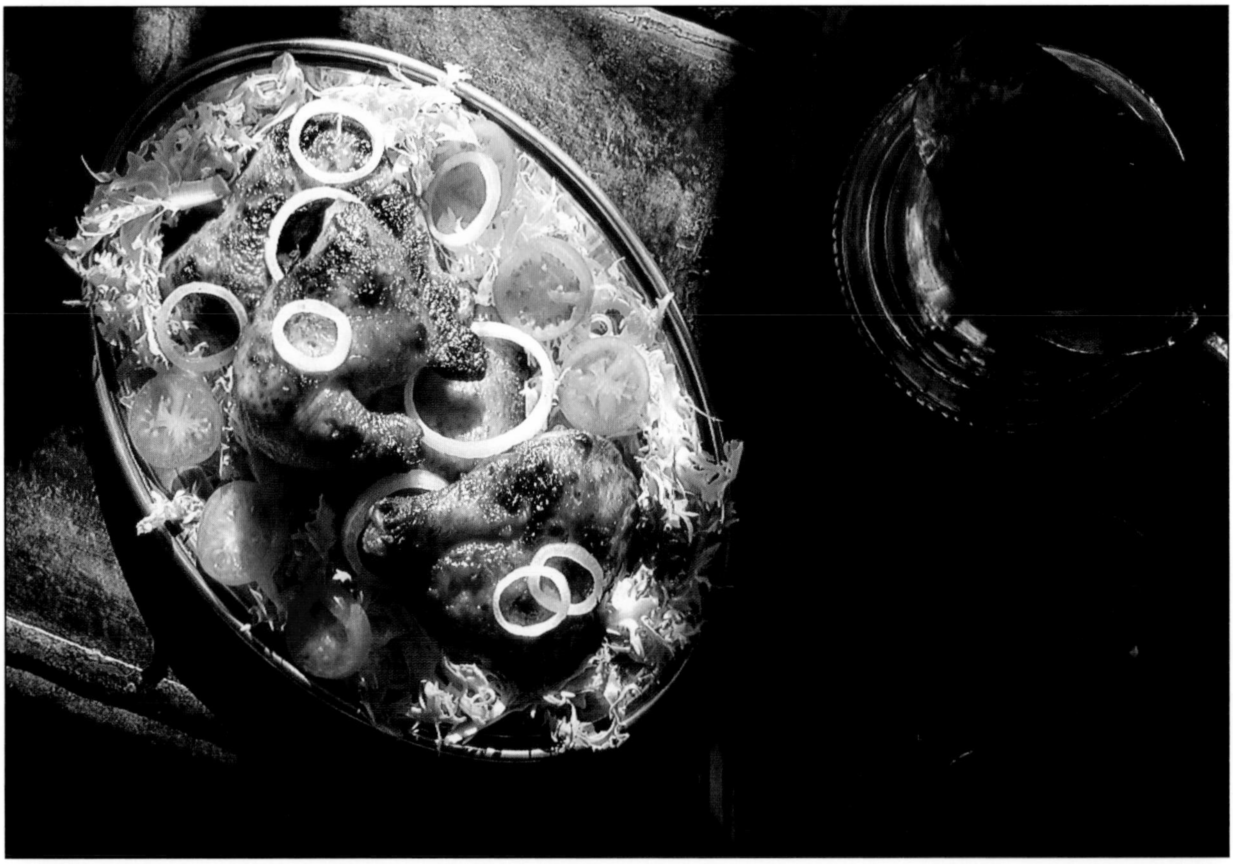

CHICKEN WITH HONEY

SERVES 4

1tbsp fresh root ginger, finely grated
2 cloves garlic, crushed
2tbsp lemon juice
5tbsp honey
1tbsp paprika
1tsp chilli powder
1tbsp cornflour
½tsp salt
8 chicken legs
2oz (50g) butter or ghee
1tbsp lemon juice
leaves from 1–2 sprigs of coriander

Combine the ginger and the next 7 ingredients in a mortar, blender or food processor and pound or purée well to make a smooth paste.

Wash the chicken pieces, dry them on absorbent kitchen paper and prick them all over with the point of a sharp knife.

Rub the spice paste all over the chicken and let stand for at least 20 minutes to marinate.

Lay the chicken pieces on a rack across a roasting pan and cook in a preheated 400°F/200°C/Gas Mark 6 oven for 45 minutes until the meat is cooked through. Sprinkle with the lemon juice and garnish with coriander leaves.

CHICKEN WITH SPICES

SERVES 4

2–3tbsp oil
2 cloves garlic, chopped
1tbsp fresh root ginger, finely grated
leaves from 1 sprig of coriander
½tsp garam masala
1tsp ground coriander
1tsp ground cumin
4 cashew nuts
1tbsp paprika

1tsp chilli powder
1tbsp lemon juice
1–2tsp salt
8 chicken legs
5oz (125g) yoghurt

In a blender or food processor, blend all the ingredients except the chicken and yoghurt to a thick paste, then stir in the yoghurt and mix thoroughly.

Wash the chicken pieces, dry on absorbent kitchen paper and prick all over with the point of a sharp knife. Smother the chicken in the spice paste and marinate for about 3 hours.

Lay the chicken pieces on a rack across a roasting pan and cook in a preheated 400°F/200°C/Gas Mark 6 oven for 45 minutes until the chicken is tender. Sprinkle with extra salt to taste.

CHICKEN, TANDOORI STYLE

SERVES 4

8 chicken legs
1–2tbsp lemon juice
salt
1tbsp fresh root ginger, finely grated
3 cloves garlic, chopped
1tsp ground coriander
½tsp ground cumin
1tsp chilli powder
2tbsp paprika
1tsp garam masala
½tsp ground black pepper
5oz (125g) yoghurt
1 lemon, sliced
1 small onion, sliced

Skin the chicken legs, wash thoroughly and dry on absorbent kitchen paper. Slash them with a sharp pointed knife.

Rub in the lemon juice and sprinkle with salt. Blend the ginger and garlic in a blender or food processor with 1 tbsp of water, then mix with the coriander, cumin, chilli powder, paprika, garam masala and pepper and stir into the yoghurt.

Smother the chicken legs in the spiced yoghurt and refrigerate, covered, to marinate overnight.

Lay the chicken legs on a rack across a roasting pan and cook in a preheated 400°F/200°C/Gas Mark 6 oven for about 45 minutes, until tender. Sprinkle with extra salt to taste and garnish with lemon and onion slices.

CHICKEN CURRY WITH YOGHURT

SERVES 4

5tbsp oil
2 onions, finely chopped
2 cloves garlic, finely chopped
1tbsp fresh root ginger, finely grated
seeds from 2 cardamom pods
1inch (2.5cm) piece of stick cinnamon
2 cloves
½tsp fennel seeds
1tsp paprika
2tsp ground coriander
½tsp ground cumin
½tsp chilli powder
½tsp turmeric
5oz (125g) yoghurt
3lb (1.5kg) chicken, skinned and cut into pieces
8oz (225g) potatoes, peeled and diced
8oz (225g) tomatoes, peeled and chopped
salt
leaves from 2 sprigs of coriander

Heat 4 tbsp of oil in a pan, add the onion, garlic, ginger, cardamom seeds, cinnamon, cloves and fennel seeds and fry until the onion is golden. Add the paprika, ground coriander, cumin, chilli powder and turmeric and continue to fry until the oil runs free from the spice mixture.

Drain off the oil, stir in the yoghurt and purée in a blender or food processor until smooth.

Fry the remaining onion in the remaining oil until golden, add the chicken and continue to fry for 5 minutes. Add the blended spice mixture, the potato, tomato, ½ tsp of salt and 1½ pt (900 ml) of boiling water and cook over low heat for about 1 hour, until the meat and vegetables are done. Add extra salt to taste and sprinkle with the coriander leaves.

CHICKEN AND TOMATO CURRY

SERVES 4

5oz (125g) butter or ghee
2 onions, chopped
3 cloves garlic, crushed
1tbsp fresh root ginger, finely grated
1 green chilli pepper, chopped
seeds from 2 cardamom pods, crushed
3 cloves
1inch (2.5cm) piece of stick cinnamon
1 bay leaf
8oz (225g) tomatoes, peeled and chopped
½tsp turmeric
½tsp chilli powder
½tsp paprika
1tsp ground coriander

CHICKEN, TANDOORI STYLE

½tsp fennel seeds
1 chicken, about 3lb (1.5kg), skinned and cut into pieces
8oz (225g) potatoes, peeled and diced
¼tsp ground pepper
¼tsp saffron
salt
leaves from 2 sprigs of coriander

Heat the butter or ghee in a pan, add the onion, garlic, ginger, green chilli, cardamom seeds, cloves, cinnamon and bay leaf and fry until the onion is golden.

Add the tomato and continue to cook, mashing it with the back of a wooden spoon to make a paste. Add the turmeric, chilli powder, paprika, coriander and fennel seeds and fry until the fat runs clear of the spices.

Add the chicken pieces and fry for 5 minutes, then pour in 1½ pt (900 ml) of boiling water, add the potato and cook over low heat, covered, for 1 hour, until the chicken is cooked and the sauce has thickened. Sprinkle on the pepper, saffron, salt and coriander leaves.

WHOLE ROAST CHICKEN

SERVES 4

1 chicken, about 3lb (1.5kg), skinned
½tsp ground black pepper
salt
2oz (50g) ground almonds
2tbsp fresh root ginger, finely grated
2 cloves garlic, chopped
leaves from 2 sprigs of coriander
1 onion, finely chopped
1tsp garam masala
1tsp paprika
1tsp chilli powder
1tsp ground coriander
¼tsp saffron
1tsp ground cumin
5oz (125g) yoghurt
1tbsp lemon juice

CHICKEN CURRY WITH YOGHURT

Skin and wash the chicken and dry with absorbent kitchen paper. Prick all over with a sharp knife, rub in the black pepper and ½ tsp of salt and let stand to absorb the flavours for about 30 minutes.

Pound, grind or blend in a blender or food processor the almonds, ginger, garlic, coriander leaves, onion, garam masala, paprika, chilli powder, ground coriander, saffron and cumin, then mix well with the yoghurt.

Smother the chicken in the spiced yoghurt and marinate for at least 4 hours. Put the chicken in a roasting pan and cook in a preheated 400°F/200°C/Gas Mark 6 oven, basting occasionally, for up to 2 hours, until the chicken is tender and the juices run clear when the bird is pierced with a skewer. Sprinkle with lemon juice and salt to taste.

CHICKEN WITH FRIED POTATOES

SERVES 4–6

2½lb (1.25kg) chicken
2lb (900g) potatoes
6tbsp oil
3 large onions, finely sliced
½inch (1cm) fresh root ginger, grated
2 cloves garlic, crushed
1½tsp chilli powder
1tsp salt
½pt (300ml) water
1tsp garam masala
oil for deep-frying

Skin the chicken and cut into 8 pieces. Wash and put to one side.

Wash the potatoes, peel and cut into strips. Soak in cold salted water for about 30 minutes. Heat 6 tbsp of oil in a saucepan over a medium high heat and fry the onions, ginger and garlic, stirring constantly, until the onions are golden brown. Add the chilli and salt, mix with the onions; fry for about 30 seconds. Add the chicken pieces and continue to fry for 8–10 minutes.

Add the water. Bring to the boil. Lower the heat, cover and cook for about 20–25 minutes until the chicken is tender and the gravy thickened. Add the garam masala and cook for a further 2–3 minutes.

While the chicken is cooking, drain the potatoes and dry on absorbent kitchen paper. Heat the oil for deep frying and fry the potatoes until golden-brown and crisp. Arrange the chicken on a flat dish and place the fried potatoes around it.

SPICED CHICKEN

SERVES 4

3tbsp coriander seeds
2 red chilli peppers, cut into 3 or 4 pieces
1inch (2.5cm) piece of stick cinnamon
2 cloves
2oz (50g) fresh coconut, grated
½tsp turmeric
2 onions, finely chopped
1tbsp fresh root ginger, finely grated
4–6 curry leaves
2lb (1kg) chicken parts, skinned
4tbsp oil
2 green chilli peppers, seeded and cut into 3 or 4 pieces
2 bay leaves
4oz (100g) tomatoes, peeled and chopped
salt

Heat a pan without any fat or oil until very hot, then add the coriander seeds, red chilli, stick cinnamon and cloves and roast them for 5–6 minutes, shaking the pan to prevent them burning. Grind or pound the roasted spices into a fine powder.

Blend the spices and coconut together in a blender or food processor. Transfer to a bowl. Stir in the turmeric, three-quarters of the onion, the ginger and half the curry leaves.

Smother the chicken with the spice mixture and let marinate for 10–15 minutes.

Heat the oil in a pan and add the remaining onion, green chilli and bay leaves. Fry until the onion is golden. Add about 1½ pt (900 ml) of water, the tomato and chicken pieces and cook gently, covered, for an hour, until the chicken is tender and the sauce is thick. Add salt to taste.

CHICKEN WITH ONIONS AND VEGETABLES

SERVES 4–6

3 medium onions
2–3tbsp oil
2 cloves garlic, crushed
½inch (1cm) fresh root ginger, grated
1lb (450g) chicken, boneless broiled or leftover roast cut into small cubes
3–4 green chillies, chopped
good pinch of turmeric
pinch of chilli powder
4oz (100g) mixed vegetables, frozen
1tsp salt
1tbsp tomato ketchup
1 small tomato, cut into 8 pieces

Chop 2 of the onions and slice the other. Heat the oil in a large frying pan over a medium heat and fry the chopped onions, garlic and ginger until lightly golden. Add the chicken, sliced onions, green chillies, turmeric, chilli powder, vegetables and salt and fry for about 10–12 minutes until the vegetables are tender. Add the ketchup and tomato and fry for 1 minute more.

CHICKEN KEBABS

SERVES 2

2tbsp soy sauce
2tbsp oil
1tsp ground black pepper
1lb (450g) boned chicken, skinned and cubed

Mix the soy sauce, oil and pepper with 1 tbsp of water, pour over the chicken, turn to coat and let marinate for at least an hour.

Thread the chicken cubes onto skewers and grill slowly for 25–30 minutes, turning and basting occasionally with the marinade, until cooked through.

CHICKEN WITH BEETS

SERVES 4–6

2½lb (1.25kg) chicken, skinned and cut into 10–12 pieces
4 medium onions, sliced
1inch (2.5cm) fresh root ginger, grated
2 cloves garlic, crushed
1½pt (900ml) water
4 cooked beets, halved and sliced
4 medium tomatoes, halved and sliced
4–5 green chillies
1tsp sugar
4–5tbsp mint leaves
juice of 2 lemons

Place the chicken, onions, ginger and garlic in a saucepan with the water and bring to the boil. Boil the chicken until tender. Add the beets, tomatoes and chillies and stir. Cook for about 15 minutes. Add the sugar and mint, and cook for a further 10 minutes. Squeeze the juice of the lemons and serve with rice.

OPPOSITE: CHICKEN KEBABS

◆ POULTRY AND MEAT ◆

FRIED CHICKEN

FRIED CHICKEN

SERVES 4–6

1 medium-sized chicken, skinned and cut into 8 pieces
4oz (100g) plain flour
1 egg
4 cloves garlic, crushed
¾inch (1.5cm) fresh root ginger, grated
8fl oz (225ml) yoghurt
1 dried red chilli, roasted and ground
¼tsp garam masala
1tsp salt
½tsp pepper
few drops red food colouring
¾tsp ground, roasted cumin seeds
oil for deep frying

Wash the pieces of chicken and pat dry. Make 2–3 slits in each piece. Mix all the other ingredients together and make sure all the pieces are fully coated. Marinate for about 6 hours.

Deep-fry over a medium heat for 12–15 minutes until nicely golden and cooked right through.

CURRIED CHICKEN SOUP

SERVES 4–6

1 breast of chicken
about 2½pt (1.5lt) water
1tsp salt
1tsp cumin seeds
2tsp coriander seeds
1tbsp channa dal (split yellow peas)
1tbsp poppy seeds
3 cloves garlic
½inch (1cm) fresh root ginger
5 peppercorns
½tsp turmeric
2–3 green chillies
1tbsp butter or ghee
1 small onion, finely sliced
16fl oz (450ml) coconut milk

Skin the chicken and cut into small pieces. Place the pieces of chicken, water and salt in a large saucepan and bring to the boil over a medium high heat. Lower the heat and simmer until it has reduced to about 14 fl oz (400 ml).

In the meantime, dry roast the cumin, coriander and channa dal until they are a few shades darker. Grind the dry roasted spices with the poppy seeds, garlic, ginger, peppercorns, turmeric and green chillies.

Remove the chicken pieces from the broth, bone them and shred into very small pieces. Add the ground spices to the broth and mix well. Sieve this mixture and put aside.

In a large saucepan, heat the butter or ghee and fry the onion until lightly golden. Add the spiced broth and cook for 2–3 minutes over a medium heat. Lower the heat to medium low.

Add the coconut milk and pieces of chicken and cook for 5–10 minutes. If the soup is too thick, add a little more water or coconut milk.

◆ ◆ ◆

LAYERED BREAD

SERVES 4–6

12oz (350g) plain flour
½tsp salt
4tbsp oil
about 6fl oz (175ml) hot water
3 heaped tbsp butter or ghee, melted

Sift the flour and salt together. Rub in the oil. Slowly add the water to form a soft dough. Knead for about 10 minutes until it is no longer sticky. Divide the dough into 16 balls. Flatten a ball on a lightly floured surface and roll into an 8 inch (20 cm) circle.

Brush a little butter or ghee on this and fold in half, brush on a little more butter or ghee and fold into a small triangle. Roll out the triangle quite thinly on the floured surface. Heat a frying pan over medium heat and place a rolled triangle on it. Heat each side for 1 minute. Keep aside. Cook each triangle in this manner.

Add the butter or ghee and gently fry one at a time for 1–2 minutes, turning once, until golden-brown.

LAYERED BREAD WITH CAULIFLOWER

SERVES 4–6

Filling
1 small cauliflower, washed
1tsp salt
½tsp amchoor (mango powder)
½tsp chilli powder

Dough
12oz (350g) flour
½tsp salt
4tbsp oil
about 6fl oz (175ml) hot water
butter or ghee for frying

To make the filling, grate the cauliflower, mix with the other ingredients and put aside.

For the dough, sift the flour and salt together. Rub in the oil. Add enough water to form a stiff dough. Knead for about 10 minutes until you have a soft dough. Divide into 20 balls. Flatten the balls slightly between the palms.

Roll out 2 balls into 4 inch (10 cm) rounds. Place about 1½–2tbsp of the filling on 1 of the rounds, spreading it evenly. Place the other round over the filling, sealing the edges with a little water. Roll out gently into 7 inch (18 cm) rounds and be careful that no filling comes out.

Heat a frying pan over a medium heat. Place a piece of bread in the frying pan and cook for about 1 minute until brown spots appear. Turn and cook the other side. Add 2 tsp of butter or ghee and cook for 2–3 minutes until golden-brown. Turn and cook the other side; add more butter or ghee if required. Make all the others in the same way.

LAYERED BREAD

CORNFLOUR BREAD

SERVES 4–6

10oz (275g) coarse cornflour
pinch of salt
about ¼pt (150ml) hot water
melted butter

Sift the flour and salt together. Add enough water to make a stiff dough. Knead with your palms for 10 minutes until soft and smooth. Divide the dough into 8–10 balls.

Take one of the balls and place it on a lightly floured surface and, with the palm of your hand, press the ball gently to about 5 inches (12.5 cm) diameter and less than ¼ inch (0.5 cm) thick. (If the dough tends to stick to your hand place a little flour on top of the dough.)

Gently lift out and place on a hot tava or frying pan and cook until lightly golden. Turn and cook the other side in the same way.

Pierce a few times with a fork, and brush with the melted butter.

LAYERED BREAD WITH RADISH

SERVES 4–6

Filling
1lb (450g) white radish, washed and scraped
1tsp salt
2–3 green chillies, finely chopped
½tsp ground, roasted cumin seeds

Dough
12oz (350g) flour
½tsp salt
4tbsp oil
about 6fl oz (175ml) hot water
butter or ghee for frying

For the filling, grate the white radish and mix with the other ingredients. Squeeze out all the water and discard it. Put aside.

For the dough, sift together the flour and salt. Rub in the oil. Add enough water to make a stiff dough and knead for about 10 minutes to make it soft and pliable. Divide into 20 balls.

Roll out 2 balls into 4 inch (10 cm) rounds. Flatten the balls slightly between the palms. Place about 1½–2 tbsp of the filling on 1 of the rounds, spreading it evenly. Place the other round over the filling, sealing the edges with a little hot water.

Roll out gently into 7 inch (18 cm) rounds and be careful that no filling comes out. Roll out all the bread in the same manner.

Heat a frying pan over a medium heat. Place a piece of bread in the frying pan and cook for about 1 minute until brown spots appear. Turn and cook the other side.

Add 2 tsp of butter or ghee and cook for 2–3 minutes until golden brown. Turn and cook the other side; add more butter or ghee if required.

DEEP-FRIED WHITE BREAD

◆ BREADS ◆

LEAVEN BREAD

SERVES 4–6

1tsp dried yeast
1tsp sugar
3fl oz (75ml) lukewarm water
10oz (275g) plain flour
½tsp salt
¾tsp baking powder
1tbsp oil
about 3tbsp yoghurt

Stir the yeast and sugar into the water and set aside for 15–20 minutes until the liquid is frothy.

Sift together the flour, salt and baking powder. Make a well in the middle, add the yeast liquid, oil and yoghurt and knead for about 10 minutes until soft and no longer sticky.

Place the dough in an oiled polythene bag and set aside in a warm place for 2–3 hours until double in size. Knead again for 1–2 minutes and divide into 12 balls. Roll into 7 inch (18 cm) rounds. Place as many as possible on a baking tray and put in a preheated 400°F/200°C/Gas Mark 6 oven, for 4–5 minutes on each side until brown spots appear. Place them for a few seconds under a hot grill until slightly browned. Wrap the cooked ones in foil while cooking the others.

DEEP-FRIED WHITE BREAD

SERVES 4–6

12oz (350g) plain flour
½tsp salt
2tbsp oil
about 6fl oz (175ml) hot water
oil for deep-frying

Sift the flour and salt together. Rub in the oil. Slowly add enough water to form a stiff dough. Knead for about 10 minutes until you have a soft, pliable dough. Divide the dough into about 40 small balls and flatten each ball.

Roll out a few balls on a slightly oily surface into rounds of 4 inches (10 cm) across (do not roll out all the balls at the same time as they tend to stick). Heat the oil in a karai or saucepan over a high heat. Put in a ball and press the middle with a slotted spoon as this causes it to puff up. Turn and cook the other side for a few seconds. Drain and serve hot.

YOGHURT BREAD

SERVES 12–14

6oz (175g) plain flour
2–3tbsp yoghurt
½tsp salt
oil for frying

Sift the flour into a bowl, make a well in the middle, add the yoghurt and salt and combine with as little warm water as possible, about 3 tbsp, to make a dough that is soft but not sticky.

Pull off a small piece of dough and roll it into a ball on a lightly floured pastry board, then roll and flatten into a pancake. Repeat with the rest of the dough.

Heat about 1 inch (2.5 cm) of oil in a pan, add the bread and fry for 2 minutes on each side, until puffy.

YOGHURT BREAD

DEEP-FRIED BROWN BREAD

SERVES 4–6

8oz (225g) wholewheat flour
½tsp salt
2tbsp oil
about 3½fl oz (100ml) hot water
oil for deep-frying

Sift together the flour and salt. Rub in the oil. Add enough water to make a stiff dough. Put the dough on a floured surface and knead for 10 minutes until soft and smooth. Divide the mixture into 20 balls.

Take one ball at a time, flatten it on a slightly oiled surface and roll into rounds of 4 inch (10 cm) across. (Do not stack the rolled breads on one another as they might stick together).

Heat oil in a karai or saucepan until very hot, add a bread, pressing the middle with a slotted spoon so that it puffs up. Quickly turn and cook the other side for a few seconds. Drain and serve hot.

STUFFED LAYERED BREAD

SERVES 4–6

Filling
1lb (450g) potatoes, boiled and mashed
1 small onion, finely chopped
1–2 green chillies, finely chopped
1tbsp coriander leaves, chopped
¾tsp salt
¾tsp ground roasted cumin

Dough
12oz (325g) plain flour
½tsp salt
4tbsp oil
about 6fl oz (175ml) hot water
butter or ghee for frying

For the filling, mix all the ingredients together and set aside. For the dough, sift the flour and salt together. Rub in the oil. Add enough water to form a stiff dough. Knead for about 10 minutes until you have a soft, smooth dough. Divide into 20 balls.

Roll out 2 balls into 4 inch (10 cm) rounds each. Place about 1½–2 tbsp of the filling on one of the rounds and spread it evenly. Place the other round over the filling, sealing the edges with a little water.

Roll out gently into 7 inch (18 cm) rounds, and be careful that no filling comes out.

Heat a frying pan over medium heat. Place a bread in the frying pan and cook for about 1 minute until brown spots appear. Turn and cook the other side. Add 2 tsp of butter or ghee and cook for 2–3 minutes until golden-brown. Turn and cook the other side. Serve warm.

STUFFED DEEP FRIED BREAD

SERVES 4–6

Filling
1tbsp butter or ghee
pinch of asafetida
¼inch (0.5cm) fresh root ginger, grated
8oz (225g) peas, boiled and mashed
¼tsp chilli powder
¼tsp salt
½tsp garam masala

Dough
8oz (225g) plain flour
½tsp salt
1½tsp butter or ghee
about. 4fl oz (100ml) hot water
oil for deep-frying

For the filling, heat the butter or ghee in a karai or saucepan over medium heat, add the asafetida and ginger and fry for a few seconds. Add the mashed peas, chilli and salt and, stirring constantly, fry for 5 minutes until the mixture leaves the sides and forms a ball. Mix in the garam masala and set aside to cool.

To make the dough, sift the flour and salt together. Rub in the butter or ghee. Add enough water to make

UNLEAVENED BREAD

a stiff dough. Knead for about 10 minutes to form a soft, pliable dough. Divide into 20 balls. Insert your thumb into the middle of each ball to form a cup. Fill with 1 tsp of the filling. Seal the top and make it into a ball again.

Flatten and roll into 4 inch (10 cm) rounds on a slightly oiled surface (take care that no holes appear when rolling). Heat the oil in a karai until very hot. Gently put in a bread, and press the middle so that it puffs up. Turn and fry the other side until lightly golden. Drain on absorbent kitchen paper and serve hot.

UNLEAVENED BREAD

SERVES 4–6

8oz (225g) plain flour
½tsp salt
boiling water

Sift the flour into a bowl with the salt and combine with as little boiling water as possible, about 3 tbsp, to make a dough that is soft but not sticky.

Form the dough into balls, roll and flatten them on a lightly floured pastry board to make small pancakes.

Heat a pan without fat or oil and cook for about 2 minutes on each side, until speckled and puffy.

DAL BREAD

SERVES 6–8

6oz (175g) channa dal (split yellow peas)
4–6 cloves garlic, finely chopped
2 green chilli peppers, finely chopped
1tsp ground cumin
½tsp turmeric
12oz (350g) plain flour
2oz (50g) butter or ghee, diced
2tbsp oil
½tsp baking powder
salt

Pick over the dal, wash well and cook in about 1½ pt (900 ml) of water for 10–15 minutes, until the dal can be mashed with the back of a wooden spoon. Drain well.

Grind, pound or blend in a blender or food processor the dal, garlic and green chilli. Mix the cumin and turmeric with 1 tsp of water and blend into the purée, which should be dry rather than loose.

Sift the flour into a bowl, make a well in the middle and add the butter

or ghee, oil, baking powder and ½ tsp of salt. Combine the ingredients to make a dough, adding as little warm water as possible, about 3 tbsp. The dough should be soft but not sticky.

Pull off a small piece of dough and roll it into a ball on a lightly floured pastry board. Make a hollow in the ball and stuff in a spoonful of dal. Stretch the dough to cover the stuffing, then roll and flatten the ball to make a small pancake. Repeat with the rest of the dough.

Heat a flat pan without any fat or oil. Cook a pancake in the hot pan for about 2 minutes on each side, until speckled and puffy.

◆ ◆ ◆

◆ CHUTNEYS, SNACKS AND SALADS ◆

TAMARIND CHUTNEY

1tbsp coriander seeds
1tsp peppercorns
½tsp cumin seeds
½tsp fenugreek seeds
1tsp mustard seeds
½tsp asafetida
5 red chilli peppers
2–3tbsp oil
1tsp urid dal (black gram)
1tsp chana dal (split yellow peas) soaked for 20 minutes, then drained
6 curry leaves
2oz (50g) shelled peanuts
2tbsp brown sugar
salt
1tbsp sesame seeds
2oz (50g) dried unsweetened coconut

Heat a frying pan without any butter or oil and add the coriander, peppercorns, cumin, fenugreek, half the mustard seeds, half the asafetida and 4 red chillies. Roast the spices for about 5 minutes, shaking the pan to prevent burning. Pound or grind the spices to a fine powder and set aside.

Heat the oil in a pan, add the remaining mustard seeds, the urid dal, channa dal, curry leaves and remaining chilli, cut into 3 or 4 pieces, and fry until all the seeds have popped.

Add the peanuts and fry for a further 3 or 4 minutes, then add the tamarind juice, the roasted spice powder, sugar, ½ tsp of salt and remaining asafetida.

Heat another pan without fat or oil, roast the sesame seeds and coconut and add to the chutney. Stir well, adding extra salt to taste.

COCONUT CHUTNEY

4oz (100g) fresh coconut, finely grated
3 red chilli peppers, chopped and seeded
2oz (50g) yoghurt
1tbsp oil
½tsp mustard seeds
4 curry leaves
salt

Grind, pound or blend in a blender or food processor the coconut and 2 red chilli peppers, then stir in the yoghurt.

Heat the oil in a pan, add the mustard seeds and fry until they have all popped, then add the remaining red chilli and the curry leaves and continue to fry for 2–3 minutes. Add to the coconut mixture with salt to taste.

GREEN CORIANDER CHUTNEY

MINT CHUTNEY

2oz (50g) mint leaves, washed
2fl oz (50ml) tamarind juice
2tbsp onions, chopped
2 cloves garlic
¾inch (1.5cm) fresh root ginger
2–3 green chillies
½tsp salt
½tsp sugar

Blend all the ingredients together until you have a smooth paste. Serve with any fried foods. (This can be stored in an airtight jar in the refrigerator for one week.)

SWEET TOMATO CHUTNEY

1lb (450g) tomatoes
2oz (50g) sugar
½tsp ground cardamom seeds
3 cloves
½tsp chilli powder
1tbsp oil
½tsp mustard seeds
1tbsp white wine vinegar
salt
4 curry leaves

Immerse the tomatoes in a bowl of boiling water for about 2 minutes, until the skins split. Drain them, allow to cool, peel and chop.

Bring ¼ pt (150 ml) of water to the boil in a small pan, add the sugar and tomato and cook for 5 minutes, stirring. Add the cardamom, cloves and chilli powder and continue cooking, mashing the tomato with the back of a wooden spoon to make a thick paste. Remove the pan from the heat.

Heat the oil in a pan, add the mustard seeds and fry until they have all popped, then add to the tomato. Stir in the vinegar, add salt to taste and sprinkle with the curry leaves.

◆ CHUTNEYS, SNACKS AND SALADS ◆

PINEAPPLE CHUTNEY

½tbsp oil
½tsp whole mustard seeds
½lb (225g) canned pineapple, crushed and drained
big pinch of salt
1tsp cornflour mixed with a little milk

Heat the oil in a small pan over medium heat. Add the mustard seeds and let them sizzle for a few seconds. Add the drained pineapple and salt and, stirring occasionally, cook for about 10 minutes. Thicken with the cornflour mixture and remove from the heat. Chill.

YOGHURT AND TOMATO RELISH

4oz (100g) tomatoes, diced
1 small onion, finely chopped
5oz (125g) yoghurt
leaves from 1 sprig of coriander
1 green chilli pepper, finely chopped
1tbsp fresh root ginger, finely grated
½tsp salt
½tsp ground cumin, roasted without fat

Mix the tomato with the onion in a bowl. Reduce the strength of the onion by rinsing it in hot water, if desired. Mix the yoghurt in another bowl. Stir the dressing into the vegetables and add extra salt to taste.

GREEN CORIANDER CHUTNEY

leaves from 3–4 sprigs of coriander
1 or 2 green chilli peppers
1tbsp fresh root ginger, grated
salt
2tbsp lemon juice
½tsp sugar

Grind, pound or blend in a blender or food processor the coriander leaves, green chilli, ginger and ½ tsp of salt to make a thick paste. Stir in the lemon juice and add sugar and extra salt to taste.

ABOVE: YOGHURT AND TOMATO RELISH BELOW: COCONUT CHUTNEY

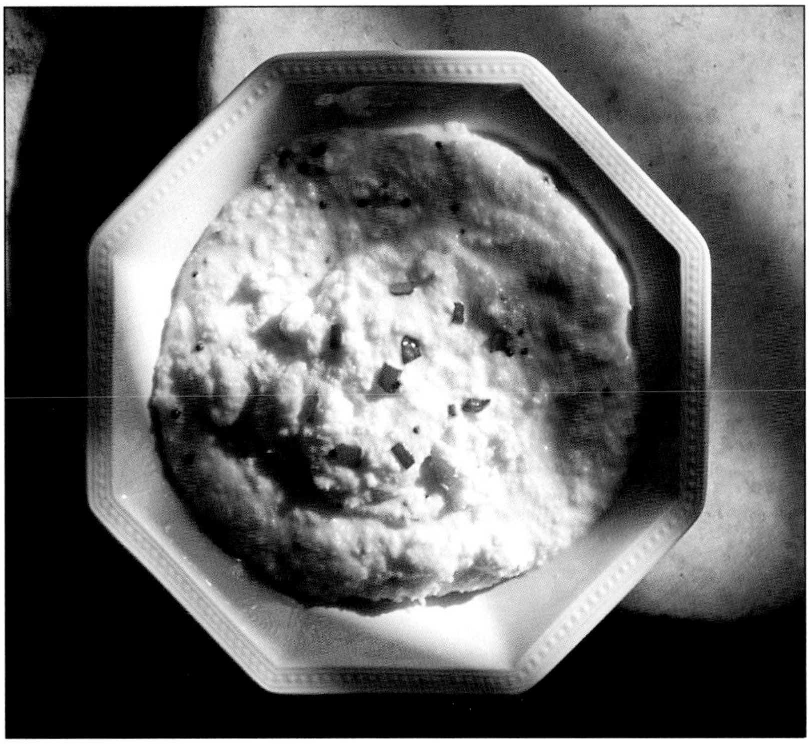

◆ CHUTNEYS, SNACKS AND SALADS ◆

CABBAGE FRITTERS

SERVES 4

4oz (100g) chickpea flour (besan)
4oz (100g) hard white cabbage, grated
1 small onion, finely sliced
2 green chilli peppers, thinly sliced
1tbsp fresh root ginger, finely grated
4–6 curry leaves, chopped
1tsp salt
½tsp chilli powder
½tsp garam masala
oil for deep-frying

Mix the flour with ¼ pt (150 ml) of water in a bowl to make a batter. Add all the ingredients except the oil and stir well to coat.

Heat a quantity of oil for deep-frying, add the cabbage in batter by the tablespoonful and fry until golden. Drain on absorbent kitchen paper. Serve with a chutney.

DATE AND PRUNE CHUTNEY

1tbsp oil
2 cardamom pods
1inch (2.5cm) piece of stick cinnamon
2 dried red chillies
4oz (100g) dates
8oz (225g) prunes
1tbsp raisins
12fl oz (350ml) water
½tsp salt
3tbsp sugar
1tsp flour
2tbsp milk

Heat the oil in a saucepan over a medium high heat. Add the cardamom, cinnamon and red chillies and let them sizzle for 8–10 seconds. Add the dates, prunes and raisins and stir-fry for 3–4 minutes. Add the water and salt and, when it comes to the boil, add the sugar and mix in well. Lower the heat, cover and cook for about 15 minutes.

In the meantime mix the flour and milk into a smooth paste. When the dates and prunes are tender, add the flour and milk paste, stirring constantly to make sure no lumps form. Remove from the heat and chill before serving.

BLACK LENTIL CHUTNEY

4oz (100g) urid dal (black gram)
1 or 2 red chilli peppers
¼tsp asafetida
2oz (50g) fresh coconut, finely grated
juice from 1tbsp seedless tamarind
salt

Pick over the dal. Heat a pan without fat or oil, add the dal, 1 chilli and the asafetida and cook, shaking the pan to prevent burning, until the dal is golden.

Pound the roasted spices together. Grind, pound or blend in a blender or food processor the coconut and tamarind with 1–2 tbsp of water, then add the roasted spice powder and grind them together, adding a little more water if necessary. Add salt to taste.

CABBAGE FRITTERS

CHICKEN AND VEGETABLE SALAD

SERVES 4–6

8oz (225g) cooked chicken, cut into manageable pieces
1 or 2 apples, cored and cut into wedges
3oz (75g) white cabbage, shredded
2 tomatoes, cut into eighths
1 green chilli pepper, finely chopped
½tsp ground pepper
¼tsp ground nutmeg
salt
2tbsp lemon juice
leaves from 1 or 2 sprigs of coriander

Mix the chicken with the apple, cabbage, tomato and green chilli. Sprinkle on the pepper, nutmeg and salt. Squeeze the lemon juice over and toss the salad. Decorate with coriander leaves.

CHEESE CUTLET

SERVES 4–6

1tbsp butter or ghee
8fl oz (225ml) milk
6oz (175g) panir (cottage cheese), drained
4oz (100g) semolina
1 medium onion, finely chopped
2 green chillies, finely chopped
1tbsp coriander leaves, chopped
½tsp salt
2tbsp flour
4fl oz (100ml) milk
breadcrumbs
oil for deep-frying

Heat the butter or ghee in a karai over medium heat, add the milk, panir, semolina, onions, chilli, coriander leaves and salt and mix thoroughly. Stirring constantly, cook until the mixture leaves the sides of the pan and a ball forms, for about 3–4 minutes.

Spread the mixture ¾ inch (1.5 cm) thick on a greased baking tin. Cut into 1 inch (2.5 cm) squares, chill for 2 hours.

Make a smooth batter with the flour and milk. Dip squares in the batter and roll in bread-crumbs.

Heat the oil in a karai over high heat and fry the cutlets for 2–3 minutes until crisp and golden.

DEEP-FRIED PASTRY

SERVES 4–6

4oz (100g) flour
½tsp salt
pinch of kalonji (onion seeds)
pinch of ground roasted cumin
1½tbsp oil
about 2fl oz (50ml) hot water
oil for deep-frying

Sift the flour and salt together. Mix in the kalonji and cumin. Rub in the 1½ tbsp of oil. Add enough water to make a stiff dough. Knead for 10 minutes until soft and smooth.

Divide the dough into 12 balls. Roll each ball into thin rounds 4 inch (10 cm) across. Make 5 or 6 small cuts in the rounds.

Heat oil in a karai or saucepan over medium heat. Add a pastry and fry until crisp and golden. Drain on absorbent kitchen paper. Serve with a chutney.

FRIED POTATO CAKES

SERVES 4–6

1lb (450g) potatoes, boiled and mashed
1–2 green chillies, chopped
½tsp salt
1tbsp coriander leaves, chopped
2tbsp onions, chopped
oil for frying

Mix the mashed potatoes with the chillies, salt, coriander leaves and onions. Form into small balls and flatten. Heat oil for shallow-frying until hot and fry the potato cakes for a few minutes on each side until golden. Serve with a chutney.

SAMOSAS

SERVES 4–6

Filling
3tbsp oil
¼tsp whole cumin seeds
1lb (450g) potatoes, diced into ½inch (1cm) cubes
1 green chilli, finely chopped
pinch of turmeric
½tsp salt
3oz (75g) peas
1tsp ground roasted cumin

Dough
8oz (225g) plain flour
1tsp salt
3tbsp oil
about 3½fl oz (90ml) hot water
oil for deep-frying

To make the filling, heat the oil in a karai or saucepan over a medium

high heat and add the cumin seeds. Let them sizzle for a few seconds. Add the potatoes and green chilli and fry for 2–3 minutes. Add the turmeric and salt and, stirring occasionally, cook for 5 minutes. Add the peas and the ground roasted cumin. Stir to mix. Cover, lower the heat and cook a further 10 minutes until the potatoes are tender. Cool.

To make the dough, sift together the flour and salt. Rub in the oil. Add enough water to form a stiff dough. Knead for 10 minutes until smooth. Divide into 12 balls. Roll each ball into a round of about 6 inches (15 cm) across. Cut in half.

Pick up one half, flatten it slightly and form a cone, sealing the overlapping edge with a little water. Fill the cone with 1½ tsp of the filling and seal the top with a little water. In a similar way make all the samosas.

Heat oil in a karai or saucepan over medium heat. Put in as many samosas as you can into the hot oil and fry until crisp and golden. Drain. Serve with a chutney.

◆ CHUTNEYS, SNACKS AND SALADS ◆

GREEN BANANA BALLS

SERVES 4–6

1 green banana, cut in half
1 green chilli, chopped
½tsp coriander leaves, chopped
½tsp salt
1tbsp onion, chopped
1tsp plain flour
oil for deep-frying

Boil the banana until soft. Peel and cool. Mash the banana with the chilli, coriander leaves, salt, onion and flour. Divide the mixture into 8 small balls and flatten. Heat the oil and fry the balls, turning once, until crisp and golden.

CURRY WITH GRAM FLOUR DUMPLINGS

SERVES 4–6

Dough
3oz (75g) gram flour
¼tsp chilli powder
½tsp ground coriander
good pinch of turmeric
¾tsp salt
2tbsp melted butter or ghee
2fl oz (50ml) water

Curry
2tbsp melted butter or ghee
½tsp cumin seeds
¼tsp mustard seeds
pinch of asafetida
4fl oz (100ml) yoghurt, beaten well
½tsp chilli powder
3tsp ground coriander
½tsp ground turmeric
1tsp salt

To make the dough, place the gram flour, chilli powder, coriander, turmeric and salt in a bowl. Rub in the butter or ghee. Add enough water to make a firm dough. Knead for 2–3 minutes. Divide into 4 parts. Roll each ball between the palms into long, round strips.

Bring some water to the boil, and place these strips into the water carefully. Boil for 5 minutes. Drain and cool. Cut into ½ inch (1 cm) pieces.

To make the curry, heat the butter or ghee in a saucepan over a medium heat. Add the cumin seeds, mustard and asafetida and let them splutter for 5–6 seconds. Remove from the heat and add yoghurt and the rest of the spices. Stirring constantly, return the pan to the heat and cook for 3–4 minutes (if you do not stir constantly the yoghurt might separate). Add the gram flour pieces, mix gently with the gravy and cook for 5 minutes.

VEGETABLE CUTLETS

SERVES 4–6

4oz (100g) beetroot, diced
4oz (100g) carrots, diced
8oz (225g) potatoes, diced
4oz (100g) cabbage, shredded
½tsp chilli powder
½tsp ground roasted cumin
½tsp ground black pepper
¾tsp salt
big pinch of sugar
1tbsp raisins (optional)
2oz (50g) flour
4fl oz (100ml) milk
breadcrumbs
oil for deep-frying

Boil the beetroot, carrots, potatoes and cabbage together until tender. Drain.

Mash the boiled vegetables with the chilli, roasted cumin, black pepper, salt, sugar and raisins. Divide into 12 balls and flatten. Chill for 1 hour.

Make a batter with the flour and milk and dip a cutlet in it. Then roll it in breadcrumbs until well coated. Heat the oil in a large frying pan and fry the cutlets for 2–3 minutes, turning once, until crisp and golden. Serve with coriander chutney.

RICE WITH GRAM FLOUR DUMPLINGS

SERVES 4–6

3oz (75g) gram flour
¼tsp chilli powder
½tsp ground coriander
pinch of turmeric
½tsp salt
2tbsp hot, melted butter or ghee
2fl oz (50ml) hot water

Rice
12oz (350g) basmati rice
2tbsp butter or ghee
1tsp cumin seeds
½tsp chilli powder
1½pt (900ml) boiling water

Sift the gram flour into a large bowl. Mix in the chilli powder, coriander, turmeric and half the salt. Rub in the butter or ghee. Add enough water to make a firm dough, knead for 2–3 minutes.

Divide into 4 parts. Roll each ball between the palms into long, round strips.

Bring some water to the boil and place these strips carefully in the water. Boil for 5 minutes. Drain and cool – cut into ½ inch pieces.

To prepare the basmati rice, wash it in several changes of water. Soak for 20 minutes in plenty of water and then drain. In a large saucepan, heat the butter or ghee over a medium high heat. Add the cumin seeds and let them sizzle for 3–4 seconds. Add the rice, chilli powder and remaining salt, and sauté for 2–3 minutes. Add the gram flour pieces carefully and gently mix with the rice. Fry for 1 minute. Add the water and, when it starts to boil rapidly, lower the heat to very low, cover and cook for about 20 minutes until the rice is tender. Fluff with a fork and serve hot.

SPICY SAGO

SERVES 4–6

7oz (200g) sago
4oz (100g) peanuts, skinned
2tbsp oil
1tsp mustard seeds
2 green chillies, chopped
pinch of asafetida
good pinch of turmeric
1tsp salt
1tsp sugar
3fl oz (75ml) water

juice of ½ lime
1tbsp coconut, grated
1tbsp coriander leaves, chopped

Wash the sago and soak in a little water for about 10 minutes. Drain and dry on absorbent kitchen paper.

Roast the peanuts and grind coarsely. Mix the sago and peanuts.

Heat the oil in a saucepan over a medium high heat. Add the mustard seeds and green chillies; when the mustard seeds start to splutter, add the asafetida and fry for 2–3 seconds. Add the sago and peanut mixture, turmeric, salt and sugar and stir-fry for 1 minute.

Lower the heat and continue to stir-fry for another 2–3 minutes. Add the water, cover and cook, stirring occasionally, until the sago is tender and nearly dry. Add the lime juice and give it a good stir. Serve garnished with coconut and coriander leaves.

VEGETABLE CUTLETS

STEAMED LENTIL CAKES

STEAMED LENTIL CAKES

SERVES 4–6

7oz (200g) channa dal (split yellow peas)
2fl oz (55ml) water
3 green chillies
½inch (1cm) fresh root ginger
1tsp salt
pinch of turmeric
¾tsp bicarbonate of soda
juice of 1 lime
1tbsp oil
½tsp mustard seeds
pinch of asafetida
1tbsp coconut, grated
1tbsp coriander leaves, chopped

Soak the dal overnight in plenty of cold water. The next morning, wash the dal 2 or 3 times. Place the dal and the water in a food processor or blender and blend until smooth.

Grind the chillies and ginger together into a paste. Add the chilli and ginger paste, salt, turmeric, bicarbonate of soda and lime juice to the blended dal and mix thoroughly.

Pour the mixture into a greased thali or a shallow cake pan, making sure that it does not come more than three-quarters of the way up. Place the thali in a steamer, cover and steam for 20 minutes. Remove from the heat and set aside for 5 minutes. Insert a skewer into the middle to test whether the lentil cakes are cooked. Cut into 1½ inch (4 cm) squares and arrange on a plate.

Heat the oil in a small saucepan, and add the mustard seeds; when they start to splutter, add the asafetida and, after 2–3 seconds, pour this over the cut lentil cakes. Garnish with the coconut and coriander leaves.

YOGHURT WITH CUCUMBER

12fl oz (350ml) yoghurt
1–2 green chillies, chopped
2tbsp coriander leaves, chopped
½ cucumber, finely sliced
½tsp chilli powder
½tsp ground roasted cumin
½tsp salt

In a bowl whisk the yoghurt until smooth. Add all the other ingredients and stir in well. Chill.

◆ ◆ ◆

GREEN MANGOES IN SPICY SYRUP

SERVES 4–6

3 small green mangoes
2tbsp oil
½tsp cumin seeds
½tsp mustard seeds
pinch of asafetida
¼tsp fennel seeds
¼tsp coriander seeds
¼tsp fenugreek seeds
pinch of turmeric
½tsp chilli powder
½pt (300ml) water
3tbsp sugar

Wash the mangoes and cut them lengthwise into quarters (do not peel). Remove the seeds.

Heat the oil over a medium high heat, add the cumin, mustard, asafetida, fennel, coriander and fenugreek and let them sizzle for a few seconds. Add the mangoes, turmeric and chilli; stir to mix all the spices and cook for 2 minutes. Add the water and sugar, bring to the boil, lower the heat and simmer for about 5 minutes. Serve hot.

FRIED SWEETS IN SYRUP (JELEBI)

SERVES 4–6

5oz (125g) plain flour
½sp baking powder
2tbsp water
7fl oz (200ml) warm water
oil for deep-frying
10oz (275g) sugar
½pt (300ml) water
few drops of yellow food colouring
few drops of rose water

Sift together the flour and baking powder. Add the yoghurt and mix well. Add enough milk to make a thick batter of pouring consistency. Keep aside in a warm place overnight.

When ready to fry the jelebis, prepare the syrup. Place the sugar and water in a large saucepan and bring to the boil. Boil for 5–6 minutes until

GRAM FLOUR BALLS

it becomes slightly thick. Remove from the heat and add colouring and rose water. Stir well and keep aside.

Heat the oil over a medium high heat. Place the batter into a piping bag with a ¼ inch (0.5 cm) plain nozzle. Squeeze the batter into the hot oil, making spiral shapes of about 2½ inches (6 cm) in diameter.

Fry until golden. Drain and add to the syrup for 1 minute. Remove from the syrup.

SOUTH INDIAN CREAMED RICE

SERVES 4–6

4oz (100g) rice
2pt (1.5lt) milk
4oz (100g) jaggery (raw palm sugar) or brown sugar
1tbsp cashew nuts, roasted

Wash the rice and set aside in a sieve to drain for 20 minutes. Bring the milk to a boil in a large saucepan, stirring constantly. Lower the heat, add the rice and stir well to mix. Simmer until the rice is tender and the milk slightly thickened. Add the jaggery or brown sugar, stir to mix and simmer for a further 5–7 minutes. Stir in the cashew nuts and remove from the heat.

CARROT HALVA

SERVES 4–6

1lb (450g) carrots, peeled and grated
1½pt (900ml) milk
5oz (125g) sugar
3 cardamom pods
4tbsp butter or ghee
2tbsp raisins
2tbsp pistachio nuts, skinned and chopped

Place the carrots, milk, sugar and cardamoms in a large saucepan and bring to the boil. Lower the heat to

medium low and, stirring occasionally, cook until all the liquid has evaporated.

Heat the butter or ghee in a large frying pan over medium heat, add the cooked carrots, raisins and pistachios and, stirring, fry for 15–20 minutes until it is dry and has turned reddish in colour.

GRAM FLOUR BALLS

SERVES 4–6

4oz (100g) gram flour
6tbsp butter or ghee
4oz (100g) sugar

Sift the gram flour. Heat the butter or ghee in a heavy-based saucepan over a medium heat and fry the gram flour until golden. Remove from the heat and cool. Add sugar and mix well. When cold, make into small balls.

◆ DESSERTS ◆

KHIR WITH ORANGES

SERVES 4

2pt (1.2lt) milk
1½oz (40g) sugar
2 oranges, peeled

Boil the milk in a large saucepan, stirring constantly. Add the sugar and stir. Reduce the heat and, stirring occasionally, simmer until it is reduced to ¾ pt (450 ml). Cool.

Remove all the pith from the oranges and slice. Add to the cooled milk. Serve chilled.

CHEESE BALLS IN SYRUP

SERVES 4–6

11oz (300g) panir (cottage cheese), drained
6oz (175g) ricotta cheese
12oz (350g) sugar
2¼pt (1.35lt) water

Rub the panir and ricotta cheese with the palm of your hand until smooth and creamy. Divide into 16 balls. Boil the sugar and water for 5 minutes over medium heat. Put the balls in the syrup and boil for 40 minutes. Cover and continue to boil for another 30 minutes. Serve warm or cold.

YOGHURT WITH SAFFRON

SERVES 4–6

20fl oz (550ml) yoghurt
¼tsp saffron
1tbsp warm milk
4oz (100g) castor sugar
2tbsp pistachio nuts, skinned and chopped

Put the yoghurt in a muslin bag and hang it up for 4–5 hours to get rid of the excess water. Soak the saffron in the milk for 30 minutes.

Whisk together the drained yoghurt, sugar and saffron milk until smooth and creamy. Put in a dish and garnish with the nuts. Chill until set. (Any seasonal fruit may be added while whisking.)

SOOJI HALVA

SERVES 4–6

4oz (100g) sugar
16fl oz (450ml) water
4tbsp butter or ghee
6oz (175g) semolina
ground cardamom seeds
3tbsp blanched almonds, slivered
few drops of rose water (optional)

YOGHURT WITH SAFFRON

Boil the sugar and water over a medium heat for about 5 minutes to make a thin syrup. Put to one side.

Heat the butter or ghee in a large saucepan over a medium heat. Add the semolina and, stirring, fry until lightly golden. Add the syrup and continue to stir until it leaves the sides of the saucepan and forms a ball. Sprinkle on the cardamom seeds, almonds and the rose water.

CHEESE FUDGE

SERVES 4–6

12oz (350g) panir (cottage cheese), drained
3oz (75g) sugar
1tbsp pistachio nuts, finely chopped

Place the panir on a plate and rub with the palm of the hand until smooth and creamy. Put the panir in a karai or saucepan over medium heat, add the sugar and, stirring constantly, cook until it leaves the sides and a ball forms. Remove from the heat and spread on a plate ½ inch (1 cm) thick. Cool slightly, sprinkle with the nuts and cut into small diamonds. Serve warm or cold.

SEMOLINA HALVA

SERVES 4–6

3tbsp butter or ghee
1oz (25g) almonds, blanched and sliced
4oz (100g) semolina
1tbsp raisins
¾pt (450ml) milk
2½oz (60g) sugar

Heat butter or ghee in a karai or saucepan over medium heat. Add the almonds and fry for 1–2 minutes until golden-brown. Remove with a slotted spoon and drain on absorbent kitchen paper.

Put in the semolina and fry, stirring continuously, until golden. Add the raisins and mix with the semolina. Add milk and sugar and stir until the mixture leaves the sides of the karai and a ball forms. Serve on a dish garnished with almonds.

CHEESE FUDGE

BAKED YOGHURT

SERVES 4

14.5oz (410g) evaporated milk
14oz (397g) condensed milk
18oz (500g) yoghurt
1tbsp pistachio nuts, skinned and chopped

Preheat oven to 450°F/225°C/Gas Mark 5. Whisk the evaporated milk, condensed milk and yoghurt together for 1 minute. Pour into an ovenproof dish and place in the preheated oven.

Turn the oven off after 6 minutes and leave the dish in the oven overnight. Chill. Serve garnished with the chopped pistachio nuts.

◆ DESSERTS ◆

FRUIT SALAD

SERVES 4

2 bananas
1 large tomato
1 apple
1 orange
1 large potato, boiled
⅓ cucumber
2–3tsp Chaat masala
1tbsp lime juice

Cut the fruit and vegetables into bite-sized pieces. Place in a bowl, sprinkle with Chaat masala and lime juice and mix gently. Serve immediately at the beginning of a meal or as a refreshing snack.

RICE PUDDING

SERVES 4–6

2pt (1.2lt) milk
1tbsp basmati rice, washed
2tbsp sugar
1tbsp raisins
½tsp ground cardamom pods
1½tbsp pistachio nuts, skinned and chopped

Bring the milk to the boil in a large pan, stirring continuously. Lower the heat and simmer for 20 minutes. Add the rice and sugar and continue simmering for another 35–40 minutes until the milk has thickened and reduced to 1 pt (1.2 lt). During the cooking time stir occasionally to stop the milk sticking to the bottom of the pan.

Add the raisins and cardamoms and, stirring constantly, cook for a further 3–4 minutes. Remove from the heat and garnish with the nuts. Serve hot or cold.

PLANTAIN JAGGERY

SERVES 4

4 ripe plantains, unpeeled
6oz (175g) jaggery (raw palm sugar; use brown sugar if jaggery is not available)

Cut the plantains into 2 inch (5 cm) lengths, place in a pan and add just enough water to cover. Add the jaggery and cook for 35–40 minutes, until all the water has evaporated.

Allow to cool, peel, then chill.

STEAMED PLANTAIN CAKE

STEAMED PLANTAIN CAKE

SERVES 4

8oz (225g) self-raising flour
1tbsp melted butter or ghee
3 or 4 ripe plantains, peeled and thinly sliced
2oz (50g) coconut, finely grated
6oz (175g) brown sugar
½tsp ground cardamom seeds

Sift the flour into a bowl, make a well in the middle and pour in the melted butter or ghee. Gradually adding as little warm water as possible (about 6 tbsp), work the ingredients into a smooth dough.

Mix the plantains with the remaining ingredients.

Cut tin foil into four 9 inch (23 cm) squares and divide the dough among them. With a finger or a spoon, dipped in water to prevent sticking, spread the dough out to within 1 inch (2.5 cm) of each edge of the foil.

Divide the plantain mixture among the sheets of dough and spread to cover. Fold each foil sheet over in the middle and fold over the edges, pressing down well to seal.

Put the foil packets in a steamer over a pan of boiling water and steam, covered, for 25–30 minutes, making sure that the foil does not touch the water.

PUMPKIN HALVA

SERVES 4

1lb (450g) pumpkin, preferably white
1pt (600ml) milk
5oz (125g) sugar
1tsp of rose water
4oz (100g) butter or ghee
¼tsp ground cardamom seeds
10–15 cashew nuts, halved

ABOVE: PUMPKIN HALVA
BELOW: PLANTAIN JAGGERY

Scrape the seeds and strings from the inside of the pumpkin, cut the flesh from the skin and chop into chunks. Grate the pumpkin coarsely, put in a square of cheesecloth and squeeze out all the moisture.

Combine the pumpkin in a pan with the milk, sugar and rose water and cook over a low heat for 30 minutes or more, stirring briskly, until all the milk has evaporated.

Stir in the butter or ghee and continue cooking until it separates. Drain off any butter or ghee not absorbed by the pumpkin mixture.

Stir in the cardamom and cashew nuts and spread the mixture about 2 inches (5 cm) deep in a greased dish with straight sides. Let stand for about 45 minutes, until set, then cut into squares.

MANGO SOUFFLÉ

SERVES 4

4 eggs
2tsp unflavoured gelatine
½pt (300ml) mango juice or 8oz (225g) mango pulp
2tbsp granulated sugar
salt
2tbsp superfine sugar
½tsp vanilla essence

Separate the eggs, placing the yolks in a heatproof mixing bowl. In a small bowl, sprinkle the gelatine over 3 tbsp of water and let stand until softened. Beat the yolks well and mix with the mango juice or pulp. Stir in the granulated sugar, gelatine and ½ tsp of salt.

Place the bowl over a pan of simmering water, taking care that the bowl does not touch the water or the eggs will scramble. Beat the mixture for 10 minutes, then take off the heat.

Whisk the egg whites with ½ tsp of salt and the superfine sugar until stiff, then fold into the yolks, adding the vanilla essence. Divide the mixture among 4 small dishes and chill before serving.

BEET HALVA

SERVES 4

1lb (450g) beetroots
1pt (600ml) milk
6oz (175g) sugar
4oz (100g) butter or ghee
¼tsp ground cardamom seeds
10 almonds, chopped

Scrape the skin from the beetroots, then grate coarsely. Put the beetroots in a pan with the milk and sugar and cook gently for 30 minutes or more, stirring briskly, until all the milk has evaporated.

Add the butter or ghee, cardamom and almonds and continue cooking, stirring constantly, until the mixture is thick and sticky. Spread the mixture about 2 inches (5 cm) deep in a greased dish with straight sides. Let stand for about 45 minutes to set, then cut into squares.

PINEAPPLE PUDDING

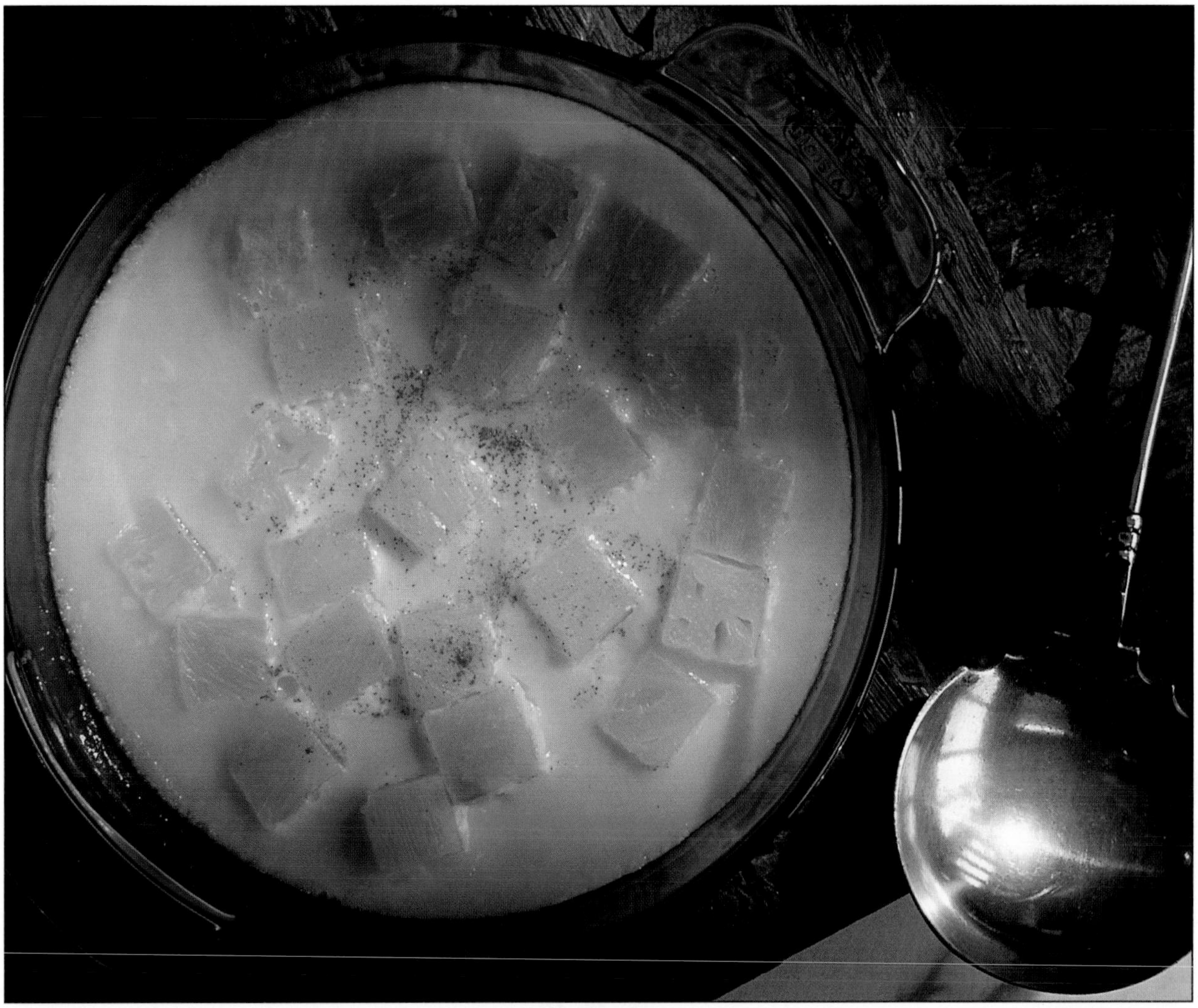

ICE CREAM WITH ALMONDS AND PISTACHIO NUTS (KULFI)

SERVES 4

2pt (1.5lt) milk
3½tbsp sugar
2tbsp ground almonds
2tbsp pistachio nuts, skinned and chopped
few drops of rose water

Bring the milk to the boil, stirring constantly. Lower the heat and simmer, stirring occasionally, until it reduces to about ¾ pt (450 ml). Add the sugar and mix thoroughly. Continue to simmer for another 2–3 minutes. Remove from the heat and let it cool completely.

Add the almonds and mix into the thickened milk, making sure no lumps form. Stir in the pistachio nuts and rose water. Place the mixture in a dish, cover it with its own lid or foil and place it in the freezer.

Take it out of the freezer after 20 minutes and give it a good stir to break up the ice crystals. Repeat twice more. After this, it may be divided up into chilled individual dishes, and covered and frozen for about 4–5 hours. Take it out of the freezer about 10 minutes before you are ready to serve.

FRITTERS IN SYRUP

SERVES 4–6

7oz (200g) plain flour
1½tsp baking powder
6fl oz (175ml) yoghurt
about 6fl oz (175ml) milk
8oz (225g) sugar
¾pt (450ml) water
oil for deep-frying

Sift together the flour and baking powder. Mix in the yoghurt. Add enough milk to make a thick batter. Boil the sugar and water together for 10 minutes.

Heat the oil in a karai or saucepan over medium high heat. Drop in 1 tbsp of the batter at a time and fry until crisp and brown. Drain on

MANGO SOUFFLÉ

absorbent kitchen paper. Soak the fried fritters in the syrup for 5 minutes. Serve in a little syrup, hot or cold.

PINEAPPLE PUDDING

SERVES 2

8oz (225g) canned pineapple chunks, drained
2 eggs
¼pt (150ml) milk
4oz (100g) sugar
¼tsp ground cinnamon
3 cloves

Arrange the pineapple pieces in a greased ovenproof dish. Beat the eggs with the milk and sugar and pour over the pineapple, then sprinkle on the cinnamon and cloves.

Set the dish in a roasting pan of boiling water and bake in a preheated 300°F/150°C/Gas Mark 3 oven for about 45 minutes, until lightly set.

◆ ◆ ◆

60円
550

JAPAN

Above: *Kyoto, the cultural capital of Japan, is famous for its zen-inspired temple cuisine.*
Far left: *Japan's land mass is split into four main islands and nearly 4,000 islets. On the fourth island Hokkaido, Lake Mashu is said to be the clearest lake in the world.*
Left: *the fish market shows some of the many types of fish supplied by the lakes, rivers and the sea.*

On first seeing a Japanese meal, one hardly dares to disturb the perfection of the tiny morsels of food arranged to form exquisite designs on the plates and bowls which form the background. The Japanese themselves tend to be more interested in the visual qualities of the meal before them than in its taste. A meal in the best restaurant in Tokyo may well taste heavenly, but what will most excite the admiration of the Japanese diner will be the way in which the chef has transformed simple vegetables, fish and meat into an edible masterpiece.

This concern with the visual quality of the meal is not the preserve of restaurants. A simple home-cooked meal will consist – not of a large plateful of food as in the West – but of tiny portions of various foods, selected as much for their variety of form, shape and colour, as for their taste. They are always neatly arranged with an eye to their appearance and carefully garnished with tiny sprigs of green or a delicate scatter of poppy seeds.

There are several levels to the design of a Japanese meal. Each individual item of food is carefully prepared to enhance its visual qualities. Lowly vegetables may be used as decorative garnish, be it a carrot, cherry blossom or a turnip chrysanthemum. The prepared foods are then artistically arranged on small plates, sometimes forming a miniature landscape. The plates and serving dishes are laid out on the lacquered trays according to prescribed rules. The setting is one of harmony and stillness.

In the West we are relatively functional in our approach to food. We eat when we are hungry, to sustain our bodies. We plan a meal in terms of taste and nutritional content, vitamins, minerals and carbohydrates. In Japan food has perhaps a wider significance than in the West. It is not just to fill the stomach and keep the body working: it has an aesthetic, ritual and social role to play too.

As with so many aspects of Japanese life, cooking techniques are neatly categorized. A Japanese meal is planned around a balance of techniques rather than nutritional considerations. A formal meal, such as one would eat in a restaurant or at a banquet, consists of a succession of dishes: first a clear soup, then a raw fish dish, followed by a simmered dish, a grilled dish, a deep-fried dish, a steamed dish and a dressed salad. A simpler home cooked meal is made up of a selection of dishes cooked using different techniques. In either case, the meal ends with the real food, rice, together with some crunchy pickles and probably a bowl of thick soup made from *miso*, a salty fermented soy bean paste.

◆ SPECIAL INGREDIENTS ◆

Basic Ingredients

Dashi: Made from dried bonito flakes and kelp *(kombu)*, is the basic stock of the Japanese kitchen. It is *dashi* which is responsible for giving the characteristic Japanese flavour to many dishes, and the ability to make well flavoured *dashi* is the essential secret of the good cook.

Ginger root: Fresh ginger root is much used in Japanese cookery as a seasoning and garnish; it is widely available, particularly in shops specializing in oriental or African foods.

Fish cake (Kamaboko): This is made from puréed white fish, pressed into solid cakes and sold ready cooked; it is usually white or tinted pink. It can be simply sliced and eaten raw, and is a popular ingredient in one-pot dishes, soups and rice and noodle dishes.

Horseradish (Wasabi): This is sold in Japanese food stores ready made in tubes, and in powder form, to be mixed up as required with a little water to a smooth paste. Horseradish is the usual accompaniment for raw fish dishes.

Kinome: The fresh-tasting young leaves of the prickly ash, is the most widely used garnish in Japan.

Kuzu: This is produced from the root of the *kuzu* vine, and is a traditional Japanese thickener.

Mirin: A sweet golden cooking wine with a very low alcohol content, is an essential item in the Japanese kitchen, giving a distinctive mild sweetness to simmering liquids, glazes and dipping sauces.

Miso: This is a rich and savoury paste produced by the fermenting action of a yeast-like mould on cooked soya beans, which are often mixed with rice or other grains. It takes at least six months and as much as three years to mature. *Miso* is a peculiarly Japanese food; indeed, as *miso* soup, it is probably eaten by every Japanese every day. It is much used in Japanese cooking as a basic flavouring, as a dressing for simmered and grilled foods and even for pickling.

Noodles: They are one of the most popular Japanese foods and come in many varieties and sizes.

Oils: The Japanese use pure vegetable oil, never animal fats, for cooking; any vegetable oil except olive oil is suitable.

Pickles (Tsukemono): No Japanese meal is complete without a dish of thinly sliced pickles of various types, colours and shapes. Pickles are made from many different vegetables; the most popular include *daikon* radish, aubergine, Chinese cabbage and *shiso* buds.

Rice cake (Mochi): Rice cakes are made by pounding glutinous rice, traditionally in big tubs, to produce a chewy white cake, which is shaped into balls or squares.

Sesame seeds: These are a characteristic Japanese flavouring and garnish. They should be lightly roasted in a dry pan to bring out the nutty flavour before use.

Seven-spice pepper: (Shichimi): This is a grainy mixture of chilli, pepper, black pepper, dried orange peel, sesame seeds, poppy seeds,

Above: *the setting for this meal is a Japanese room with its muted colours and sparse furnishings, creating an atmosphere of harmony and stillness.*

◆ SPECIAL INGREDIENTS ◆

slivers of *nori* seaweed, and hemp seeds; the exact blend of spices varies.

Soy sauce: A fermentation of soya beans, wheat and salt, is one of the primary seasonings of Japanese cooking. The thinner, lighter Japanese soy sauce, should be used in preference to the Chinese.

Soya bean curd: This is one of the most common ingredients in Japanese cooking, used in a wide variety of dishes. It has a delicate, slightly nutty, flavour and is an easily digestible source of vegetable protein.

Vinegar: Japanese rice vinegar has a light, delicate flavour. It is available in delicatessens as well as Japanese and Chinese food stores.

Yuzu: This is a tiny citrus fruit with a distinctively flavoured rind, much prized as a garnish and flavouring.

Food From The Land

Aubergine: These are much used, in a variety of different types of dishes. They come in many shapes and sizes, all of which are smaller than those available in the West.

Bamboo shoots: The shoots of the young bamboo, which grow at an amazing rate, are a symbol of spring in Japan. A very common ingredient throughout the East, they are prized for their crunchiness and delicate taste.

Burdock: This long slender root vegetable with a crunchy texture and earthy taste, is much used in Japanese cooking.

Chestnuts: Both large and small chestnuts are a popular food in Japan, roasted and eaten as a snack or included in a variety of sweet and savoury dishes.

Napa or celery cabbage (Hakusai): This has a somewhat milder flavour than Western cabbage and is much used in Japanese cooking.

Chrysanthemum leaves: This delicious leaf vegetable is much used in one-pot dishes, particularly in *sukiyaki*.

Daikon: Huge white *daikon* roots – a kind of giant white radish – are a common sight in Japanese fields and markets.

Gingko nuts: These have a delicate flavour and texture and are a regular ingredient in steamed dishes.

Leeks: The Japanese leek is smaller, sweeter and finer than the Western leek. It is widely used as an ingredient in soups, simmered dishes and grilled dishes and, finely sliced, is a common garnish and condiment. Use long, slender leeks or large spring onions.

Lotus root: This crunchy root vegetable is served as *tempura* and in vinegared and simmered dishes.

Mushrooms: Many different varieties of fresh mushrooms, both wild and cultivated, are used in Japan – in soups, simmered dishes and one-pot dishes.

Yams: Many different varieties of yam and sweet potato are used in Japanese cooking in simmered and one-pot dishes and in *tempura*.

◆ EQUIPMENT AND TECHNIQUES ◆

Equipment

Japanese meals may be successfully prepared using utensils available in any well equipped Western kitchen, with just a little improvisation. In fact, most Japanese kitchens are cramped and somewhat less complete and convenient than the average Western kitchen. However, with their characteristic love of precision and the right tool for each task, the Japanese have developed a range of kitchen utensils which, although not essential, are very useful in preparing Japanese dishes. They also make an aesthetically pleasing addition to the kitchen.

It is not essential to use Japanese knives, but you should have several good sharp knives which perform the same functions. Japanese knives are made of carbon steel, and are always honed on a whetstone.

Left: *Both metal steamers and bamboo steamers are used in Japan. Stacking bamboo steamers are readily available in Chinese stores and are most efficient. Bamboo makes a better insulator than metal, ensuring that more heat is retained.*
Steamers may be simply improvised. Use a large covered saucepan containing some support to keep the cooking vessels above the level of the water. A cloth stretched under the lid will absorb excess moisture.

Below left: *a fine-meshed strainer is used for draining noodles.* ***Below:*** *a small round frying pan is sometimes used for making omelettes.*

◆ EQUIPMENT AND TECHNIQUES ◆

Above *This vegetable knife* ***(top)*** *performs all manner of delicate vegetable cutting operations – from chopping and slicing to fine paring – with efficiency and speed. It has no Western equivalent, and is a worthwhile investment. The long thin-bladed knife* ***(centre)*** *is used for cutting fish fillets. A Western meat slicer may be used instead. A basic kitchen knife* ***(bottom)*** *is used for both general fish and meat cutting and also for more delicate work. It is available in many sizes.*

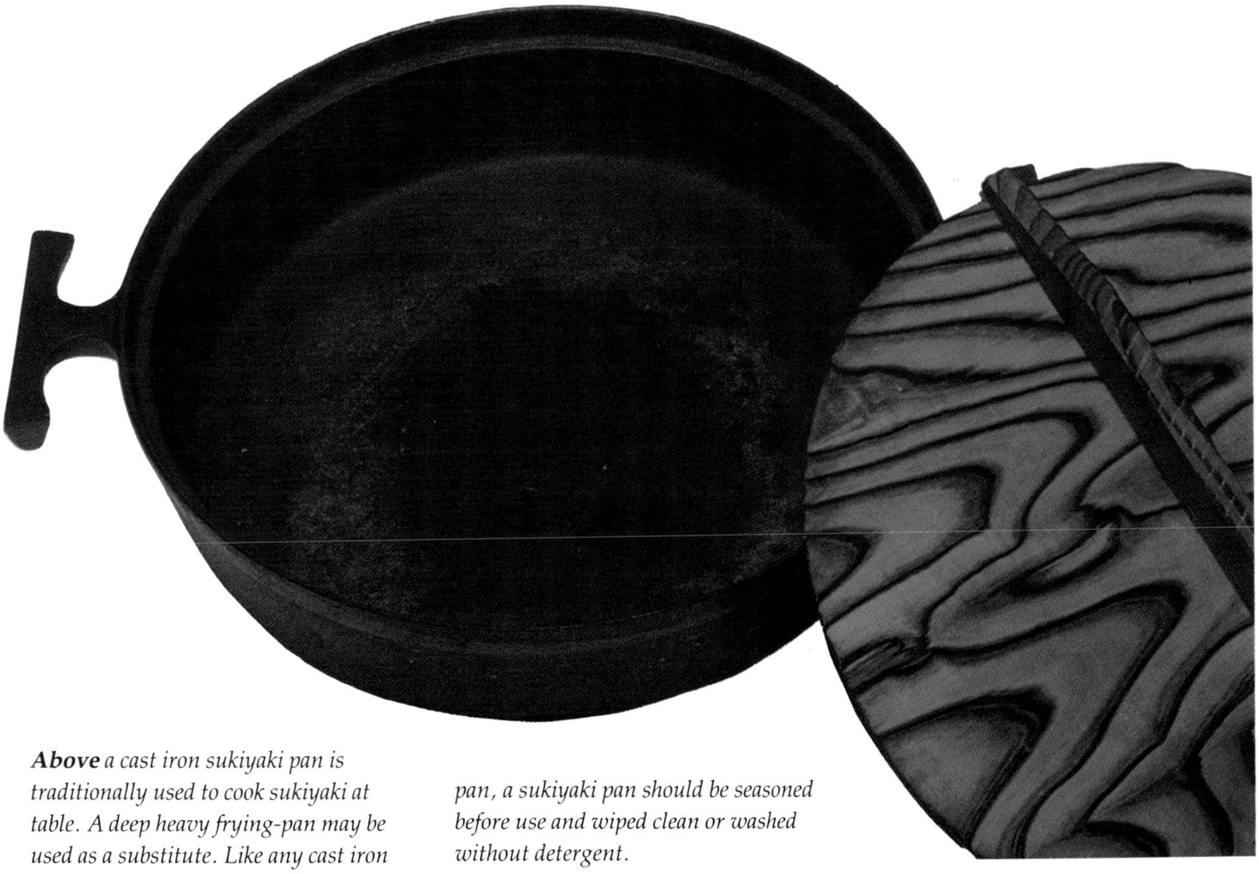

Above *a cast iron sukiyaki pan is traditionally used to cook sukiyaki at table. A deep heavy frying-pan may be used as a substitute. Like any cast iron pan, a sukiyaki pan should be seasoned before use and wiped clean or washed without detergent.*

◆ EQUIPMENT AND TECHNIQUES ◆

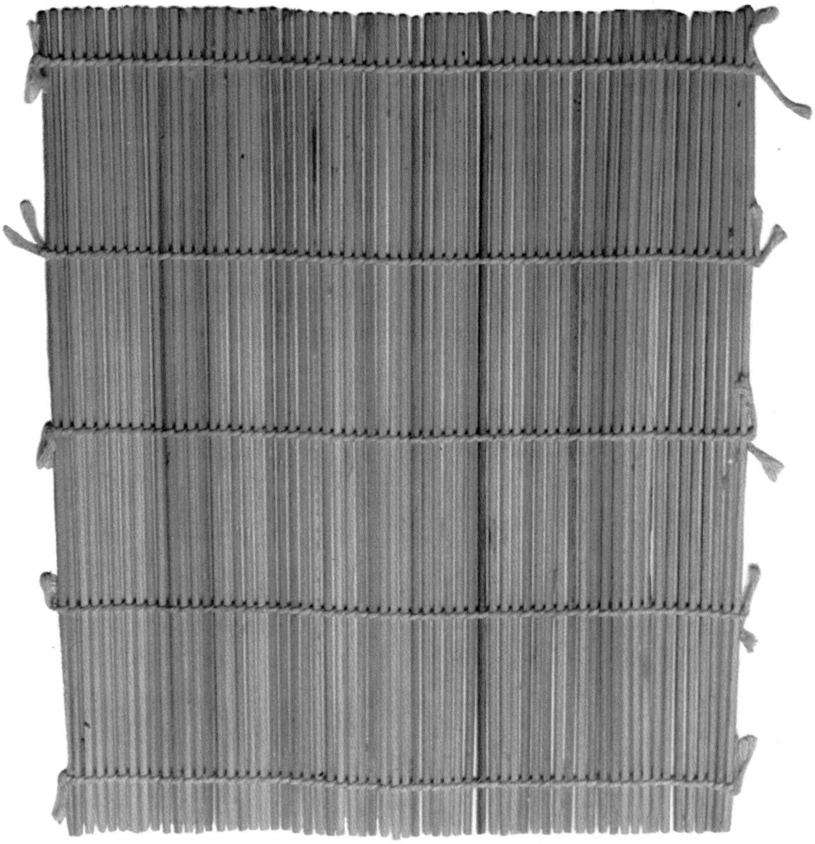

Left: *a small flexible bamboo mat is used for making sushi. Sushi may be rolled by hand, but will be less firmly and evenly packed.*

Left: *one-pot dishes are traditionally made in a heavy lidded earthenware casserole, which is ideal for the purpose. An even distributor of heat, it can be placed over a direct flame if the outside surface is completely dry.*

◆ EQUIPMENT AND TECHNIQUES ◆

Right: *cooking chopsticks are usually made of bamboo. Chopsticks for table use include plain bamboo serving chopsticks and eating chop-sticks made of lacquered wood or bamboo, which are often decorative.*

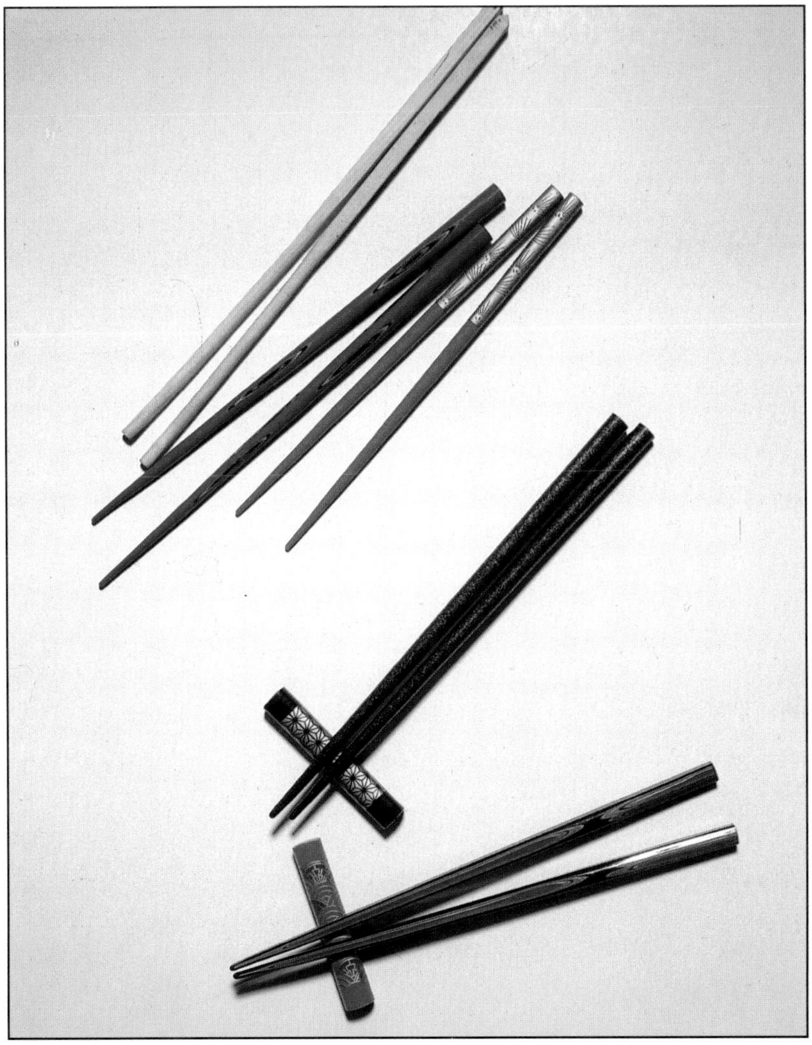

Right: *the Japanese mortar and pestle is a beautiful utensil as well as being extremely efficient. Foods such as nuts and sesame seeds are ground in this.*

Far right: *the Japanese grater is extremely fine-toothed, made of metal or ceramic, it often has a sill to collect the draining juices. Ideal for grating ginger and horseradish.*

Right: *a small flat bamboo rice paddle is used to turn and fluff cooked rice, and to mix seasonings into sushi rice. A flat wooden spoon is a good substitute.*

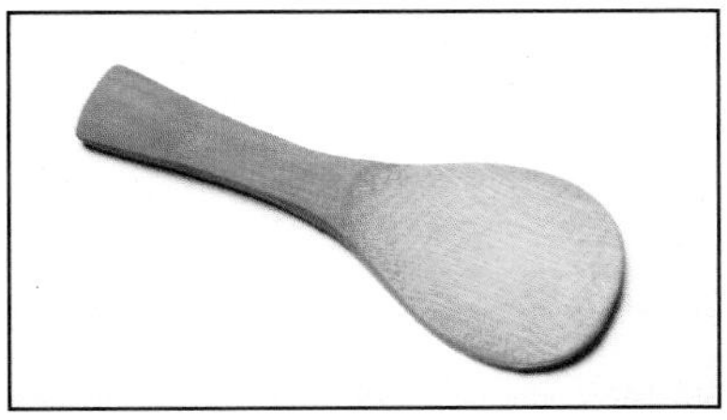

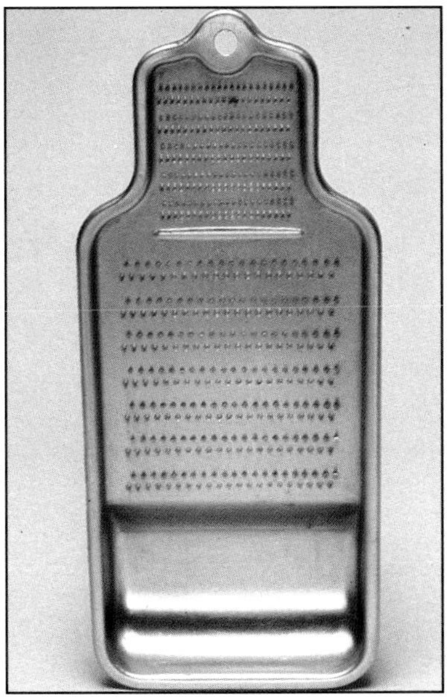

◆ EQUIPMENT AND TECHNIQUES ◆

Techniques

In Japanese cuisine, with its minimal approach to actual cooking, cutting techniques assume a greater importance than in the West. Foods are transformed more in cutting than in the cooking. The Japanese home-cook will often buy ready cut foods, deeming cutting to be one art best left to the experts. Many of the basic techniques are quite straightforward and within the reach of any home cook.

Preparing fish: Small fish look most attractive served whole, and need simply to be gutted. Larger fish are filleted according to their shape.

Salting fish: Fish is salted in order to firm the flesh and reduce odour. Thick fillets need more and longer salting than thin. Immerse fillets of white fish in a salt solution of 2 tbsp salt in 5 cups of water, for 20–30 minutes. For heavier salting dredge the fish in salt and set aside for 60–90 minutes.

Dried foods: In general, dried foods are first rinsed in cold water, then soaked in lukewarm water. After this they are shredded and simmered with fish, meat or vegetables.

Vegetable cutting: Decoratively cut vegetables add a great deal to the visual appeal of a dish. The main requirement for vegetable cutting is a good knife, a Japanese vegetable knife is ideal but any good, sharp knife will do.

Preparing fish to be served in fillets:
The shape of a fish determines how it should be gutted and filleted. Round-bodied fish such as trout and mackerel are cut along the spine to produce two boneless fillets. Wide flat fish, such as sole, give four thin fillets.

Gutting:
1 *Wash the fish in lightly salted water and scrape away the scales. Rinse and pat dry.*

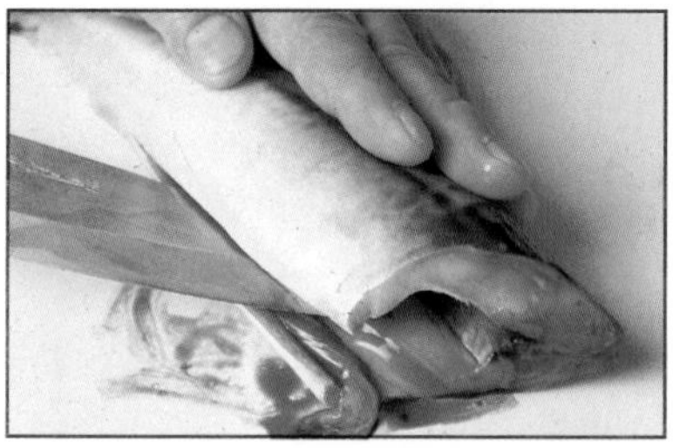

2 *Place the fish with the head facing to the left. Make a diagonal cut at the base of the head. Make a second diagonal cut to remove the head.*

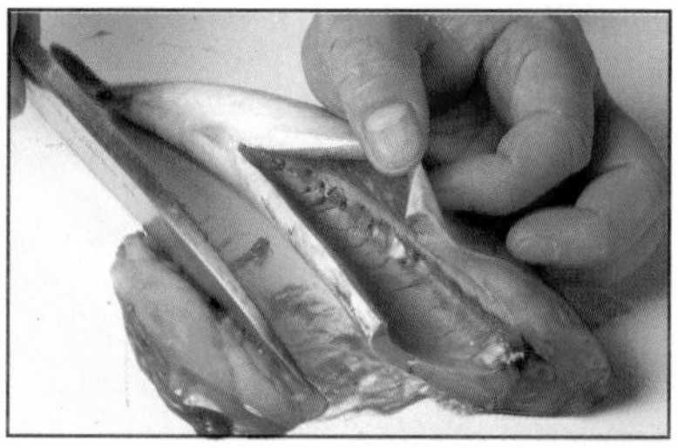

3 *Slit along the entire belly of the fish and carefully remove the stomach and intestines. Scrape the knife along the inside of the body to break blood pockets. Rinse thoroughly with cold water.*

Two-piece filleting:
1 *Rest the left hand gently on top of the fish and draw the knife lightly from the head to the tail. Retrace the cut several times, each time cutting closer to the spine; do not use a sawing motion.*

2 *Turn the fish and cut smoothly from the tail to the head.*

3 *Cut through to separate the fillets. The fish separates into two halves, one boneless and one containing the backbone.*

◆ EQUIPMENT AND TECHNIQUES ◆

Vegetable cutting:

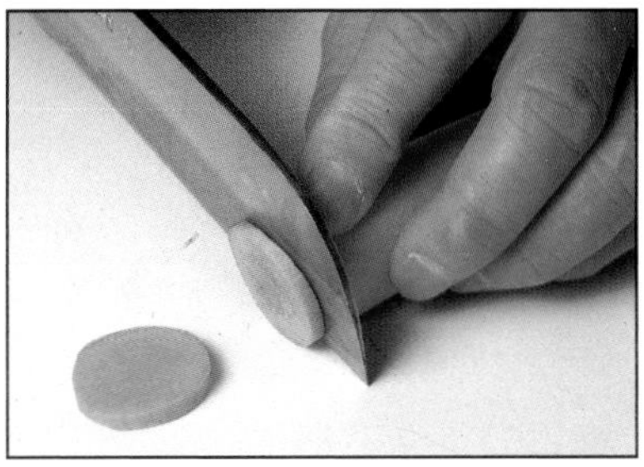

ROUNDS Cylindrical vegetables like daikon *radish and carrot are simply sliced through to make rounds.*

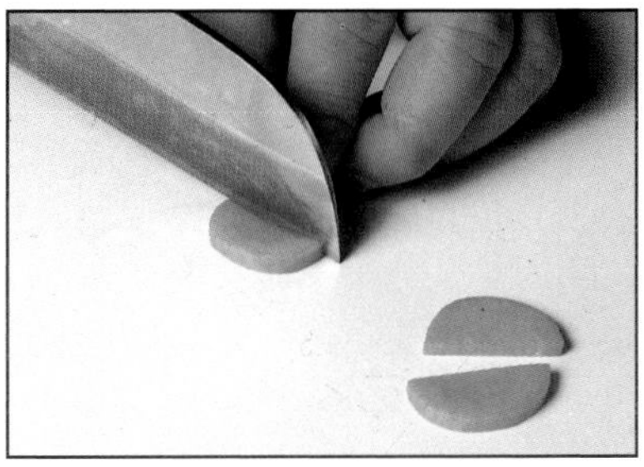

HALF-MOON CUT Cut rounds in half to make half moon slices; or halve the vegetable length-wise and slice.

GINGKO LEAVES Cut rounds into quarters to make gingko leaves. This cut is used for large or tapering vegetables such as bamboo shoots and carrots.

CLAPPER CUT Thick rectangles are reminiscent of the wooden blocks clapped together at moments of excitement in Kabuki plays. Cut the vegetable into 2 inch lengths. Then cut into slices ⅛–⅜ inch thick. Turn and cut again to make small.

POEM CARD CUT These thin rectangles are the same shape as the little poem cards which feature in the New Year's festivities. Halve the vegetable and slice into thin slices. Trim into slender rectangles.

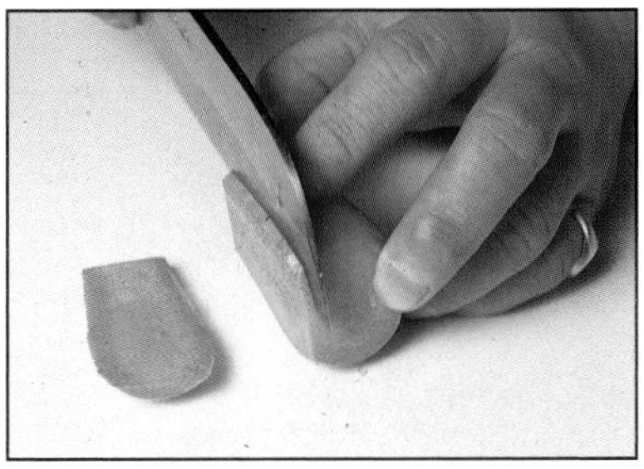

DICE CUT Cut thick rectangles. Then cut across to make cubes of even size. These dice are about ⅜ inch square.

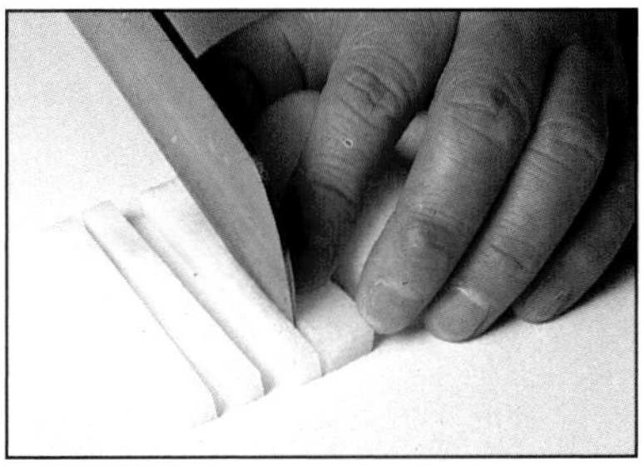

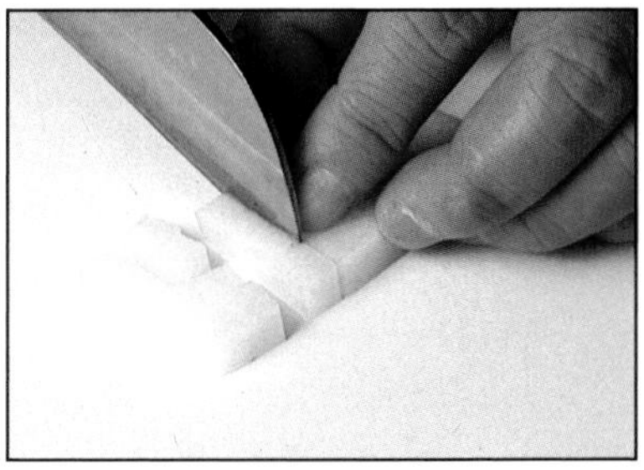

◆ EQUIPMENT AND TECHNIQUES ◆

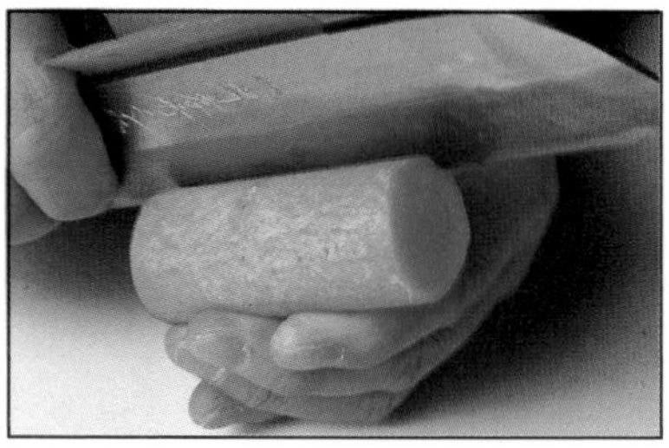

SHEET PARING In this technique the vegetable – usually a carrot or daikon *radish – is peeled in a long continuous motion until it becomes a single large paper-thin sheet. Hold the carrot in your left hand and pare with your right, using the thumb of your right hand to control the knife.*

MINCING Shred the vegetable very finely. If the vegetable is thick, first cut into thin strips and then chop very finely, balancing the knife on the point and moving it up and down as you slide the vegetable underneath.

NEEDLE CUT Cut the vegetable into segments and slice the segments very finely. Cut the slices into very thin threads.

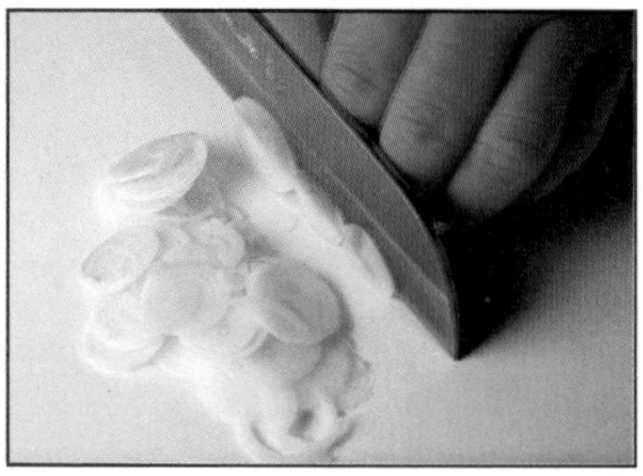

PAPER-THIN LEEK SLICES To use as a garnish, the white part of young leeks or spring onions are cut into paper-thin slices. The green part of spring onions or young leeks are slivered very finely.

The shredded vegetable is then rinsed in cold water, drained and patted dry.

The Japanese leek is sweet tasting and is used as a common garnish.

Fancy cutting:

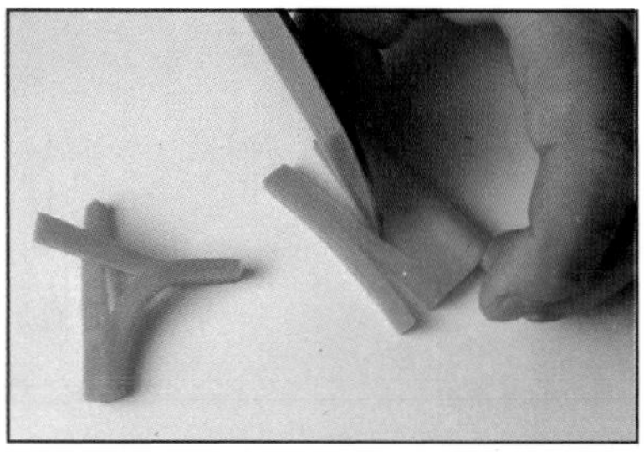

DECORATIVE CARROT TWIST Lemon peel as well as carrot is often formed into a decorative twist. Make two thin slits in a slice of carrot and twist.

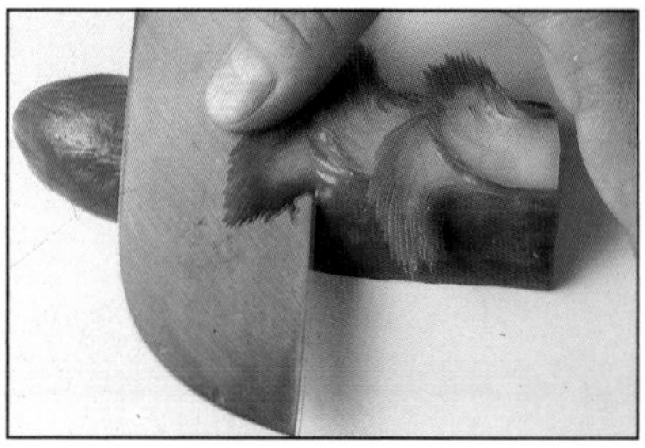

PINE NEEDLES This particularly beautiful garnish makes use of the contrast of light and dark green in the cucumber.

Divide the vegetable into 3 inch lengths and halve it lengthwise. Score the top part of the cucumber very closely with 1/4 inch deep cuts.

Peel back a 3/4 inch strip of skin and push to the side with your thumb. Repeat the cut, pushing the skin to alternate sides to form the pine needles.

◆ EQUIPMENT AND TECHNIQUES ◆

Above: *assorted garnishes are relatively easy to make and form an attractive accompaniment to a wide variety of dishes.*

DASHI I

SERVES 4–6

2pt (1lt) cold water
⅓oz (10g) piece kombu seaweed
1tbsp dried bonito flakes

Put 2 pt (1 lt) cold water in a large saucepan and add the kombu. Bring slowly to the boil. Remove the kombu just before the water boils, and reserve to use in Dashi II.

Add the bonito flakes. Bring the water to a full boil and immediately remove from the heat. Allow the flakes to settle. Strain off the bonito flakes through a cheesecloth-lined sieve. Reserve the bonito flakes to use in Dashi II.

DASHI II

Dashi II is a heavier stock, made by simmering the kombu and bonito that have been used to make Dashi I. It is used for simmered dishes, seasoned stocks and miso soups, where a stronger flavour is required.

SERVES 6

3pt (1.75lt) cold water
kombu and bonito flakes reserved from Dashi I (see recipe)
1tbsp dried bonito flakes

Put the reserved kombu and bonito flakes with the cold water in a large saucepan and heat just to the boil. Lower the heat and simmer for about

CLEAR SOUP WITH SHRIMPS AND SPINACH

20 minutes, until the stock is reduced by a third.

Add the dried bonito flakes and immediately remove the saucepan from the heat. Allow the flakes to settle, then strain off through a cheesecloth-lined sieve.

EGG DROP SOUP WITH MANGE TOUT

SERVES 4

4oz (125g) mange tout
1½pt (900ml) Dashi I (see recipe)
½tsp light soy sauce
salt
2 eggs

Wash the mange tout, pat dry and slice diagonally into very thin slices. Parboil in lightly salted water for 1 minute, remove and plunge into cold water to stop further cooking. Drain and pat dry.

Bring the dashi just to the boil; turn the heat to low and season to taste with soy sauce and salt. Beat the eggs lightly in a small bowl.

Add the mange tout to the simmering dashi, and pour over the egg in a thin stream. Remove from the heat immediately and ladle into warmed soup bowls.

CLEAR SOUP WITH SHRIMPS AND SPINACH

SERVES 4

4 medium shrimps
salt
3tbsp kuzu, potato flour or cornflour
2oz (50g) spinach leaves
1½pt (900ml) Dashi I (see recipe)
a few slivers yuzu or lemon rind

Shell and devein the shrimps, leaving the tail attached. Wash and pat dry. Slit the back of the shrimps open and press out flat.

EGG DROP SOUP WITH MANGE TOUT

Cut a lengthwise slit in the middle and push the tail through this slit to make a shrimp flower. Repeat with the remaining shrimps.

Salt the shrimps lightly, and dredge in kuzu or cornflour. Drop the shrimps into lightly salted boiling water and parboil for 2 minutes. Drain on absorbent kitchen paper.

Wash the spinach and parboil in lightly salted boiling water for 2 minutes, until just tender. Plunge immediately into cold water to retain the brilliant green colour.

Lay the leaves of spinach evenly on a bamboo rolling mat and roll firmly to squeeze out moisture. Unroll the spinach from the bamboo mat and cut it into four 2 inch (5 cm) pieces.

Warm 4 soup bowls and arrange a roll of spinach in each. Arrange a shrimp beside each roll.

◆ SOUPS ◆

MISO SOUP WITH MUSHROOMS AND LEEKS

SERVES 4

4 large or 8 small mushrooms
1 young leek
1½pt (900ml) Dashi II (see recipe)
3tbsp white miso

Wipe the mushrooms, trim away the hard stem and slice the caps finely. Wash the leek, pat dry and slice very finely.

Bring the dashi to the boil, add the mushrooms and simmer for just 30 seconds. Ladle a little of the hot dashi into a bowl and cream the miso into it.

Strain the miso mixture into the hot dashi; do not reboil. Ladle the soup into 4 warmed soup bowls, distributing the mushrooms evenly. Sprinkle over a little chopped leek and serve immediately.

BEAN PASTE SOUP

SERVES 4

1½pt (900ml) dashi II (see recipe)
1 cake of fresh bean curd
2oz (50g) miso
a little chopped spring onion

Heat the dashi in a pan. When boiling reduce the heat and add the bean curd, which has been cut into dice. Cook for 3–4 minutes. Stir in the miso, which has been mixed to a thin cream with water. Cook for 1 minute without boiling, then pour into bowls with a little spring onion.

MISO SOUP WITH BEAN CURD AND LEEKS

SERVES 4

1 young leek
8oz (225g) bean curd
½pt (900ml) Dashi II (see recipe)
3tbsp red miso

Wash the leek and slice very finely; divide among 4 soup bowls. Cut the bean curd into small cubes and distribute among the 4 bowls. Heat the dashi in a small saucepan. Put a little of the hot dashi in a bowl, add the miso and soften with a wire whisk. Strain the miso mixture into the hot dashi. Do not reboil. Ladle the dashi over the bean curd and leeks in each bowl and serve immediately.

MISO SOUP WITH WAKAME AND BEAN CURD

SERVES 4

⅔oz (20g) dried wakame seaweed
8oz (225g) bean curd
1½pt (900ml) Dashi II (see recipe)
3tbsp red miso

Rinse the wakame and soak in lukewarm water for 10–15 minutes. Drain and cut into 1 inch (2.5 cm) pieces. Cut the bean curd into cubes.

Bring the dashi to the boil, add the wakame and bean curd and simmer for just 1 minute. Ladle a little of the hot dashi into a bowl, and cream the miso. Strain the miso into the hot dashi; do not reboil. Ladle the soup into 4 warmed soup bowls, distributing the bean curd and wakame evenly, and serve.

CLEAR SOUP WITH CLAMS

SERVES 4–6

4 large hard-shelled clams
1½pt (900ml) cold water
4 × 4inch (10cm) pieces of kombu seaweed
pinch of salt
small bunch of curly parsley
4 pieces yuzu or lemon peel

Put the clams in lightly salted water to cover and leave in a dark place for 4–5 hours. Wash the clams thoroughly, wipe the kombu and put in a saucepan with the cold water. Bring to the boil, adding 1 tsp salt just before the water boils. Remove the kombu and discard. Simmer for 2 minutes, until the clams open. Remove the pan from the heat.

Remove the clams and separate the clam meat from the shells with a sharp paring knife. Wash the shells and arrange one shell in each soup bowl. Place a clam in each shell.

Wash the curly parsley, pat dry and arrange in the 4 bowls. Lay a slice of lemon rind in each bowl. Strain the stock and reheat, adding a little salt to taste. Ladle the hot stock carefully into the soup bowls and serve immediately.

THICK NEW YEAR'S SOUP WITH CHICKEN

SERVES 4

½lb (225g) boned chicken, leg and breast, with skin
2 young leeks
1½pt (900ml) Dashi II (see recipe)
3tbsp white miso

Trim the chicken and slice into thin strips. Blanch in a little lightly salted water for 2 minutes, and drain. Slice the leeks diagonally into fine slices.

In a large saucepan, bring the dashi to the boil; add the chicken pieces and simmer until tender.

Ladle a little of the hot soup into a bowl, add the miso and soften with a wire whisk. Strain the miso into the soup. Reheat the soup but do not boil. Warm 4 soup bowls. Ladle the soup into the bowls, distributing the chicken pieces evenly. Top with thin slices of leek and serve immediately.

THICK VEGETABLE SOUP WITH BEAN CURD

SERVES 4

8oz (225g) bean curd
2 medium carrots
3 medium potatoes
1 bamboo shoot, fresh or canned
8 fresh or dried and reconstituted shiitake mushrooms
1 cake konnyaku (arum root)
2tbsp vegetable oil
1½pt (900ml) Dashi II (see recipe)
4tbsp red miso

◆ SOUPS ◆

First drain the bean curd: set a weight such as a chopping board or dinner plate on the bean curd and set aside for at least 30 minutes to drain.

Prepare the vegetables. Wash and peel the carrots and potatoes and cut into small chunks. Cut the bamboo shoot into pieces of the same size. Trim away the hard stems of the mushrooms and cut into quarters.

With a teaspoon, cut the konnyaku into chunks. Heat the vegetable oil in a frying pan, add the vegetables and sauté over high heat, until lightly browned and evenly coated with oil.

Turn the vegetables into a saucepan and ladle the dashi over them. Bring to the boil. Squeeze the drained bean curd through your fingers and into the soup. Ladle a

THICK VEGETABLE SOUP WITH BEAN CURD

little of the hot soup into a bowl and add the miso. Soften with a wire whisk.

Strain the miso into the soup. Reheat the soup until nearly boiling, but do not boil. Ladle the soup into warmed soup bowls and serve immediately.

◆ ◆ ◆

◆ RICE AND NOODLES ◆

COOKING RICE

SERVES 4

14oz (400g) short grain white rice
¾pt (450ml) water

Wash the rice well about 1 hour before cooking. Rinse several times and stir it with the hand until the rinsing water is clear. Combine with the water and set aside to soak for at least 30 minutes.

Cover and bring to the boil over high heat. Reduce the heat to very low and simmer for 8–10 minutes. Turn off the heat and leave the pan on the cooker for another 15 minutes to steam. Do not lift the lid of the pot while the rice is cooking.

Dampen a wooden rice paddle or wooden spoon. Turn and fluff the rice with it before serving.

LONTONG

SERVES 4–6

1 × 4oz (100g) packet boil-in-the-bag rice
1pt (600ml) boiling salted water

Place the boil-in-the-bag rice in the water and boil for 1¼ hours or until the whole bag is puffy and firm and the rice fills the whole of it. The bag must be covered in water all the time. You can place a saucer or plate on top to weigh it down if necessary. Allow to cool completely before stripping off the bag, leaving a cushion of rice which can then be cut into neat cubes and served with spiced and deep fried chicken or with sate.

As an alternative use this recipe which uses short grain rice.

8oz (225g) short grain rice
¾pt (450ml) water
salt

Place the washed rice, water and salt in a pan. Bring to the boil, stir, cover and simmer for 30–35 minutes over the gentlest heat until the rice is tender. Cool, then turn into a 1 inch (2.5 cm) deep dish. Press down, cover with foil, a plate and a weight. Leave until firm. Remove the weights and foil and cut into cubes or diamond shapes.

PORK CUTLET ON RICE

PORK CUTLET ON RICE

SERVES 4

14oz (400g) short grain white rice
¾pt (450ml) water
4 breaded pork cutlets
1 small onion
1pt (600ml) Dashi II (see recipe)
3½fl oz (100ml) mirin
3fl oz (75ml) soy sauce
6 eggs

Cook the rice in the water (see recipe). While the rice is cooking and resting, prepare the topping. Prepare and deep-fry the pork cutlets; drain on absorbent kitchen paper and slice diagonally into 1 inch (3 cm) strips. Set aside and keep warm.

Peel and slice the onion. Combine the dashi, mirin and soy sauce in a saucepan and bring to the boil. Add the onion and simmer until soft.

Lightly mix the eggs with chopsticks and slowly pour over the onion. Stir once when the egg is nearly set.

Half fill 4 large bowls with hot rice and neatly arrange a sliced breaded pork cutlet on each bowl. Before the egg is completely set, ladle a quarter of the egg mixture over each bowl, distributing all the liquid, and taking care that the egg mixture does not completely cover the cutlets.

VINEGARED RICE FOR SUSHI

SERVES 4

14oz (400g) shortgrain white rice
¾pt (450ml) water
4tsp rice vinegar
2tbsp sugar
2tsp salt

Cook the rice in the water (see recipe). Cool to room temperature. When the rice has rested, place in a wide, shallow container.

Combine the vinegar, sugar and salt and heat to dissolve the sugar

and salt. Sprinkle the rice with the vinegar mixture.

Quickly and lightly cut and toss the rice with a wooden rice paddle or spoon. Ideally, you should fan the rice as you toss it, so that it becomes glossy. Vinegared rice should be used immediately. Otherwise cover with a damp cloth and use within a few hours.

THIN SUSHI ROLLS

SERVES 4

vinegared rice made from 7oz (200g) uncooked rice
2oz (50g) takuan pickle
½ cucumber, 6inches (15cm) long
2 sheets nori seaweed
1tsp rice vinegar, mixed with 3tbsp water
freshly made wasabi horseradish (see recipe)

Prepare the vinegared rice (see recipe). Shred the takuan pickle. Slice the cucumber into narrow strips. Toast the nori by moving it over a flame for a few seconds until it changes colour and becomes fragrant, and halve each sheet of nori.

To make the takuan pickle rolls, lay one half sheet of nori on a bamboo rolling mat. Moisten your hands with the vinegar, place one-fourth of the vinegared rice on the nori and spread to cover the edges, leaving the top 1 inch (2.5 cm)

uncovered. Lay half the takuan pickle in a line along the centre of the rice.

Holding the takuan in place with your fingers, roll up the bamboo mat to form a firm roll. Press the mat around the roll to shape it, remove the mat and with a sharp knife cut the roll into 6 slices, cutting either diagonally or straight downward. Repeat with the takuan.

To make cucumber rolls, lay a sheet of nori on the bamboo mat and spread over a quarter of the rice. Smear a thin line of wasabi horseradish along the centre of the rice, and lay 1 or 2 strips of cucumber on the wasabi. Roll up and cut as before.

◆ RICE AND NOODLES ◆

THICK SUSHI ROLLS

SERVES 4

vinegared rice made from 7oz (200g) uncooked rice
2 cakes dried bean curd
2 dried gourd strips, each 12inches (30cm) long
4 dried mushrooms
1½pt (900ml) Dashi II (see recipe)
3tbsp soy sauce
3tbsp sugar
2tbsp mirin
½ cucumber, 6inches (15cm) long
2 sheets nori seaweed
1tsp rice vinegar
3tbsp water

Prepare the vinegared rice (see recipe). Soak the bean curd in hot water for a few minutes, then squeeze, and repeat until the water which is squeezed out is clear. Reconstitute the gourd strips and mushrooms. Put the dried bean curd in a saucepan with ¾ pt (450 ml) of dashi, 1 tbsp soy sauce and 1 tbsp of sugar. Combine the gourd strips with ½ pt (300 ml) of dashi and 1 tbsp each of soy sauce, mirin and sugar. Remove the mushroom stems and slice the caps finely; combine the caps with 3½ fl oz (100 ml) of dashi and 1 tbsp each of soy sauce, mirin and sugar.

Bring each of the 3 mixtures to the boil and simmer for 20 minutes, until the simmering liquid is nearly absorbed. Leave to cool in the simmering liquid, then drain. Slice each cake of dried bean curd into 6 strips. Slice the cucumber into narrow strips and set aside in lightly salted water to soak for 20 minutes. Drain and pat dry with absorbent kitchen paper. This can all be done beforehand.

Toast the nori by waving it over a high flame for a few seconds until it changes colour and becomes fragrant. Lay on a bamboo rolling mat. Combine the vinegar and water and use to keep your fingers moistened. Place half the rice on the nori.

Keeping your fingers moist, spread the rice to cover three-quarters of the nori, extending right to the edges. Spread half the dried bean curd, gourd strips, mushrooms and cucumber in a thick strip across the rice. Holding the ingredients in place with your fingers, begin to roll firmly, using your thumbs to roll up the bamboo mat. Try to keep the ingredients in the centre of the roll. Continue rolling, taking care not to trap the bamboo mat inside the roll.

Complete the roll and gently but firmly press the mat around the roll for a few seconds to shape it. Unroll. Wet a sharp knife and cut the roll in half. Then cut each half into 4 slices. Repeat with the remaining ingredients.

GOLDEN SUSHI POUCHES

SERVES 4

vinegared rice made from 7oz (200g) uncooked rice
4 cakes deep-fried bean curd
2 dried gourd strips, each 12inches (30cm) long

Simmering stock
3tbsp mirin
3tbsp sugar
4tbsp soy sauce
½pt (300ml) Dashi II (see recipe)
½ carrot
salt

Prepare the vinegared rice (see recipe). Pour boiling water over the deep-fried bean curd cakes to remove oil; when cool enough to handle, halve each cake across. Ease each half open to make 8 pouches. Reconstitute the gourd strips. Combine the bean curd pouches and gourd strips with the simmering stock ingredients in a saucepan and bring to the boil. Cover with a drop lid and simmer for 20 minutes. Leave to cool in the simmering stock. Remove the bean curd pouches and gourd ribbon, squeeze and drain. Parboil and shred the carrot.

Mix the rice with the shredded carrot. With moistened hands pick up a small ball of rice and shape into an oval. Open a bean curd pouch and gently slide the rice ball into the pouch. Fold the sides and then the top flap of the pouch over the rice to close it. Fill all the bean curd pouches in the same way.

Cut the prepared gourd strips in half and use to tie 4 bean curd pouches.

CHESTNUT RICE

SERVES 4

16 large fresh chestnuts
14oz (400g) short grain white rice
¾pt (450ml) water
½tsp salt

Soak the chestnuts overnight. With a sharp knife, pare away the peel and remove the inner skin. Neatly halve and soak in fresh water for another 3 or 4 hours.

Wash the rice thoroughly and soak for 1 hour. Place in a saucepan and add the water, chestnuts and salt. Cover, bring to the boil and simmer for 8–10 minutes. Turn off the heat and leave to steam for another 15 minutes. Serve, distributing the chestnuts evenly.

RICE WITH CHICKEN

SERVES 4

14oz (400g) short grain white rice
4oz (100g) boned chicken breast or thigh
2tbsp soy sauce
4 dried mushrooms, reconstituted
¾pt (450ml) chicken stock
4tsp sake
4 sprigs of fresh coriander

Wash the rice thoroughly and put in a strainer to drain for at least 30 minutes. Cut the chicken into short, ½ inch (2 cm) strips, sprinkle with the soy sauce and set aside to marinate for 30 minutes. Discard the mushroom stems and slice the caps finely.

Put the rice in a saucepan and pour the chicken stock and sake over it. Add the chicken and mushroom pieces. Bring to the boil over high heat, stirring occasionally. Cover tightly and reduce the heat to very

low. Simmer for 8–10 minutes, then turn off the heat and leave, still covered, to steam for 15 minutes. Mix well and serve, garnishing each bowl with coriander leaf.

CHICKEN AND EGG ON RICE

SERVES 4

14oz (400g) short grain white rice
¾pt (450ml) water
4oz (100g) boned chicken breast or thigh
4 leeks or spring onions
4 dried mushrooms, reconstituted
1pt (600ml) Dashi I (see recipe)
5fl oz (150ml) soy sauce
3tbsp mirin
1tbsp sugar
4 eggs

Cook the rice in the water (see recipe). Prepare the topping while the rice is cooking and resting. Cut the chicken into bite-sized pieces; cut the leeks or spring onions diagonally into 2 inch (5 cm) lengths. Drain the mushrooms, cut off the stems and finely slice the caps.

Prepare each portion separately. Measure out a quarter of the dashi into a small frying pan, and add a quarter of the chicken and mushrooms. Bring to the boil and simmer for 5 minutes.

Add a quarter of the leeks or spring onions and simmer for 1 more minute. Season with a quarter of the soy sauce, mirin and sugar.

Lightly mix the eggs with chopsticks and slowly pour a quarter of the egg mixture over the chicken and vegetables. Wait until the egg is half set, then stir only once.

Half fill a large bowl with hot rice and pour the egg mixture over the rice before the egg is fully set; the heat of the rice will continue to cook the egg. Make 3 more portions in the same way with the remaining ingredients.

CHICKEN AND EGG ON RICE

RICE WITH FIVE VEGETABLES

SERVES 4

14oz (400g) short grain white rice
½ medium carrot
½ burdock root
1 cake thin deep-fried bean curd
½ cake konnyaku (arum root)
4 dried mushrooms, reconstituted
4tbsp soy sauce
2tbsp sugar
¾pt (450ml) Dashi II (see recipe)

Wash the rice thoroughly, drain and soak in fresh water for 1–2 hours. Prepare the 5 vegetables. Scrape the carrot and burdock root. Douse the deep-fried bean curd with boiling water to remove excess oil. Cut the carrot, konnyaku and deep-fried bean curd into julienne strips.

Shred the burdock on the diagonal; place in cold water immediately. Remove the stems of the mushrooms and slice the caps finely.

Combine the soy sauce, sugar and dashi in a large bowl. Drain the burdock and add all 5 shredded vegetables to the dashi. Set aside for a few minutes to allow the flavours to mingle. Drain the rice well and put into a saucepan. Pour the dashi together with the vegetables over the rice and stir well to mix. Bring to the boil, then cover tightly, reduce the heat to low and simmer for 10 minutes. Turn off the heat and leave the pan, still tightly covered, for another 15 minutes. Mix the rice with a wooden rice paddle or spoon to distribute the vegetables evenly before serving.

COOKING NOODLES

SERVES 4

14oz (400g) dried buckwheat noodles

Noodles are always cooked *al dente*, that is, they are cooked through to the centre but are removed from the water when still quite firm. White wheat noodles (udon) are cooked as we cook spaghetti, in plenty of rapidly boiling salted water, for about 10 minutes, until just cooked. Buckwheat noodles (soba) may be cooked in the same way, but here is the traditional Japanese way of cooking buckwheat noodles:

Bring plenty of unsalted water to a rolling boil in a large, deep saucepan. Gradually add the noodles. Stir slowly to stop the noodles from sticking. When the water returns to the boil, add ¼ pt (150 ml) of cold water. Bring back to the boil and repeat. When the water boils a third time, lower the heat and simmer for 2–3 minutes until the noodles are just cooked.

Drain the noodles and immerse in cold water, stirring gently to separate the strands and remove the starch. Place the noodles in hot water to reheat before using.

FOX NOODLES

SERVES 4

14oz (400g) dried udon noodles

Noodle broth
2pt (1lt) Dashi II (see recipe)
2tbsp light soy sauce
2tsp salt
1tbsp sugar
2tsp sake
2 spring onions
4 cakes thin deep-fried bean curd

Simmering stock
⅓pt (200ml) Dashi II (see recipe)
2tbsp soy sauce
1tbsp sugar

Cook the noodles (see recipe). Combine the noodle broth ingredients and bring to the boil; keep warm. Shred and rinse the spring onions.

Pour boiling water over the deep-fried bean curd to remove oil. Drain and combine with the simmering ingredients in a small saucepan and bring to the boil. Cover with a drop lid and simmer for 10 minutes.

Warm 4 deep bowls. Put the noodles in a sieve and immerse in boiling water for a few seconds to reheat; divide among the 4 bowls. Arrange one folded cake of deep-fried bean curd and a quarter of the spring onion in each bowl, ladle the hot broth over them and serve.

NOODLES IN SMALL CASSEROLES

SERVES 4

14oz (400g) dried udon noodles
4oz (100g) boned chicken, skin intact
1tsp each soy sauce and sake
1 cake kamaboko (fish cake)
4 dried mushrooms, reconstituted

ABOVE LEFT: FOX NOODLES
ABOVE RIGHT: MOON VIEWING NOODLES

Simmering stock
3½fl oz (100ml) Dashi II
1tbsp each soy sauce, mirin and sugar

4 spring onions
4 pieces prawn tempura

Noodle broth
2pt (1lt) Dashi II (see recipe)
4tbsp light soy sauce
3tbsp mirin
½tsp salt
4 eggs

Cook the noodles (see recipe). Cut the chicken into small chunks, sprinkle with soy sauce and sake and set aside for 10 minutes to marinate. Cut the kamaboko into slices. Remove the mushroom stems and cut a decorative cross in the top of each mushroom cap. Combine with the simmering stock ingredients and simmer for 15 minutes. Slice the green part of the spring onions on the diagonal into slices. Prepare the prawn tempura. Combine the noodle broth ingredients and bring to the boil; keep warm.

Put the noodles into 4 small ovenproof casseroles with lids. Divide the chicken, kamaboko, mushrooms and spring onions among the 4 casseroles; ladle the noodle broth over them.

Cover the casseroles and bring to the boil; carefully scoop off any foam. With the back of a spoon make a small hollow in the noodles in each casserole and break an egg into the hollow. Immediately cover the casserole and turn off the heat; the egg will semi-set. Add a piece of prawn tempura to each casserole and serve immediately.

MOON VIEWING NOODLES

SERVES 4

14oz (400g) dried udon noodles

Noodle broth
2pt (1lt) Dashi II (see recipe)
2tbsp light soy sauce
2tsp salt
1tbsp sugar
2tsp sake
4 spring onions
½ sheet nori
4 eggs

Cook the noodles in plenty of rapidly boiling salted water for 10 minutes, until just cooked. Drain and immerse in cold water, stirring gently to separate the strands. Drain and set aside.

Combine the noodle broth ingredients and bring to the boil; keep warm. Slice the green part of the onions on the diagonal into 2 inch (5 cm) slices. Toast the nori and cut with scissors into rectangles 1 × 2 inch (2 × 5 cm).

Warm 4 deep bowls. Put the noodles in a sieve and immerse in boiling water for a few seconds to reheat; divide among the 4 bowls and top with slices of spring onion. Gently break an egg onto each bowl of noodles, taking care not to break the yolk. Immediately ladle the hot broth over the noodles; the hot broth will slightly cook the egg. Garnish each bowl with nori and serve immediately.

BUCKWHEAT NOODLES IN HOT BROTH

SERVES 4

14oz (400g) dried buckwheat noodles

Noodle broth
1½pt (900ml) Dashi II (see recipe)
3tbsp dark soy sauce
2tbsp sugar
2tbsp mirin
2tsp salt
2 young leeks or spring onions

Cook the noodles (see recipe). Combine the noodle broth ingredients and bring to the boil; keep warm. Shred and rinse the leeks or spring onions. Warm 4 deep bowls. Immerse the noodles in a sieve in boiling water for a few seconds to reheat. Divide among the 4 bowls.

Ladle the hot broth over the noodles and top with a mound of shredded leek or spring onion.

CHILLED BUCKWHEAT NOODLES

SERVES 4

14oz (400g) dried buckwheat noodles

Dipping sauce
1pt (600ml) Dashi II (see recipe)
3½fl oz (100ml) dark soy sauce
4tbsp mirin
1tsp sugar
2 young leeks or spring onions
1tsp freshly made wasabi horseradish
½ sheet nori seaweed

Cook the noodles (see recipe). Combine the dipping sauce ingredients and bring to the boil; chill. Shred and rinse the leeks or spring onions. Prepare the wasabi horseradish. Toast the nori seaweed and cut with scissors into thin strips.

Divide the chilled dipping sauce among 4 small bowls. Mound portions of leeks and wasabi in 4 small containers. Put the drained cold noodles in 4 containers or plates and scatter strips of nori seaweed over each portion.

ABOVE TOP: BUCKWHEAT NOODLES IN HOT BROTH
ABOVE BOTTOM: CHILLED BUCKWHEAT NOODLES

◆ ◆ ◆

◆ VEGETABLES, SALADS AND EGGS ◆

EGG ROLL MADE OF SEVERAL OMELETTES

SERVES 4–6

4 eggs
4tbsp cold Dashi II, depending on egg size
½tsp thin soy sauce
½–1tbsp sake
½tsp salt
1tbsp sugar
2 sheets nori (seaweed) (optional)
a little oil for cooking

Beat the eggs. Heat the dashi, soy sauce, sake, salt and sugar and cool, then mix with the eggs. If you are using the nori, pass one side of each sheet over a gas flame to intensify the colour and flavour, then divide into 2 or 3 strips. Lightly oil the pan. Pour in enough egg mixture to just cover the base of the pan, top with a strip of the nori, if using, and when the egg is set roll it up or fold. Lift to the end of the pan, lightly brush the pan with oil, if necessary, and again flood enough egg mixture into the pan to cover the base, lifting the rolled omelette at one end to allow the egg mixture underneath. Add nori again, if using. Fold up in the same way when the mixture is set and repeat until all the mixture is used up and you have a large roll.

If you have a bamboo mat cover with a sheet of kitchen paper. Place the omelette on it and roll up fairly firmly. Leave for several minutes then unfold. Cut across into slices to serve at breakfast, lunch or supper.

WHITE SALAD

SERVES 4

3 dried mushrooms, reconstituted
2tsp soy sauce
1tsp mirin
4oz (100g) daikon radish
1 small carrot
salt
½ cake konnyaku (arum root) (optional)
2oz (50g) French beans

Dressing
7oz (200g) bean curd
1tbsp white sesame seeds
2½tbsp white miso
1tbsp mirin
1tsp sugar

Garnish
1 sheet nori seaweed

Remove the stems of the mushrooms and slice thinly. Place in a small saucepan and add the soy sauce and mirin; simmer over very low heat for 10–15 minutes. Leave the mushrooms in any remaining stock to cool.

Cut the daikon radish and carrot into threads. Salt and set aside for 10 minutes, then knead until the vegetables become soft. Rinse, squeeze out excess moisture and pat dry.

Rub the konnyaku with salt, then rinse and pound with a rolling pin or a wooden pestle. Cut into julienne strips. Sauté in a dry frying pan for a few minutes, then set aside to cool. Top and tail the beans and parboil.

Wrap the bean curd in clean dry towels, weight with a chopping board and set aside for 20–30 minutes to drain. Press the bean curd through a sieve.

Toast the sesame seeds with a little salt in a dry frying pan. When they give off a nutty aroma, transfer to a suribachi or heavy frying-pan and grind until oily. Blend in the bean curd and the remaining dressing ingredients.

Make sure the vegetables are all perfectly dry, and stir into the dressing. Mound the salad in small deep individual bowls. Lightly toast the nori seaweed and cut with scissors into threads. Set a small mound of nori on each serving to garnish.

RIGHT: WHITE SALAD

AUBERGINES WITH SESAME SEEDS

SERVES 12

1¼lb (575g) aubergines (long and thin, preferably)
1tbsp salt
4tbsp corn oil
2tbsp sesame seed oil
2–3tbsp miso
2tbsp mirin
2tbsp sugar
about 5tbsp Dashi II
1–2tsp roasted sesame seeds

Wipe the aubergine and trim the ends. Cut into 1 inch (2.5 cm) thick slices and sprinkle with salt. Leave for 30 minutes. Rinse and dry well on absorbent kitchen paper. Fry in hot oil, turning all the time until they are brown. Stir the miso with the mirin, sugar and dashi. Cook without a cover to reduce in a small pan. Cool rapidly. Spread this mixture onto each aubergine slice, then mark in a criss-cross pattern with a knife. Cool rapidly. Sprinkle each one with a few sesame seeds. Turn onto a serving dish and scatter with the remaining sesame seeds. Eat as a snack or part of lunch; it is a refreshing way of preparing aubergines.

ABOVE LEFT: RED AND WHITE SALAD
ABOVE RIGHT: CUCUMBER AND WAKAME SALAD

FRENCH BEANS WITH PEANUT DRESSING

SERVES 4

6oz (175g) French beans
salt

Dressing
1½oz (40g) peanuts, roasted
1½tbsp sugar
2tbsp soy sauce
1–2tbsp Dashi II, if required (see recipe)

Garnish
½tsp dried bonito flakes

Wash and trim the beans. Parboil in lightly salted boiling water until just tender. Drain and refresh in cold water. Slice diagonally into 1½ inch (4 cm) lengths. Pat dry.

Place the peanuts in a suribachi and grind finely. Blend in the remaining dressing ingredients, adding enough dashi to make a thick paste.

Add the beans and stir well to coat with dressing. Arrange small portions of the salad in deep individual bowls and garnish with bonito flakes.

CUCUMBER AND WAKAME SALAD

SERVES 4

1 cucumber or 2 small Japanese cucumbers
½tsp salt
1tbsp dried wakame seaweed, reconstituted

Dressing
3tbsp rice vinegar
2tbsp Dashi II (see recipe)
2tbsp soy sauce
1tbsp sugar
½tsp salt
2tbsp mirin

Garnish
1tbsp fresh root ginger, chopped into fine needles

Slice the cucumber in half lengthwise. Scrape out the seeds. Cut into paper-thin slices. Dissolve ½ tsp of salt in 3½ fl oz (100 ml) of cold water, add the cucumber and leave to soak for 20 minutes. Put the

cucumber into cheesecloth to drain.

Squeeze the cucumber gently to remove excess moisture.

Combine the dressing ingredients in a small saucepan, and heat to dissolve the sugar. Remove from heat and chill. Trim the wakame seaweed and chop coarsely. Combine the wakame and cucumber in a bowl and spoon the chilled dressing over them. Toss gently.

Arrange neat mounds of salad in individual bowls. Garnish with a little chopped ginger.

STUFFED FRIED BEAN CURD

SERVES 6

2×2oz (50g) packets fried bean curd
¼pt (150ml) Dashi II
2tbsp sugar
1–2tbsp soy sauce

Filling
Sushi rice (see recipe)
2 dried mushrooms soaked in 4fl oz (120ml) water for 30 minutes. Drain and reserve soaking juice
1tbsp soy sauce
1tbsp sugar
1tbsp roasted sesame seeds
pickled ginger to garnish

Pour the boiling water over the bean curd. Drain and dry on absorbent kitchen paper. Cut in half and open each one into a pocket shape. Mix the dashi, sugar and soy sauce together and cook with the bean curd over a low heat until the bean curd has soaked up the stock. When the prepared rice is cool, place in a bowl. Slice the mushrooms finely. Pour the soaking juices from the mushrooms into a pan. Add soy sauce and sugar.

Cook the mushrooms until the liquid has evaporated. Cool quickly and add to the rice with the sesame seeds. Use this mixture to stuff the bean curds. Rub your hands with vinegar to make it easier to form the rice into a neat ball before popping it into the pocket-shaped bean curd. Tuck in the flaps and turn over. Set on a serving plate and garnish with pickled ginger and serve.

RED AND WHITE SALAD

SERVES 4

4inches (10cm) daikon radish
1 medium carrot
½tsp salt

Dressing
3tbsp rice vinegar
3tbsp mirin
1tbsp Dashi II (see recipe)
pinch of salt

1 piece 1½inch (4cm) kombu seaweed
orange or lemon rind, shredded, to garnish

Scrape the daikon radish and carrot. Cut into needles. Salt the vegetables and set aside for 10 minutes. Knead thoroughly until the daikon radish becomes soft and translucent, then squeeze to press out as much water as possible.

Combine the dressing ingredients in a small saucepan and bring to the boil. Remove from the heat and chill. Add 2 tbsp of the chilled dressing to the vegetables. Mix and knead; squeeze to press out the dressing. Discard the excess dressing.

Put the kombu in a clean bowl and put the vegetables on top. Pour the remaining dressing over them. Cover the bowl and refrigerate for at least 30 minutes — the salad will have a better flavour if it is left overnight. Refrigerated in a tightly sealed container, it will keep for up to 2 weeks.

Serve cold or at room temperature in small portions, garnished with a few shreds of orange or lemon peel.

AUBERGINES SAUTÉED AND SIMMERED

SERVES 4

2 small aubergines
2tbsp vegetable oil
¾pt (450ml) Dashi II (see recipe)
1tbsp sugar
4tbsp dark soy sauce
1tsp dried bonito flakes

Wash and trim the aubergines. Halve lengthwise and score the skin finely so that the bitter juices can drain away. Cut into 1 inch (2 cm) slices.

Place the slices in a strainer and blanch with boiling water to remove the bitter juices. Cover with a light weight — such as a chopping board — and set aside for 20 minutes to drain. Rinse and pat dry.

In a frying pan, heat the vegetable oil and sauté the aubergines over medium heat for 7 minutes until they are tender. Pour in the dashi, stir, and add the sugar and soy sauce. Cover with a drop lid and simmer for 10 minutes until the simmering liquid is reduced. Serve individual portions in small bowls and garnish with dried bonito flakes.

MIXED SALAD PLATE

SERVES 4

4oz (100g) boned white chicken meat
pinch of salt
1tbsp sake
2oz (50g) harusame noodles
½ cucumber
4 leaves red cabbage
1 medium carrot
8 leaves lettuce
1 bunch of watercress
1 lemon
½tbsp wakame seaweed, reconstituted
1 kiwi fruit

Dressing
3 pickled plums (umeboshi)
3tbsp Dashi II
3tbsp mirin
4tbsp rice vinegar
1tsp salt
2tsp sugar
1tsp kuzu, potato flour or cornflour

Season the chicken with salt and sake. Place in a bowl and steam in a preheated steamer over a high heat for 20 minutes. Allow to cool. Shred the chicken.

Drop the harusame noodles into rapidly boiling salted water and boil for 4–5 minutes until soft. Rinse in cold water several times and set aside to drain.

Cut the cucumber into strips. Slice the cabbage and carrot into threads. Place in cold water.

Wash the lettuce and watercress and pat dry. Slice the lemon. With a sharp knife, cut the wakame seaweed into 1 inch (2.5cm) lengths. Peel and slice the kiwi fruit.

Seed the pickled plums and rub the plum flesh through a sieve. Stir in the other dressing ingredients. Cook the mixture over a very low heat, stirring frequently, until it thickens.

Drain the cucumber, cabbage and carrot and pat dry. Arrange all the ingredients on an attractive tray or platter. Serve the dressing separately as a dipping sauce.

DEEP-FRIED POTATO

SERVES 4

4 medium potatoes
vegetable oil for deep-frying

Slice the potatoes into ¼ inch (0.5 cm) thick slices. Cut each slice into a roughly triangular shape. Cut a notch in each triangle to make a leaf.

Fill a heavy-bottomed saucepan with oil to a depth of 2 inches (5 cm), and heat to 315°F/160°C/Gas Mark 2, or slightly higher. Put in a few potato slices and deep-fry quite slowly for 3–4 minutes, or until crisp and brown. Remove and drain on absorbent kitchen paper. Deep-fry the remaining slices a few at a time in the same way.

AUBERGINE TOPPED WITH SWEET MISO

SERVES 4

2 medium aubergines
vegetable oil

White miso sauce

4oz (100g) white miso
1tbsp sugar
3fl oz (75ml) mirin

Red miso sauce
4oz (100g) red miso
1½tbsp sugar
3fl oz (75ml) mirin

white sesame seeds, toasted
black sesame seeds or poppy seeds, toasted

Prepare the 2 miso sauces. Combine the ingredients for the white miso sauce in the top of a double boiler, and cook very gently over simmer-

LEFT: DEEP-FRIED BEAN CURD IN BROTH

ing water, stirring with a wooden spoon, until the sugar is dissolved and the sauce is the consistency of mayonnaise. Set aside. Repeat for the red miso sauce. (These quantities give enough miso sauce for several meals. The sauces will keep for 1 month).

Trim the stems of the aubergines and halve lengthwise. Score the flesh so that heat will penetrate more quickly.

Heat 2 tbsp of vegetable oil over medium heat in a frying pan and fry the aubergines until well cooked, turning occasionally. Add more oil if necessary. Drain on absorbent kitchen paper.

With a knife, spread the cut face of alternate aubergine halves with the two miso sauces.

Sprinkle a few black sesame seeds or poppy seeds on the white miso sauce to garnish. Sprinkle white sesame seeds on the red miso sauce.

DEEP-FRIED BEAN CURD IN BROTH

SERVES 4

11oz (300g) bean curd
2tbsp kuzu, potato flour or cornflour

Dipping sauce
⅓pt (200ml) Dashi II (see recipe)
1tbsp light soy sauce
3tbsp mirin

Garnishes
⅔oz (20g) daikon radish
1tbsp fresh root ginger
1 spring onion or young leek
1tbsp dried bonito flakes
vegetable oil for deep-frying

First drain the bean curd; set a weight such as a chopping board or dinner plate on the bean curd. Set aside for at least 30 minutes to drain.

Grind the kuzu or flour finely in a suribachi or mortar and pestle; or simply crush with a rolling pin to make a fine powder.

Cut the drained bean curd into 4 pieces and roll in the kuzu flour. Set aside.

Make the dipping sauces by combining the ingredients in a small saucepan, bring just to a simmer and keep warm.

Peel and grate the ginger. Set aside. Peel and grate the daikon radish and set aside. Slice the spring onion or leek into very fine slices. Place the bonito flakes in a small bowl.

Fill a small saucepan or deep-fryer with vegetable oil to a depth of 3 inches (7 cm) and heat to 350°F (180°C). Deep-fry each piece of bean curd separately for 6–8 minutes, until golden. Drain the bean curd briefly on absorbent kitchen paper. Arrange each piece of bean curd on a serving dish, and top with the garnishes. Either pour the warm dipping sauce over or serve separately.

ROLLED OMELETTE WITH PEAS

SERVES 4

5 eggs
⅓pt (200ml) Dashi II (see recipe)
1tbsp mirin
1½tbsp light soy sauce
pinch of salt
1tbsp peas
vegetable oil
1½tbsp daikon radish, grated
soy sauce

Break the eggs into a bowl. Add dashi, mirin, soy sauce and salt. Mix lightly with a whisk and stir in the peas.

Brush the omelette pan lightly with oil, and heat over moderately high heat. Pour in just enough of the egg mixture to coat the pan, tilting the pan so that the egg mixture forms an even layer. As soon as the egg is set, tilt the pan and roll the top of the omelette toward you, to form a roll at the front of the pan.

Push the roll to the back of the pan. Brush the pan with oil and pour in a little more of the egg mixture, lifting the roll to allow the egg mixture to flow underneath it.

Allow the egg mixture to set and proceed as before, tilting the pan and rolling the omelette toward you to form a roll, then pushing to the back of the pan. Repeat until all the egg mixture is used and there is a thick roll at the end of the pan.

Place a bamboo rolling mat over the omelette and remove the omelette from the pan; or use a fish slice. Roll the omelette in the bamboo mat, press gently, and leave to rest for 1 minute.

Unroll the omelette and slice into 1 inch (2 cm) pieces. Arrange on small serving plates. Moisten the grated daikon with a little soy sauce, and place a small mound on each plate to garnish.

◆ ◆ ◆

◆ FISH AND CRUSTACEANS ◆

SUSHI

SERVES 4

vinegared rice, prepared from 7oz (200g) uncooked rice
1lb (450g) fresh raw fish (tuna, prawns, salmon, etc)
1tsp wasabi horseradish
1tsp rice vinegar mixed with 3tbsp water
soy sauce

Prepare the vinegared rice (see recipe). Clean, fillet and slice the fish into ⅛ inch (2 mm) thick slices. Prepare the wasabi horseradish.

Keeping your hands moistened with the vinegar mixture, dab a little wasabi horseradish in the centre of a slice of fish. Form a small ball of rice in your fingers and quickly shape into a rectangle. Press onto the slice of fish.

Press the rice and fish together with both hands to firm and neaten the rectangle. Carefully set aside. Continue to make the fish and rice rectangles in the same way until all the ingredients are used.

SALMON STEAMED WITH ROE

SERVES 4

12oz (350g) salmon fillets, boned and skinned
salt
vegetable oil
2oz (50g) salmon roe
2tbsp sake
2oz (50g) grated daikon radish, drained
1 egg

Sauce
½pt (300ml) Dashi II
3tbsp mirin
2tbsp rice vinegar
2tbsp light soy sauce
2tsp cornflour mixed with 2tsp water
1 lemon
1 young leek, shredded and rinsed

Salt the salmon and slice it thinly. Place in a lightly oiled frying-pan and fry for 1–2 minutes on each side to seal the flavour. Immediately remove to a sieve and rinse with cold water.

Mix the roe with the sake in a small bowl to clean the roe; strain and discard the liquid. Mix the radish with the egg and season with a little salt. Stir the roe into the radish and egg mixture.

Divide the salmon pieces evenly among 4 small bowls, and spoon the roe mixture over the salmon. Cover with cling film or tin foil, sealing the edges tightly. Place in a preheated steamer; steam for 5 minutes over high heat.

While the salmon is steaming, prepare the sauce. In a small saucepan, bring the dashi, mirin, vinegar and soy sauce to a simmer. Turn the heat to low, add the cornflour solution and stir continuously until the sauce thickens.

Remove the bowls from the steamer, uncover, and spoon the thickened sauce over the salmon pieces. Squeeze a little lemon juice onto each portion, top with a few shreds of leek and serve.

CRAB AND CUCUMBER ROLLS

◆ FISH AND CRUSTACEANS ◆

CRAB AND CUCUMBER ROLLS

SERVES 4

½ cucumber
½tsp salt
2 large or 4 small rectangular egg sheets (omelettes)
6oz (175g) crab meat
3tbsp rice vinegar
2tbsp fresh root ginger, grated

Cut the cucumber into 2 inch (5 cm) lengths and slice thinly. Dissolve ½ tsp of salt in 3½ fl oz (100 ml) of cold water, add the cucumber and leave to soak for 20 minutes. Squeeze gently to remove excess moisture and pat dry with absorbent kitchen paper.

Arrange all the ingredients in preparation for the roll. Lay one egg sheet on a bamboo rolling mat. Arrange a wide band of crab meat along the near end; lay a line of cucumber slices along the crab meat.

Holding the crab meat and cucumber firmly in place with your fingers, roll the bamboo mat over with your thumbs to enclose them, making sure that they remain in the centre of the roll (this may be a little tricky the first time). Gently press the mat around the roll to shape it. Leaving the mat behind, continue to roll up the egg sheet until the roll is nearly complete.

Brush a little vinegar along the edge of the roll and finish rolling, pressing gently to seal. Leave the roll to rest for a few minutes with the sealed edge underneath. Repeat with the remaining ingredients to make another large or 3 small rolls.

Wet a very sharp knife and cut each roll into slices 1–2 inches (2–5 cm) long, wetting the knife several times as you cut. Arrange 2 or 3 slices in individual dishes and serve.

SAKE-STEAMED CLAMS

SERVES 4

8 large hard-shelled clams
4 pieces kombu seaweed
3½fl oz (100ml) sake
½tsp salt
1 bunch of watercress, divided into 4
4 thin slices lemon

Put the clams in lightly salted water to cover. Leave in a dark, cool place for 24 hours, to allow the clams to expel sand. Rinse the clams thoroughly, wipe the kombu and place in 4 deep plates for steaming. Sprinkle sake over the clams and kombu and season lightly with salt.

Cover with cling film or tin foil, sealing the edges tightly, and place in a preheated steamer. Steam for 10 minutes, until the clams open. Remove the wrap or foil, add the watercress and steam uncovered for a few seconds. Serve with a slice of lemon.

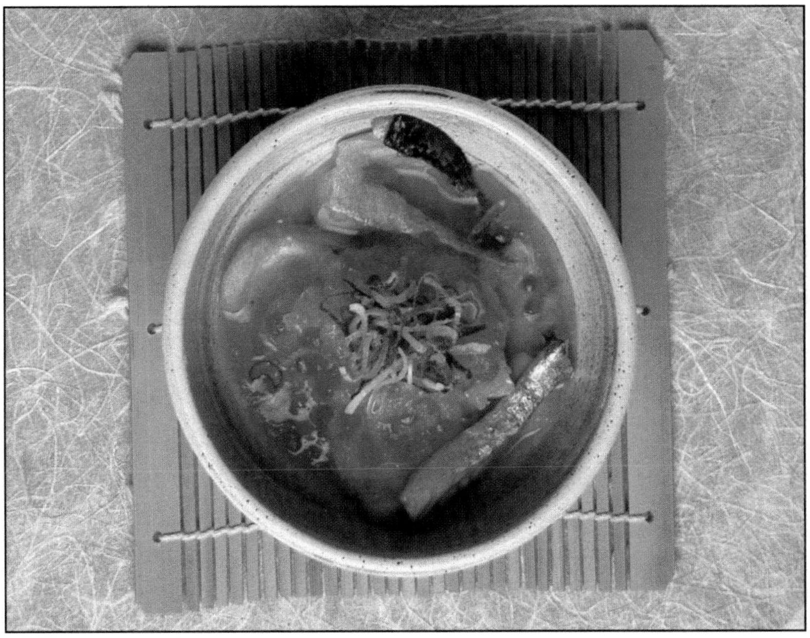

SALMON STEAMED WITH ROE

SAKE-STEAMED SOLE

SERVES 4

4 × 3oz (75g) fillets of sole
salt
1 piece kombu seaweed
⅓pt (200ml) sake

Dipping sauce
⅓pt (200ml) ponzu sauce
⅓pt (200ml) light soy sauce
2fl oz (50ml) mirin
3½fl oz (100ml) Dashi II (see recipe)

Condiments
1 young leek, shredded and rinsed
red maple radish

Lay the fillets on a cutting surface with the dark side uppermost. With a sharp knife make a shallow cross about ¼ inch (5 mm) deep in the top of each fillet. Sprinkle the fillets with a little salt and set aside to drain for at least 1 hour. Rinse in cold water and pat dry.

Prepare 4 deep plates for steaming. Wipe the kombu and place 1 piece in each plate. On each put 1 fillet scored side up. Pour sake generously over the fillets and kombu. Cover with cling film or tin foil, sealing the edges tightly. Place in a preheated steamer and steam for 15 minutes.

While the fish is steaming, prepare the dipping sauce. Combine the dipping sauce ingredients in a small saucepan and bring to a simmer; pour into 4 small bowls. Arrange small mounds of the condiments on individual plates. Serve the fish piping hot with the dipping sauce and condiments.

SHINSHU-STYLE STEAMED SEA TROUT

SERVES 4

1 sea trout, weighing about 18oz (500g)
salt
4 dried mushrooms, reconstituted
1 young leek, shredded and rinsed
4oz (100g) buckwheat noodles
4 × 2inch (5cm) pieces kombu seaweed, wiped
sake
wasabi horseradish, freshly made

Sauce
1½pt (900ml) Dashi II (see recipe)
⅓pt (200ml) dark soy sauce
¼pt (150ml) mirin

Fillet the fish. Cut the fish into 4 slices; or use 4 ready-cut fillets. Slice each fillet and open it out like a book. Lightly salt both sides and set aside for 40 minutes to 1 hour. Simmer the mushrooms in their soaking water for 20 minutes until tender, and prepare the leek.

Separate the noodles into 4 bunches and tie each bunch securely at the base. Put into plenty of rapidly boiling salted water. Boil for 10 minutes until the noodles are tender; do not add cold water. Remove the noodles and immediately place in cold water.

Rinse the fish slices and pat dry. Lay the free end of the noodles over the open fish slice, and fold over the fish to enclose the noodles like a sandwich.

Fold the tied end of the noodles over the fish, then cut away the tied end. Repeat with the remaining slices of fish.

Divide the kombu pieces among 4 ovenproof bowls, and carefully place the fish and noodles on the kombu. Place a drained mushroom in each bowl. Sprinkle a little sake over each piece of fish. Cover the bowls tightly with cling film or tin foil, and steam in a preheated steamer for 10 minutes.

Combine the dashi, soy sauce and mirin in a small saucepan and bring to the boil. Remove the fish from the steamer and ladle the hot sauce over the fillets. Garnish with shredded leek and a little wasabi, and serve immediately.

DEEP-FRIED SHRIMPS IN THICKENED BROTH

SERVES 4

14oz (400g) shrimps
cornflour or potato flour
vegetable oil for deep-frying
4oz (100g) daikon radish, grated

SHINSHU-STYLE STEAMED SEA TROUT

1/3pt (200ml) Dashi II (see recipe)
4tbsp mirin
4tbsp light soy sauce
1 dried red chilli pepper, seeded and very finely sliced
1 1/2oz (40g) fresh peas

Peel the shrimps, leaving just the tails attached. To devein, insert a toothpick under the vein in the centre of the back and pull up gently. Rinse the shrimps and pat dry. Sprinkle cornflour or potato flour over the shrimps.

Preheat plenty of oil to 325°F (170°C). Carefully lower the shrimps into the oil by spoonfuls and deep-fry for 2–3 minutes, until golden. Remove and drain on absorbent kitchen paper.

Place the grated radish in a sieve and rinse in cold water. Squeeze the radish firmly and shape into a ball.

In a small saucepan, bring the dashi to a simmer. Add the mirin, soy sauce and the ball of grated radish with sliced chilli pepper on top. Parboil the peas and add together with the shrimps. Bring back to a simmer and serve immediately in individual bowls.

DEEP-FRIED SHRIMPS IN THICKENED BROTH

TEMPURA

SERVES 4

8 large prawns or jumbo shrimp, shelled and deveined, tails attached
2 medium onions
1 green pepper
1 medium carrot
4oz (100g) mushrooms, wiped and trimmed, stems removed
1 aubergine
1 sheet nori seaweed
2oz (50g) rice vermicelli (harusame) (optional)
4 sea scallops, washed and patted dry
vegetable oil for deep-frying

Dipping Sauce
1/2pt (300ml) Dashi II (see recipe)
3tbsp light soy sauce
2tbsp mirin

Batter
2 egg yolks
1/3pt (200ml) ice water
4oz (100g) sifted flour
extra flour for dusting ingredients

Condiments
6tbsp daikon radish, grated
2tbsp fresh root ginger, grated

Score the belly of the prawns to prevent curling. Peel and halve the onions and cut across in slices, piercing with toothpicks to hold the rounds together. Core and deseed the pepper; halve and cut into strips. Cut the carrot into twists. Score a neat cross in the top of each mushroom. Cut the aubergine into fans. With scissors, cut the nori seaweed in half. Cut one half into wide strips and set aside. Cut the other half into narrow strips and use to tie the rice vermicelli into bunches. Arrange all the ingredients, together with the batter ingredients, conveniently on a tray.

Combine the dipping sauce ingredients in a small saucepan, bring to the boil and keep warm. Prepare the condiments.

Fill a small saucepan with oil to a depth of 3 1/4 inches (8 cm) and heat to 325°F (170°C). While the oil is heating, prepare the batter. Place the egg yolks in a mixing bowl, add the ice water and mix very lightly. Do not beat. Add the flour all at once. Mix very lightly with chopsticks. The batter will be very lumpy.

Make sure that all the ingredients are perfectly dry. Dip the item of food to be fried in flour, and shake to remove excess.

Dip the food in the batter and place in the hot oil. Deep-fry for about 3 minutes until golden. Continue until all the ingredients are cooked, frying only a few items at a time.

Drain the cooked pieces of tempura on a rack or on absorbent kitchen paper for a few minutes. Arrange attractively on a neatly folded paper napkin and serve with warm dipping sauce and the condiments. The diners mix the condiments into the dipping sauce, and dip the tempura pieces into it before eating.

◆ FISH AND CRUSTACEANS ◆

DEEP-FRIED SOLE

SERVES 4

4 × 3oz (75g) fillets of sole
salt
vegetable oil for deep-frying
3tbsp kuzu or cornflour
4tbsp daikon radish, grated
2tbsp fresh foot ginger, grated
ponzu sauce

Lay the fish fillets on a cutting surface, dark side uppermost. With a sharp knife, make a shallow cross, about ¼ inch (2 mm) deep, in the top of each fillet. Sprinkle with a little salt and set aside to drain for at least 1 hour. Prepare the condiments while the fish is draining. Rinse in cold water and pat dry.

Heat plenty of oil in a small heavy saucepan to 340°F (170°C). Coat both sides of each fillet evenly with kuzu or cornflour. Set the fish aside for a few minutes so that the coating can set.

Deep-fry the fillets one at a time for 4–5 minutes. Remove and drain on absorbent kitchen paper. Arrange each fillet on a folded napkin on a small plate, and serve the condiments and sauce separately. The condiments are combined into the sauce, and then the fish dipped into the sauce before eating.

SQUID STUFFED WITH VEGETABLES

SERVES 4

4 squid
1 small carrot
1½oz (40g) peas or French beans
vegetable oil
3 eggs, beaten

Gut and trim the squid and rinse well. Parboil the vegetables and chop the carrot and beans finely.

Brush a small pan with oil, add the vegetables and sauté lightly. Stir in the egg over low heat, and continue to stir until the egg mixture is nearly set. Remove from the heat and season to taste with a little salt.

Stuff each squid about half full with the vegetable mixture, and use a toothpick to close the 'bag'. Brush each squid with miso topping.

Grill the squid over high heat for 3–4 minutes, and serve immediately.

SWEET GLAZED SALMON

SCALLOPS IN GREEN SAUCE

SERVES 4

4–8 sea scallops
salt
vegetable oil

Miso sauce
5 leaves spinach
2oz (50g) white miso
2tbsp mirin
3tbsp water

Wash the scallops, pat dry and salt them lightly. Brush a shallow baking dish with oil, and arrange the scallops in it.

Prepare the miso sauce; wash the spinach leaves and pat them dry. Chop them roughly, place them in a food processor and grind them into a paste. Stir in the miso, mirin and water. Blend to make a smooth green sauce.

Spread the miso sauce in a thick layer on the scallops. Bake for 3–4 minutes in a preheated hot oven, so that the scallops are just heated. If overcooked, the scallops will become tough.

SWEET GLAZED SALMON

SERVES 4

4 salmon fillets
teriyaki sauce

Cut the fillets in 1 inch (2.5 cm) slices and skewer, being careful not to pierce the skin. Grill the salmon over very high heat, cooking the flesh side first.

Turn the salmon to grill the skin side, and brush with teriyaki sauce. Serve immediately, and spoon over a little more teriyaki sauce.

GOLDEN PRAWNS

SERVES 4

8 large prawns or jumbo shrimp
8 small potatoes
1pt (600ml) Dashi II (see recipe)
3tbsp sake
6tbsp mirin
4tbsp light soy sauce
6oz (175g) green beans
3tbsp cornflour
3 egg yolks
yuzu or lemon peel (optional)

Shell and devein the prawns, leaving the tail intact. Slit open the back of the prawn. Score the back of each prawn and press it out flat.

Peel and trim the potatoes and cut into small equal-sized balls. Parboil in lightly salted water covered with a drop lid until just tender. Drain and refresh in cold water.

Combine the dashi, sake, mirin and soy sauce in a saucepan; add the potatoes and bring to the boil. Remove from the heat and set aside, so that the potatoes cool in the simmering stock and absorb the flavour.

Trim the beans and cut diagonally into 2 inch (5 cm) pieces. Parboil in lightly salted water until the beans are just tender. Drain and refresh immediately in cold water to prevent further cooking.

Bring the stock to a simmer again. Holding the prepared prawns by the tail, brush each prawn with corn flour to make an even coating.

Separate the egg yolks into a small bowl, and beat until frothy. Holding the bowl of egg yolks over the simmering stock, dip the prawns into the egg yolk, holding each prawn by the tail.

Carefully lay the prawns in the stock and simmer gently, uncovered, until the egg is set and the tails are bright pink. The egg yolk coating will puff up a little as the prawns cook. Put the beans into the simmering stock to reheat.

Arrange the prawns against the potatoes in small serving bowls and place the beans in front. Ladle over the simmering stock. This dish may be garnished with yuzu or lemon peel.

GOLDEN PRAWNS

◆ FISH AND CRUSTACEANS ◆

SALT-GRILLED FISH

SERVES 4

4 sweetfish (ayu), mackerel, trout or other medium-sized fish
salt
lemon wedges
soy sauce
4 pickled ginger shoots

Scale and gut the fish, leaving the head and tail intact. Hold the fish with the head pointing to the right, so that the back of the fish is facing you, and thread 1 or 2 skewers through the fish, making sure that the skewers do not pierce the front of the fish. Prick the skin a few times with a needle.

Take a pinch of salt and rub it into the tail and fins, so that they are heavily coated with salt. This is known as 'cosmetic' salting, and prevents the tail and fins from burning.

Lightly salt the entire fish. Grill over high heat, grilling the front of the fish first and turning only once.

Remove the skewers and arrange fish facing to the left, with the head slightly toward the front. Garnish with lemon wedges or soy sauce and pickled red ginger shoots.

CRAB AND NAPA CABBAGE SIMMERED YOSHINO STYLE

SERVES 4

6 leaves napa cabbage
1pt (600ml) Dashi II (see recipe)
2tsp salt
1tsp light soy sauce
1tbsp mirin
1tbsp sake
7oz (200g) fresh crab meat (or 5oz [150g] canned crab meat)
2tbsp kuzu, arrowroot or cornflour

SOLE SIMMERED IN SAKE

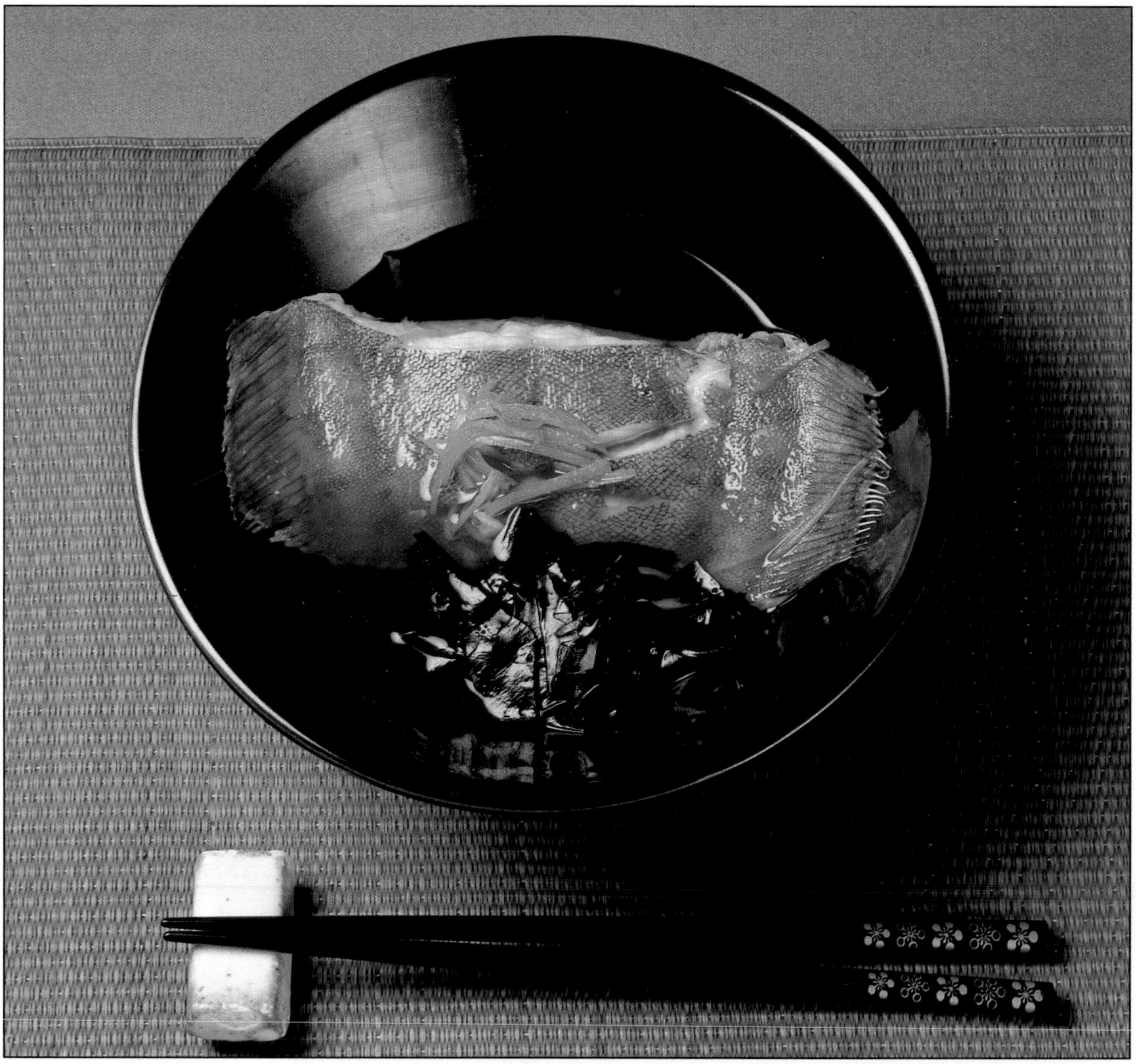

Wash the cabbage leaves and parboil in plenty of lightly salted water for 3 minutes. Drain and cut into 2 inch (5 cm) pieces.

Put the dashi into a medium-sized saucepan and bring to a simmer. Add the napa cabbage, and stir in the salt, soy sauce, mirin and sake.

Flake the crab meat and add to the simmering stock. Cover with a drop lid and simmer for 3 minutes.

Dissolve the kuzu in 3½ fl oz (100 ml) of cold water, and pour gradually into the simmering stock, stirring continuously. Continue to stir over very low heat until the sauce thickens.

Remove the napa cabbage and crab meat and arrange in small, deep bowls; ladle over the thickened sauce and serve hot.

SOLE SIMMERED IN SAKE

SERVES 4

4 × 3oz (75g) fillets of sole
salt
⅓oz (10g) fresh root ginger
⅓pt (200ml) Dashi II (see recipe)
4tbsp sake
4tbsp dark soy sauce
4tbsp mirin
1tsp salt
⅓oz (10g) piece dried wakame seaweed, reconstituted

Lay the fish fillets on a cutting surface with the dark side uppermost. With a sharp knife make a shallow cross, about ¼ inch (5 mm) deep, in the top of each fillet, to allow the fish to absorb the flavour of the simmering liquid more thoroughly.

Arrange the fillets on a strainer and sprinkle with a little salt; set aside to drain for at least 1 hour. Rinse in cold water and pat dry. Peel the ginger and slice thinly.

Combine the dashi, sake, soy sauce, mirin and salt in a large saucepan and bring to the boil. Arrange the fish in a single layer in the simmering stock, with the dark side on top.

Add the ginger. Return to the boil, carefully skim the surface, cover with a drop lid and cook over medium heat, occasionally ladling the simmering stock over the fish pieces, until the stock is reduced by half.

Cut the reconstituted wakame into 1 inch (2.5 cm) pieces and add to the simmering stock. Continue to simmer for a few more minutes until the stock is thick and much reduced. Turn off the heat and leave the fish for a few minutes in the hot stock before serving.

With a fish slice, remove the fish. Arrange in individual bowls and distribute the wakame and ginger evenly. Pour over a little of the simmering stock and serve.

MACKEREL SIMMERED IN SAKE

SERVES 4

4 mackerel fillets
pinch of salt
⅓pt (200ml) sake
3½fl oz (100ml) mirin
2fl oz (50ml) dark soy sauce
2tbsp fresh root ginger, grated

Rinse the fillets in cold water and pat dry. Arrange the fillets in a colander and sprinkle with a little salt; set aside to drain for at least 1 hour. Rinse in cold water and pat dry.

With a sharp knife, cut each fillet into 3 or 4 pieces. In a large saucepan bring the sake to a simmer. Arrange the fish in a single layer in the simmering sake, dark side uppermost, and bring the sake rapidly back to the boil. This process blanches the mackerel.

Add the remaining ingredients, bring to the boil and carefully skim the surface. Cover with a drop lid and cook over high heat for about 10 minutes until the flesh is tender and the stock is reduced by two-thirds.

Turn off the heat and leave the fish in the hot stock before serving. After a few minutes, carefully remove the fish from the stock with a fish slice and arrange the fillets in individual bowls. Garnish with the ginger and spoon stock over the fish.

MACKEREL SIMMERED IN MISO

SERVES 4

4 mackerel fillets, skin intact
salt
1oz (25g) fresh root ginger
½pt (300ml) Dashi II (see recipe)
2tbsp sake
5tbsp red miso
2oz (50g) sugar

Rinse the fillets in cold water and pat dry. Arrange the fillets in a colander and sprinkle with 2 tbsp of salt; set aside to drain for at least 1 hour.

With a sharp knife, cut each fillet into 3 or more pieces. Bring plenty of water to the boil. Place the fillets in a strainer and immerse in boiling water for a few minutes. Remove, drain and set aside.

Peel half of the ginger and slice into paper-thin slices. Arrange the fillets in a single layer in a frying pan.

Pour the dashi and sake over the fillets, add the ginger slices and bring to a simmer. Cover with a drop lid and simmer over very low heat until the fillets are firm and white.

Combine the miso and sugar in a small bowl. Add a little of the hot stock and mix well with a whisk to dissolve the miso. Add the miso mixture to the simmering mackerel liquid, and stir.

Cover with the drop lid and continue to simmer, occasionally spooning the miso stock over the fish, until the stock becomes thick and glossy. Remove the saucepan from the heat and set aside to allow the mackerel to cool in the stock.

Peel and shred the remaining ginger and put into a little water to soak. Remove the mackerel fillets from the miso stock and arrange in individual serving bowls. Ladle the miso stock over the fillets, garnish with ginger shreds and serve.

◆ ◆ ◆

◆ POULTRY AND MEAT ◆

CHICKEN SIMMERED CHIKUZEN STYLE

SERVES 4

10oz (275g) boned chicken, with skin
4 fresh shiitake or standard mushrooms, wiped
2 medium carrots
5oz (150g) bamboo shoots, fresh or canned
4 small potatoes, scrubbed
1 cake konnyaku (arum root)
1–2tbsp vegetable oil
⅓pt (200ml) Dashi II (see recipe)
2tbsp sugar
2tbsp mirin
3tbsp light soy sauce
2oz (50g) mange tout

Cut the chicken into ¾ inch (2 cm) cubes. Wash and trim the vegetables and cut into small chunks. Knead the konnyaku with a little salt; rinse, pat dry and tear into small pieces.

For the best flavour, the vegetables should be parboiled separately in lightly salted water, rinsed and drained. Heat the oil in a large saucepan over high heat.

Drop the chicken pieces into the oil and stir-fry to coat in oil. Add the carrots and konnyaku, and then the mushrooms, bamboo shoots and potatoes, in that order.

Stir-fry for 3 minutes, until the chicken and vegetables are lightly cooked and evenly coated with oil. Ladle the dashi over them, add the sugar, mirin and soy sauce, and bring to the boil.

Cover with a drop lid and simmer for 15 minutes, until the simmering stock is glossy and reduced by one-third.

Trim the mange tout and slice diagonally into 1 inch (3 cm) slices. Parboil in lightly salted water, and add to the chicken and vegetables just before serving.

Serve hot or at room temperature in individual bowls, arranging the vegetables attractively.

GRILLED CHICKEN

SERVES 4

2¼lb (1kg) boned chicken thigh
4 young leeks, washed and trimmed

Yakitori sauce
¾pt (450ml) dark soy sauce
⅓pt (200ml) chicken stock
⅓pt (200ml) sake
4oz (100g) sugar
3½fl oz (100ml) mirin

Combine the yakitori sauce ingredients in a saucepan. Bring to the boil, and simmer gently for 5 minutes. Remove from the heat and cool to room temperature. Transfer the sauce to a deep jar.

Cut the chicken into 1 inch (2.5 cm) pieces, and cut the leeks into 1½ inch (4 cm) lengths. Thread the chicken and leeks alternately onto bamboo skewers.

Grill over the hottest flame, turning frequently to avoid burning. When the juices begin to drip, dip the skewered chicken into the sauce and return to the grill. Repeat this several times until the chicken is lightly cooked. Be careful not to overcook the chicken; it should remain moist.

Serve the chicken piping hot, on

SWEET GLAZED CHICKEN

the skewers, and spoon over a little of the yakitori sauce. Traditionally, yakitori is sprinkled with a little dash of seven-spice pepper, and eaten with the fingers straight from the skewer.

SWEET GLAZED CHICKEN

SERVES 4

2 chicken legs and thighs, boned
vegetable oil
teriyaki sauce

Pierce the skin of the chicken with a fork to allow the sauce to penetrate. Brush a frying pan with oil and fry the chicken over high heat, turning, until well browned.

Remove the chicken from the heat and rinse with boiling water. Return the chicken pieces to the pan and pour over the teriyaki sauce. Cook until the sauce is glossy, turning the chicken so that it is well coated in sauce. Remove from the heat when the sauce is well reduced and thick.

Cut the chicken into ½ inch (2 cm) slices, and arrange the slices on individual plates. Serve hot.

SAKE-STEAMED CHICKEN

SERVES 4

11oz (300g) boned chicken breast, skin attached
1tbsp salt
2tbsp sake
½ cucumber
4 leaves lettuce
4 lemon wedges
wasabi horseradish, freshly made
3tbsp dark soy sauce
ponzu sauce
red maple radish
1 young leek, shredded and rinsed

SAKE-STEAMED CHICKEN

Put the chicken in a bowl, skin side up, and score the skin with a fork. Sprinkle with salt and sake and set aside for 20 minutes to marinate.

Steam the chicken, uncovered, in a preheated steamer over high heat for 15–20 minutes, until just cooked. Allow to cool and slice into ¾ inch (2 cm) pieces.

Cut the cucumber into 2 in (5 cm) lengths, and cut lengthwise into paper-thin slices. Salt lightly, knead, rinse and pat dry.

Wash the lettuce leaves and pat dry. Lay them on 4 small plates. Arrange the chicken slices on the lettuce leaves, and garnish with cucumber slices and lemon wedges.

Prepare the wasabi and serve with soy sauce. Serve the ponzu sauce with red maple radish and shredded leek.

DEEP-FRIED CHICKEN TATSUTA STYLE

SERVES 4

1½lb (700g) boned chicken, skin attached
6tbsp cornflour
vegetable oil for deep-frying
1 lemon, washed, dried and quartered
4 sprigs of parsley, washed and patted dry

Marinade
4tbsp soy sauce
2tbsp sake
1tbsp sugar
1tbsp ginger juice

Cut the chicken into large bite-sized chunks. Mix the marinade ingredients and pour over the chicken. Mix well so that the chicken is evenly covered. Set aside to marinate for 30 minutes.

Drain the chicken and coat with cornflour. Wait for a few minutes so that the coating can set.

In a small saucepan, heat oil for deep-frying to 350°F (180°C). Carefully place the chicken in the oil, a few pieces at a time, and deep-fry for about 3 minutes, until crisp and brown.

Remove piece by piece and drain. Arrange a few pieces of chicken on a neatly folded paper napkin. Garnish with lemon quarters and sprigs of parsley.

BRAISED BEEF WITH BROCCOLI

SERVES 4

7oz (200g) sirloin of beef, thinly sliced
11oz (300g) broccoli
4oz (100g) button mushrooms
2 cloves garlic
2tbsp vegetable oil
1tbsp each sake, rice vinegar, sesame seed oil, water and sugar
2tsp cornflour

With a sharp knife, cut the beef into small even chunks. Wash and trim the broccoli and divide into florets. Wipe and trim the mushrooms and halve them. Peel the garlic and slice finely.

Heat the oil in a large saucepan over medium heat. Add the garlic and fry for a few minutes to flavour the oil. Add the mushrooms and sauté lightly. Stir in the broccoli and beef and sauté to brown the beef. Add the remaining ingredients and bring to the boil.

Cover with a drop lid and simmer over medium heat for 5 minutes

BRAISED BEEF WITH BROCCOLI

until the beef is cooked, occasionally ladling the sauce over the beef. Arrange in small, deep serving bowls to serve, and ladle over a little of the stock.

BEEF AND VEGETABLE ROLLS

SERVES 4

1 medium carrot
4oz (100g) asparagus
4oz (100g) French beans
12oz (350g) prime beef, sliced paper-thin
cornflour or potato flour
vegetable oil

Sauce
1tbsp sugar
3tbsp water
1tbsp sake
1tbsp mirin
3tbsp soy sauce

Scrape the carrot and cut into long, narrow strips. Trim the asparagus. Top and tail the beans.

Parboil the vegetables separately in lightly salted water until just tender. Drain immediately and refresh in cold water. Drain and pat dry.

On a chopping board, lay half the meat slices side by side with edges overlapping to form a sheet of even width. Press the overlapping sections gently so that they stick. Brush with cornflour.

Lay a few strips of each vegetable at one end of the beef sheet. Roll up

firmly. Tie securely with white cotton string. Repeat the process with the remaining beef and vegetables.

Combine the sauce ingredients in a bowl and stir well to blend. Put a little oil into a frying pan and heat over high heat. Add the rolls and sauté until lightly browned.

Pour the sauce over the rolls and bring to a simmer. Continue to simmer over low heat for 5 minutes, until the beef is tender and well flavoured.

To serve, cut the strings and slice the rolls into 1 inch (2.5 cm) rounds. Arrange on individual serving dishes and spoon over a little of the sauce.

◆ POULTRY AND MEAT ◆

CHICKEN PIECES AND CHICKEN LIVERS ON SKEWERS

SERVES 4

8 chicken livers (optional)
4 chicken thighs, boned
4 spring onions, or ½ green pepper, deseeded and cut into 8 pieces

Marinade
6tbsp soy sauce
2fl oz (50ml) sake
3½fl oz (100ml) mirin (or sweet sherry if unobtainable)

Heat the soy sauce, sake and mirin together, stirring all the time until it comes to the boil. Cook without a cover for 2–3 minutes until it has reduced to two-thirds, then cool.

Meanwhile clean the chicken livers, cutting away any threads with scissors. Remove the chicken thighs from the bone, then cut into even-sized pieces for grilling (1 inch/ 2.5 cm).

Cut the spring onions into the same size lengths. Thread the halved chicken livers, if you are using them, onto skewers with the chicken pieces and spring onion or green pepper. Pour the marinade into a jam jar and dip each skewer of food into this. Set under a hot grill or over a barbecue.

Dip in the marinade 3 or 4 times during the 10-minute cooking period. Serve at once to enjoy this succulent dish at its best.

BEEF SALAD IN HOT CHILLI DRESSING

SERVES 4

2oz (50g) Japanese yam (or 4–5 okra, parboiled)
½ cucumber
1 young leek or spring onion
1in (2.5cm) piece fresh root ginger
10oz (275g) beef fillet
salt and pepper
vegetable oil for frying

Dressing
2 pickled plums (umeboshi)
1tbsp miso
3tbsp rice vinegar
1 red chilli pepper, seeded and very finely sliced
1tbsp sugar
1tsp sesame seed oil

4 sprigs of watercress to garnish

Wash the vegetables and pat dry. Cut up the yam and cucumber. Lightly salt and set aside to drain. Sliver the leek or spring onion and cut the ginger into threads.

Lightly brush a frying pan with oil and fry the beef until both sides are lightly browned. Slice the beef very finely and season with salt and pepper.

Seed the pickled plums. Mash the plum flesh with the miso in a suribachi. Combine the vinegar, ½ the chilli pepper and the sugar in a small saucepan and heat to dissolve the sugar. Remove from the heat and cool. Blend the cooled vinegar mixture with the pickled plum and miso, and finally stir in the sesame seed oil.

Rub the mixture through a sieve to purée. Rinse the yam and cucumber and pat dry. Arrange the beef and vegetables in 4 small, deep bowls and pour the dressing over them. Garnish each dish with a sprig of watercress and a few slices of red chilli pepper.

MIXED GRILL

SERVES 4

4 small 4oz (100g) boneless steak fillets
4 sea scallops
2 medium onions
2oz (50g) mushrooms
2oz (50g) mange tout
1 green pepper
4 prawns or jumbo shrimps, shelled and deveined
4 white fish fillets or steaks
vegetable oil

Sauce
1¾pt (1lt) soy sauce
¾pt (450ml) mirin
1pt (600ml) sake
3fl oz (75ml) ginger juice
1½tbsp sesame seed oil

Condiments
daikon radish, grated
red maple radish
ponzu vinegar
mustard, freshly made

Trim the steaks. Wash the scallops and pat dry. Peel and slice the onions. Cut a cross in the top of each mushroom. Trim the mange tout. Deseed the pepper and cut lengthwise into eighths. Put the sauce ingredients into a jar and shake well.

Set a griddle in the centre of the table. Set a small bowl containing a little of the sauce at each place, and arrange bowls of each condiment on the table.

Heat the griddle and brush with oil. Fry the meat, shellfish, prawns, fish and vegetables — a few at a time — over medium heat, turning, until done. The diners help themselves to the various foods as they please, adding sauce and condiments to taste.

SUKIYAKI, TOKYO STYLE

SERVES 4

7oz (200g) bean curd
12 flat mushrooms, wiped and trimmed
1 package shirataki noodles
7oz (200g) napa cabbage
1 onion
4 leeks, washed and trimmed
1¼lb (550g) top sirloin beef, in paper-thin slices

Sauce
⅓pt (200ml) Dashi II (see recipe)
⅓pt (200ml) soy sauce
⅓pt (200ml) mirin
1tbsp sugar

4 eggs
vegetable oil

Cut the bean curd into 1½ inch (4 cm) squares. Remove the stems of the mushrooms and cut a cross in the top of each. Parboil the shirataki for 1–2 minutes and drain. Wash the cabbage, slice across into 1½ inch

(4 cm) lengths, then quarter each segment. Pat dry. Peel the onion, halve and slice. Cut the leeks diagonally into 1½ inch (4 cm) lengths. Arrange the ingredients attractively on a large platter; do not mix the ingredients.

Combine the sauce ingredients and bring to the boil; transfer to a jug. Each diner breaks an egg into a bowl and beats it.

A large, deep frying pan or an electric frying pan is best for sukiyaki. Heat the pan over a medium heat and brush with oil. Add slices of beef in a single layer and brown both sides.

Add small quantities of all the other ingredients and pour over a little of the sauce. Continue to cook over a medium heat, replenishing the pot with meat, vegetables and sauce as required. Before eating, dip the cooked meat and vegetables into raw egg.

BEEF SALAD IN HOT CHILLI DRESSING

SHABU SHABU

SERVES 4

7oz (200g) bean curd
7oz (200g) napa cabbage
4oz (100g) spinach, washed and trimmed
4oz (100g) bamboo shoots
12 flat mushrooms, wiped and trimmed
1 package shirataki noodles
4 leeks, washed and trimmed
1¼lb (500g) top sirloin of beef, in paper-thin slices

Sesame sauce
2tbsp white sesame seeds
salt
3tbsp Dashi II (see recipe)
2tbsp rice vinegar
2tbsp light soy sauce
1tbsp mirin

soy sauce
red maple radish
daikon radish, grated
lemon wedges
spring onions or leeks, shredded and rinsed
1 piece kombu seaweed

Cut the bean curd into 1½ inch (2 cm) squares. Wash the cabbage and cut into large chunks; parboil in plenty of rapidly boiling salted water for 2–3 minutes, then drain well and pat dry. Wash the bamboo shoots and cut into strips.

Remove the stems of the mushrooms and cut a cross in the top of each. Parboil the shirataki for 1–2 minutes and drain. Cut the leeks diagonally into 1 inch (3 cm) lengths. Arrange the ingredients attractively on a large platter, grouping each type of ingredient together.

Lightly toast the sesame seeds with a little salt until golden-brown. Transfer to a suribachi and grind until oily. Gradually blend in the remaining sesame sauce ingredients. Pour into small individual bowls for dipping. Fill 4 other small bowls with soy sauce and prepare and distribute the condiments in yet more bowls.

Wipe the kombu and make a few slashes in it to help release the flavour. Place in a large ovenproof casserole and fill three-quarters full of water. Bring to the boil and remove the kombu. It is now up to the diners to cook the meal. With chopsticks, pick up slices of beef and move them around in the simmering stock for ½ minute, until the meat becomes pink. Dip into sauces and eat.

Continue to cook the ingredients. Allow the vegetables to cook for a little longer than the meat. When ingredients have been consumed, ladle the broth into bowls, season with a little salt and serve as soup.

EATING SHABU SHABU

SIMMERED PORK NAGASAKI STYLE

SERVES 4–6

2¼lb (1kg) pork shoulder
1pt (600ml) water
piece fresh root ginger, peeled and crushed
1pt (600ml) Dashi II (see recipe)
4tbsp sugar
5–6tbsp dark soy sauce
½pt (300ml) sake
1tbsp mirin
mustard

Chop the pork into manageable pieces. Place them in a steamer and steam for 30 minutes. Remove the pork from the steamer and place in a large saucepan. Cover with the water and add the ginger.

Bring to the boil, skim the surface carefully and cover with a drop lid. Simmer over the lowest possible heat for at least 2 hours, topping up the water if necessary, until the pork is very tender.

Drain the pork, discarding the cooking water and ginger. Rinse well and refrigerate for at least 3 hours, preferably overnight.

An hour before you are ready to cook the pork, remove it from the refrigerator and allow it to come to room temperature. Cut the pork into small chunks.

In a dry frying pan, sauté the pork to brown it lightly. Transfer the browned pork to a saucepan.

Ladle the dashi over the pork. Add the sugar, soy sauce, sake and mirin. Bring to a rapid boil, reduce

the heat, cover with a drop lid and simmer for 30–40 minutes, until the simmering stock is considerably reduced.

Arrange a few pieces of pork on each serving dish and ladle a little of the thickened simmering stock over them. Serve with a dab of mustard.

NAMBA-STYLE BACON AND LEEK ROLLS

SERVES 4

8 rashers Canadian bacon
cornflour
6 young leeks
vegetable oil

Trim the bacon, and lay 3 or 4 rashers side by side with edges overlapping to form a sheet of even width. Press the overlapping sections gently so that they stick. Brush the bacon with cornflour.

Trim the leeks. Place 3 leeks at one end of the bacon sheet, alternating tops and tails of the leeks. Carefully roll the leeks in the bacon. Tie the rolls securely with white cotton string.

Put a little oil into a frying pan and heat over a high heat. Place the tied rolls in the pan and fry, turning, for about 7 minutes, until the bacon is cooked to taste and the leeks are tender. Repeat with the remaining bacon and leeks. Remove the strings and cut the rolls into ½ inch (2 cm) slices.

BREADED PORK CUTLET

SERVES 4

4 slices pork loin or tenderloin, 4–5oz (120–150g) each
salt and pepper
4tbsp flour
2 eggs, lightly beaten
4oz (100g) homemade breadcrumbs
vegetable oil for deep-frying
4 lettuce leaves
1 lemon
mustard, freshly made

Dipping sauce
Worcestershire sauce
ketchup
dark soy sauce
sake
mustard, freshly made

SIMMERED PORK NAGASAKI-STYLE

Place each piece of loin or tenderloin between 2 sheets of waxed paper. Pound until flattened into a thin cutlet. Trim the cutlets and score the edges in a few places to prevent curling. Season both sides.

Coat each cutlet lightly with flour, dip into beaten egg and finally coat both sides with breadcrumbs.

Fill a heavy-bottomed saucepan with oil to a depth of 3 inch (8 cm), and heat to 350°F (180°C). Deep-fry the cutlets one at a time for 5–7 minutes, turning once or twice until the meat is well cooked and golden-brown.

Drain the cooked cutlets briefly on absorbent kitchen paper. Slice into 1 inch (2.5 cm) slices. Arrange each cutlet on a lettuce leaf so that it looks as though it is uncut. Garnish with lemon wedges and freshly made mustard.

Make tonkatsu sauce by combining Worcestershire sauce with ketchup, soy sauce, sake and mustard, adjusting the quantities to taste. Serve in small bowls as a dip.

◆ ◆ ◆

◆ FRUITS AND DESSERTS ◆

JELLIED PEACHES

SERVES 8

1 stick agar (kanten)
¾pt (450ml) water
12oz (350g) sugar
4fl oz (120ml) fresh peach pulp
2tbsp fresh lemon juice
2 egg whites

Rinse the agar and soak in cold water for 20 minutes. Then squeeze and tear into small pieces. Combine with the measured water in a saucepan and bring slowly to the boil. Simmer, stirring occasionally, until the agar dissolves. Add the sugar and continue to simmer, stirring, until the sugar has dissolved.

Line a fine sieve with cheesecloth and strain the agar mixture through it into a bowl. Stir in the peach pulp and lemon juice and leave to cool.

Beat the egg whites until stiff, and gradually fold in the cooled peach mixture. Pour into a straight-sided square or rectangular tin and refrigerate until set. Cut into 1 inch (2.5 cm) squares or diamonds and serve 1 or 2 on small plates.

SWEET BEAN GELATIN

SERVES 8

½ stick agar (kanten)
10fl oz (300 ml) water
4oz (100g) sweet bean paste
sugar (optional)
¼tsp salt

Rinse the agar and soak in cold water for 20 minutes. Then squeeze the agar and tear into small pieces. Combine with the measured water in a saucepan and bring slowly to the boil. Simmer, stirring occasionally, until the agar dissolves.

Add the sweet bean paste and sugar and boil for 3 minutes, stirring continuously with a wooden spoon. Stir in the salt and remove from the

CLOCKWISE FROM TOP: ZIGZAG ORANGE HALVES AND ORANGE BASKETS, APPLE PETALS, HARLEQUIN APPLE, AND BANANA MOUNTAIN PEAKS

heat. Allow to cool slightly.

Pour into a straight-sided square or rectangular container about 6 inches (15 cm) square and put aside to cool and set. Refrigerate the tin to speed up this process. Cut the gelatin into oblongs and serve on small plates.

APPLE PETALS

SERVES 4–6

1 large red apple
1 large green apple

Choose a large, firm, red apple. Wash and dry the apple and slice it neatly in half.

Divide the apple into sixths or eighths, depending on the size of the apple. Make a straight cut down the inside of each segment to remove the core.

Make 2 very shallow diagonal cuts through the skin of the apple, meeting in the centre of the segment. With a paring motion, slide the knife between the skin and flesh of the apple to the point where the 2 diagonal cuts meet, releasing the central diamond of skin. Remove and discard the central diamond, leaving two red petals.

Prepare a green apple in the same way, making 4 instead of 2 petals, and arrange 1 or 2 apple segments of each colour on small plates. This technique is also used for oranges and pears.

ZIGZAG ORANGE HALVES

SERVES 2

1 medium orange

Wash and dry an orange and level off the base. Cut the orange in a zigzag all the way around, cutting right through to the centre.

Gently ease apart the 2 halves of the orange. One half equals one serving.

ORANGE BASKETS

1 medium orange for each basket

Wash and dry an orange and level off the base. Set the orange on its base and make 2 parallel cuts downward, about ½ inch (1 cm) apart, to form the handle, cutting through the top third of the orange. Make 2 horizontal cuts from the sides of the orange to meet the vertical cuts, forming the top of the basket.

Remove the 2 segments. Slide the knife under the handle and neatly remove the flesh. Carefully remove as much of the flesh of the orange as possible, keeping the flesh in large chunks. The remaining orange skin will now be in the form of a basket. Neatly chop the flesh and pile into the basket, filling it just to the rim.

SWEET BEAN SOUP WITH RICE CAKES

SERVES 4

4oz (100g) aduki beans
4oz (100g) sugar
¼tsp salt
4 rice cakes

Wash the beans and put in a large saucepan with water to cover. Bring to the boil, then drain and discard the water. Cover again with water, bring to the boil, then reduce the heat and simmer for 1–1½ hours until the beans are soft.

Add the sugar and enough water to make a thick, soupy consistency. Simmer over medium heat for 15 minutes, stirring frequently.

Grill the rice cakes under a hot grill or over a hot flame, turning once so that the cakes do not burn, until both sides are crisp and brown. Put 1 rice cake in each of 4 deep bowls and ladle over the hot soup. The rice cakes should be eaten with chopsticks; the soup is then drunk directly from the bowl.

HARLEQUIN APPLE

SERVES 1

1 large red apple

Choose a large, firm, red apple. Wash and trim the apple and level off the base. Neatly score the skin in a zigzag all the way around the apple.

Carefully pare away the skin with a single stroke between each point, so that the remaining white flesh is neatly contoured.

BANANA MOUNTAIN PEAKS

SERVES 1

1 banana

Cut the banana just before serving to avoid discolouration. Trim the end of the banana and make a lengthwise cut halfway through the fruit.

Leave the knife in the banana as a guide and with a second knife make a diagonal cut through to the centre.

Turn the banana and repeat on the other side. Separate the two halves to make mountain peaks, and arrange two halves decoratively on one plate for a single serving.

◆ ◆ ◆

ORIENTAL TOUR

In the countries of the East can be found a fascinating diversity of peoples, religions, cultures, traditions, and, of course, cuisines. This Oriental tour demonstrates that despite centuries of exchange between these different countries and their customs, and various influences from the West, each cuisine continues to retain its own special character and charm.

This section contains recipes from the regions: Malaysia, Singapore, Indonesia, the Philippines, Thailand, Korea, Burma, Kampuchea, Vietnam and Laos. Perhaps the main reason for the continued vigour of these regional cuisines is the way that they use to the full all the local food resources available to them. Rice is the staple ingredient throughout the Far East, but these lands also produce an abundance of delicious fruits and vegetables, which can be seen displayed in teeming markets from Burma to Indonesia. The sea and richly stocked rivers provide an endless source of fresh and unusual fish and shellfish. In fact, from wild herbs and spices to chicken feet and shark fins, everything edible is ingeniously transformed into exotic and mouth-watering delicacies.

With years of experience in the culinary field, cooking utensils throughout each of the countries have been kept to a minimum: the wok, for example, is common to all Oriental cuisines. However, presentation and table etiquette are unique to each specific area, and make their own special contribution to the experience of a truly local cuisine.

Top far left: *farming rice fields, Indonesia.* ***Bottom far left:*** *throughout Thailand these large nets are used by fishermen both in rivers and canals to catch small fish.* ***Top left:*** *Malaysia is lush and green as a result of its monsoon climate. The landscape is often broken up by the appearance of these long-trunked trees and spectacular mountain ranges.* ***Left:*** *terraced paddy-fields are common throughout the Philippines. Fields are surrounded by levees or bunds and submerged in water. The water is present through the rice growing period, after which the rice is harvested by hand.*

Sunset over Singapore. The island of Singapore, set at the tip of the Malayan Peninsula, is known as the cross-roads of the east.

Many countries throughout the Orient rely on boats like these klongs from Burma to ferry produce to and from the markets.

◆ SPECIAL INGREDIENTS ◆

This section lists special ingredients not already listed in previous sections.

Annatto seeds: Also known as achuete seeds, they look like reddish brown grape pips and are used to give colour to shellfish in Philippino cooking.

Asam jawa (tamarind pulp): This is used to give a tartness to Malay, Nonya and Indian dishes. It is sold in 1lb (450g) packets and can be kept for several months in a jar in the base of the refrigerator or a very cool place.

Asam keping (tamarind): Dried tamarind fruit resembles dried apple slices. They are used to give a sourness to some dishes and are especially useful if added to a soup.

Bagoong: A Philippino fish paste usually of anchovies or shrimps, this rather lurid, pink-coloured sauce is made by putting the fish and salt in a ceramic pot and letting the mixture ferment for days or weeks.

Banana leaves: These are used as plates in some restaurants, but also as a wrapping for some Malay and Indonesian food, giving it a special flavour.

Blachan (balachan, terasi or **trasi, kapi, ngapi):** Tiny prawns are caught near the shore, which are then fermented in enormous barrels with salt. When they have rotted and formed a paste they are formed into blocks, dried and packaged.

The blachan varies in colour from dull pink to a darker brown. It must always be cooked before eating. This can be done by wrapping the suggested quantity in a small foil parcel and frying over a gentle heat in a dry frying pan for 5 minutes, or shaping it into a neat cube around the edge of a skewer and holding it over the gas flame to cook the outside. It can also be grilled to achieve the same result.

Buah keras (macadamia nut, candlenut, kemiri): This chunky, hard-shelled nut, crushed, is frequently used in Malay and Indonesian cooking as a thickening for sauces.

Cayenne pepper: This is made from a particular type of capsicum, originally found in Cayenne in French Guinea. It is much hotter and less brightly coloured than paprika, but does not have the depth of true chilli, which is also coarser in texture.

Chick-peas (kabli channa, channa dal): These are usually available whole and sometimes split or ground (gram flour). They are used ground in Burmese cooking as a thickening agent.

Chorizo: This Spanish pepper sausage is used in Philippino cooking. It is available in delicatessens.

Citrus leaves (lime leaves): The leaves of the kaffir lime, *papeda* or *magrut* as it is also known, give a very distinctive flavour to many Thai and some Malaysian fish dishes.

Coconut milk and cream: Coconut milk is a very important ingredient in the traditional recipes of South East Asia.

Daun kesom: This herb gives its strong, pungent flavour to soups. Do

The markets of the east are renowned for the freshness and variety of their produce –fruits, vegetables and meat, always displayed in immaculate rows.

◆ SPECIAL INGREDIENTS ◆

not try to find a substitute, but if you visit Malaysia, Singapore or Thailand look out for it, even if only to smell it.

Daun pandan (screw pine): This is a long, pointed leaf, which is tied into a knot and put into many Malay and Indonesian sweet recipes.

Ikan bilis: Ikan bilis fish are an indispensible part of Malay cuisine. They are deep fried and sprinkled over food, served as an accompaniment, or added to vegetable dishes. Buy the cleaned variety.

Kecap manis: This is the Indonesian soy sauce and is a sweet, thick variety.

Konnyaku: A yam-based product that comes in two types, either grey or white; those in the know favour the grey. Blanch in boiling water before using then drain and cut into shapes. It has no particular flavour and is used more for texture.

Krupuk (prawn crackers): These can be bought in 8 oz (225 g) packets from most oriental stores.

Laos (lengkuas, 'greater galangal'): Laos is a member of the ginger family and has an earthy, rather a pine-like smell and flavour.

Lemon grass (serai, sereh): Clumps of this grass grow profusely in eastern gardens. The bulbous stem, which is about the size of a spring onion or miniature leek, is generally sold in bundles. Use one teaspoon for each stem in the recipe.

Oyster sauce: This thick, brown sauce of varying quality is made basically from an extract of oysters, salt and also starches. It accentuates flavours and accompanies meat and vegetable dishes very successfully.

Many of the special ingredients require some simple preparation before use. These are some of the basic preparation techniques.

Sambal rojak (harko, petis): This thick, treacle-like paste is made up from soya paste and fermented shrimp.

Sambal ulek: A ready made paste of chillies and salt, this is a convenient substitute for all that pounding and grinding – two chillies make up one teaspoon. It is also sold commercially in jars.

Seasame seed oil: A rich, dark brown oil made from crushed, roasted sesame seeds. Used a great deal in Korean and Japanese cooking.

Sesame paste: This is used in Korean recipes. To make it, roast and grind two or three tablespoons of sesame seeds, and add three teaspoons of sesame seed oil, mixing it to a paste.

Star anise: Used ground in five-spice powder, this is a very attractive, round, star shape with eight sections, which can all be used separately.

Tangerine peel: This adds another dimension to chicken or duck dishes. Soak the small pieces for 30 minutes before cooking. You can make your own by drying out tangerine peel in a slow oven until dry. Store in an airtight container.

◆ SPECIAL INGREDIENTS ◆

Making coconut milk:

1 *Measure out the correct amount of boiling water into a measuring jug and add it to the prescribed quantity of desiccated coconut in a food processor.*
2 *Blend for several seconds in the processor until the two are well mixed.*
3 *Pour out this coconut mixture into a bowl and allow it to cool – otherwise you will scald your hands at the next stage.*
4 *Lift out handfuls of the coconut and squeeze over a sieve into a measuring jug. Place the spent , desiccated coconut into another bowl as this may be used again, although it will not make such rich milk on the second occasion. Squeeze until you have the required quantity of coconut milk. This is usually ¼pt/150ml less than the amount of hot water.*

1

2

3

4

Deep frying spices:

1 *As with dry frying coconut, place the spices in a wok or pan without oil. Use a slice for turning. Cook until they begin to give off a distinctive aroma, do not brown.*
2 *Transfer to a pestle and mortar and pound until fine. Then use immediately to capture all the flavour.*

1

2

Cleaning a chilli:

1 *Whether you are using a red or green chilli, slice off the stalk end of it. Place it under running water and, using a knife, slit up one side of the chilli, from top to bottom.*
2 *Make sure that you keep it under running water to prevent the oils affecting the eyes and throat, and, with the help of the knife, remove all the seeds from the inside. It is then ready to use.*

1

2

◆ SPECIAL INGREDIENTS ◆

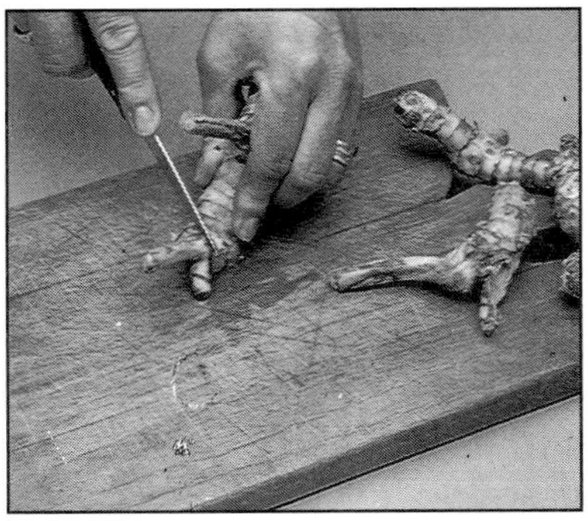

Preparing Laos:
1 *Trim off any knobbly bits from the root of the laos so that you are left with the central core.*

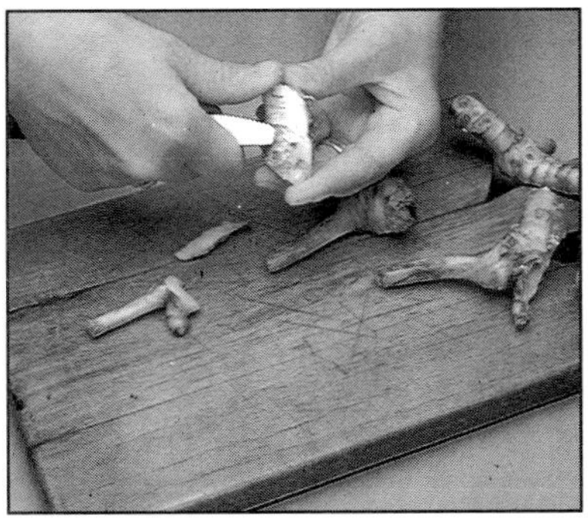

2 *Take a knife and peel off the skin carefully, as, unlike the ginger, it is tough and unpleasant if left on.*

3 *After slicing it, place in a pestle and mortar and pound well, then use immediately to retain maximum flavour.*

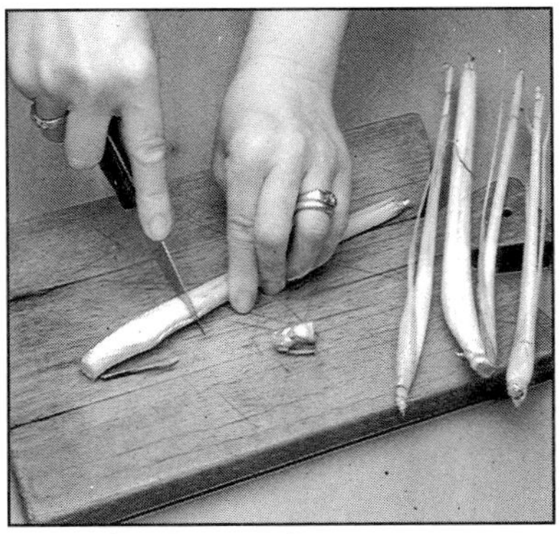

Preparing Lemon Grass:
1 *Taking a piece of lemon grass, trim 2 inches (5 cm). Reserve the top section for adding to casserole dishes.*

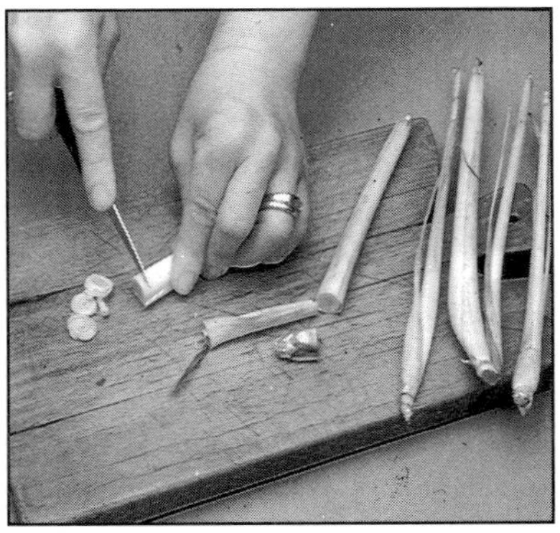

2 *Take this bottom section, which is to be used for pounding, and slice it into rings, as you would do for the laos and ginger. It is now ready for pounding.*

3 *Transfer these rings to a pestle and mortar and pound them finely. Use immediately, otherwise the root will lose some of its flavour.*

Preparing ginger:
1 *Scrape or peel the outside of the ginger root. You do not need to be too meticulous.*

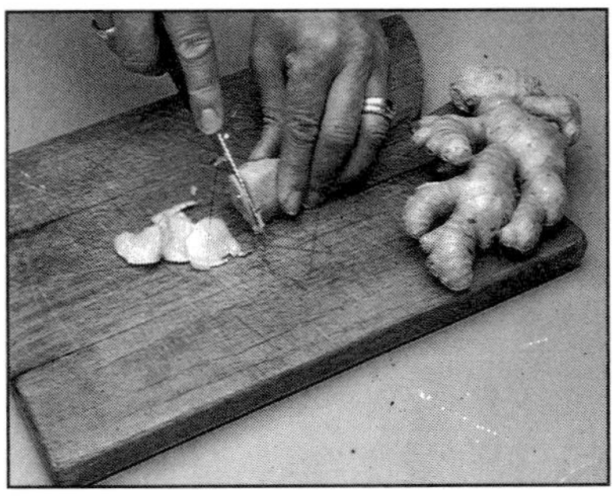

2 *Thinly slice the root with a sharp knife so that you are left with slender rings, which will be used for pounding.*

3 *The ginger is then ready for pounding in a pestle and mortar. It should be used immediately.*

PRAWN SOUP À LA CAMBODGIENNE (KAMPUCHEA)

SERVES 8

½lb (225g) cooked prawns
2½pt (1.5lt) fish stock
5–8 dried tamarind slices
3 stems of lemon grass, cut in half and bruised
½inch (1cm) lengkuas root, peeled and pounded
salt to taste
1 chicken stock cube
3 green tomatoes, peeled and quartered
2–3 slices fresh pineapple, not too ripe chopped into neat cubes
6 green chillies, or less if preferred, deseeded and chopped
2tbsp fish sauce
1–2 cloves garlic
2tbsp oil
2tbsp cumin seeds, dry fried and pounded
½ bunch of spring onions, trimmed into 1inch (2cm) lengths
1 handful of coriander leaves and stems

Set the prawns and stock aside. Soak the tamarind slices in water while preparing the other ingredients. Leave them for at least 20 minutes, then remove and add the tamarind juice to the stock. Prepare the lemon grass, lengkuas, tomatoes, pineapple and chillies.

Bring the stock to the boil with the bruised stems of lemon grass, lengkuas, salt and stock cube. Cook gently for 2–3 minutes, then add the tomatoes, pineapple and chillies. Simmer for 10 minutes. Add the prawns and fish sauce. Cook for a further 5 minutes, but no longer, otherwise the prawns will be tough. Meanwhile fry the garlic in the oil, add the cumin and stir into the soup with the spring onion and coriander. Serve hot.

PORK SOUP WITH GINGER (KAMPUCHEA)

SERVES 6

2½pt (1.5lt) pork or chicken stock
2tbsp light soy sauce
1 clove garlic, crushed
1inch (2.5cm) fresh root ginger, sliced
1 medium-sized onion, sliced
1tbsp sugar
1tbsp fish sauce, or to taste

PORK SOUP WITH GINGER

◆ SOUPS ◆

1tbsp lime juice or vinegar
4oz (100g) pork fillet, shredded finely
1–2tbsp seasoned cornflour
2–3tbsp oil
seasoning
spring onions or coriander leaves to garnish

Simmer the stock and soy sauce together while preparing the other ingredients. Pound the garlic, ginger and onion together in a pestle and mortar or blender and add them to the soup. Cook for 5 minutes, then add the sugar, fish sauce and lime juice or vinegar. Dip the pork in seasoned cornflour.

Fry in hot oil until the meat changes colour, keeping the pieces of meat as separate as possible. Pour off any excess oil and add the meat to the soup. Simmer for 20–30 minutes or until the meat is tender. Taste for seasoning and serve garnished with chopped spring onions or coriander leaves.

SOUR SOUP (BURMA)

SERVES 4

10 pieces dried tamarind, soaked in 1¼pt (1lt) warm water for 30 minutes
2–3tbsp peanut oil
1 onion, very finely sliced
2 cloves garlic, crushed
¼tsp ground turmeric
3 green tomatoes, peeled, deseeded and chopped

SOUR SOUP

½inch (1cm) ngapi (blachan), dry fried then mixed to a paste with tamarind juice, or fish sauce to taste
salt and freshly ground black pepper
handful of shredded sorrel or spinach leaves

Strain the tamarind into a jug and reserve. Heat the oil, fry the onions, garlic and turmeric together without browning. Add the tomatoes and strained stock. Bring to the boil, stir in the ngapi or fish sauce and seasoning. Simmer for several minutes. Add the leaves, taste for seasoning and cook until the sorrel or spinach leaves are tender.

◆ SOUPS ◆

VEGETABLE AND PRAWN SOUP (BURMA)

SERVES 6

2½pt (1.5lt) water
2oz (50g) powdered, dried shrimp or whole, dried shrimps, pounded in pestle and mortar
pepper, freshly ground
2–3 cloves garlic, crushed
1tbsp fish sauce
dash of soy sauce (optional)
salt to taste
courgette, diced
4oz (100g) green leaves such as spinach, sorrel, Chinese leaves or watercress

Pour the water into a pan and bring to the boil. Add the prepared, powdered shrimp, pepper, garlic, fish sauce, soy sauce if using and salt to taste. Simmer for a few minutes while preparing the courgette. Add these and cook for several minutes until tender. Taste for seasoning.

CURRIED FISH SOUP WITH NOODLES (BURMA)

SERVES 8

1½lb (650g) huss, pilchard or mackerel
3 stems of lemon grass
1inch (2.5cm) fresh root ginger, scraped
2tbsp fish sauce
3 onions
4 cloves garlic
2–3 chillies, deseeded
1tsp ground turmeric
peanut oil for frying
1½pt (900ml) coconut milk
1oz (25g) rice flour
1oz (25g) chick pea flour
1lb 3oz (540g) canned bamboo shoot
fresh coriander leaves
1lb (450g) rice noodles, prepared according to packet directions

Accompaniments
3 eggs, hard-boiled and cut into wedges
1–2 onions, peeled and finely sliced
lemon, cut into wedge shapes
1 bunch of spring onions, finely chopped
fried chillies (see below)
crisp fries (see below)

Ask the fishmonger to clean the fish, but leave on the bone. Place in a pan with cold water to cover. Add 2 stems of lemon grass and half the ginger, just bruised. Bring up to the boil, add fish sauce and cook for 10 minutes. Lift out the fish and allow to cool while straining the remaining stock into a bowl. Discard the skin and bones from the fish and reserve the flesh, which will be in small pieces.

Pound the lower stem of the reserved lemon grass together with the remaining piece of ginger, the onions, garlic, chillies and turmeric to a smooth paste in a food processor or with a pestle and mortar.

Heat the oil and fry all these ingredients in it until they give off a rich aroma. Draw the pan off the heat and add the pieces of fish. Add coconut milk to the reserved fish stock. Add sufficient water to make up to 4 pt (2.4 lt). Blend the rice and chick pea flours to a thin cream with some of the stock. Stir this into the remaining stock and allow it to come to the boil over a medium heat, stirring all the time. Add the bamboo shoot and cook for 10 minutes until just tender. Stir in the fish and spice mixture.

Taste for seasoning, cover and leave until the rice noodles are cooked and the accompaniments are assembled. Do not allow the soup to cook for more than a few minutes or the fish will break up.

Each person puts a helping of noodles in a deep bowl and pours or ladles over some of the prepared soup which has been scattered with coriander leaves at the last minute. Choose from the accompaniments as you wish.

Fried chillies
8–10 dried red chillies
2tbsp peanut oil
1tsp powdered prawns

Dry roast the chillies over a gentle heat; the seeds can be removed to make them less hot. Pound the chillies, fry them in hot oil and stir in the powdered prawns. Turn into a small bowl together with other accompaniments — make sure you use with discretion.

Crisp fries
2oz (50g) canned chick peas
3oz (75g) plain flour
1oz (25g) gram flour
1oz (25g) rice flour
¼tsp ground turmeric
salt
few pinches of sugar
¼tsp bicarbonate of soda
5fl oz (150ml) water
oil to ¼inch (5mm) depth for frying

Drain the chick peas. Blend the flours together with the turmeric, salt, sugar and bicarbonate of soda. Mix to a smooth batter with water. Add the chick peas. Fry in small spoonfuls in hot oil until they pale, then drain well. Return to the hot fat for a further minute to crisp up and turn golden-brown. Guests break these over the fish soup at the table.

CLEAR SOUP WITH STUFFED MUSHROOMS (THAILAND)

SERVES 8

3pt (1.75lt) homemade clear, beef or chicken stock
18 small, dried Chinese mushrooms
1 small piece of winter melon

Stuffing for mushrooms
½lb (225g) finely minced pork with a little pork fat
2 cloves garlic, crushed
4 stems of coriander, finely chopped with leaves chopped separately
salt and freshly ground black pepper
2tsp soy sauce
1 spring onion root, trimmed and chopped
6 water chestnuts, peeled and chopped

few coriander leaves to garnish

Prepare the stock or use a stock cube with a little soy sauce for colour. Soak the mushrooms for 30 minutes until soft. Remove the stalks and set aside on absorbent kitchen paper. Peel and cube the melon and set aside.

Meanwhile prepare the stuffing for the mushrooms. Mix the pork,

garlic, coriander stems and leaves, seasoning, soy sauce, spring onions and water chestnuts together. Divide the mixture between the soaked mushrooms. Place the stuffed mushrooms in a bamboo steamer over a wok with a lid on a sheet of greaseproof paper. Cook for 20 minutes. While this is happening bring the stock to the boil, then add the cubes of melon and cook until just tender.

Place the stuffed mushrooms and a few cubes of melon in each serving bowl. Pour on the soup and scatter with a few coriander leaves.

NOODLE SOUP (SINGAPORE)

SERVES 6–8

Fish stock

1 fish head or shells and heads from the fresh prawns (see below)
2½pt (1.5lt) water
½inch (1cm) piece root ginger, sliced
1 stick celery
1 small onion
salt and pepper

Soup

2 cloves garlic, crushed
½inch (1cm) piece fresh root ginger, finely chopped
3tbsp oil
6oz (175g) cooked pork, cut into shreds or small pieces
½lb (225g) prawns, fresh if possible or frozen
6oz (175g) bean sprouts
stock
4oz (100g) fine rice noodles (beehoon), soaked for 10 minutes
4oz (100g) crab meat, or any white fish if liked

spring onions or coriander, finely chopped, and slivers of chilli to garnish

NOODLE SOUP

Place all the ingredients for the stock into a large pan. Bring to the boil, then cover and simmer for 20 minutes. Strain and reserve.

Fry the garlic and ginger in oil without browning. Add the pork pieces, prawns and bean sprouts and stir-fry for 1–2 minutes. Strain in the stock and bring to the boil before adding the noodles. Cook uncovered for 3–4 minutes or until the noodles are just cooked.

Place the crab meat or white fish pieces in a warm serving bowl and top up with the soup. Garnish with spring onion or coriander. Eat with chopsticks, to cope with all the pieces, and a Chinese soup spoon out of warmed bowls.

◆ SOUPS ◆

PRAWN SOUP (THAILAND)

SERVES 4–6

1lb (450g) raw prawns, head and shell removed
2pt (1lt) cold water
2 stems lemon grass, bruised or 1tsp serai powder
1tsp salt
3 lime leaves, reserve one for garnish
3 chillies, deseeded and two bruised, the other cut into rings for garnish
1tbsp fish sauce
juice 2 large lemons or limes

Reserve the shelled prawns and put the head and shells into a pan with water. Add lemon grass or serai powder, salt and two of the lime leaves, and the chillies. Bring to the boil (do not cover) and simmer for 15 minutes. Strain off the stock and return it to the rinsed pan. Allow it to come to the boil, add the raw prawns and simmer for 3–4 minutes or until the prawns are pink and cooked. Stir in the fish sauce and enough lemon or lime juice to make the soup taste sharp. Taste for seasoning. Pour into a serving bowl or tureen and scatter the top with sliced chilli and torn lime leaves if using.

STUFFED BABY SQUID IN A BROTH (THAILAND)

SERVES 6–8

1lb (450g) baby squid, cleaned but left whole for stuffing
½lb (225g) raw pork meat, finely minced
4 stems coriander, leaves reserved for garnish
1–2 cloves garlic, peeled and crushed
salt and freshly ground black pepper
2½pt (1.5lt) fish stock
2 stems of lemon grass, bruised
2 or 3 lime leaves
2tbsp fish sauce or lime juice
1–2 chillies, deseeded and cut into rings

Prepare the squid by removing the heads, rubbing of the purplish skin and pulling out the quill. Turn inside out and wash well. Turn back to the original side and drain well. Cut the tentacles from the head and squeeze out the centre bone. Wash and reserve the tentacles. Mix the pork, finely chopped coriander, garlic and seasoning together. Stuff the squid with this mixture, but do not overfill. Replace the tentacles at the opening of the squid. Secure with wooden cocktail skewers if liked.

Bring the fish stock to the boil with the lemon grass. Cook for a few minutes. Drop in the squid with torn lime leaves and cook gently for 10–15 minutes. Remove lemon grass and lime leaves. Taste for seasoning and add fish sauce or lime juice. Serve in bowls topped with slices of chilli and coriander.

VEGETABLE SOUP (INDONESIA)

SERVES 6

½lb (225g) chicken breast
4oz (100g) peeled prawns
1 onion
2 cloves garlic, crushed
1 fresh red or green chilli, deseeded and sliced
½inch (1cm) terasi or blachan
3 macadamia nuts
½inch (1cm) laos root or 1tsp laos powder
1tsp sugar
oil for frying
½pt (300ml) coconut milk
2pt (1.2lt) chicken stock

Vegetables
1 aubergine, cut into small dice and sprinkled with salt
½lb (225g) French beans, cut small
small wedge of crisp white cabbage, shredded
1 red pepper, deseeded and cut finely

Cut the chicken into dice and set aside with the prawns. Cut half of the onion into slices; pound the remainder with the garlic, chilli, terasi, macadamia nuts, laos and sugar into a paste.

Fry in a little oil in a wok until the mixture gives off a rich aroma. Add the sliced onion and chicken pieces and cook for 3–4 minutes. Now stir in the coconut milk and stock. Bring to the boil and simmer for a few minutes.

Rinse the aubergine and dry. Add to the soup with the beans and cook for only a few minutes until the beans are almost tender. At the last minute add the cabbage and red pepper and prawns. The vegetables should still be crisp when the soup is served.

CHICKEN SOUP (INDONESIA)

SERVES 6–8

2 fresh chicken breasts or quarters
1 medium-sized onion, sliced
seasoning
4 shallots or equivalent white onion
4 macadamia nuts or blanched almonds
3 cloves garlic, crushed
½inch (1cm) piece fresh root ginger, sliced
½tsp ground turmeric
½tsp ground chilli powder
3–4tbsp oil
1tbsp light soy sauce
4oz (100g) bean sprouts or Chinese cabbage

Garnish
1 large cooked potato, cut into dice
oil for frying
4 spring onions, shredded
1 hard-boiled egg, chopped

Cover the chicken pieces with 3 pt (1.75 lt) of water. Add the onion and seasoning. Bring to the boil and simmer for 40 minutes or until the chicken pieces are tender. Lift the chicken from the soup and, when cool enough to handle, remove the meat (discard skin and any bones) and shred or cut it into small pieces. Skim the stock and reserve.

Meanwhile pound the shallots or onions and nuts with the garlic and ginger. Stir in the turmeric and chilli. Heat the oil and fry this spice mixture. Add the chicken pieces and 2 pt (1.2 lt) of the reserved stock and soy sauce. Taste for seasoning and bring to the boil. Simmer for a further

8 minutes. Add the cleaned bean sprouts for the final 2 minutes of cooking. Serve hot.

While the soup is simmering and before adding the bean sprouts prepare the garnishes. Fry the potato dice until they are brown all over; drain on absorbent kitchen paper. Arrange portions of potato, spring onion and hard-boiled egg in large soup bowls. The diners help themselves from a tureen at the table.

SOUP WITH COCONUT MILK (MALAYSIA)

SERVES 6

4 × 8oz (225g) packets unsweetened, desiccated coconut to make 1¾pt (1lt) coconut milk and 4fl oz (100ml) coconut cream
4oz (100g) shallots, peeled
4 cloves garlic
2 buah keras or shelled, blanched almonds
6tbsp coconut oil
3 stems of lemon grass
½inch (1cm) square blachan
1oz (25g) mild curry powder
a few curry leaves
salt to taste
1pt (600ml) ikan bilis stock (see below)

Accompaniments

2oz (50g) ikan bilis and 1½pt (900ml) water to make stock
3 aubergines
1½lb (675g) shelled prawns, sprinkled with 2tsp sugar
1 shredded cos-type lettuce
4oz (100g) bean sprouts
2 spring onions, finely chopped
2oz (50g) crispy fried onions
2 bunches of fried bean curd or 1 packet

Selection of noodles

laksa noodles
mee
beehoon (about 4oz [100g] per person)
½ × 8oz (225g) packet prawn crackers; dry in very low oven first, then deep-fry in oil

Prepare the coconut milk and cream. Pound half of the shallots with the garlic, nuts and one sliced and bruised stem of lemon grass. Fry the remaining half of the shallots, sliced, in coconut oil until they give off a good smell, then add the pounded mixture and stir well. Add the bruised lemon grass stems, blachan and curry powder — mixed to a paste with the coconut milk — and fry to bring out the full flavour. Stir all the time, as you add half of the coconut cream and all the coconut milk, to prevent the soup curdling. Add the curry leaves.

Simmer for 10 minutes without covering. Taste for seasoning of salt. Finally, add the ikan bilis stock and stir in the remaining coconut cream as it comes to the boil. Add the halved, fried bean curd as described below.

To prepare the accompaniments first cook the ikan bilis in water for 30 minutes to make a stock. Strain and discard the fish. Add the aubergines to the stock and cook for 5 minutes until tender and the skins can be peeled off easily. Cut into quarters and pieces about 3 inches (7.5 cm) long. Arrange on a serving platter.

Next, cook the prawns in the stock for 4 minutes until just tender. Arrange on a platter with the shredded lettuce, bean sprouts, spring onions and crispy fried onions. Rinse the fried bean curd in boiling water and squeeze to remove excess oil. Add to the soup.

Finally prepare the noodles, drain and arrange them on a platter. Serve the soup in a large tureen.

SOUP WITH COCONUT MILK

◆ SOUPS ◆

SOUR SOUP WITH PRAWNS AND VEGETABLES (PHILIPPINES)

SERVES 6

½lb (225g) raw prawns with shells and 2pt (1.2lt) water
4oz (100g) cooked, shelled prawns and 2pt (1.2lt) prepared fish stock
1 level tbsp tamarind pulp and ¼pt (150ml) warm water to make tamarind juice
½ sweet potato, peeled and finely diced
4oz (100g) green beans, trimmed and cut into ½in (1cm) lengths
2 tomatoes, skinned, deseeded and chopped
4oz (100g) spinach leaves, stems removed and leaves torn
salt and pepper

Rinse the prawns and place in a large pan with the water. Bring to the boil and gently cook, uncovered, until they are tender. Lift them out, then strain the stock into another pan. Alternatively, use the cooked prawns together with a ready made up pot of fish stock.

Meanwhile prepare the tamarind juice and shell the prawns. Discard the shells. Add the sweet potato to the stock in the pan and cook for 5–10 minutes. Add the beans and cook for 5 minutes. At the last minute add the tamarind juice, tomato and spinach. Just before serving, stir in the shelled prawns to reheat, and season to taste.

COLD NOODLE SOUP (KOREA)

SERVES 8

2pt (1.2lt) chilled beef stock
1lb (450g) fresh or dried Chinese egg noodles

To garnish
4oz (100g) pressed beef or cold roast beef
½ cucumber, cut into even-sized slices
1 unripe pear, peeled and sliced and brushed with vinegar
¼–½ white radish, peeled and grated
1 hard-boiled egg
4 spring onions, trimmed and chopped, reserve 2 for dressing
a little chopped red chilli
1tbsp roasted sesame seeds

Soy dressing
2fl oz (50ml) soy sauce
1 clove garlic, crushed
2tbsp rice vinegar
2 spring onions, finely sliced, from above
sugar to taste

Mustard dressing

1tbsp dry mustard
water or vinegar to mix to a soft paste

Prepare the beef stock as much as a day ahead, if possible, so that it can cool and be skimmed thoroughly. Measure and reserve. Boil the noodles for 1 minute if fresh; soak for 10 minutes if dried, then cook for 3–5 minutes; drain and rinse with cold water. Leave to drain thoroughly. Cut the beef into even-sized pieces, about 2×3 inches (5×7½cm). Prepare the cucumber, pear and radish; reserve. Slice the egg. Chop the spring onions and keep on one side together with both the chilli and sesame seeds.

Divide the noodles between the deep soup bowls. Arrange the beef, cucumber and radish artistically on top of the noodles, but toward the outer edges of the dish. Set the egg slices in the centre and scatter with chilli, spring onion and sesame seeds. Pour in the chilled beef stock, taking care not to disturb the garnish.

Prepare the soy dressing by blending together the soy sauce, garlic, rice vinegar, spring onions and sugar to taste. Turn into a serving bowl. Prepare the mustard dressing and spoon it into a small bowl. Serve all at room temperature.

BEEF SOUP WITH SPRING ONIONS (KOREA)

SERVES 8–10

Stock
¾lb (350g) shin of beef
1–2 beef bones (if available), cut small
1inch (2.5cm) fresh root ginger, bruised and cut in half
salt
4pt (2.4lt) water
1–2 fresh red chillies, deseeded and pounded

1–2 cloves garlic, crushed
1tbsp sesame seed oil
1tbsp roasted sesame seeds, ground to a paste
3–4tbsp soy sauce
1 bunch of spring onions, trimmed and cut into 2inch (5cm) lengths
salt and pepper to taste

Cut the beef into 3 equal pieces. Place these in a pan with the beef bones, ginger, salt and water. Bring to the boil, skim well then lower the heat, cover and simmer for 1½–2 hours on a low heat or until the meat is tender. Strain the stock and skim away any fat. Discard the bones and ginger, but reserve the meat and shred finely. Mix well with the chilli, garlic, sesame seed oil and paste, and soy sauce.

Return the stock to a pan and add all but a handful of the spring onions, then cook for 5 minutes. Meanwhile fry the meat mixture in another pan for just a minute, then pour on the hot stock. Bring to the boil, season and cook for a further 5–10 minutes.

Throw in the reserved spring onions just before the end of cooking. These will add both colour and flavour to the finished dish, and are worth taking the trouble over.

SOUP WITH TAMARIND (MALAYSIA)

SERVES 6–8

6 small or 2 medium-sized mackerel, gutted, rinsed and dried

Fish stock
1 fish head
3pt (1.75lt) water
1 onion, sliced
1 stick of celery
1 piece fresh root ginger
1 stem and bud of the ginger plant flower

◆ SOUPS ◆

4 stems of daun kesom or basil
seasoning to taste

Soup
6 pieces asam keping, soaked in 1pt (600ml) warm water
10 red chillies, pounded, or 1–2tbsp chilli powder, mixed to a paste with oil
½inch (1cm) square piece blachan
20 peeled and chopped shallots about 4oz [100g]
4tbsp coconut oil
1tbsp sugar

Noodles
8oz (225g) fresh laksa noodles or rice vermicelli

Accompaniments
1 lettuce, washed, dried and shredded
3 fresh red chillies, seeded and sliced into rings
4 shallots, cut into slices
½ cucumber, diced
2 limes, each cut into 6 wedges
6 sprigs of fresh mint
1 stem and bud of the ginger plant flower, sliced finely
prawn crackers

Wash the fish head. Remove the flesh from 3 of the smaller fish or 1 of the medium-sized fish. Shred finely and leave in the refrigerator. Place the fish bones and head and the remaining whole fish into a pan with the onion, celery, bruised root ginger chopped ginger flower, daun kesom and salt to taste. Bring to the boil and cook for at least 1 hour until the fish have disintegrated. Strain and reserve the stock.

Soak the asam in the water for at least 30 minutes, then squeeze and reserve the juice. Prepare the chillies, toast the piece of blachan on a skewer over a gas flame until it dries on the outside and gives off a strong smell. Pound with half the shallots. Fry the remaining shallots in the oil until they are just turning colour. Add the chilli, blachan and onion mixture. Reduce the heat and cook for several minutes to bring out the flavour. Add asam juice and sugar and leave to cook for about 10 minutes. Add 2–2½ pt (1.25–1.5 lt) of fish stock and adjust the seasoning. Just before serving add one ladleful of stock to the shredded fish flesh to make it into a creamy consistency, before stirring it all into the pan. Cook, stirring, for 3–4 minutes.

Prepare the accompaniments and arrange them in separate small bowls or in piles on a large platter. Serve the shrimp paste in a bowl and prawn crackers in a dish. Prepare the noodles. Bring the stock or salted water to the boil, soak the noodles for 1–2 minutes then stir, but do not cover. Strain through a colander with boiling water.

Each person takes a helping of noodles and places them in the bowl. Add a selection of accompaniments. Top with soup and eat with prawn crackers.

◆ ◆ ◆

◆ RICE AND NOODLES ◆

COCONUT RICE (SINGAPORE)

SERVES 4

1pt (600ml) coconut milk, made from 8oz (225g) desiccated coconut and 1¼pt (750ml) boiling water
1 stem of lemon grass
8oz (225g) long grain rice
salt to taste
ring of fresh chilli and sprigs of fresh coriander to garnish

Prepare the coconut milk. Rinse a heavy-based pan with water, then pour in the coconut milk. Add the bruised stem of lemon grass and allow to come to the boil. Lift off the heat, then stir in the rice and salt. Bring to the boil, stirring occasionally, then cover and cook over the lowest possible heat for 12 minutes or until the rice is tender. Stir with a chopstick or fork.

Turn off the heat – leave still covered in a warm place until required. Remove the stem of lemon grass before serving. Garnish with rings of fresh chilli and coriander.

FRIED RICE (SINGAPORE)

SERVES 4

8–10oz (225–250g) cold, cooked rice
4 dried mushrooms
1 egg, beaten
cooking oil
8 shallots, sliced
3 cloves garlic, crushed
4oz (100g) small prawns, peeled
4oz (100g) Chinese sausage (optional), steamed and sliced
4oz (100g) cold roast pork (optional)
1–2tbsp light soy sauce
salt and pepper
few frozen peas
chopped spring onion and red chilli
shredded lettuce leaves

Prepare the rice a few hours ahead or the night before. Soak the mushrooms in water for 1 hour, then drain and chop. Fry the beaten egg in a little hot oil in a frying pan to make an omelette, then remove it and shred finely. Set aside.

Fry the shallots in a wok until they are crisp and brown, stirring all the time. Lift out and reserve. Fry the prawns and garlic for just a few minutes. Set aside.

Fry the Chinese sausage, pork and mushrooms, then lift out and reserve. Fry the rice in sufficient hot oil so that the grains are coated, turning all the time. Add the soy sauce and seasoning to taste, plus half the cooked ingredients, and mix well. Stir in the frozen peas and some of the spring onion.

Turn onto a warm platter and garnish with the remaining cooked ingredients, chillies, omelette and lettuce.

CUBES OF COMPRESSED RICE (INDONESIA)

4oz (100g) packet boil-in-the-bag rice
boiling, salted water

Place the boil-in-the-bag rice in the water and boil for 1¼ hours or until the whole bag is puffy and firm and the rice fills the whole of it. The bag must be covered in water all the time. You can place a saucer or plate on top to weight it down if necessary. Allow to cool completely before stripping off the bag, leaving a cushion of rice which can then be cut into neat cubes and served with spiced and deep-fried chicken or with sate.

INDONESIAN FRIED RICE (INDONESIA)

SERVES 4

8oz (225g) rice, cooked and allowed to go cold
1 egg
4–6oz (100–175g) pork fillet
4oz (100g) peeled prawns (optional)
2 fresh red chillies, deseeded and shredded
¼inch (0.5cm) square blachan, prepared
1 onion, sliced
2 cloves garlic, crushed
6–8tbsp oil
2tbsp sweet soy sauce
spring onions and prawn crackers to garnish

Make an omelette with a beaten egg (or fry it whole when the dish is ready) in a tbsp of fat in a wok or frying pan; roll up the omelette and turn out, then, when cold, cut it into fine strips and set aside. Trim and cut the pork into fine strips and set aside with the prawns, if you are using them.

Prepare the chillies, pound the blachan with onion and garlic, then fry with the chillies in hot oil without browning. Add the meats and cook for 2–3 minutes, stirring all the time. Add the prawns, if using, and the rice. Turn all the time to prevent the rice sticking to the pan. Stir in soy sauce and taste for seasoning.

Turn the mixture out onto a hot platter, garnish with the omelette or fried egg, spring onions and a few prawn crackers.

COCONUT RICE (INDONESIA)

SERVES 4

6oz (175g) long grain rice
8oz (225g) desiccated coconut and 1pt (600ml) boiling water to make ¾pt (450ml) coconut milk
½tsp ground coriander
1 piece of stick cinnamon
1 stem of lemon grass, bruised
1 salam or bay leaf (optional)
salt
fried onion flakes to garnish

Wash the rice if necessary, then place in a pan with the prepared coconut milk, coriander, stick cinnamon, lemon grass and salam, bay. Add salt. Bring to the boil over a medium heat, stirring a few times. Cook over the lowest heat for 12–15 minutes or until all the coconut milk has been absorbed.

Fork through carefully and remove the cinnamon, lemon grass and leaf. Cover with a tight-fitting lid, then cook over the lowest heat for a further 10 minutes. Garnish with crispy fried onions.

STEAMED RICE (THAILAND)

SERVES 4

8oz (225g) long grain rice
1pt (600ml) cold water

Rinse the rice in a sieve, then place it in a pan with water. Bring to the boil, lower the heat and cook uncovered until the water has been absorbed and a series of holes appear in the surface of the rice.

Line the base of a steamer within ½ inch (1 cm) of the edges with tin foil and raise the edges into a shallow, bowl-like shape. Puncture all over base with a skewer. Turn the rice into the foil in the steamer and place over a pan of fairly fast-bubbling water. Cover and cook for 30 minutes until the rice is just tender and fluffy. Refill the base pan with boiling water as necessary.

Notice that no salt is added to this recipe — this is quite traditional as the real Thai rice is of such excellent quality, with a fragrant flavour, that salt detracts from this.

CURRIED FRIED RICE (THAILAND)

SERVES 4–6

½lb (225g) cooked meats, chicken, pork and/or prawns
1lb (450g) cold, cooked rice from 8oz (225g) long grain rice
4oz (100g) long beans or French haricot beans, cut into 2inches (5cm) lengths and blanched
nam pla (fish sauce) and sugar to taste

Curry paste
3–5 dried red chillies, deseeded and pounded, or 1–2tsp chilli powder
6 shallots, chopped finely
2 cloves garlic, chopped
2 stems of lemon grass, use bottom part of bulb, sliced
½inch (1cm) khaa (lengkuas) root, sliced finely
4 stems of coriander, chopped, with the leaves reserved for garnish
a little grated lime peel
6–8tbsp vegetable oil

STEAMED RICE

Cut the meats into fine slices and leave the prawns, if using, whole. Set the rice on one side. Prepare and blanch the beans.

Meanwhile pound the chillies with shallots, garlic, lemon grass, laos and coriander stems and peel. This can be done in a food processor. If using the chilli powder add it to these pounded ingredients. Heat the oil and fry this paste until it gives off a fragrant aroma. Add the cooked meats then the rice, stirring all the time until the fried rice is well mixed. Add more oil if necessary.

Season with salt, fish sauce and sugar, if liked, to taste. Finally add the green beans. Serve garnished with coriander leaves.

◆ RICE AND NOODLES ◆

RICE FRITTERS (PHILIPPINES)

MAKES 25

4oz (100g) long grain rice
2 eggs, beaten
2oz (50g) caster sugar
few drops of vanilla essence
3oz (75g) plain flour
1tbsp baking powder
salt
¼tsp ground cinnamon
2oz (50g) desiccated coconut
oil for deep-frying
icing sugar for dredging

Cook the rice and cool. Turn it into a bowl, add the beaten eggs, sugar and flavouring. Mix well. Sift in the flour, baking powder, salt and cinnamon with the coconut. Mix thoroughly. Drop teaspoonfuls into hot oil and cook until golden-brown.

Cook 3 or 4 fritters at a time, draining them on absorbent kitchen paper. Dredge with icing sugar. Serve hot.

STEAMED GLUTINOUS RICE (LAOS)

SERVES 4

8oz (225g) glutinous rice, soaked in water to cover for up to 6 hours

Drain the rice, then place in a steamer lined with muslin. Set over bubbling water and cover. Replenish with boiling water as necessary. Cook until the rice grains are soft. The longer the soaking period the shorter the cooking time. Serve hot.

COOKING RICE (MALAYSIA)

SERVES 3

6oz (175g) quality rice
¾pt (450ml) hot water
salt to taste

Wash the rice very thoroughly in lots of cold water. Place in a saucepan with water, and salt if liked. Bring to the boil, do not cover, and cook over a medium heat for approximately 10 minutes, until the majority of the water has either been absorbed or evaporated.

Now cover with a tight-fitting lid and place over the lowest possible heat. Cook for a further 10 minutes.

FRIED NOODLES WITH PORK (MALAYSIA)

SERVES 4

1lb (450g) packet kway teow (sheets of white noodles)
a piece of pork fat
2tbsp cooking oil
2 cloves garlic, crushed
1 red chilli, deseeded and chopped finely
1tbsp light soy sauce
1tbsp dark soy sauce
1tbsp oyster sauce
4oz (100g) bean sprouts
2oz (50g) cooked prawns
2oz (50g) cooked pork, cut into shreds
Chinese chives or coriander leaves to garnish

Cut the noodles into strips ½ inch (1 cm) wide and set aside. Gently heat the pork fat in the wok until the fat runs out. Leave the liquid fat in the pan, but take out and cut the crisp fat into small pieces to add to the pan later. Heat the fat with the oil. Fry the garlic and chilli without browning, then stir in the sauces.

Pour boiling water over the noodles. Drain well and add to the wok with the bean sprouts, prawns and pork and crisp fat. Taste for seasoning. Toss well and serve on a hot platter, garnished with Chinese chives or fresh coriander.

CHINESE RICE PORRIDGE (MALAYSIA)

SERVES 4

4oz (100g) short grain rice
1oz (25g) skinned, raw peanuts
1¾pt (1lt) chicken stock
4oz (100g) lean pork
1tsp soy sauce
1tsp sesame seed oil
2tsp seasoned cornflour

Accompaniments
2 cloves garlic, cut into slivers
6 small onions, finely sliced
4tbsp oil
2 red chillies, deseeded and finely chopped
sprigs of fresh coriander
small dish of light soy sauce
1 fresh egg per person (optional)

Rinse the rice and put it in a large pan with the peanuts and chicken stock. Bring to the boil, cover and simmer gently for 35 minutes or until the mixture is a soft, creamy consistency. Slice the pork into fine strips; dip these in a mixture of soy sauce and sesame seed oil and then into seasoned cornflour. Prepare the garlic and onions, then fry them separately in hot oil, drain and serve in small bowls. Fry the pork in the pan oil for 2–3 minutes. Add to the cooked porridge and cook for 2–3 minutes.

Prepare the chillies, coriander and soy sauce. Spoon the porridge into serving bowls. A whole egg can be broken into the porridge and stirred around to cook it, before scattering some of each of the other accompaniments on top.

CURRY NOODLES (SINGAPORE)

SERVES 4–6

1lb (450g) fresh yellow noodles
4–6tbsp oil
1 square bean curd, well drained, cut into dice
2 beaten eggs, seasoned
1 medium onion, sliced
1 clove garlic, crushed
1tbsp soy sauce
2–3tbsp ketchup
1tbsp chilli sauce (or to taste)
1 large cooked potato, diced
4 spring onions
1–2 green chillies, deseeded and shredded

Cook the noodles in boiling water in a large pan for just 2–3 minutes. Do not overcook. Drain and rinse with

cold water to halt cooking; set on one side. Heat 2 tbsp of the oil and fry the bean curd until brown. Drain and set aside. Pour the beaten eggs into the pan. When it has set like an omelette, roll it up on a board and chop finely.

Spoon the remaining oil into the wok and fry the onion and garlic for 2–3 minutes. Add the drained noodles, soy sauce, ketchup and chilli sauce. Toss well over a medium heat. Add the potato dice, most of the spring onion, some of the chilli

CURRY NOODLES

and all the bean curd. Keep tossing. When hot, add pieces of the cooked egg. Serve on a hot platter, garnished with the remaining spring onion and chilli.

FRIED NOODLES WITH PRAWNS, MEAT AND VEGETABLES (PHILIPPINES)

SERVES 8

1–1½lb (450–675g) egg noodles, fresh or dried
1lb (450g) whole, fresh prawns, or 8oz (225g) thawed, frozen prawns
½lb (225g) cooked chicken breast
½lb (225g) cooked ham or lean pork
2oz (50g) lard or 4–6tbsp cooking oil
1 medium onion, chopped
2 cloves garlic, crushed
½ small Chinese cabbage, finely shredded, or 8oz (225g) bean sprouts
¼pt (150ml) fish stock from prawns or chicken stock
2tbsp fish sauce
seasoning
spring onions, chopped
bagoong (anchovy or shrimp paste), served in a separate dish at the table

Cook the fresh noodles in boiling water for 1–2 minutes, rinse with cold water and drain thoroughly, or cook dried noodles according to packet directions and drain in the same way.

Cover the fresh prawns, if using, with cold water. Bring to the boil and cook gently for 5 minutes. Lift out with a slotted spoon, remove the heads and shells and reserve the prawns. Discard the shells. Strain the cooking liquid. If using frozen prawns, thaw well. You will need to substitute the prawn stock with chicken stock later in the recipe. Using a very sharp knife, finely slice the chicken meat and ham or pork.

Heat half the oil in a wok and fry the drained noodles for 2–3 minutes, stirring. Lift out of the pan onto a platter and keep warm. Heat the remaining oil in the pan, fry the onion and garlic until soft and just beginning to turn golden. Add the cabbage or bean sprouts, cook for 1–2 minutes, mix well, then stir in most of the chicken, ham or pork and prawns, reserved fish or prepared chicken stock and fish sauce. Turn the mixture all the time.

Return the noodles to pan, taste for seasoning and serve on a hot platter garnished with the reserved prawns, the chicken, ham or pork and the spring onions. Serve the bagoong separately.

CRISP FRIED NOODLES (THAILAND)

SERVES 6–8

Sauce
4oz (100g) raw chicken breast, finely chopped
2oz (50g) cooked pork, sliced
4oz (100g) cooked prawns, shelled
6 shallots, chopped
2 cloves garlic, crushed
oil for frying

1 square bean curd, yellow or white, cut into neat cubes
½ × 12oz (340g) can salted soya beans
4 beaten eggs
1fl oz (25ml) cider or wine vinegar
1–2tbsp icing sugar
nam pla (fish sauce) to taste

Noodles
12oz (350g) rice vermicelli
fat for deep-frying
¼tsp chilli powder

Garnish
spring onions
2–3 red chillies, deseeded and finely sliced
fresh coriander leaves
chopped, pickled garlic or fried garlic flakes
rind of lime or strip of grapefruit peel, cut into fine shreds
6oz (175g) bean sprouts, tails removed for best effect

Prepare the chicken breast, cut the cooked pork into fine slices and set aside with the prawns. Fry the shallots and garlic in hot oil in a wok; do not colour. Add the chicken and stir for 3–4 minutes, then stir in the pork and prawns. Turn the ingredients all the time.

Add the bean curd cubes and salted soya beans and cook for 2–3 minutes. Then add the beaten eggs little by little, stirring throughout and adding extra oil if necessary to the sauce.

At this stage stir in the vinegar, icing sugar and fish sauce. Toss in the pan for 1–2 minutes, then check the flavour. It should have a sweet, salty taste. Set aside.

Heat oil to 375°F (190°C) in a large pan and deep-fry the noodles for just a few seconds. This is best done in several stages in a frying basket or wok. The noodles will become puffy and crisp. Remove them from the fat, drain and keep warm.

Just before serving, put half the sauce and a sprinkling of the chilli powder in a large wok or pan with half the noodles. Toss together without breaking up the noodles too much. Repeat this tossing procedure with the remaining sauce, chilli and noodles.

Pile onto a large serving platter and garnish attractively with spring onions, chillies, coriander, garlic and lime rind or grapefruit shreds. Arrange the bean sprouts all around the base.

MIXED VEGETABLES WITH NOODLES (KOREA)

SERVES 4

½lb (225g) rump or sirloin steak, sliced thinly

Marinade
1tbsp sugar
2tbsp soy sauce
1tbsp spring onion, finely chopped
1 clove garlic, crushed
few crushed, roasted sesame seeds

4oz (100g) transparent noodles, soaked in water for 20 minutes
4 dried Chinese mushrooms, soaked in water for 30 minutes
1 onion, sliced
1 carrot, peeled and cut into fine matchstick-like pieces
2 courgettes or ½ cucumber, trimmed and cut into sticks
½ red pepper, seeds removed and cut into strips
4 button mushrooms, sliced
3oz (75g) bean sprouts, washed and drained
3 spring onions
sesame seed oil for cooking

Garnish
1–2 eggs, separated whites and yolks
1tbsp soy sauce
salt and pepper
roasted sesame seeds

Chill the steak so that it is easier to slice finely and cut it into 2 inch (5 cm) strips. Soak in marinade. Cook the soaked and drained noodles in boiling water for 5 minutes. Drain well and separate by pulling apart. Drain the mushrooms and slice.

Prepare the onion, carrot, courgettes or cucumber, red pepper, button mushrooms, bean sprouts and spring onions. Reserve one of the spring onions for garnish.

Heat a little oil in the pan. Break the egg yolks and pour them into the pan. When they are set, remove them onto absorbent kitchen paper. Heat the pan again and pour in the egg whites. When these are set, drain, then cut up the yolk and the white into strips or diamond shapes to use as garnish.

Drain the marinade from the beef. Heat a little more oil and stir-fry the beef until it changes colour. Add the carrot and onion next. Cook for 2 minutes, then add the other vegetables, tossing all the time until they are just cooked. Add noodles and soy sauce and taste for seasoning. Cook for 1 more minute. Turn out onto a serving dish and garnish attractively with egg strips, chopped spring onion and sesame seeds.

◆ ◆ ◆

◆ VEGETABLES AND PULSES ◆

VIETNAMESE SALAD

SERVES 4

8oz (225g) Chinese leaves
2 carrots
½ cucumber
salt
2 red chillies, deseeded and finely sliced
1 small onion, sliced into fine rings
4 pickled gherkins, sliced, plus 3tbsp of the liquid
1 clove garlic, chopped
1tsp sugar
2tbsp cider or white vinegar
2oz (50g) peanuts, lightly pounded
8oz (225g) cooked chicken, shredded
few stems of fresh coriander

Wash and shred the Chinese leaves thinly. Peel and cut the carrots into matchstick-like strips. Trim the ends from the cucumber, cut in half lengthwise and scoop out the seeds. Cut in pieces the same size as the carrot, sprinkle with salt and leave for 15 minutes.

Place the chillies, onion and gherkin slices together in a bowl. Blend the gherkin liquid with the garlic, sugar and vinegar. Rinse and dry the cabbage, carrot and cucumber, then add these to the liquid ingredients with the nuts and chicken, toss altogether and taste. Add more vinegar, if you wish, for a sharper taste. Garnish with coriander leaves.

KOREAN PIZZA

MAKES 16

8oz (225g) split mung beans, washed
2oz (50g) glutinous rice

1tbsp soy sauce
1tbsp roasted sesame seeds, crushed
½tsp bicarbonate of soda
4oz (100g) bean sprouts, blanched and dried
1 clove garlic, crushed
4 spring onions, trimmed and chopped
4oz (100g) cooked lean pork, shredded
salt and pepper to taste
sesame seed oil for frying
soy dressing for dipping

Pick over, then soak the split (or whole) mung beans and glutinous rice in the water for at least 8 hours. Rinse well, removing as many green skins as possible, drain, then put into a food processor and grind to a batter the consistency of double cream. Add soy sauce, sesame seeds and bicarbonate of soda. When ready to cook, add the bean sprouts, garlic, spring onion and pork. Season to taste.

Heat the sesame seed oil in a pan. Spoon or ladle in just over ¼ pt (150 ml) of the mixture and, using the back of a spoon, spread it into a thick pancake. Drizzle a little of the oil over the surface, cover and cook over a medium heat until the underside is cooked.

Now invert a lightly oiled plate over the pancake. Remove from the heat and turn the frying pan over so that the pancake is on the plate. Slip the pancake, uncooked side down, back into the pan, and continue cooking for a further 3–4 minutes. Keep warm while cooking the remaining batter and serve in quarters with the dipping sauce.

CUCUMBER SALAD (KOREA)

SERVES 4–6

1 large cucumber
2tsp salt
3 spring onions, finely chopped
1tbsp sesame seed oil
1tsp chilli powder
2tbsp soy sauce
sugar to taste
1tbsp roasted sesame seeds, lightly crushed

Halve the cucumber, trim the ends, cut it into 2 in (5 cm) lengths, then into stick-like pieces. Sprinkle with salt and after 30 minutes squeeze to drain off any excess liquid. Fry the cucumber and two-thirds of the onion in hot sesame seed oil without browning. Add chilli powder and cook for 1 minute.

Stir in the soy sauce, sugar to taste and the sesame seeds. Turn onto a serving dish and leave for 2–3 hours before serving so that the flavours blend, then sprinkle with the remaining spring onions.

KIMCHI (KOREA)

MAKES 2lb (900g)

1½lb (675g) Chinese leaves
1½lb (675g) Chinese turnips or hard pears
4tbsp salt
⅓pt (200ml) water
4 spring onions, trimmed and finely chopped
4 cloves garlic, crushed
1inch (2.5cm) piece fresh root ginger, sliced and finely chopped
2–3tsp chilli powder

Shred the cabbage into pieces the length of your little finger. Peel and thinly slice the Chinese turnip or pears evenly. Sprinkle the vegetables with salt. Mix well, then press into a glazed or glass bowl and pour over water. Cover with a lid and leave overnight.

On the following day drain off the salt water from the vegetables and reserve. Mix the vegetables with the spring onions, garlic, ginger and chilli powder; use rubber gloves if you have sensitive hands. Pack these into a large 2 lb (900 g) jar or 2 smaller ones. Pour over the reserved salt water. Cover with clingfilm and store in the warm sun or an airing cupboard for 2–3 days. Thereafter store in the refrigerator where it can be kept for several weeks.

BEAN CURD SALAD, NONYA STYLE (SINGAPORE)

SERVES 4

3 pieces hard bean curd
oil for deep-frying
4oz (100g) bean sprouts, blanched
4oz (100g) Chinese cabbage, blanched
½ cucumber, sliced and sprinkled with salt

Sauce
2fl oz (50ml) juice made from 1tsp tamarind paste
1–2 fresh chillies, deseeded
small red onion, chopped
1tbsp thick soy sauce
½oz (15g) brown sugar
2 good tbsp crunchy peanut butter

Cut the bean curd into quarters or slices and fry in hot oil until crisp and brown. Drain and leave to cool.

Blanch the bean sprouts in a pan of boiling water for just 30 seconds. Drain and put into a bowl of iced water for 2 minutes. Drain well. Blanch the cabbage in the same way. Slice the cucumber and sprinkle with salt. Leave while preparing the sauce, then rinse and dry. Arrange the cucumber slices on a platter. Top with bean curd and bean sprouts and cabbage.

Prepare the sauce. First make the tamarind juice, then pound the chillies and onion to a paste in a food processor. Add the soy sauce, brown sugar and peanut butter. Add a little water if necessary so that the sauce pours. Just before serving, pour the sauce over the arranged salad vegetables or serve separately, if preferred.

KOREAN PIZZA

◆ VEGETABLES AND PULSES ◆

FRIED ONION FLAKES (SINGAPORE)

shallots or onions, peeled
oil for deep-frying

Finely slice the shallots or onions. Dry on absorbent kitchen paper and leave in a dry place, preferably the sun, for an hour. Deep-fry until golden. Drain on absorbent kitchen paper; do not add salt. When cold and crisp, store in an airtight jar.

SAMOSAS (SINGAPORE)

MAKES 30

1/3 packet spring roll wrappers, 10inches (25cm) square
2tbsp flour, mixed to a paste with water
oil for deep-frying

Filling
8oz (225g) potato, peeled and boiled
2oz (50g) cooked cauliflower (optional)
1 small onion, chopped finely
1/2inch (1cm) fresh root ginger, chopped
1 clove garlic, crushed
1oz (25g) melted ghee or unsalted butter
1/2tsp chilli powder
1–2tsp garam masala
2oz (50g) frozen peas, thawed
1tbsp chopped coriander leaves and stems
squeeze of lemon juice
salt to taste

Let the wrappers thaw out. Make a paste from the flour and water and set aside. Prepare the filling by dicing the potato finely and evenly and cutting the cauliflower into small pieces. Fry the onion, ginger and garlic in ghee or butter. Do not brown. Add the chilli powder and cook for a minute, then stir in the potato, cauliflower and peas. Sprinkle with garam masala and set aside to cool. Add the coriander and lemon juice. Taste for seasoning and add salt as required.

Cut the spring roll wrappers into 3 inch (7.5 cm) strips. Brush the edges of each piece with paste. Fold over one corner to make a triangle. Fill this with a small spoonful of the filling. Fold the whole strip over and over to make a triangular-shaped samosa. Seal any open edges with more flour and water paste, if necessary. You may have to add more water to this. Fry the samosas a few at a time in deep oil until golden and crisp. Drain well and serve hot, with a few slivers of carrot, cucumber and celery.

If you are making these for a party, fry until they are cooked through, but not golden, and then plunge them into hot fat for a few minutes before serving.

NAM PRIK SAUCE FOR RAW VEGETABLES (THAILAND)

1/2inch (1cm) square kapi (blachan)
4tbsp dried shrimps, soaked for 15 minutes until soft, then drained
4 cloves garlic, crushed
4tbsp freshly cooked prawns (optional)
4–6 fresh red chillies, deseeded and chopped
1 sprig coriander, stalks and leaves
nam pla (fish sauce) to taste
1tbsp brown sugar
juice of 1/2–1 lemon or lime

Dry fry the shrimp paste. Pound it with the drained, dried shrimps and garlic to a paste. Add freshly cooked prawns if you are using them and pound again. Add the chillies and repeat. Bruise the coriander stems and leaves with the mixture. Season with fish sauce, sugar and lime or lemon juice. More chillies can be added, but try these quantities first.

SALAD OF TART FRUITS (THAILAND)

SERVES 4–6

2 green apples
2 green mangoes
1/2 small pineapple
4oz (100g) cooked pork, cut into strips
2oz (50g) cooked prawns

Dressing
2–3tbsp lemon juice
2tsp sugar
1tbsp fish sauce or to taste
mint or coriander leaves to garnish

Peel and cut the apples and mangoes into even-sized pieces. Slice the pines from the pineapple, remove the core and cut the flesh up into bite-sized pieces. Arrange these attractively with the pork and prawns on a serving dish. Blend the dressing ingredients together and pour over the salad. Garnish with mint or coriander leaves.

FRESH CUCUMBER ACCOMPANIMENT (THAILAND)

1 medium-sized cucumber
1tbsp salt
2tbsp distilled vinegar
2tsp caster sugar
1 small onion, cut into fine strips
1–2 fresh red or green chillies, deseeded and chopped

Wash the cucumber and score the flesh lengthwise with a fork. Then slice it finely and put the slices into a glass dish. Sprinkle with salt and leave for 15 minutes. Drain off the juices, rinse with cold water and drain thoroughly. Arrange in a serving dish and sprinkle over vinegar and sugar. Scatter with onion rings and chopped chillies. Serve with curry of your choice.

GREEN VEGETABLE SALAD WITH COCONUT DRESSING (MALAYSIA)

SERVES 4

Salad
1lb (450g) prepared mixed green vegetables such as: beans, Chinese cabbage, bean sprouts, 1/4–1/2 cucumber

Sauce
4oz (100g) desiccated coconut
5fl oz (150ml) water
1/2inch (1cm) blachan, prepared
1 clove garlic, crushed
1 green chilli, prepared

salt
juice of ½ lemon or 1tbsp tamarind juice
sugar to taste
sprigs of mint to garnish

Trim ends from the beans and blanch in boiling water for 2–3 minutes until just cooked. Rinse in cold water to retain the colour. Wash the cabbage and shred, not too finely. Plunge the bean sprouts into cold water for a few minutes and drain.

Cut the cucumber into 1 inch (2.5 cm) lengths and each chunk into 10 pieces. Cook the coconut and water together for 5 minutes. Cool. Pound the blachan with garlic and chilli to a paste. Add to the grated coconut. Add salt, lemon or tamarind juice and sugar to taste. Transfer to a large bowl, then add the prepared vegetables. Toss well and serve garnished with mint leaves. Do not keep.

NAM PRIK SAUCE FOR RAW VEGETABLES

◆ VEGETABLES AND PULSES ◆

SAGO PUDDING (MALAYSIA)

SERVES 4

10oz (275g) sago
2tbsp coconut cream

Syrup
5oz (150g) palm sugar or dark brown sugar
¼pt (150ml) butter
slice fresh root ginger
½pt (300ml) thick coconut milk from 12oz (350g) desiccated coconut and ¾pt (450ml) boiling water

Bring a large pan of water to the boil. Wash the sago thoroughly in a sieve and immediately add it to the boiling water; cook until the granules become clear, stirring frequently. This will take 12–15 minutes. Strain through a sieve, washing well with cold running water until all the starch is removed. Drain well, then turn the sago into a bowl, add the coconut cream and pour the mixture into a 1 pt (600 ml) mould or 4 individual serving dishes. Leave at least 6 hours in the refrigerator to set.

Prepare the syrup by dissolving the palm sugar with water in a pan. Add the slice of ginger. Stir until the syrup thickens. Remove the ginger and leave to cool. Prepare the coconut milk and stir before serving as the cream will have floated to the top. Unmould the pudding to serve or leave it in individual bowls. Guests help themselves to the sugar syrup and coconut milk at the table.

SAMBAL BLACHAN (MALAYSIA)

2–4 fresh red chillies
salt
½inch (1cm) square blachan
juice of ½ lemon or lime

Prepare the chillies, removing the seeds, and cut each one in half lengthwise. Pound in a pestle and mortar with a little salt. Add the prepared blachan and lemon or lime juice to taste. Serve as an accompaniment to rice meals.

SALAD OF BEAN SPROUTS AND BEAN CURD (BURMA)

SERVES 4–6

8oz (225g) can bean sprouts
1 square bean curd, cut into small dice
oil for frying
1½tbsp powdered shrimp
2 dried red chillies, dry roasted, seeds removed and pounded, or ½tsp chilli powder
2tbsp oil
dash of fish sauce
juice 1 lemon
fried onion flakes

Soak the bean sprouts in cold water. Toss into boiling water for 1 minute, then drain and rinse with cold water. Fry the bean curd in fat until it is crisp; drain. Place the bean sprouts, powdered shrimp, chilli powder, oil and fish sauce in a bowl and toss together. Squeeze over lemon juice. Taste for seasoning and, at the last minute, add crisp bean curds and top with fried onion.

PICKLED CUCUMBER AND SESAME SEED ACCOMPANIMENT (BURMA)

1 large cucumber
juice of ½ lemon
1tsp salt
4tbsp peanut oil
1tbsp sesame seed oil
3 cloves garlic, finely sliced
1 onion, finely sliced and dried on absorbent kitchen paper
1tbsp roasted sesame seeds

Peel the cucumber, cut it in half and scoop out the seeds. Cut into even-sized chunks. Put 1 pt (600 ml) of water into a pan (stainless steel or enamel if possible). Add lemon juice and salt. Bring to the boil, then lightly cook the cucumber pieces in this, but take care not to overcook. Drain and leave to cool.

Heat the oils and fry the garlic, then lift out the pieces and fry the onion until crisp; lift out and drain. Reserve the oil and when cool pour over the cucumber. Toss well, then mix with the garlic, onion and sesame seeds. Serve with curries.

CRUSHED CHILLIES (INDONESIA)

½lb (225g) fresh red chillies, deseeded
2tsp salt

Plunge the chillies into a pan of boiling water and cook for 5–8 minutes. Drain, then pound in a blender without making the paste too smooth. Turn into a glass jar, stir in salt and cover with a piece of greaseproof paper or clingfilm, then screw on the lid and store in the refrigerator.

Spoon into small dishes to serve as an accompaniment or use in recipes where suggested. It is fiercely hot and should you get any of the chilli on your fingers wash them well in soapy water immediately.

COOKED SALAD WITH HOT PEANUT SAUCE (INDONESIA)

SERVES 4–6

Peanut sauce
4oz (100g) salted peanuts
½pt (300ml) coconut milk
1tsp tamarind and 4tbsp water to make tamarind juice
¼inch (5mm) blachan, prepared
1 clove garlic, crushed
3 shallots or 1 small red onion
oil for frying
1tsp chilli powder or sambal ulek
1tbsp brown sugar
1tsp dark soy sauce
salt to taste

Salad
2 medium potatoes, peeled, boiled and diced
4oz (100g) bean sprouts, blanched, rinsed and drained
4oz (100g) cabbage, shredded, blanched and rinsed
4oz (100g) each green beans and florets of cauliflower, boiled until just tender and drained

½ cucumber, sliced
1 small carrot, cut into matchstick-like pieces
Chinese leaves, shredded
watercress (optional)
2 hard-boiled eggs

Grind the salted peanuts until gritty but not a paste; set aside. Prepare the coconut milk, tamarind water and blachan. Pound the blachan with the garlic, shallots or onion. Fry in 3 tbsp of hot oil without browning. Stir in the chilli powder or sambal ulek and cook for 1 minute. Add the coconut milk and allow to come to the boil. Stir in the tamarind water, sugar and soy sauce, and the ground

peanuts, which will thicken the sauce. Taste for seasoning.

Allow to simmer until creamy in consistency. Set aside. Arrange the vegetables in piles on a large platter with egg quarters. Heat up the sauce and serve separately in a sauce boat.

◆ ◆ ◆

◆ FISH AND CRUSTACEANS ◆

FISH IN BEAN PASTE SAUCE (SINGAPORE)

SERVES 2–3

1½lb (675g) ikan merah, snapper or bream
½ medium onion, chopped
2 cloves garlic, crushed
2tbsp bean paste
½oz (15g) fresh root ginger
oil for frying
1tsp sugar
3 green chillies, deseeded and roughly chopped
½pt (300ml) water
seasoning to taste

Wipe the fish, then make 3 incisions on each side with a sharp knife. Pound half the onion, one garlic clove and the bean paste together until creamy. Slice and shred the ginger. Half fry the fish in oil on both sides, then lift out. Fry the reserved onion and garlic in the fat in the pan until just browning.

Stir in the bean paste mixture and fry for 1–2 minutes to bring out the flavour. Add the sugar and green chillies. Cook until you can smell the aroma from the chillies. Pour in the water. Bring to the boil, then lower the fish into the sauce. Cover and cook for 5–10 minutes further or until the fish is cooked through. Garnish with chopped spring onion or fresh coriander leaves.

KING PRAWNS COOKED IN SHELLS (SINGAPORE)

SERVES 2

1lb (450g) whole, uncooked prawns in shell
1tbsp sugar
1inch (2.5cm) piece fresh root ginger, sliced
1tbsp Chinese rice wine or dry sherry
1tbsp light soy sauce
3tbsp oil
4tbsp ketchup
1tbsp chilli sauce or to taste
water
salt and freshly ground black pepper
coriander leaves and slices of cucumber

Rinse and dry the prawns in their shells. Sprinkle them with sugar then squeeze the ginger through a garlic press onto the prawns. Add the rice wine or sherry and soy sauce. Leave to marinate for 30 minutes.

Heat the oil and fry the drained prawns for 3–4 minutes until the colour changes, then add the marinade, ketchup, chilli sauce and water. Season to taste, adding more sugar if desired. Cook for 2–3 minutes and serve garnished with coriander and wedges of cucumber.

FISH CURRY (BURMA)

SERVES 6

1½lb (675g) haddock or cod fillet
1tsp turmeric
salt
1lb (450g) tomatoes, peeled, deseeded and roughly chopped
3–4 fresh red chillies, deseeded
1inch (2.5cm) fresh root ginger
2 onions
a few dried garlic flakes or 2 fresh cloves garlic
6–8tbsp peanut oil
1tbsp fish sauce
¼pt (150ml) water
4 spring onions, chopped

Skin the fish fillet and rub the surface with turmeric and salt. Cut into 1 inch (2.5 cm) cubes. Prepare the tomatoes and reserve. Place the chillies, ginger, one of the onions (slice the other and set aside) and garlic flakes or fresh garlic in a food processor. Do not allow this mixture to become too fine.

Heat two-thirds of the oil and fry the pieces of fish in it for 2–3 minutes. Turn over once. Lift out onto a plate. Add the remaining oil to the pan and fry the spice paste, then, after 1 minute, add the sliced onion. When the onion looks transparent, add the tomato and fish sauce.

Pour in the water. Cover and cook gently for 15 minutes. Now add the fish and chopped spring onion. Taste for seasoning. Shake the pan from time to time (if you stir you will break up the fish). Cook for 5 minutes then serve.

FISH CURRY (MALAYSIA)

SERVES 4

1½lb (675g) tengirri or ikan merah, monkfish or halibut
2 × 8oz (225g) packets unsweetened, desiccated coconut
3oz (75g) small red onions
3 cloves garlic
5 shelled bush keras (macadamia nuts) or almonds
1oz (25g) fresh root ginger
2 stems of lemon grass
3tsp ground turmeric
3tbsp coconut oil or vegetable oil
3 chillies, deseeded and finely shredded
salt to taste

Remove the skin and any bones from the fish and reserve. Cut the fish into chunks and sprinkle them with salt. Dry fry 2 oz (50 g) of the coconut in a wok, stirring all the time until it browns. Pound, using a pestle and mortar or blender, until the oil in the dry coconut begins to show. Make 2 fl oz (50 ml) of coconut cream and 1 pt (600 ml) coconut milk with the remaining coconut. Peel and slice the onions. Set one-third aside with the finely chopped garlic. Dry fry the remaining onions with chopped nuts, fresh ginger slices and sliced lemon grass to bring out the flavours fully. Pound until fine then, add the turmeric.

Heat the oil, fry the reserved onion slices and garlic until they are just turning golden. Add the pounded paste and fry well without browning. Stir in the coconut milk and bring just to the boil. Now add the fish cubes, shredded chilli, pounded dry coconut and the fish trimmings in a muslin bag if preferred. These are used to give additional flavour, but are removed before serving, of course. Cook for only 5 minutes. Taste for seasoning and stir in the coconut cream just before serving. Sprinkle with shredded chilli in a serving dish.

STEAMED POMFRET (MALAYSIA)

SERVES 2–4

2 pomfret, plaice, bream or sole, gutted but head, fins and tail left on
salt and pepper
2 dried mushrooms, soaked in warm water
1inch (2.5cm) piece fresh root ginger, cut into shreds
2 spring onions
1tbsp oil

Sauce
stock from cooked fish
1tbsp sesame seed oil
1tbsp oyster sauce
sugar and salt to taste

Garnish
shredded chilli
fresh coriander leaves
spring onion curls

Clean the fish and lay each one on a piece of oiled tin foil. Slash twice, season and set aside. Drain and cut the mushrooms into fine slivers. Trim the green from the spring onions and reserve for the garnish. Slice the white part finely and sprinkle it over the fish with the ginger and mushroom.

Drizzle over the oil and set in the steamer with the foil turned up at the edges to retain the cooking juices or in a shallow casserole. Steam for about 15 minutes. Lift out and set on a warm serving dish.

Strain the sauce into a measuring jug and make up to ¼ pt (150 ml) of stock by adding hot water. Heat the sesame seed oil and add the stock, oyster sauce, sugar and salt to taste. Pour over the cooked fish and serve with garnishes.

CHILLI CRAB (MALAYSIA)

SERVES 4

2 cooked crabs (1½lb [675g] each)
1inch (2.5cm) piece fresh root ginger
2 fresh red chillies or 2tsp chilli sauce
2 cloves garlic, crushed
4–6tbsp vegetable oil
8fl oz (225ml) ketchup
1tbsp brown sugar
¼pt (150ml) hot water
1 beaten egg (optional)
salt

CHILLI CRAB

fresh coriander to garnish
chunks of cucumber and pieces of toast to serve

Remove the large claws and turn each crab onto its back, with the head facing away from you. Use your thumbs to push the body up from the main shell. Discard the stomach sac and dead men's fingers (the lungs and any green matter); leave the creamy brown meat in the shell and cut in half. Cut the body section in half with a strong knife and crack the claws with a sharp tap from a hammer or cleaver. Crack, but do not splinter, them.

Pound the ginger, prepared chillies and garlic together. Fry in hot oil for 1–2 minutes without browning. Add the ketchup, chilli sauce, sugar and water, and mix well. When almost boiling add all the crab over a high heat. Just before serving stir in the beaten egg, which will scramble in the sauce if desired; taste for seasoning and serve at once garnished with fresh coriander leaves, together with the cucumber and toast.

◆ FISH AND CRUSTACEANS ◆

SQUID SAMBAL (MALAYSIA)

SERVES 4–6

8–10 squid (about 1½lb [675g])
8 nuts, either macadamia, almond or cashew
8tbsp oil
2tsp chilli powder
2 medium red onions
½in (1cm) blachan
2 stems of lemon grass
½pt (300ml) tamarind water from 2tsp tamarind pulp
1tbsp brown sugar
salt to taste

Remove the tentacles from each squid, clean well, trim and remove the eyes. Reserve. Wash and peel off the reddish-purple skin on the outside of each one. Remove the transparent bone from the pocket of the squid, then turn each one inside out and clean well. Score the flesh into a criss-cross pattern on the inside, then cut into long strips from tip to base.

Grind the nuts and add chilli powder, with 1 tbsp of the oil. Peel, chop and pound the onions finely, then pound further with blachan. Slice the lemon grass stems into 2 or 3 and bruise with a cleaver to release the flavour. Prepare the tamarind water. Heat the wok and fry the squid without oil, stirring all the time until the liquid has evaporated. Lift out and reserve.

Heat the oil, fry the chilli and nut paste, then the onion and blachan and lemon grass. Cook, stirring all the time to bring out the flavour of the spices. Add tamarind water and sugar. Reduce the heat and cook for a further few minutes. Increase the heat, add the squid and salt to taste. Reduce the heat and cook, uncovered, for about 5 minutes, when the sauce should be dark red and oily and the squid just tender.

FRIED FISH WITH TAMARIND (THAILAND)

SERVES 4

1 whole bream or red snapper, weighing 2lb (900g), cleaned and scaled
2–3tbsp seasoned cornflour
oil for frying
1oz (25g) tamarind pulp, soaked in ¼pt (150ml) warm water
2–3 cloves garlic, chopped
4–6 spring onions, root removed and the white bulb cut from green tops; make tops into curls

Preparing a squid:

1 Use a sharp knife to cut away the tentacles, making your incision just above the eyes.

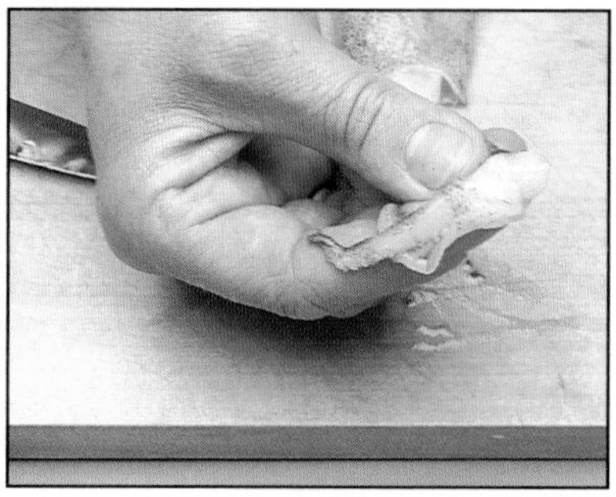

2 With your fingers press up on the tentacle to squeeze out the little central bone, which should come out fairly easily.

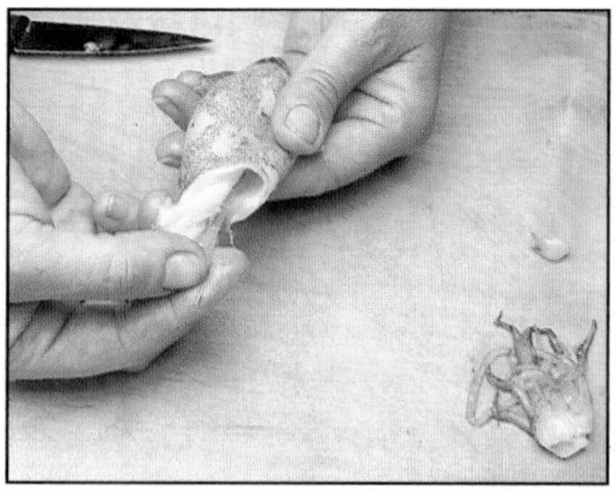

3 Again with your fingers, remove the quill and innards from the body cavity of the squid. These may then be discarded.

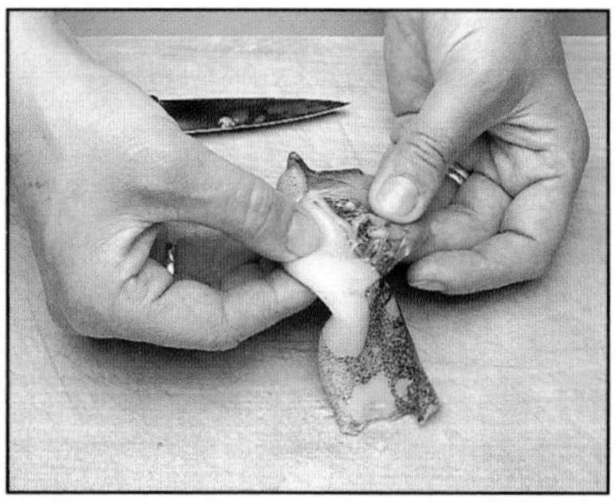

4 Pull away the thin outer skin from the flesh, which should come off easily and in one piece, leaving the flesh intact.

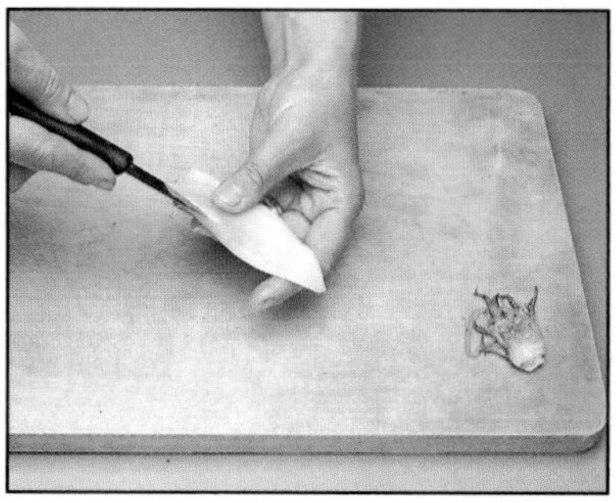

5 Take the knife and slit through the side of the skinned piece so that you are able to open it out flat.

6 Wash it well, then open it out, inside uppermost, and score the surface. Then, cut it into even-sized ribbons.

◆ FISH AND CRUSTACEANS ◆

½inch (1cm) fresh root ginger, shredded
1tbsp soy sauce
1–2tbsp dark brown sugar
1–2tbsp fish sauce
1–2 fresh red chillies, deseeded and shredded

Ask the fishmonger to leave the fish head and tail on. Rinse and pat dry on absorbent kitchen paper. Dredge with seasoned cornflour and fry on both sides in a large pan for 10–15 minutes in all, or until cooked through. Set aside and keep warm.

Meanwhile strain the tamarind juice through a sieve, then discard the seeds and pulp. Fry the garlic, white bulbs of the spring onion and ginger in a little oil in the cleaned pan without browning. Add soy sauce, sugar and fish sauce, along with the tamarind juice. Stir well. Pour over the cooked fish and garnish with red chillies and the reserved, chopped spring onion tops or curls.

STUFFED BABY SQUID IN A BROTH (THAILAND)

SERVES 6–8

1lb (450g) baby squid, cleaned but left whole for stuffing
½lb (225g) raw pork meat, ⅔ meat, ⅓ fat, finely minced
4 stems of coriander, leaves reserved for garnish
1–2 cloves garlic, crushed
salt and freshly ground black pepper
2½pt (1.5lt) prepared fish stock
2 stems of lemon grass, bruised
2 or 3 lime leaves
2tbsp nam pla (fish sauce) or lime juice
1–2 chillies, deseeded and cut into rings

Prepare the squid by removing the heads, rubbing off the purplish skin and pulling out the quill. Turn inside out and wash well. Turn back to the original side and drain well. Cut the tentacles from the head and squeeze out the centre bone. Wash and reserve the tentacles.

Mix the pork, finely chopped coriander, garlic and seasoning together. Stuff the squid with this mixture, but do not overfill. Replace the tentacles at the opening of the squid. Secure with wooden cocktail sticks if liked.

Bring the fish stock to the boil with the lemon grass. Cook for a few minutes. Drop in the squid with torn lime leaves and cook gently for 10–15 minutes. Remove lemon grass and lime leaves. Taste for seasoning and add fish sauce or lime juice. Serve in bowls topped with slices of chilli and coriander.

BOEMBOE BALI OF FISH (INDONESIA)

SERVES 6

2lb (900g) cod or haddock fillet
½inch (1cm) terasi or blachan
2 medium-sized red (or white) onions
1inch (2.5cm) fresh root ginger
½inch (1cm) piece laos, peeled, or 1tsp laos powder
2 cloves garlic
1–2tbsp chilli powder
6–8tbsp oil
1tbsp Indonesian sweet soy sauce
1tsp tamarind pulp, soaked in 2tbsp warm water
½pt (225ml) water

Skin the fish and cut into bite-sized cubes. Drain on absorbent kitchen paper and set aside while preparing the other ingredients. Pound the terasi, onions, ginger, laos and garlic to a paste in a pestle and mortar or food processor. Stir in the chilli powder and laos powder, if you are using it instead of the fresh laos. Cook this mixture in 2 tbsp of the oil until it gives off a rich aroma. Remember to stir the mixture all the time.

Add the soy sauce, strained tamarind juice and water. Cook for 2–3 minutes. In a separate pan, fry the cubes of fish for 4–5 minutes. Do not turn too much or the flesh will break up. Lift out of the pan on a draining spoon and put into the sauce. Cook for 3 minutes and serve with boiled rice. Garnish with a little chopped chilli, if liked, or celery leaves.

VINEGAR FISH (INDONESIA)

SERVES 4

2 small to medium-sized mackerel, filleted
2–3 fresh red chillies, deseeded
4 macadamia nuts or almonds
1 red onion
2 cloves garlic, crushed
½inch (1cm) piece fresh root ginger
1tsp turmeric
3tbsp coconut or vegetable oil
3tbsp vinegar
5fl oz (150ml) water
salt
fried onion or finely shredded chilli to garnish

Wipe the fish fillets and set aside. Pound the chillies and nuts with the onion, garlic, ginger, turmeric and 1 tbsp of the oil to a paste. Fry the mixture in the remaining oil without browning, then stir in vinegar and water; season and bring to the boil.

Place the fish fillets in the pan. Cover and cook for 10–12 minutes or until the fish is tender. Lift the fish onto a plate and keep warm. Reduce the sauce by boiling rapidly for 1 minute, then pour over the fish and serve. Garnish the vinegar fish with fried onion flakes or finely shredded chilli.

SUMATRAN-STYLE PRAWN CURRY (INDONESIA)

SERVES 4

1lb (450g) fresh prawns
2–3 courgettes
2 fresh red chillies, deseeded
1 medium-sized onion
¼inch (5mm) slice fresh lengkuas or ¼tsp laos powder
1 stem of lemon grass
½tsp ground turmeric
⅓pt (200ml) water
squeeze of lemon juice
salt
8oz (225g) packet desiccated coconut and ¾pt (450ml) boiling water to make ½pt (300ml) coconut milk

◆ FISH AND CRUSTACEANS ◆

Peel the prawns and set them aside. Trim the ends from the courgettes and cut into strips 2 inch (5 cm) long. Pound the chillies and onion to a paste with the lengkuas and the lower 2 inch (5 cm) part of the lemon grass. Add laos powder, if using, with the turmeric. Add water to the mixture with lemon juice and salt.

Pour into a pan — adding the rest of the lemon grass stem — bring to the boil and cook for 1–2 minutes, stirring all the time. Add the chayote or courgette pieces and cook for 2 minutes, stirring all the time, then add the coconut milk. Taste again for seasoning.

Now add the prawns and cook until they are tender, which will only take 3–4 minutes. Remove the stem of lemon grass. Serve at once with plain rice.

PRAWN SATE (INDONESIA)

SERVES 3

12 king prawns

Marinade

¼inch (5mm) terasi (blachan)
1 clove garlic, crushed
1 stem of lemon grass, lower 2½inches (6cm) only
3–4 macadamia nuts or almonds
½tsp chilli powder
¼tsp salt
oil for frying
8tbsp coconut milk
½tsp tamarind and 2tbsp water to make tamarind juice

To serve

Lontong (see recipe)
cubes of cucumber
wedges of lemon

Peel the prawns and remove the spinal cord if desired. Make an incision along the underbody without cutting the prawn in half. Open them up like a book and thread 2 onto each skewer. Prepare the marinade by preparing the terasi, then pound with the garlic, lemon grass, nuts, chilli powder and salt to a paste in a pestle and mortar or food processor. Fry this paste in a little oil, stirring all the time, until it gives off a good smell. Then add the coconut milk and tamarind juice. Allow to simmer for 1 minute.

Cool, then leave the prawns on 6 skewers in the marinade. Leave for 1 hour before cooking under a hot grill for 3 minutes or until cooked through. Baste with any remaining marinade. Turn once. Serve on a platter with the Lontong, cucumber and lemon wedges to complement the flavour of the shellfish.

GRILLED SQUID WITH LIME (PHILIPPINES)

SERVES 3–4

2–3 large squid 1½–2lb (750–900g) uncleaned weight, cleaned
salt and pepper to taste
oil
6–10 pieces lemon or lime

Season the squid, then brush with oil before grilling over a barbecue for 8–12 minutes. They can also be cooked under a grill or in a frying pan with oil. Slice them into rings after cooking and serve with the lemon or lime.

PICKLED FISH (PHILIPPINES)

SERVES 6

1½–2lb (675–900g) red snapper, bream or white fish fillets
3–4tbsp seasoned flour
oil for frying

Sauce

1inch (2.5cm) fresh root ginger, shredded
2–3 cloves garlic, crushed
1 onion, cut into thin rings
½ large green pepper, deseeded
½ large red pepper, deseeded
¾pt (450ml) water
1 rounded tbsp cornflour
3–4tbsp herb or cider vinegar
1tbsp brown sugar
patis to taste, if available
seasoning

Wipe the fish and cut into serving portions. Pat dry on absorbent kitchen paper then dust lightly with seasoned flour. Fry in shallow, hot oil in a frying pan until golden-brown

GRILLED SQUID WITH LIME

and almost cooked through.

In a separate pan fry the ginger, garlic and onion in clean oil until soft and transparent, but not browned. Add the green and red pepper, cut into cubes, and cook for just 1 minute. Lift out and reserve.

Blend a little water with cornflour to a paste. Add the remaining water, vinegar and sugar. Stir into the pan in which the vegetables were cooked and stir until the sauce is smooth and thickens a little. Add the fish sauce and seasoning to taste. Pour the sauce over the fish and reheat without stirring. Transfer to a warmed serving platter and pour over the sauce. Serve hot or cold.

FISH À LA CAMBODGIENNE (KAMPUCHEA)

SERVES 8

2 medium-large mackerel, filleted
salt and pepper
4 cloves garlic
½inch (1cm) piece lengkuas, peeled and sliced
1tsp sugar
½inch (1cm) cube kapi or blachan, dry fried
6–8tbsp lemon juice
6tbsp boiled water
2tbsp fish sauce
extra fish stock or boiled water, if necessary, to get the right consistency
1 small onion, chopped
1–2oz (25–50g) roasted peanuts, pounded (unsalted)
3–6 spring onions, chopped
handful of coriander leaves, chopped

Raw vegetables to serve
finger shapes of carrots, cucumber and green pepper
under-ripe tomatoes, quartered
florets of cauliflower
slices of green apple, tossed in lemon juice
green mango
green chillies

Season and grill the mackerel fillets on both sides until brown and just cooked. Cool, remove the skin and bones and flake finely. Meanwhile grill the garlic and lengkuas, then pound together and add to the fish mixture with sugar. Set aside.

Dry fry the kapi or blachan. Remove from its foil parcel and blend to a paste with the lemon juice, water and fish sauce. Stir the 2 mixtures together. They should be the consistency of a thick batter, slightly sour and salty. Add fish stock or water if necessary.

Stir in the finely sliced onion, peanuts, spring onion and coriander. This can be done the day before and stored in a covered container in the refrigerator. Serve with a selection of raw vegetables, attractively arranged on a platter.

◆ FISH AND CRUSTACEANS ◆

CRAB-FILLED ROLLS (VIETNAM)

MAKES 15

1oz (25g) cellophane noodles, soaked in water to cover for 10 minutes
10 wood ears (tree fungus), soaked in water to cover for 10 minutes
½lb (225g) minced pork
½lb (225g) crab meat, fresh or canned
4 spring onions, trimmed and finely chopped
1tsp fish sauce
salt and pepper to taste
flour and water paste to seal
spring roll wrappers
oil for deep-frying

Sauce
2 fresh red chillies, deseeded and pounded
2 cloves garlic, crushed
1tbsp sugar
3tbsp fish sauce (nuoc mam)
juice of ½ large lemon or lime

To serve
lettuce leaves
mint and coriander leaves
matchstick-like pieces of cucumber
sauce

Drain the noodles and cut into 1 inch (2.5 cm) lengths. Drain the wood ears and slice finely. Then add both of these ingredients to the pork and set aside.

Remove any cartilage from the crab and add the meat to the pork mixture with the spring onions, fish sauce and seasoning to taste. Place a spring roll wrapper in front of you like a diamond. Spoon some of the mixture just below the centre; fold over the point nearest to you and roll once. Bring the side points toward the centre to enclose the filling, then brush the top edges with the paste and roll up to completely seal.

Deep-fry in hot oil for 8–10 minutes or until cooked through. If the oil is too hot the outside will be ready before the filling is cooked through. Drain well on absorbent kitchen paper and repeat until all the rolls are cooked.

To make the sauce blend chillies, garlic, sugar and fish sauce (nuoc mam) together. Add lemon or lime juice to taste, and a little water if liked.

Serve the crab-filled rolls Vietnamese style by wrapping each one in a lettuce leaf with a few sprigs of mint and coriander and a stick of cucumber. Dip in the sauce.

MARINATED AND CURRIED PRAWNS WITH CUCUMBER (KAMPUCHEA)

SERVES 4

16 large prawns, head and body shell removed, but tail left on
½ cucumber, sliced and dried

Marinade
1tsp cumin seeds
1tsp fennel seeds
1tbsp coriander seeds
2 cloves garlic, crushed
½inch (1cm) fresh root ginger, sliced
4 shallots, sliced
½–1tsp chilli powder
1tsp turmeric
1tbsp sugar
¼pt (150ml) fish stock or water
2tbsp light soy sauce
1tbsp fish sauce
juice 1 lemon or lime
salt

Batter for prawns
2oz (50g) plain flour
1oz (25g) cornflour
salt
3fl oz (75ml) water

Filling the crab-filled Rolls

1 *Having made up the filling, take one of the wrappers, place on a tray and brush over with a brush, dampened with flour and water paste.*

2 *If you are using these circular wrappers, you will need to fold over a piece of the edge nearest you. Then place a line of the filling on this edge.*

3 *Roll over this filling once, then fold over the two outside edges.*

4 *You may now continue to roll up the remainder of the wrapper. It should stick as a result of the brushed-on paste.*

MARINATED AND CURRIED PRAWNS WITH CUCUMBER

1 egg white, whisked
fat for deep-frying prawns

Prepare the prawns and cucumber. Dry fry the spices for the marinade. Pound and add them to the garlic, ginger and shallots in a food processor, and blend to a paste. Add chilli powder, turmeric, sugar, fish stock, soy and fish sauces, lemon or lime juice and salt. Pour over the prawns and leave to marinate while preparing the batter.

Sift the flours together, then add sufficient water to make a creamy batter, but do not add the egg until the last minute. Heat the oil. Dry the prawns on absorbent kitchen paper. Fold the egg white into the batter, dip prawns in this and pop them straight into the hot oil to fry until they are golden and cooked through.

Meanwhile bring the marinade to the boil, then simmer for 5–8 minutes. Add some of the cucumber to the sauce if desired and reserve some for garnish. Pour over the prawns and serve hot.

◆ ◆ ◆

◆ POULTRY AND MEAT ◆

CHICKEN SATAY (MALAYSIA)

SERVES 12

4 boned chicken breasts, about 6oz (175g) each
about 12 bamboo or coconut skewers — soak in water before using to prevent burning

Spice marinade
½tsp each cumin, fennel and coriander seeds
6 small red shallots, peeled and chopped
1 clove garlic, crushed
1 stem of lemon grass
3 macadamia, almond or cashew nuts
½tsp ground turmeric
1tsp brown sugar
salt to taste

Peanut sauce
4oz (100g) peanuts
4 shallots, peeled and chopped
2 cloves garlic
½tsp blachan
6 macadamia, almond or cashew nuts
2 stems of lemon grass
3tbsp coconut oil or peanut oil
2–3tsp chilli powder
½pt (300ml) thick coconut milk
4tbsp tamarind water made from 1tbsp tamarind pulp or dried tamarind
1tbsp brown sugar
salt to taste

Leave the skin on the chicken breasts, then cut them into ½ inch (1 cm) cubes. Fry the spices with quarter of a teaspoon of oil over a medium heat to bring out the flavour, then grind or pound. Add the shallots, garlic, lemon grass (which has been bruised and sliced) and roughly chopped nuts. Grind or pound until fine. A little oil can be added if necessary when grinding by machine. Stir in the turmeric.

Sprinkle the chicken pieces with sugar, then mix thoroughly with the pounded ingredients until they are well coated. Leave at least 4 hours to marinate. Thread about 5 cubes onto each skewer and sprinkle with salt.

To make the peanut sauce, roast the peanuts in a hot oven (400°F/200°C/Gas Mark 6) for about 20 minutes. Rub off the skins in a tea towel and grind for just a few seconds in a liquidizer. Do not reduce the nuts to a powder — this would spoil the consistency of the sauce. Grind or pound the onions and garlic with the blachan. Grind or pound the macadamia nuts and lemon grass.

Fry the onion mixture in hot oil, then add the nut and lemon grass paste. Reduce the heat, add chilli powder and cook for 2 minutes. Stir all the time while adding the coconut milk. Allow it to come to the boil, then reduce the heat and add tamarind water, sugar, salt to taste and peanuts. Cook for 2–3 minutes and stir frequently until the sauce thickens.

To cook satay, place skewers of chicken satay on a barbecue or hot grill and brush with a little coconut oil or peanut oil. Turn as necessary until cooked. Serve on a large platter with chunks of cucumber and onion, and the hot peanut sauce in a separate bowl. For lunch serve with a bowl of rice.

CHICKEN CURRY FROM PENANG (MALAYSIA)

SERVES 4

1 × 3lb (1.5kg) fresh chicken, divided into 8 pieces
8oz (225g) unsweetened, desiccated coconut and just over ¾pt (450ml) boiling water to make coconut milk
¼pt (150ml) tamarind juice from pulp or dried tamarind
½inch (1cm) square blachan, dry fried
2–4 fresh chillies or 1–2tsp chilli powder
2 macadamia nuts or almonds
2 stems of lemon grass
1inch (2.5cm) piece fresh root ginger
2 cloves garlic
1–2tsp ground turmeric
4tbsp coconut oil or cooking oil
salt
piece of stick cinnamon
6 green or white cardamom pods, bruised but left whole
2 large onions, finely sliced and deep-fried, or chopped coriander to garnish

Wipe the chicken and set aside. Prepare the coconut milk and tamarind juice. Dry fry the blachan. Pound the prepared and chopped chillies, nuts, lemon grass, ginger and garlic into a paste with the blachan; if using dried chilli, add it to the paste. Stir in the turmeric.

Heat the oil and fry the spice mixture for a few minutes without browning. Stir in the chicken pieces until they are all coated with the spices. Add salt. Pour in the coconut milk and tamarind juice. Add the cinnamon and cardamom pods.

Cook uncovered over a gentle heat for 35–45 minutes until almost all the sauce has cooked away. Taste for salt. Test the chicken pieces with a skewer. When tender serve in a hot bowl. Traditionally it is served with a topping of crispy fried onions.

CHICKEN CASSEROLE WITH GINGER (PHILIPPINES)

SERVES 4

3lb (1.5kg) chicken
1inch (2.5cm) piece fresh root ginger, chopped
1 large onion, sliced
2 cloves garlic, crushed
4–6tbsp oil or pork fat
1pt (600ml) water or chicken stock
1 unripe papaya (paw-paw)
2tbsp patis (fish sauce) or to taste
good handful of washed spinach leaves
a few fresh chilli leaves if available
salt and pepper

Cut the chicken into 8 or more pieces, dry on absorbent kitchen paper and set aside. Fry the ginger, onion, and garlic in hot oil or pork fat until soft and tender, but not coloured. Lift out and reserve. Reheat the fat in the pan and fry the chicken pieces on all sides until golden, turning frequently. Add water or stock and seasoning.

Stir in the onion, garlic and ginger. Cover and cook over a gentle heat until the chicken pieces are almost cooked — about 35–45 minutes depending on the size.

Wash and cut the papaya in half,

remove the seeds and outer skin. Slice evenly and add to the chicken. Cover and cook until the papaya is tender — about 5 minutes. Bring up to a rapid boil, add the fish sauce, spinach and chilli leaves if using. Cover and cook for 1 minute. Taste for seasoning and serve.

CHICKEN CASSEROLE WITH COCONUT MILK (PHILIPPINES)

SERVES 4

3lb (1.5kg) chicken or 4 chicken quarters
4 cloves garlic, crushed
⅓pt (200ml) cider vinegar
½–1tsp black peppercorns, crushed
sprinkling annatto seeds
¾pt (450ml) chicken stock or water
½pt (300ml) prepared coconut milk, made from 8oz (225g) desiccated coconut and ¾pt (450ml) hot water
1 chayote, peeled, seed removed, cut into thin slices then blanched and drained
oil or pork fat for frying
1tbsp light soy sauce
cucumber and tomato matchsticks to garnish

Wipe the chicken and cut into 8 pieces, thigh and drumstick into 2 pieces and the breast and wing into a further 2 portions. Similarly cut each of the chicken quarters, if using, into 2. Place in a glass or glazed bowl, add the garlic, vinegar, peppercorns and annatto seeds. Mix well, then leave to marinate for 1 hour. Meanwhile prepare the coconut milk and chayote.

Turn the marinated chicken pieces into a pan with the stock or water. Bring to the boil, but do not cover, then simmer for 25–30 minutes, adding a little extra water if necessary to keep the chicken moist.

When the chicken is tender lift out and reduce the cooking liquid to ¼ pt (150 ml) and set aside. Clean the pan, add oil and fry the chicken pieces until they are brown all over. Keep warm on a serving dish.

Add the coconut milk and chayote to the reduced sauce in another pan. Add soy sauce. Cook for 4–5 minutes until the chayote is just tender. Pour over the chicken pieces and garnish with cucumber and tomato sticks. Serve with freshly boiled rice.

CHICKEN CASSEROLE WITH COCONUT MILK

◆ POULTRY AND MEAT ◆

CHICKEN CURRY (KAMPUCHEA)

SERVES 8

8 chicken legs, cut into drumstick and thigh portions
6–8tbsp oil
4 small onions, cut into quarters
4 small potatoes, peeled and cut into quarters
2 × 8oz (225g) packets desiccated coconut and 1½pt (900ml) hot water to make coconut milk
full quantity green or red curry paste
1 stock cube
salt
sugar
fish sauce
curry leaves (optional)
handful of coriander, stems chopped and leaves separated
1–2tbsp ground almonds (optional)
1 aubergine, sliced, salted for 1½ hours and rinsed
coriander leaves for garnish

Brown the chicken all over and lift out onto a plate. Fry the onions and potatoes until brown. Set these on one side and pour off the oil from the pan. Spoon ¼ pt (150 ml) of the coconut cream from the top of the coconut milk into a large pan or wok and add the prepared red or green curry paste. Lower the heat and cook, stirring all the time until the spices give off a rich aroma. Add a stock cube, salt, sugar and fish sauce to taste, along with curry leaves, if you are using them, and chopped coriander stems.

Add the meat to the pan, turning the pieces in the sauce until well coated. Add onions, potatoes and coconut milk. Bring to the boil, then reduce to simmer for 45–60 minutes. Shake the pan rather than stir to prevent the meat from breaking up.

When the chicken pieces are tender, thicken, if desired, with the ground almonds mixed to a paste and stirred into the mixture. Reheat for a few minutes. If you have chosen to cook a green curry, pieces of aubergine can be added 5–10 minutes before the end of cooking and before thickening with ground almonds. Serve in a large bowl scattered with coriander leaves to garnish attractively.

CHICKEN CURRY WITH NOODLES (BURMA)

SERVES 6–8

3lb (1.5kg) chicken, cut into quarters
salt
1lb (450g) onions
3 cloves garlic, crushed
4 fresh red chillies, deseeded or 2tsp chilli powder
1–2tsp ground turmeric
peanut oil for frying
1¼pt (700ml) coconut milk
3–4tbsp chick pea flour
salt
1–2tbsp fish sauce
coriander leaves
1lb (450g) egg noodles or rice noodles

Break some of the rice noodles into 1 inch (2.5 cm) lengths and deep-fry until crisp. Drain on absorbent kitchen paper. Place the chicken joints in a pan. Add 3½ pt (2 lt) of water and salt. Bring to the boil, then cover and simmer for 45–60 minutes or until the chicken is tender.

Lift the chicken joints from the pan, cool and remove the meat and cut into small pieces. Discard the skin and bones. Strain the stock and reserve. Meanwhile pound the onions, garlic and chillies, or chilli powder, to a paste in a food processor. Add the turmeric. Fry in hot oil until it gives off a rice aroma. Stir in the coconut milk and 2 pt (1.2 lt) of the reserved chicken stock. Simmer for 15 minutes.

Blend the chick pea flour with a little of the cold stock or water to make a cream. Slowly stir one ladleful of liquid from the pan into the cream, then pour this back into the pan. Simmer over a low heat, stirring until the soup thickens a little. Add the chicken pieces, salt and fish sauce if liked. Turn into a serving tureen scattered with fresh coriander leaves.

Cook the noodles. Spoon the noodles into the bowl first and top with the curried chicken.

CHICKEN RENDANG (MALAYSIA)

SERVES 4

3lb (1.5kg) fresh chicken, jointed into 8 pieces
1tbsp sugar
12oz (350g) unsweetened, desiccated coconut and just over 1pt (600ml) boiling water to make coconut milk and cream
4 small red onions
2 cloves garlic
1inch (2.5cm) piece fresh root ginger
2inch (5cm) piece fresh lengkuas
2 stems of lemon grass
5tbsp coconut oil or vegetable oil
2tbsp dry chilli powder or to taste
salt to taste

Rinse the pieces of chicken and dry them on absorbent kitchen paper. Place in a bowl, sprinkle with sugar and toss in the bowl to release their juices.

Dry fry 3 oz (75 g) of coconut in a large frying pan or wok, turning all the time until it becomes dry, crisp and golden. Pound with a pestle and mortar until the oil begins to 'show'. Turn the remaining coconut into a deep bowl. Prepare the coconut milk and cream. Leave to stand for 15 minutes and spoon off 4 tbsp of the thickest coconut cream. You should have approximately ¾ pt (450 ml) of coconut milk.

Peel the onions and garlic and scrape the ginger and lengkuas. Roughly chop up these ingredients and pound with the lemon grass until fine. Heat the oil in the wok. Fry the pounded ingredients for several minutes to bring out the flavour. Lower the heat, add the chilli powder and cook for 3–4 minutes, stirring all the time. Add the thick coconut cream and salt. Stir as the mixture comes to the boil to prevent curdling.

Add the chicken pieces, turning frequently so that the rendang mixture coats each piece. Reduce the heat and stir in the remaining coconut milk. Cook over a gentle heat for 45–50 minutes or until the chicken is tender.

Just before serving spoon some of the sauce into the pounded coconut. Mix well, then return this to the pan. Stir without breaking up the chicken and cook for a further 5 minutes.

DEEP-FRIED CHICKEN (INDONESIA)

SERVES 6

6 chicken drumsticks and 6 thighs
1oz (25g) sugar
12oz (350g) packet desiccated coconut, blended with ¾pt (450ml) boiling water to obtain ½pt (300ml) coconut milk
2tsp coriander seeds, dry fried
1tsp chilli powder
1tsp ground turmeric
1tsp salt
1 medium onion
1 clove garlic
½inch (1cm) piece fresh root ginger
1 stem of lemon grass
1–2tbsp flour
fat for deep-frying

Sprinkle the chicken pieces with sugar and set on one side. Make the coconut milk. Grind the coriander seed and add it to the chilli, turmeric and salt. Mix to a smooth paste with a little coconut milk.

Finely chop the onion, garlic and ginger in a food processor. Fry these in a little oil in a deep pan for 1–2 minutes. Add the spice paste and fry, then stir in the coconut milk. When just boiling reduce the heat and add the chicken pieces and bruised stem of lemon grass. Cover and cook very gently for about 30 minutes or until the pieces are tender.

Transfer to a container and leave in the refrigerator or a cool place overnight. Carefully lift the chicken pieces out of the spice mixture. Scrape off any excess mixture. Dust the chicken lightly with flour.

Deep-fry the pieces in hot oil until they are golden. Cool before taking on a picnic. Sprinkle with juice from wedges of lemon if desired, and eat with pieces of cucumber and crisp lettuce leaves.

LAP, KENG SOM AND TCHÉO (LAOS)

SERVES 6–8

5lb (2.25kg) turkey (approx) or 4lb (1.75kg) chicken

Keng som soup
skin, bones and giblets from above
3pt (2lt) water
2tbsp tamarind pulp, soaked in ½pt (300ml) warm water for 15 minutes
1 stem of lemon grass, bruised
3 green tomatoes, washed and cut into wedges
1–2tbsp fish sauce
salt and sugar, if liked
fresh coriander leaves and spring onion tops to garnish

Lap
4oz (100g) glutinous rice
flesh from the above turkey or chicken
juice of 1 lemon
2tbsp padek or bagoong (anchovy)
½–1tbsp chilli powder, made from 4–8 roasted red chillies
½inch (1cm) fresh laos, scraped and sliced
1 stem of lemon grass, use lower 2in (5cm)
½–1 onion
fish sauce, if liked
salt and a little sugar to taste
coriander leaves and spring onion to garnish

Tchéo chilli pepper sauce
5 green chillies, deseeded and pounded
2 cloves garlic, crushed
2tbsp fish sauce
handful of fine coriander leaves
platter of raw vegetables: carrot, cucumber, cauliflower, cut into small pieces

Set the flesh from the turkey or chicken on one side while the soup is prepared. Put the skin, bones and rinsed giblets into a large pan. Bring to the boil, skim, then add the juice from the tamarind, lemon grass and tomatoes. Bring to the boil again, then reduce to simmer and cook for 30 minutes. Lift out the chicken liver and gizzard and finely slice to add to the soup later. Continue cooking for a further 30 minutes.

Add the fish sauce, sliced liver and gizzard from the chicken or turkey and seasoning. Then, when the lap is ready, skim and strain into a hot tureen. Garnish with coriander leaves and spring onion tops.

To prepare the lap, dry fry the rice in a frying pan or wok, turning all the time until the rice is roasted and golden. Pound or put in a blender or food processor until fine. Finely chop or mince the turkey or chicken flesh. Half fry the turkey or chicken in the wok, breaking up with a fish slice so that the meat begins to change colour.

Add the pounded rice to the meat little by little along with the lemon juice and the padek or bagoong and some of the chilli. Pound the laos root and lemon grass together, stir into the mixture with very finely chopped onion and more chilli, if liked. Add fish sauce, salt and sugar to taste. Mix well with your hands, adding a little of the soup if necessary. The mixture should be moist not wet.

To prepare the tchéo, pound the chillies, garlic and coriander leaves together, then add as much fish sauce as is necessary to suit individual taste.

BARBECUED, SPICED CHICKEN (INDONESIA)

SERVES 4

3lb (1.5kg) chicken, cut into 4 pieces
8 shallots
2 cloves garlic, crushed
6 candlenuts (buah keras)
½inch (1cm) fresh root ginger, sliced
1 stem of lemon grass
1tsp chilli powder
4tbsp light soy sauce
2tbsp sweet soy sauce
3tbsp oil
salt
oil for frying
¼pt (150ml) chicken stock

Slash the flesh of the chicken quarters several times. Finely chop the shallots and set aside. Pound the garlic, candlenuts, ginger, lemon grass and chilli powder together. Mix with soy sauces and oil, and pour onto the chicken pieces. Leave to marinate for 30 minutes.

Heat oil in a wok, fry the onions without browning, lift the chicken pieces out of the marinade and fry on both sides to seal. Reduce the heat, cook for 10 minutes. Transfer to the barbecue to complete cooking. Add the marinade to the remaining ingredients in the pan. Fry, then add stock. Cook for 5 minutes and serve this sauce with the chicken.

SPICED BEEF IN COCONUT MILK (INDONESIA)

SERVES 6–8

2lb (1kg) good quality beef
2 onions, chopped
4 cloves garlic, crushed
3tbsp oil
1 stem of lemon grass
4–8 red chillies, deseeded, or 2tbsp sambal ulek
8 cardamom pods
1tsp coriander seeds
1tsp cumin seeds
½tsp cinnamon
1tsp tamarind, mixed with 6tbsp water to make tamarind juice
1lb (450g) desiccated coconut and 1½pt (900ml) boiling water to make just over 1pt (600ml) coconut milk
salt
crispy onions or spring onions to garnish

Cut the beef into neat cubes. Fry the onions and garlic in oil for 3–4 minutes in a large pan. Draw from the heat. Pound the lower part of the stem of the lemon grass with the chillies. Spoon onto the meat. Remove the seeds from the cardamom pods and dry fry with coriander and cumin. Pound or grind. Add cinnamon.

Spoon this mixture onto the meat and mix thoroughly to impregnate the meat with spices. Prepare the tamarind juice and coconut milk, then pour these into the pan containing the softened onions. Allow to come to the boil, stirring all the time, then stir in the spiced meat.

Add salt, bring back to the boil, then reduce to the lowest heat so that the liquid is just bubbling, and simmer for 2½–3 hours or until the meat is tender and the sauce greatly reduced. Taste for seasoning. Transfer to a warmed serving dish. Garnish with crispy or spring onions.

STUFFED ROLLED BEEF (PHILIPPINES)

SERVES 8

3½lb (1.6kg) brisket of beef in one piece, suitable for rolling
1tbsp Japanese soy sauce
1tbsp lemon juice
2 cloves garlic, crushed
salt and pepper

Filling
2 slices cooked ham
1 chorizo (Spanish sausage), skinned and then chopped finely
2 large carrots, peeled and cooked in boiling water for 3 minutes
2 hard-boiled eggs
1–2oz (25–50g) raisins
a few stuffed olives
2 whole large gherkins, cut in half lengthwise

For cooking
4tbsp oil
1 large onion, chopped
14oz (400g) canned, crushed tomatoes
1tbsp tomato purée
2tbsp vinegar
1 bay leaf
5fl oz (150ml) beef stock or water

chopped spring onions to garnish

Order the beef a day or two before you need it so that the butcher can select a good piece of meat. Sprinkle the meat with soy sauce, lemon juice and garlic. You can then leave it to marinate while you are preparing the filling. It should then soak up plenty of flavour.

When ready, season the meat then arrange the ham and finely chopped sausage over half the meat. Lay the carrots along from end to end and the hard-boiled egg left whole. Scatter with raisins and olives and, finally, place the gherkins on top. Now roll up very carefully like a Swiss roll and tie securely with string to make a firm roll; otherwise you will find that it unravels during cooking.

Fry the roll in hot oil until brown all over. Add the onions, cook until soft, then add the tomatoes, purée, vinegar, bay leaf and stock or water. Taste for seasoning. Cover and cook in a moderate oven (325°F/160°C/Gas Mark 3) for 2½–3 hours or until tender. Lift the meat onto a serving dish and keep warm. Pass the vegetables and stock through a vegetable mill. Return to the pan and taste for seasoning. When hot serve with the beef, cut into neat slices and scattered with spring onions. It may be accompanied by rice or noodles.

BEEF AND VEGETABLE SALAD (KAMPUCHEA)

SERVES 8

½lb (225g) rump steak, cut into thin slices, or use best quality minced beef, if preferred
¼pt (150ml) vinegar
pinch of salt
½lb (225g) tripe
¾pt (450ml) milk and water, to cover tripe
salt

Sauce
3 cloves garlic
3 shallots
½inch (1cm) lengkuas
good handful of coriander, stems chopped and leaves set aside
reserved marinade from beef
1–2tbsp fish sauce
1tsp sugar
seasoning
lemon juice (optional)
6–8oz (175–200g) roasted peanuts, skins removed and ground coarsely, or salted peanuts
fish stock or water

Vegetables for serving
½ daikon radish or moolie (long white radish), peeled and cut into strips
½ box bean sprouts, rinsed and drained
1–2 stems of lemon grass, use lower 2½in (6cm), finely chopped
ground peanuts
½ red pepper, deseeded and cut into strips
½ onion, sliced
¼ iceberg lettuce, shredded into 1in (2.5cm) strips
coriander leaves
handful of mint leaves
bunch of red radishes, cut into flower shapes

Marinate the seasoned steak slices or minced beef in the vinegar for 30 minutes. The vinegar should cover the meat. When the meat looks cooked, squeeze any excess juices from it and reserve these with the marinade for the sauce. Cut the meat into fine strips. Meanwhile cook the tripe in salted milk and water to cover for 45 minutes, or until quite tender. Drain and cut into strips the same size as the beef.

Now prepare the sauce. Grill the garlic, shallots and lengkuas. Cool, skin and pound with the chopped coriander stems to a paste. Heat the reserved vinegar marinade from the meat in a small pan. Add this paste, cook for 1–2 minutes, then stir in the fish sauce, sugar, seasoning and lemon juice, if a tangy flavour is preferred. Thicken the sauce with ground peanuts. Stir in sufficient fish stock or water to reduce the sauce to just the consistency of thin cream, but no runnier.

SPICED BEEF IN COCONUT MILK

To serve the salad, mix the beef, tripe, white radish, bean sprouts and lemon grass together. Taste for seasoning. Pile the mixture into the centre of a large serving platter and scatter with some of the ground peanuts. Arrange the red pepper on top attractively and the onion slices around the meats. Place the lettuce, coriander and mint leaves around the edge with the radishes. Serve the sauce separately so that each person takes some meat and salad and tops with spoonfuls of the sauce. It is easier for diners to satisfy their own desires and take as much or as little as they require.

◆ POULTRY AND MEAT ◆

BEEF SPARERIBS (KOREA)

SERVES 4

3lb (1.4kg) meaty ribs of beef, cut into chunky pieces
1–2tbsp sugar
¼pt (150ml) soy sauce
2tbsp sesame seed oil
2 cloves garlic, crushed
1tbsp sesame seeds, roasted and crushed
3–4 dried Chinese mushrooms, soaked in 1pt (600ml) water for 30 minutes
2 spring onions, trimmed and chopped
1 small Chinese turnip, peeled and cut into chunks
½ × 20oz (567g) can of water chestnuts
seasoning
1 egg, separated and made into garnish

Score the meaty pieces of the ribs and rub all over with sugar. Mix the soy sauce, sesame seed oil, garlic and sesame seeds together and rub into the pieces of beef. Marinate for 1 hour. Pour off the marinade and reserve.

Drain and reserve the liquid from the mushrooms and slice the mushrooms. Fry the meat in a wok without oil to seal it on all sides, then pour over the marinade and reserved soaking water.

Bring to the boil and cook over a gentle heat for 1 hour until the beef is almost tender. Remove the cover and add the mushrooms, spring onions, turnip and water chestnuts. Cook for a further 30 minutes when much of the liquid will have evaporated. Taste for seasoning. Garnish on a hot platter with the egg strips or, if desired, cut them into diamond shapes, which is quite traditional.

MARINATED AND BARBECUED BEEF (KOREA)

SERVES 8

2lb (900g) beef fillet or rump, cut thinly

Marinade
¼pt (150ml) soy sauce
2tbsp sesame seed oil
2tbsp sake
1 clove garlic, crushed
1tbsp sugar
2tbsp crushed, roasted sesame seeds
4 spring onions, trimmed and chopped
freshly ground black pepper and salt to taste
a little oil for cooking
slivers of garlic and raw chopped onion and lettuce to garnish if liked

Place the meat in the freezer to firm it up so that the slices can be cut more thinly. Keep them all as even as possible. Mix all the ingredients for the marinade together and pour over the meat in a shallow glass or glazed dish. Leave at least 3 hours and preferably overnight. When required, grill over charcoal or in a heavy frying pan with a minimum of oil to just cook the beef. Serve at once.

KOREAN HOTPOT

SERVES 4–6

Marinade
2tbsp soy sauce
2 cloves garlic, crushed
1tbsp sesame seed oil
1tbsp roasted sesame seeds, pounded
1tsp sugar
freshly ground black pepper

4oz (100g) beef fillet, partially frozen and thinly sliced
4oz (100g) minced pork
4oz (100g) minced beef
4oz (100g) calves' liver, partially frozen and thinly sliced
4–6 dried Chinese mushrooms, soaked in water for 30 minutes
half a 18oz (500g) can of bamboo shoots, drained and finely sliced
1 onion, sliced
2 carrots, peeled and sliced
4 spring onions, trimmed and chopped into 2inch (5cm) lengths
sesame seed oil for frying
4–6tbsp flour
2 beaten eggs
1¾pt (1lt) beef stock, made from can of condensed consommé and water

Garnish
1oz (25g) pine kernels
gingko nuts (optional)

Marinate the beef slices in the marinade ingredients for 15 minutes. Lift out and set on one side. Add the marinade to the minced beef and pork. Roll the mixture into 12 even-sized balls and set aside. Slice the liver. Drain the mushrooms and slice.

Prepare the bamboo shoot, onion, carrot and spring onions.

Now the cooking begins. Stir-fry the beef slices in some sesame seed oil and then put aside. Wipe the pan in between frying. Repeat with the liver, which has been dipped in flour

and then quickly into the beaten egg. Dip the meat balls in flour and beaten egg and again cook in a little sesame seed oil until cooked through; reserve. Drain the bamboo shoots. Lightly fry the onion first, lift out and then separately fry the carrots, spring onions and sliced mushrooms.

Just before you take the hotpot to the table arrange the meats and vegetables together with the meat balls attractively in the moat of the hotpot, making sure that each layer is arranged in the same way so that each guest has a helping identical to his neighbour. Scatter the pine kernels and gingko nuts on top, if liked. Just before serving, flood in a little of the stock, cover and heat up rapidly. Add more hot stock before taking to the table.

When the hotpot is in position at the table and the heat is satisfactory, carefully pour in boiling stock, taking care not to disturb the foods. Guests help themselves with chopsticks and drink the soup at the end from bowls.

STIR-FRY PORK (LAOS)

SERVES 4–6

1lb (450g) pork fillet
1 piece of pork fat or oil
1 onion, chopped
1 clove garlic, crushed
2 green chillies, deseeded and pounded
½lb (225g) green beans, cut into 1in (2.5cm) lengths
1½tsp fish sauce
salt and sugar to taste
coriander leaves to garnish
plain boiled rice to serve

Trim the pork and cut into small pieces. Render the fat from the pork. When all the fat is in the pan, discard it or heat the oil, if preferred. Fry the onion, garlic and chilli until it gives off a rich aroma; do not allow to brown. Push to the side of the pan and stir in the pork fillet pieces. Turn all the time until the meat changes colour. Cook for 2–3 minutes.

Now add the beans and toss all the ingredients well. Add the fish sauce, sugar and salt to taste. Garnish with fresh coriander leaves and serve with plain rice and a raw vegetable platter and perhaps Tchéo sauce.

◆ POULTRY AND MEAT ◆

PORK CURRY (BURMA)

SERVES 6

2lb (900g) lean pork, cut into 1in (2.5cm) pieces
1lb (450g) onions
8 cloves garlic, crushed
2inches (5cm) fresh root ginger, chopped
2½tsp chilli powder
4 stems of lemon grass
1inch (2.5cm) ngapi (blachan)
1tsp turmeric
4tbsp peanut oil for frying
salt to taste
½pt (300ml) stock or water
coriander leaves to garnish

Place the pork pieces on a dish. Slice half the onions and put the remainder into a food processor with the garlic, ginger, chillies, the lower 2½ inches (6 cm) of the lemon grass (bruise and reserve the top of the stem), ngapi and turmeric. Make these ingredients into a coarse paste.

Fry the pork pieces in the hot oil to change colour, then increase the heat and add the paste. Fry for 2 minutes, then add the remaining onion slices. When the pork is well coated with the spice mixture, pour on the stock or water. Add salt and the lemon grass tops.

Cover and cook for 1½ hours or until the pork is tender. Cook, uncovered, for a further 15 minutes, if liked, to reduce the liquid. Remove the lemon grass. Add more chilli if a hotter curry is preferred. Sprinkle with fresh coriander and eat with rice.

SPICED PORK IN COCONUT MILK (SINGAPORE)

SERVES 3

1lb (450g) lean pork, cut into cubes
8oz (225g) desiccated coconut, and ¾pt (450ml) boiling water to make ½pt (300ml) coconut milk
½inch (1cm) square blachan
2 medium-sized red onions, chopped
1½–2tsp chilli powder
3tbsp coconut oil or vegetable oil
1 stem of lemon grass
salt to taste
juice of ½ lemon
pinch of sugar

Set the pork on one side. Prepare the coconut milk. Dry fry the blachan. Pound the onions with the blachan and chilli powder. Fry in oil without browning. Add the pork and fry until the meat changes colour and is well covered with the spices.

Stir in the prepared coconut milk over a gentle heat and the bruised stem of lemon grass. Slowly bring to the boil, stirring to prevent curdling. Add salt to taste. Simmer until the pork is tender. Remove the lemon grass stem. Add lemon juice and sugar to taste. Serve with plain boiled rice and a cucumber salad.

LONG COOK PORK LEG STEW (SINGAPORE)

SERVES 4

3½–4lb (1.5–1.75kg) meaty pigs' trotters
1tbsp tamarind pulp, soaked in ¼pt (150ml) water
6 red chillies, deseeded
6 cloves garlic, crushed
2–3 medium-sized onions
8tbsp oil
2tbsp soya bean paste
2tbsp light soy sauce
2tbsp dark soy sauce
1 star anise
½inch (1cm) piece fresh root ginger, shredded finely
2tsp dark brown sugar
just under 1pt (600ml) water
salt
fresh coriander leaves or shredded spring onion to garnish

Ask the butcher to cut the trotters into chunky pieces through the bone. Prepare the tamarind juice. Set one whole chilli aside for garnish and pound the remainder with garlic and onions. Fry in oil for 2–3 minutes. Stir in the bean paste, then turn the trotters in this mixture to coat them on all sides. Add the soy sauces, prepared tamarind juice, star anise, ginger, sugar and water. Add salt if necessary, but go carefully as the bean paste is quite salty.

Cover and cook gently for at least 2 hours or until the pork is tender. Cool and leave overnight. Skim away any excess fat. Cover and cook in an ovenproof casserole in a moderatley hot oven (325°F/160°C/Gas Mark 3) for an hour or until the pork is cooked through and the sauce is bubbling. Scatter with fresh coriander leaves or spring onion and the reserved chilli, cut into rings.

CRISPY PORK KNUCKLE (PHILIPPINES)

SERVES 1–2

1–2 pieces pork knuckle
salt to taste
oil for frying

Sauce
3½fl oz (100ml) vinegar
1½ cloves garlic
salt and black pepper to taste
5–7 pieces chilli, sliced

Allow 14–18 oz (400–500 g) (raw weight) of pork knuckle per person. Cook the pork knuckle in salted water over a low heat until tender (1–1½ hours, depending on their size). Remove and pat dry with absorbent kitchen paper. Then fry in medium hot oil for 15 minutes until they have acquired a crispy consistency. Mix together all the vinegar sauce ingredients and serve as an accompaniment.

SPICY LAMB CURRY (INDONESIA)

SERVES 4–6

5oz (150g) shallots
4 cloves garlic
8 chillies
5 candlenuts (buah keras)
¾inch (2cm) fresh root ginger
6tbsp cooking oil
1tsp coriander
½tsp fennel
½tsp nutmeg

¼tbsp cumin
4 cloves
1 piece of stick cinnamon
2 pieces of lemon grass, broken up
2lb 3oz (1kg) shoulder of lamb, cut into cubes
1¼pt (750ml) lamb or chicken stock
1pt (600ml) coconut milk
salt and pepper to taste

Heat the oil in a wok. Meanwhile, pound together the shallots, garlic, chillies, candlenuts and ginger and fry them for 3 minutes in the oil. Then add the coriander, fennel, nutmeg, cumin and cloves. Add the lamb for browning, then the cinnamon and lemon grass. Pour on the stock and half the coconut milk.

Cook for 1 hour until the liquid has reduced by half. Stir in the remaining coconut juice, simmer for 10 minutes. Taste for seasoning and serve with plain rice.

◆ ◆ ◆

CRISPY PORK KNUCKLE

◆ SNACKS AND DESSERTS ◆

PRAWN AND SWEET POTATO FRITTERS (PHILIPPINES)

MAKES 16

16 medium-sized fresh prawns
water to just cover
½lb (225g) plain flour
1tsp baking powder
½tsp salt
1 egg, beaten
small sweet potato, peeled (about 4oz [100g])
1 clove garlic, crushed
2 handfuls of bean sprouts, soaked in cold water for 10 minutes and well drained
small bunch of spring onions, shredded
oil for shallow- and deep-frying

Dipping sauce
1 clove garlic, crushed
3tbsp good quality vinegar
1–2tbsp water
salt to taste

Place the whole prawns in a pan of water. Bring to the boil, then simmer for 4–5 minutes or until the prawns are tender. Lift the prawns from the pan with a draining spoon. Discard the heads and body shell, but leave the tails on if liked. Strain and reserve the cooking liquid and allow to cool. Sift the flour, baking powder and salt into a bowl.

Add the beaten egg and enough of the cooked stock to make a batter, the consistency of double cream. Grate in the sweet potato (this discolours on standing so add only at the last minute), stir in the garlic and bean sprouts.

Chop the spring onions. Heat the oil, ¼ inch (5 mm) in depth, in a large frying pan and put more oil in a large pan for deep-frying. Spoon a good tablespoonful of the mixture into fritter shapes in the shallow oil (about the size of a large dropped scone), top with a few chopped spring onions and one prawn in the centre.

Cook over a medium heat until almost cooked through. Transfer to the hot 375°F (190°C) oil in the large pan, flip over when crisp and brown, then drain on absorbent kitchen paper. Fry several at a time and serve hot or warm, garnished with a little more chopped spring onion. Mix all the ingredients for the dipping sauce and divide among tiny dishes.

ICED COCONUT MILK WITH SAGO (BURMA)

SERVES 4

4oz (100g) tapioca or sago
4oz (100g) jaggery or dark brown sugar
few tbsp water
1½pt (900ml) coconut milk
ice cubes

Rinse the tapioca or sago, drain and put into a large pan with plenty of water. Bring to the boil and reduce to a simmer. Stir often, cooking until the pearls of sago or tapioca become clear. Allow 10 minutes for sago and 20 minutes for tapioca. Drain and rinse with plenty of cold water until all the starch is removed.

Dissolve the jaggery or dark brown sugar in water over a gentle heat, then cool. Spoon some of the sago or tapioca into a tall glass. Add syrup to taste, then the coconut milk and sufficient ice cubes to suit individual taste. It is important to serve this at once so that you are able to enjoy it at its very best.

JACKFRUIT PUDDING (KAMPUCHEA)

SERVES 8

8oz (225g) packet desiccated coconut and ½pt (300ml) hot water to make just under ½pt (300ml) coconut milk
16oz (454g) can jackfruit in syrup
2–3tbsp sugar
pinch of salt
5 eggs, whisked

Prepare the coconut milk. Open the can of jackfruit and reserve the syrup. Cut into thin slices. Mix the reserved syrup with the prepared coconut milk and sugar. Stir until the sugar dissolves. Add a pinch of salt. Taste the mixture, which should be quite sweet, but not excessively so.

Add the syrup mixture to the beaten eggs to form a creamy mixture. Strain into a buttered ovenproof dish, 10 × 8 inches (25 × 20 cm). Cover with tin foil and set in a steamer over gently boiling water. When set, remove from the steamer and finish baking in the oven. Alternatively, place the dish in a roasting tin of water, to come halfway up the sides of the dish, and bake in a moderate oven (325°F/160°C/Gas Mark 3) for about 40 minutes.

ICED COCONUT MILK DESSERT (PHILIPPINES)

MAKES 1 LARGE SUNDAE GLASS

1tbsp each: jackfruit, coconut flesh, sweet kidney beans, chick peas, plantain or yam, leche flan, sweetcorn kernels
crushed ice
⅓pt (200ml) evaporated milk
ice cream (optional)

maraschino cherries to garnish

Spoon the fruits, beans and so on into the base of a tall sundae-type glass. Add the crushed ice and then top with evaporated milk, ice cream, if using, and maraschino cherries to garnish. Eat with a long spoon.

CARAMEL AND LIME CUSTARD (PHILIPPINES)

SERVES 8

Caramel

8oz (225g) sugar
8tbsp water

Custard
14½oz (410g) can of evaporated milk
½pt (300ml) fresh milk
5 large eggs
1oz (25g) sugar
few drops of vanilla essence
a little lime rind, finely grated

Place the sugar and water in a heavy-based pan. Stir over heat until the sugar has dissolved. Bring to the boil and boil until the caramel turns a deep golden-brown. The caramel will continue to cook even when it is removed from the heat so speed is essential. Remove it from the heat and immediately pour it into 8 individual ramekin dishes and rotate each one so that the caramel coats the sides of the dishes as well as the base. Leave on one side.

Meanwhile heat the evaporated and fresh milk without boiling. Pour the mixture onto the beaten eggs, sugar and vanilla essence. Stir well, then strain into a large jug and pour into the ramekin dishes when the caramel is set. Any extra custard can be cooked in a separate ovenproof dish and used up as an extra quantity.

Place in a roasting tin of warm water that comes halfway up the sides of the dishes. Set in a moderately hot oven (320°F/160°C/Gas Mark 3) and cook for 35–45 minutes or until it is quite set. Serve hot or cold with cream. If serving cold, pipe a whirl of cream on top of each and add a piece of lime, or spike with a little caramel, which you can make at the same time as the caramel for the base of the ramekins (that is, 1oz [25g] sugar, 1 tbsp water). Pour onto a piece of foil. Leave to set and crush with the end of a rolling pin when required.

Store the caramel in the refrigerator for several weeks, wrapped in tin foil. If you prefer one large crème caramel instead of the individual servings, use a 2½ pt (1.5 lt) ovenproof soufflé dish and cook for about 1 hour in the water bath or until set. It is quite delicious served in either dish!

SWEET RICE WITH COCONUT (PHILIPPINES)

SERVES 4–6

1pt (600ml) thin coconut milk
9oz (250g) glutinous rice
½tsp salt
5oz (150g) brown sugar
¼pt (150ml) coconut cream
1tsp anis seed
¾oz (20g) grated coconut

Bring the thin coconut milk to the boil and add the rice and salt, cooking gently until the rice is soft, about 1 hour. Add two-thirds of the brown sugar and stir it into the rice. Pour the rice into a 2 lb (900 g) loaf tin. Pour over the coconut cream and the remaining sugar, together with the anis seed.

Bake in the oven at 400°F/200°C/Gas Mark 6 for 30 minutes. Leave to cool overnight. Cut into long, square-shaped sticks and roll in shredded coconut. Arrange on a platter.

SWEET RICE WITH COCONUT

◆ SNACKS AND DESSERTS ◆

Opening a coconut:

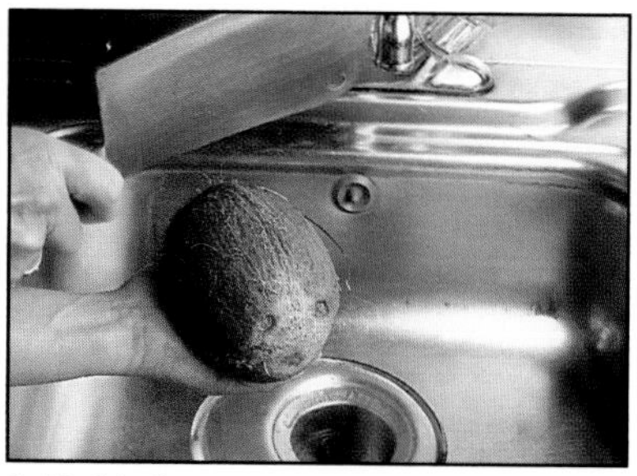

1 Hold the coconut in the left hand, positioning it over a bowl to catch the juice.

2 Make sure the eyes are just above the thumb and, using the back of a cleaver, strike the top or crown of the nut.

3 The coconut will fall apart easily and the juice will be caught in the bowl, if you wish to drink it.

Making coconut chips:

1 Slit open the coconut and ease the 2 halves apart. Crack into smaller pieces if necessary.

2 Slide the blade between the white flesh and brown husk of the coconut to ease away the hard, outer casing.

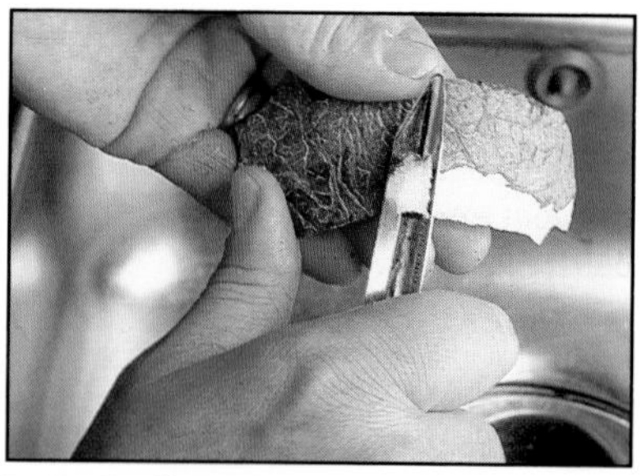

3 Peel off the remaining brown skin with an ordinary potato peeler, leaving you with just the flesh.

4 Feed the peeled pieces of coconut into a food processor. Make sure you use the slicing attachment.

5 Switch the processor on and leave for a few seconds so that you are left with thin slices of coconut.

6 Place these slices on a baking tray, sprinkle with salt and bake in the oven for 30 minutes. Cool before serving.

◆ SNACKS AND DESSERTS ◆

BANANA FRITTERS (INDONESIA)

SERVES 4

2oz (50g) rice flour
2oz (50g) plain flour
1 egg, beaten
5fl oz (150ml) coconut milk, prepared
4 bananas, depending on size
oil for deep-frying

Sauce
5oz (150g) palm sugar or brown sugar
¼pt (150ml) water
slice of fresh ginger
1 bay leaf

Sift the rice and plain flours into a bowl. Add the beaten egg and mix to a thick coating batter with coconut milk. Set aside. Peel and cut the bananas in half diagonally. Dip in the batter and fry for 3–4 minutes in hot oil until the outside is crisp and golden. Drain on absorbent kitchen paper. Then, fry the remainder and serve together with the sauce.

To make the sauce dissolve the palm sugar with water in a pan. Add the bay leaf and slice of ginger. Stir until the syrup thickens. Remove bay leaf and ginger and leave to cool before serving.

CUCUMBER PICKLE (INDONESIA)

1 cucumber
salt
1 tomato, skinned, deseeded and diced
1 small onion, finely sliced
1 red chilli, deseeded and chopped
3tbsp good quality vinegar
2tsp sugar
pinch of salt

Trim the ends from the cucumber, peel lengthwise but leave some of the skin on to make the salad look more attractive. Cut into thin slices and lay on a large plate. Sprinkle with salt and leave for 15 minutes. Rinse and dry. Meanwhile prepare the tomato, onion and chilli. Arrange all the vegetables in a bowl and pour over vinegar, sugar and salt blended together. Chill before serving.

PEANUT SNACKS (INDONESIA)

MAKES 20

3 cloves garic, crushed
½tsp coriander seeds, pounded
½tsp turmeric
pinch of salt
1½oz (40g) rice flour
about 6–8tbsp coconut milk
2oz (50g) salted peanuts, lightly crushed
oil for frying

Mix the garlic, coriander, turmeric and salt together, then stir in the rice flour. Mix to a creamy batter with coconut milk. Add the peanuts — they should still be in fairly large pieces. Heat a little oil in a frying pan and spoon some of the mixture into a pan, about the size of a dropped scone. Fry on both sides, then lift onto absorbent kitchen paper on a cooling rack. Leave until cold. Store in an airtight tin if there are any left-overs.

CURRY PUFFS (SINGAPORE)

MAKES 20–25

14oz (400g) puff pastry, thawed

Filling
½ onion, finely crushed
1 clove garlic, crushed
½inch (1cm) piece fresh root ginger, pounded
1 chilli, deseeded and pounded or 1tsp chilli powder
1oz (25g) ghee or unsalted butter
4oz (100g) minced fresh lamb or beef
½tsp turmeric
½tsp ground coriander seeds
small potato, grated
1 tomato, skinned and chopped finely
stock to moisten
seasoning to taste

Leave the pastry to thaw while preparing the filling. Fry the onion, garlic, ginger and fresh chillies, if using, in hot fat without browning. Stir in the meat and cook until it changes colour, stirring all the time. Add the turmeric and coriander. Stir in the potato and tomato and a little stock if necessary to just moisten. Cover and cook for 5 minutes, then taste for seasoning. Cook without a cover for a further 5 minutes. Set aside to cool.

Roll out the pastry thinly on a floured board and cut it into 4 inch (10 cm) rounds. Put a spoonful of filling on one half, avoiding the edges. Damp the edges and seal. Alternatively cut into 3½ inch (9 cm) squares and fold into triangles. Set on a baking sheet and cook in a hot oven (420°F/220°C/Gas Mark 7) for 10 minutes or until puffy and golden-brown. Serve as soon as possible.

COCONUT CHIPS (MALAYSIA)

1 fresh coconut
salt

Select a fresh coconut, which sounds full of juice when it is shaken. This juice is quite pleasant to drink so, if you wish to save it, either pierce one of the 'eyes' of the coconut and drain off or open it carefully and collect the juice in a bowl.

When open use a palette or broad-bladed knife to ease the flesh away from the hard outer shell. Peel away the brown skin with a potato peeler. Slice the flesh into wafer-thin shavings in the food processor, then scatter these evenly all over a couple of baking sheets and sprinkle with salt. Crisp in a moderately slow oven (325°F/170°C/Gas Mark 3) for about 30 minutes; but turn them over occasionally during this time. Cool and store in airtight containers. Serve with drinks.

◆ ◆ ◆

◆ INDEX ◆

◆ INDEX ◆

◆ INDEX ◆

◆ INDEX ◆

◆ INDEX ◆

◆ ◆ ◆